SCHAUM'S OUTLINE OF

THEORY AND PROBLEMS

OF

STATICS AND MECHANICS OF MATERIALS

•

WILLIAM A. NASH, Ph.D.

Professor of Civil Engineering
University of Massachusetts

•

SCHAUM'S OUTLINE SERIES
McGRAW-HILL, INC.

New York   St. Louis   San Francisco   Auckland   Bogotá   Caracas
Lisbon   London   Madrid   Mexico   Milan   Montreal   New Delhi
Paris   San Juan   Singapore   Sydney   Tokyo   Toronto

Dedicated to my daughter, Rebecca Nash McKay, and my son,
Phillip Arthur Nash, and their families

WILLIAM A. NASH is Professor of Civil Engineering at the University of Massachusetts, Amherst. He received his B.S. and M.S. from the Illinois Institute of Technology and his Ph.D. from the University of Michigan. He served as Structural Research Engineer at the David Taylor Research Center of the Navy Department in Washington, D.C., and was a faculty member at the University of Florida for 13 years prior to his present affiliation. He has had extensive consulting experience with the U.S. Air Force, the U.S. Navy Department, Lockheed Aerospace Corp., and the General Electric Co. His special areas of interest are structural dynamics and structural stability.

Schaum's Outline of Theory and Problems of
Statics and Mechanics of Materials

1 2 3 4 5 6 7 8 9 10 11 12 13 14 15 16 17 18 19 20 SHP SHP 9 2 1

ISBN 0-07-045896-0

Sponsoring Editor: David Beckwith
Production Supervisor: Louise Karam
Editing Supervisors: Meg Tobin, Maureen Walker
Cover design by Amy E. Becker.

Library of Congress Cataloging-in-Publication Data

Nash, William A.
    Schaum's outline of theory and problems of statics and mechanics
of materials/William A. Nash.
        p. cm. (Schaum's outline series)
    Includes index.
    ISBN 0-07-045896-0
    1. Statics—problems, exercises, etc. 2. Strength of materials-
-Problems, exercises, etc. 3. Statics—Outlines, syllabi, etc.
4. Strength of materials—Outlines, syllabi, etc. I. Title.
II. Title: Theory and problems of statics and mechanics of
materials.
TA351.N37   1991
620.1'12—dc20   91-13201
                                                            CIP

Preface

Statics and Mechanics of Materials covers the subject matter of courses with that name as well as those whose names include one or another of the terms *statics, mechanics of materials, strength of materials,* or *solid mechanics.* The chapters are approximately equally divided between the mechanics of rigid bodies and that of deformable bodies. The treatment of the mechanics of deformable bodies is general in nature; it begins with the differential equations of equilibrium applicable to any elastic body, and then shows how special cases of these equations lead to solutions of common engineering problems.

Each chapter begins with an outline of important concepts; continues with a series of fully worked-out problems that utilize and, in some cases, extend those concepts; and ends with a number of unsolved problems (with answers only). The problems are of a somewhat advanced nature and are about equally divided between the modern SI units and the traditional USCS units. Most important, eleven computer programs are developed in detail and used in problems to show how tedious computations are readily treated with modern computer methods. These programs have been implemented on a mainframe CYBER system. Only minor changes in input format would be needed to make them suitable for use on most PCs.

The author would like to acknowledge the contributions of several people who aided greatly in the preparation of this book. In particular, most sincere thanks are due Kathleen Derwin for the preparation of many of the computer programs, as well as for the careful checking of essentially all problems and computations. Thanks also go to B. S. Ravindra and Gao-Qui Zhu for the preparation of certain computer programs. Much of the book was written while the author was a visiting professor at the Technical University of Darmstadt, West Germany. Thanks must go to the Alexander von Humboldt Foundation of Bonn for making that stay possible, and to the faculty in Darmstadt for its hospitality. The capable editorial assistance of Mr. Edward Millman is also acknowledged with thanks.

Lastly, the author is deeply indebted to his wife, Verna B. Nash, for her patience and encouragement during the preparation of the manuscript.

WILLIAM A. NASH

Amherst, Massachusetts
November 1991

Contents

Chapter 1

Properties of Forces and Force Systems

COMPONENTS OF A FORCE

The *components* (or *scalar components*) of a force **F** in the *x* and *y* directions are denoted by F_x and F_y, respectively (Fig. 1-1), and are

$$F_x = |\mathbf{F}| \cos \theta \qquad F_y = |\mathbf{F}| \sin \theta \qquad (1.1)$$

where the vertical bars denote the magnitude of the vector **F**.

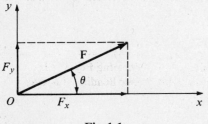

Fig. 1-1

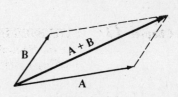

Fig. 1-2

VECTOR ADDITION

Two vectors **A** and **B** may be added by taking **A** and **B** as adjacent sides of a parallelogram, as indicated in Fig. 1-2. The vector sum (or *resultant*) of **A** and **B** is then the vector from the origin of **A** and **B** along the diagonal to the opposite corner. This defines the *parallelogram rule* for vector addition. We sometimes refer to **A** and **B** of Fig. 1-2 as *vector components* of **A** + **B**.

DOT PRODUCT

The *dot product* (or scalar product) of two vectors **A** and **B** is the product of the magnitudes of the two vectors multiplied by the cosine of the acute angle α between them, as shown in Fig. 1-3:

$$\mathbf{A} \cdot \mathbf{B} = |\mathbf{A}||\mathbf{B}| \cos \alpha \qquad (1.2)$$

It is frequently convenient to work with unit vectors (i.e., vectors of unit length) directed along the *x*, *y*, and *z* axes, as shown in Fig. 1-4. These are denoted **i**, **j**, and **k**, respectively. From (*1.2*) we obviously have

$$\mathbf{i} \cdot \mathbf{i} = \mathbf{j} \cdot \mathbf{j} = \mathbf{k} \cdot \mathbf{k} = 1$$
$$\mathbf{i} \cdot \mathbf{j} = \mathbf{j} \cdot \mathbf{k} = \mathbf{i} \cdot \mathbf{k} = 0 \qquad (1.3)$$

Figure 1-5 shows the extension of these ideas to three-dimensional space.

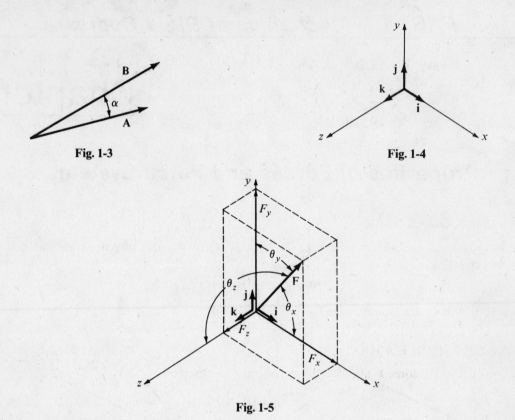

Fig. 1-3

Fig. 1-4

Fig. 1-5

DIRECTIONS OF VECTORS

The direction of the vector $\mathbf{F}$ in Fig. 1-5 is specified by the three angles θ_x, θ_y, and θ_z, where

$$\cos \theta_x = \frac{F_x}{|\mathbf{F}|} \qquad \cos \theta_y = \frac{F_y}{|\mathbf{F}|} \qquad \cos \theta_z = \frac{F_z}{|\mathbf{F}|} \qquad (1.4)$$

The numbers $\cos \theta_x$, $\cos \theta_y$, and $\cos \theta_z$ are called the *direction cosines* of $\mathbf{F}$, and they completely specify its direction.

CROSS PRODUCT

The *cross product* (or *vector product*) of two vectors $\mathbf{A}$ and $\mathbf{B}$ is defined as the vector that is perpendicular to the plane containing $\mathbf{A}$ and $\mathbf{B}$ and that has magnitude equal to the product of the magnitudes of $\mathbf{A}$ and $\mathbf{B}$ multiplied by the sine of the acute angle α between $\mathbf{A}$ and $\mathbf{B}$. Thus,

$$|\mathbf{A} \times \mathbf{B}| = |\mathbf{A}||\mathbf{B}| \sin \alpha \qquad (1.5)$$

The cross product is illustrated in Fig. 1-6. The sense of $\mathbf{A} \times \mathbf{B}$ is determined with a right-hand rule.

For the unit vectors $\mathbf{i}$, $\mathbf{j}$, $\mathbf{k}$ (Fig. 1-4), we have the following cross products:

$$\begin{array}{lll}
\mathbf{i} \times \mathbf{i} = 0 & \mathbf{j} \times \mathbf{i} = -\mathbf{k} & \mathbf{k} \times \mathbf{i} = \mathbf{j} \\
\mathbf{i} \times \mathbf{j} = \mathbf{k} & \mathbf{j} \times \mathbf{j} = 0 & \mathbf{k} \times \mathbf{j} = -\mathbf{i} \\
\mathbf{i} \times \mathbf{k} = -\mathbf{j} & \mathbf{j} \times \mathbf{k} = -\mathbf{i} & \mathbf{k} \times \mathbf{k} = 0
\end{array} \qquad (1.6)$$

We can write the cross product of $\mathbf{A}$ and $\mathbf{B}$ in terms of components and unit vectors as

$$\mathbf{A} \times \mathbf{B} = (A_x\mathbf{i} + A_y\mathbf{j} + A_z\mathbf{k}) \times (B_x\mathbf{i} + B_y\mathbf{j} + B_z\mathbf{k})$$

By (1.6), this becomes

$$\mathbf{A} \times \mathbf{B} = (A_y B_z - A_z B_y)\mathbf{i} + (A_z B_x - A_x B_z)\mathbf{j} + (A_x B_y - A_y B_x)\mathbf{k} \tag{1.7}$$

$$= \begin{vmatrix} \mathbf{i} & \mathbf{j} & \mathbf{k} \\ A_x & A_y & A_z \\ B_x & B_y & B_z \end{vmatrix} \tag{1.8}$$

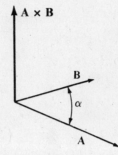

Fig. 1-6

MOMENT OF A FORCE ABOUT A POINT

The moment of the force $\mathbf{F}$ about point A is defined as the cross product

$$\mathbf{M}_0 = \mathbf{r} \times \mathbf{F} \tag{1.9}$$

where $\mathbf{r}$ is the vector from A to any point on $\mathbf{F}$. From the definition of the cross product, (1.5), the moment $\mathbf{M}_0$ is a vector perpendicular to the plane of $\mathbf{r}$ and $\mathbf{F}$, with $\mathbf{r}$, $\mathbf{F}$, and $\mathbf{M}_0$ forming a right-handed system. The three are shown in Fig. 1-7, where we have introduced the double-headed vector to distinguish moments from forces.

If we construct a perpendicular from A to the line of action of $\mathbf{F}$ and call the perpendicular distance d as shown in Fig. 1-7, then the magnitude of $\mathbf{M}_0$ is, by (1.5),

$$|\mathbf{M}_0| = |\mathbf{r}||\mathbf{F}| \sin \alpha = d|\mathbf{F}|$$

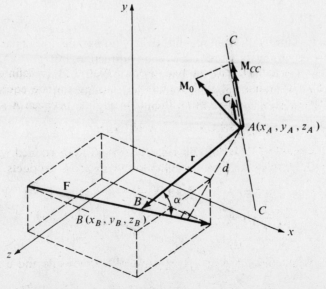

Fig. 1-7

This last form is convenient for use in two-dimensional problems, where it is customary to omit the absolute-value signs and write

$$M_0 = Fd \qquad (1.10)$$

(An example is given in Problem 1.7.)

MIXED TRIPLE PRODUCT

The *mixed triple product* (or *triple scalar product*) of vectors $\mathbf{A}$, $\mathbf{B}$, and $\mathbf{C}$ is defined as

$$\mathbf{A} \cdot (\mathbf{B} \times \mathbf{C}) \qquad (1.11)$$

This can be shown to be

$$\mathbf{A} \cdot (\mathbf{B} \times \mathbf{C}) = A_x(B_y C_z - B_z C_y) + A_y(B_z C_x - B_x C_z) + A_z(B_x C_y - B_y C_x)$$

$$= \begin{vmatrix} A_x & A_y & A_z \\ B_x & B_y & B_z \\ C_x & C_y & C_z \end{vmatrix} \qquad (1.12)$$

MOMENT OF A FORCE ABOUT AN AXIS

Consider again the force $\mathbf{F}$ of Fig. 1-7. Previously we defined the moment of $\mathbf{F}$ about the *point A*. We shall also have use for the moment of $\mathbf{F}$ about an *axis* through A. Since the moment of $\mathbf{F}$ about A is represented by the vector $\mathbf{M}_0$, we now define the moment $\mathbf{M}_{CC}$ about any axis CC (passing through A) as the projection of $\mathbf{M}_0$ on CC. Thus,

$$|\mathbf{M}_{CC}| = \mathbf{C} \cdot \mathbf{M}_0 = \mathbf{C} \cdot (\mathbf{r} \times \mathbf{F}) \qquad (1.13)$$

This may be shown to be

$$|\mathbf{M}_{CC}| = \begin{vmatrix} C_x & C_y & C_z \\ x_B - x_A & y_B - y_A & z_B - z_A \\ F_x & F_y & F_z \end{vmatrix} \qquad (1.14)$$

MOMENT OF A COUPLE

A *couple* consists of two forces of equal magnitude having parallel lines of action but opposite senses (Fig. 1-8). A couple produces no overall force effect in any direction, but it does tend to produce rotation. The moment of a couple may be found by applying (1.9) to each of the forces and then adding.

Since a couple is in essence a moment vector, the vector representation for a moment (the double-headed arrow) is a convenient way to represent the couple in three-dimensional space.

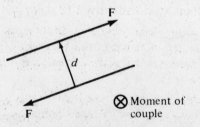

Fig. 1-8

Again, since a couple is a moment vector, the sum of two couples $\mathbf{M}_1$ and $\mathbf{M}_2$ is readily found by vector addition:

$$\mathbf{M} = \mathbf{M}_1 + \mathbf{M}_2 \qquad (1.15)$$

This sum may be represented as in Fig. 1-9.

A couple may be broken down into components directed along any set of axes, such as the x, y, z coordinate axes. This is done exactly as for a force.

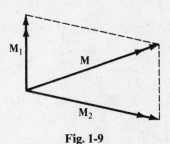

Fig. 1-9

VARIGNON'S THEOREM

Consider a single force $\mathbf{F}$ which has the vector components $\mathbf{F}_1$ and $\mathbf{F}_2$. *Varignon's theorem* states that *the moment of $\mathbf{F}$ about any point O is equal to the sum of the moments of $\mathbf{F}_1$ and $\mathbf{F}_2$ about the same point O*. It is important to observe that $\mathbf{F}$, $\mathbf{F}_1$, and $\mathbf{F}_2$ must be *concurrent* (i.e., all intersect at the same point).

EQUIVALENT FORCE SYSTEMS; RESULTANTS

It is often desirable to reduce a given force system to its simplest equivalent form, called its *resultant*. The resultant can take various forms, depending upon the type of force system involved. Important cases are as follows.

1. *Concurrent forces*, i.e., those meeting at a common point, may be added as shown in Fig. 1-2. The resultant (their sum) naturally passes through the common point. (See Problems 1.18 and 1.24.)

2. *Coplanar forces*, i.e., those lying entirely in one plane, can also be added by the method of Fig. 1-2. Alternatively, one can add the components of the given forces to find the components of the resultant (their sum). It is then necessary to locate the line of action of the resultant. This is done by equating the moments of the given forces about some convenient point to the moment of the resultant force about that same point. Thus, the resultant of a coplanar system of forces and couples is a single force acting along a specified and unique line of action. (See Problems 1.21 and 1.23.)

3. *Parallel forces, all in the same plane*, yield a resultant force that is found as the algebraic sum of the forces of the system. The line of action of this resultant is found by equating the moments of the given forces about some convenient point to the moment of the resultant force about the same point. (This follows from an extension of Varignon's theorem.) In some cases, such a parallel force system may have a couple as a resultant. (See Problems 1.19, 1.20, and 1.22.)

4. *Parallel forces, not all in the same plane*, yield a resultant force that is found as the algebraic sum of the forces of the system. The line of action of this resultant is located by equating the moments of the given forces about each of two axes in a plane perpendicular to the given forces to the moments of the resultant about these same axes.

5. In the *general case* of forces and couples in three-dimensional space, it is possible to reduce a given force system to a single force acting at any specified point together with a couple, neither of which is zero.

Solved Problems

1.1 A cable-stayed bridge over the Ohio River has the configuration shown in Fig. 1-10. The cables are arranged symmetrically about the tower. Each of the four cables ① is tensioned to 6,000,000 lb; each of the four cables ② is tensioned to 3,800,000 lb; and each of the four cables ③, to 2,300,000 lb. Determine the total of the vertical components of all 12 of these cable forces, since that value would be needed to design the tower.

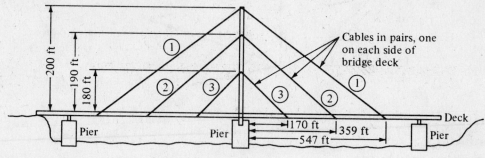

Fig. 1-10

For each set of three cables, we have the situation shown in Fig. 1-11. We first need the lengths of the cables. For cable ①,

$$L_1 = \sqrt{(200)^2 + (547)^2} = 582.4 \text{ ft}$$

Similarly, $L_2 = 406.1$ ft and $L_3 = 247.6$ ft.

The total y component of the tensions in the three cables is now found to be

$$F_y = 6,000,000 \cos \theta_1 + 3,800,000 \cos \theta_2 + 2,300,000 \cos \theta_3$$

$$= 6,000,000 \frac{200}{582.4} + 3,900,000 \frac{190}{406.1} + 2,300,000 \frac{180}{247.6}$$

$$= 5,510,000 \text{ lb downward}$$

Since there are two sets of cables on the right side of the central tower and another two sets on the left, the total downward vertical component of *all* twelve cable tensions is $4 \times 5,510,000 = 22,040,000$ lb.

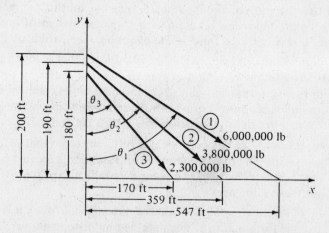

Fig. 1-11

1.2   During the hot rolling of aluminum slabs to yield finished aluminum plate, the slab thickness is reduced by approximately 40 percent and enormous forces are generated. A triangle marked on the side of a slab was found, experimentally, to be subjected to the normal and tangential forces shown in Fig. 1-12. Determine the vector sum (resultant) of these four forces.

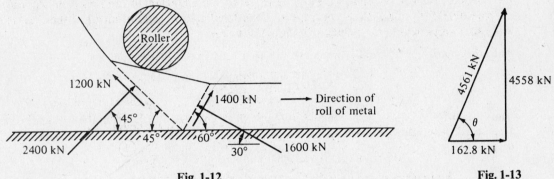

Fig. 1-12   **Fig. 1-13**

Here,

$$R_x = 2400 \cos 45° - 1200 \cos 45° - 1600 \cos 30° + 1400 \cos 60°$$
$$= 2400(0.707) - 1200(0.707) - 1600(0.866) + 1400(0.500)$$
$$= 162.8 \text{ kN}$$

$$R_y = 2400 \sin 45° + 1200 \sin 45° + 1600 \sin 30° + 1400 \sin 60°$$
$$= 2400(0.707) + 1200(0.707) + 1600(0.500) + 1400(0.866)$$
$$= 4558 \text{ kN}$$

Hence, $$|\mathbf{R}| = \sqrt{(162.8)^2 + (4558)^2} = 4561 \text{ kN}$$

Now, from Fig. 1-13, $\theta = \arctan(4558/162.8) = 87.95°$.

1.3   Find the x, y, and z components of the 40-kN force vector shown in Fig. 1-14.

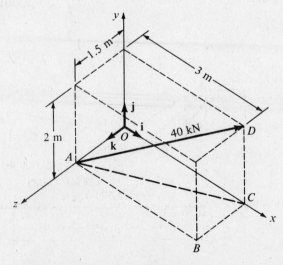

Fig. 1-14

The displacement **AD** has components 3, 2, and -1.5 m in the x, y, and z directions, respectively. The distance from A to D is then

$$|\mathbf{AD}| = \sqrt{(3)^2 + (2)^3 + (-1.5)^2} = 3.905 \text{ m}$$

The vector **AD** may then be written in terms of its components as

$$\mathbf{AD} = \frac{3}{3.905}\mathbf{i} + \frac{2}{3.905}\mathbf{j} + \frac{-1.5}{3.905}\mathbf{k} = 0.768\mathbf{i} + 0.512\mathbf{j} - 0.384\mathbf{k}$$

The force vector, call it **V**, differs from **AD** only by a scale factor. Hence,

$$\mathbf{V} = 0.768(40)\mathbf{i} + 0.512(40)\mathbf{j} - 0.384(40)\mathbf{k}$$
$$= 30.72\mathbf{i} + 20.48\mathbf{j} - 15.36\mathbf{k}$$

Thus the 40-kN force has components of 30.72 kN, 20.48 kN, and -15.36 kN in the x, y, and z directions, respectively. As a check, we have

$$\sqrt{(30.72)^2 + (20.48)^2 + (-15.36)^2} = \sqrt{1599.08} \approx 40$$

The direction cosines of the 40-kN force are 0.768, 0.512, and -0.384.

1.4   In Problem 1.3, find the projection of the 40-kN force on the xz plane.

The length AC is

$$AC = \sqrt{(1.5)^2 + (3)^2} = 3.35 \text{ m}$$

The projection of the 40-kN force is then

$$F_{xz} = 40\,\frac{3.35}{3.905} = 34.31 \text{ kN}$$

1.5   Find the x, y, and z components of the 100-kN·m moment vector shown in Fig. 1-15.

The displacement **OF** has components 5, 3, and -2 in the x, y, and z directions, respectively. The distance from O to F is thus

$$|\mathbf{OF}| = \sqrt{(5)^2 + (3)^2 + (-2)^2} = 6.16 \text{ m}$$

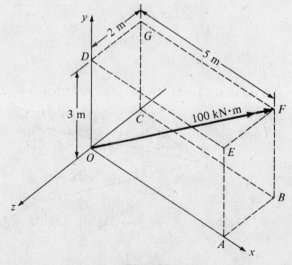

Fig. 1-15

The direction cosines of **OF** are then

$$\frac{5}{6.16} = 0.812 \qquad \frac{3}{6.16} = 0.487 \qquad \frac{-2}{6.16} = -0.325$$

The 100-kN · m moment vector **M** is then

$$\mathbf{M} = (0.812)(100)\mathbf{i} + (0.487)(100)\mathbf{j} + (-0.325)(100)\mathbf{k}$$
$$= 81.2\mathbf{i} + 48.7\mathbf{j} - 32.5\mathbf{k}$$

Its components are thus

$$M_x = 81.2 \text{ kN·m} \qquad M_y = 48.7 \text{ kN·m} \qquad M_z = -32.5 \text{ kN·m}$$

1.6   In Problem 1.1, find the moment of the tension in each of the cables ① about the base of the tower at the bridge deck level.

To apply Varignon's theorem, we replace the cable tension by its x and y components:

$$F_x = 6{,}000{,}000\,\frac{547}{582.4} = 5{,}635{,}000 \text{ lb} \qquad F_y = 6{,}000{,}000\,\frac{200}{582.4} = 2{,}060{,}000 \text{ lb}$$

We must be careful to place both these components at the *same* point on the line of action of the 6,000,000-lb force. Let us select the tower top, point A in Fig. 1-16. Then the moment of the tension about point O is the sum of the moments of its components:

$$|\mathbf{M_0}| = (5{,}635{,}000 \text{ lb})(200 \text{ ft}) + (2{,}060{,}000 \text{ lb})(0 \text{ ft})$$

The last term on the right vanishes because F_y passes through the moment center. The desired moment is thus $|\mathbf{M_0}| = 11{,}270 \times 10^5 \text{ lb·ft}$.

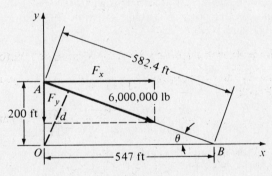

Fig. 1-16

1.7   Rework Problem 1.6 using the perpendicular distance from O to line AB.

This distance d, shown in Fig. 1-16, is found by first solving for θ:

$$\theta = \arctan \frac{200}{547} = \arctan 0.3656 = 20.08°$$

Hence $d = 547 \sin \theta = 547(0.3434) = 187.8 \text{ ft}$

Now, from (*1.10*),

$$M = Fd = (6{,}000{,}000 \text{ lb})(187.8 \text{ ft}) = 11{,}270 \times 10^5 \text{ lb·ft}$$

1.8   Find the moment of the force $\mathbf{F} = 80 \text{ kN}$ about the origin of the coordinate system in Fig. 1-17.

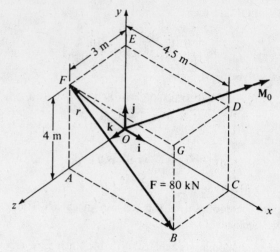

Fig. 1-17

We must first find the x, y, and z components of the 80-kN force. The length of the diagonal FB is $\sqrt{(4)^2 + (4.5)^2} = 6.021$ m. Then, from the figure,

$$F_z = 0 \qquad F_x = \frac{4.5}{6.021}\, 80 = 59.79 \text{ kN} \qquad F_y = \frac{-4}{6.021}\, 80 = -53.15 \text{ kN}$$

Thus, $\mathbf{F} = 59.79\mathbf{i} - 53.15\mathbf{j}$.

The position vector $\mathbf{r}$ may extend from the origin O to any convenient point on the line of action of the 80-kN force. Let us select point F, which, relative to O, has the vector representation $\mathbf{r} = 4\mathbf{j} + 3\mathbf{k}$. Then, from (1.8) and (1.9) we have

$$\mathbf{M}_0 = \begin{vmatrix} \mathbf{i} & \mathbf{j} & \mathbf{k} \\ 0 & 4 & 3 \\ 59.79 & -53.15 & 0 \end{vmatrix}$$

$$= (0 + 159.5)\mathbf{i} - (0 - 179.4)\mathbf{j} + (0 - 239.2)\mathbf{k}$$

$$= (159.4\mathbf{i} + 179.4\mathbf{j} - 239.2\mathbf{k}) \text{ kN·m}$$

This moment is a vector passing through O and perpendicular to the plane of $\mathbf{r}$ and $\mathbf{F}$ as shown in Fig. 1-17. Also, $|\mathbf{M}_0| = 338.9$ kN·m.

If the block shown in dotted lines were supported in a ball-and-socket joint at point O, the force $\mathbf{F}$ would tend to rotate the block about an axis coinciding with $\mathbf{M}_0$.

1.9   A television transmission tower consists of three tubular legs held together with both horizontal and diagonal cross members. The tower is braced by guy cables as indicated in Fig. 1-18. Cable ① is tensioned with a force of 30,000 lb. Determine the moment of this force about the tower base O.

The distance AC is found from right-triangle relationships to be 1038 ft. The 30,000-lb force lies in the xy plane and has components

$$F_x = -\frac{494}{1038}\, 30{,}000 = -14{,}280 \text{ lb} \qquad F_y = -\frac{913}{1038}\, 30{,}000 = -26{,}390 \text{ lb} \qquad F_z = 0$$

Thus $\mathbf{F} = (-14{,}280\mathbf{i} - 26{,}390\mathbf{j})$ lb.

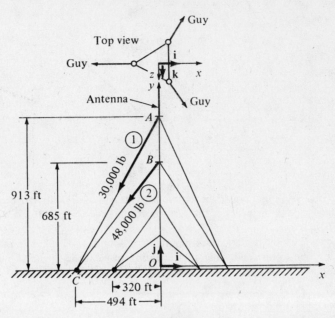

Fig. 1-18

We place the position vector **r** from O to A, so that $\quad$ **r** $= 913\mathbf{j}$ ft. $\quad$ Then, from (1.8) and (1.9), we have

$$\mathbf{M}_0 = \begin{vmatrix} \mathbf{i} & \mathbf{j} & \mathbf{k} \\ 0 & 913 & 0 \\ -14{,}280 & -26{,}390 & 0 \end{vmatrix}$$

$$= (0 + 13{,}038{,}000)\mathbf{k} = 13{,}038{,}000\mathbf{k} \ \text{lb·ft}$$

This moment is a vector passing through O and acting in the direction of the z axis. From the top, it appears as shown in Fig. 1-19.

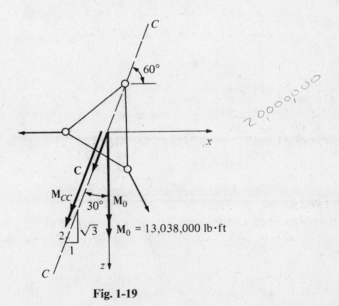

Fig. 1-19

1.10 Develop a computer program in the BASIC computer language to determine the moment of a force in three-dimensional space about an arbitrary point.

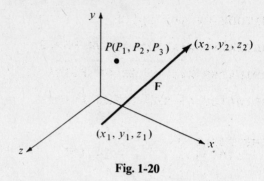

Fig. 1-20

Let the force of magnitude F be represented as a vector with tail coordinates (x_1, y_1, z_1) and tip coordinates (x_2, y_2, z_2), as in Fig. 1-20. The coordinates of the point about which the moment is desired are (P_1, P_2, P_3).

The moment of the force about point P is found from *(1.9)*, most easily by using *(1.8)*. The simple program that follows will solve that equation to yield the x, y, and z components M_1, M_2, and M_3 of the moment.

```
00100 REM *** THIS PROGRAM DETERMINES THE MOMENT OF ANY GIVEN FORCE    ***
00110 REM *** IN SPACE ABOUT ANY GIVEN POINT P                         ***
00120 REM
00130 REM ***             READ IN DATA                                 ***
00140 PRINT "ENTER THE MAGNITUDE OF THE FORCE "
00150 INPUT F
00160 PRINT "ENTER THE COORDINATES X1, Y1, Z1 OF FORCE "
00170 INPUT X1,Y1,Z1
00180 PRINT "ENTER THE COORDINATES X2, Y2, Z2 OF FORCE "
00190 INPUT X2,Y2,Z2
00200 PRINT "ENTER THE COORDINATES OF THE POINT P "
00210 INPUT P1,P2,P3
00220 REM
00230 REM *** CALCULATE THE LENGTH OF VECTOR                           ***
00240 REM
00250 LET L=SQR((X2-X1)**2+(Y2-Y1)**2+(Z2-Z1)**2)
00260 REM
00270 REM *** CALCULATE THE X, Y, AND Z COMPONENTS OF FORCE            ***
00280 REM
00290 LET F1=((X2-X1)/L)*F
00300 LET F2=((Y2-Y1)/L)*F
00310 LET F3=((Z2-Z1)/L)*F
00320 REM
00330 REM *** CALCULATE MOMENT ABOUT THE POINT                         ***
00340 REM
00350 LET M1=((Y1-P2)*F3)-((Z1-P3)*F2)
00360 LET M2=((Z1-P3)*F1)-((X1-P1)*F3)
00370 LET M3=((X1-P1)*F2)-((Y1-P2)*F1)
00380 PRINT
00390 PRINT "MOMENT ABOUT THE POINT P "
00400 PRINT M1,M2,M3
00410 END
```

1.11   Rework Problem 1.8 using the computer program of Problem 1.10.

The coordinates of the tail of the force vector are $(0, 4, 3)$, and those of the tip of the vector are $(4.5, 0, 3)$. The coordinates of P are $(0, 0, 0)$. We enter these data to obtain

```
ENTER THE MAGNITUDE OF THE FORCE
? 80
ENTER THE COORDINATES X1, Y1, Z1 OF FORCE
? 0,4,3
ENTER THE COORDINATES X2, Y2 Z2 OF FORCE
? 4.5,0,3
ENTER THE COORDINATES OF THE POINT P
? 0,0,0

MOMENT ABOUT THE POINT P
 159.447          179.378          -239.171
```

The three values on the last line are, respectively, the x, y, and z components of the desired moment. They agree with those found in Problem 1.8.

1.12   A force of 250 kN acts along the diagonal of a hollow box as indicated in Fig. 1-21. Determine the moment of the force about the base diagonal EA.

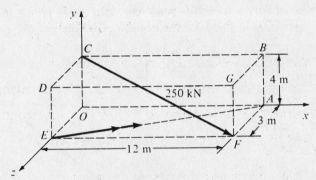

Fig. 1-21

Let us refer to Fig. 1-7. Axis CC in that figure corresponds to the line EA in the present problem. The desired moment is then given by (1.14). In that equation, the elements of the first row of the determinant are the direction cosines of CC (or, what is essentially the same thing, the direction cosines of the unit vector **C**). To find the direction cosines of EA in Fig. 1-21, we first note that its length is 12.37 m. Then its direction cosines are 12/12.37, 0, and $-3/12.37$; the minus sign is inserted because, in moving from E to A one moves in the negative z direction.

The elements of the second row of the determinant represent the coordinates of a position vector from the axis to the line of action of the force. We select (for convenience) the vector from E (0, 0, 3) to C (0, 4, 0); hence the elements of the second row are 0, 4, -3.

The elements of the last row of the determinant are the x, y, and z components of the force (here the 250-kN force). From the geometry, $CF = 13$ m, so the x, y, and z components of the force are 250 (12/13), -250 (4/13), and 250 (3/13), respectively. Thus, from (1.14), we have

$$|\mathbf{M}_{EA}| = \begin{vmatrix} \dfrac{12}{12.37} & 0 & -\dfrac{3}{12.37} \\[2mm] 0 & 4 & -3 \\[2mm] 250\dfrac{12}{13} & -250\dfrac{4}{13} & 250\dfrac{3}{13} \end{vmatrix} = 223.9 \text{ kN·m}$$

The fact that the resulting numerical value is positive indicates that the 250-kN force tends to produce clockwise rotation about the axis EA as viewed toward E from A. This is in accordance with the sense of rotation indicated in Fig. 1-7, where the force **F** obviously produces counterclockwise rotation about the CC axis as viewed down along the axis from above.

1.13 For the situation of Problem 1.9, find the moment of the 30,000-lb force about the axis C-C, which lies in the xz plane of Fig. 1-19.

We introduce a unit vector $\mathbf{C}$ along C-C. From the geometry, $\mathbf{C} = -0.5\mathbf{i} + 0.866\mathbf{k}$.

From (1.14) together with the component-wise representation of $\mathbf{F}$ in Problem 1.9, we have

$$|\mathbf{M}_{CC}| = \begin{vmatrix} -0.5 & 0 & 0.866 \\ 0 & 913 & 0 \\ -14{,}280 & -26{,}390 & 0 \end{vmatrix}$$

$$= (0.866)(0 + 13{,}038{,}000) = 11{,}291{,}000 \ \text{lb·ft}$$

The validity of this result is evident from Fig. 1-19, since $|\mathbf{M}_{CC}|$ is merely the component of $\mathbf{M}_0$ in the direction of C-C; that is, $|\mathbf{M}_0|\cos 30 = |\mathbf{M}_{CC}|$. The vector $\mathbf{M}_{CC}$ is shown in Fig. 1-19.

1.14 Develop a computer program in BASIC to determine the moment of a force in three-dimensional space about an arbitrary line in that space.

Let the force of magnitude F be represented as a vector with tail coordinates (x_1, y_1, z_1) and tip coordinates (x_2, y_2, z_2), as in Fig. 1-22. The moment about the axis C-C is desired.

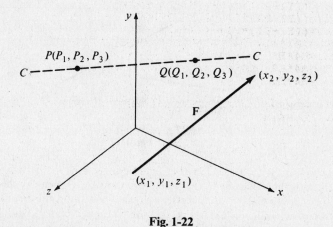

Fig. 1-22

Let point P, with coordinates (P_1, P_2, P_3), be any point on C-C, and let Q, with coordinates (Q_1, Q_2, Q_3), be a second point on C-C. The moment of $\mathbf{F}$ about C-C is given by (1.14). That equation is solved with the following program, which yields the components M_x, M_y, M_z of the desired moment:

```
00100 REM *** THIS PROGRAM DETERMINES THE MOMENT OF ANY GIVEN FORCE   ***
00110 REM *** IN SPACE ABOUT ANY GIVEN LINE 'PQ'                       ***
00120 REM
00130 REM ***                READ IN DATA                             ***
00140 REM
00150 PRINT "ENTER THE MAGNITUDE OF THE FORCE "
00160 INPUT F
00170 PRINT "ENTER THE COORDINATES X1, Y1, Z1 OF FORCE "
00180 INPUT X1,Y1,Z1
00190 PRINT "ENTER THE COORDINATES X2, Y2, Z2 OF FORCE "
00200 INPUT X2,Y2,Z2
00210 PRINT "ENTER THE COORDINATES OF THE POINT P "
00220 INPUT P1,P2,P3
00230 PRINT "ENTER THE COORDINATES OF THE POINT Q "
00240 INPUT Q1,Q2,Q3
```

```
00250 REM                                                        ***
00260 REM *** CALCULATE THE LENGTH OF VECTOR
00270 REM
00280 LET L=SQR((X2-X1)**2+(Y2-Y1)**2+(Z2-Z1)**2)
00290 REM
00300 REM *** CALCULATE THE X,Y,AND Z COMPONENTS OF FORCE        ***
00310 LET F1=((X2-X1)/L)*F
00320 LET F2=((Y2-Y1)/L)*F
00330 LET F3=((Z2-Z1)/L)*F
00340 REM
00350 REM *** CALCULATE THE COMPONENTS OF VECTOR QP              ***
00360 REM
00370 LET L1=P1-Q1
00380 LET L2=P2-Q2
00390 LET L3=P3-Q3
00400 REM
00410 REM ***CALCULATE THE COMPONENTS OF UNIT VECTOR E-QP        ***
00420 REM
00430 LET E=SQR((L1**2)+(L2**2)+(L3**2))
00440 LET E1=L1/E
00450 LET E2=L2/E
00460 LET E3=L3/E
00470 REM                                                        ***
00480 REM *** CALCULATE MOMENT ABOUT THE POINT
00490 REM
00500 LET M1=((Y1-P2)*F3)-((Z1-P3)*F2)
00510 LET M2=((Z1-P3)*F1)-((X1-P1)*F3)
00520 LET M3=((X1-P1)*F2)-((Y1-P2)*F1)
00530 LET M4=(M1*E1)+(M2*E2)+(M3*E3)
00540 LET M5=M4*E1
00550 LET M6=M4*E2
00560 LET M7=M4*E3
00570 PRINT
00580 PRINT "MOMENT ABOUT THE LINE PQ"
00590 PRINT M5,M6,M7
00600 END
```

1.15　Rework Problem 1.12 using the computer program of Problem 1.14.

　　　Referring to Fig. 1-21, we select C and F as the tail and tip of the force vector; hence　$(x_1, y_1, z_1) = (0, 4, 0)$ and $(x_2, y_2, z_2) = (12, 0, 3)$.　For the two points on the line EA about which the moment is sought, we select E and A; hence　$(P_1, P_2, P_3) = (0, 0, 3)$ and $(Q_1, Q_2, Q_3) = (12, 0, 0)$.　The program of Problem 1.14 then produces the following output:

```
ENTER THE MAGNITUDE OF THE FORCE
? 250
ENTER THE COORDINATES X1, Y1, Z1 OF FORCE
? 0,4,0
ENTER THE COORDINATES X2, Y2, Z2 OF FORCE
? 12,0,3
ENTER THE COORDINATES OF THE POINT P
? 0,0,3
ENTER THE COORDINATES OF THE POINT Q
? 12,0,0

MOMENT ABOUT THE LINE PQ
 217.195          0            -54.2986
```

Hence the components of the required moment are $M_x = 217.2$ kN·m, $M_y = 0$, $M_z = -54.3$ kN·m. These may be combined to yield

$$|\mathbf{M}_{EA}| = \sqrt{(217.2)^2 + 0^2 + (-54.3)^2} = 223.9 \text{ kN·m}$$

which agrees with the result of Problem 1.12.

1.16 Find the moment of the couple in Fig. 1-23. Both its forces lie on the inclined plane *AB*.

Taking moments about a point on either force of the couple yields

$$|\mathbf{M}| = (2 \text{ kN})(3 \text{ m}) = 6 \text{ kN·m}$$

The vector representation of this moment follows from the right-hand rule. The vector is *perpendicular* to the inclined plane *AB* and appears as indicated by the dashed moment vector in the figure.

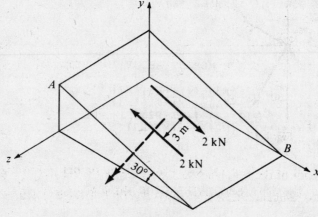

Fig. 1-23

1.17 A reinforced-concrete beam is being tested to failure by applying two couples. Cracking begins when one couple has the value 452 kN·m while simultaneously a perpendicular couple has the value 172 kN·m (Fig. 1-24). Find the sum of these two couples.

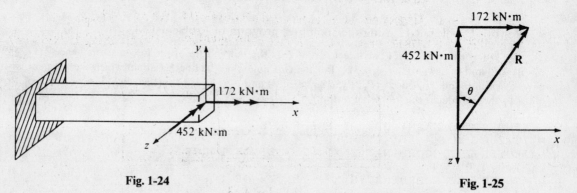

Fig. 1-24   **Fig. 1-25**

The vector representations of these two couples are added as indicated in Fig. 1-25:

$$\mathbf{R} = \sqrt{(172)^2 + (452)^2} = 483.6 \text{ kN·m} \qquad \theta = \arctan \frac{172}{452} = 20.8°$$

Their sum is thus a couple of magnitude 483.6 kN·m directed 20.8° from the transverse axis of the beam.

1.18   Find the resultant of the four concurrent forces in Fig. 1-26.

Denoting the resultant by **R**, we have, for its components,

$$R_x = -9 \cos 30° - 15 \cos 45° + 6 \cos 60° + 4 \sin 30°$$
$$= -7.79 - 10.61 + 3 + 2 = -13.40 \text{ kN}$$

$$R_y = -9 \sin 30° + 15 \sin 45° + 6 \sin 60° - 4 \cos 30°$$
$$= -4.50 + 10.61 + 5.20 - 3.46 = 7.85 \text{ kN}$$

Hence, $$|\mathbf{R}| = \sqrt{(-13.40)^2 + (7.85)^2} = 15.53 \text{ kN}$$

The direction of the resultant is found with Fig. 1-27 to be $\theta = \arctan 7.85/13.40 = 30.4°$.

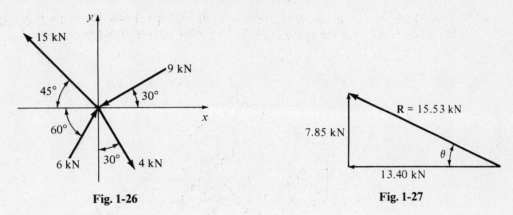

Fig. 1-26   **Fig. 1-27**

1.19   Find the resultant of the four parallel forces acting on bar AB in Fig. 1-28.

Denoting the resultant (which is obviously a vertical force) as **R** and summing forces (treating upward as positive), we have

$$R = -20 - 30 + 20 - 15 = -45 \text{ kN}$$

We must now determine the location of the line of action of **R**. To do this we select any convenient point, say A, and use Varignon's theorem to indicate that the moment of the resultant about A is equal to the sum of the moments of the various forces of the system about that same point. Let the distance of **R** from A be designated d. Then, arbitrarily taking clockwise as positive, we have

$$(45 \text{ kN})(d) = (30 \text{ kN})(2 \text{ m}) - (20 \text{ kN})(5 \text{ m}) + (15 \text{ kN})(8 \text{ m}) = 80 \text{ kN·m}$$

from which $d = 1.778$ m.   The resultant is thus a downward force of 45 kN acting 1.778 m to the right of point A.

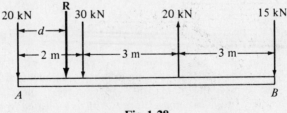

Fig. 1-28

1.20   Find the resultant of the four parallel forces acting on bar AB in Fig. 1-29.

Summing forces vertically yields

$$R = -30 - 10 + 20 + 20 = 0$$

The resultant is thus not a force, but the given force system may still have some turning effect. In that case the resultant would be a couple. Selecting a convenient moment center, say A, and taking clockwise moments about A to be positive, we have

$$M_A = (10 \text{ kN})(3 \text{ m}) - (20 \text{ kN})(6 \text{ m}) - (20 \text{ kN})(10 \text{ m}) = -290 \text{ kN·m}$$

The resultant of the given system is thus a counterclockwise couple of moment 290 kN·m.

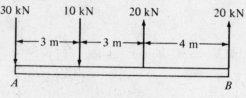

Fig. 1-29

1.21 Find the resultant of the system of two forces and one couple in Fig. 1-30.

Summing forces horizontally and vertically and remembering that the couple has no force effect in any direction, we obtain

$$R_x = -20 \cos 45 - 25 \cos 80 = -18.48 \text{ kN}$$
$$R_y = -20 \sin 45 + 25 \sin 80 = 10.48 \text{ kN}$$

and
$$|\mathbf{R}| = \sqrt{(-18.48)^2 + (10.48)^2} = 21.24 \text{ kN}$$

As indicated in Fig. 1-31, the resultant $\mathbf{R}$ acts at the angle $\theta = \arctan(10.48/18.48) = 29.56°$.

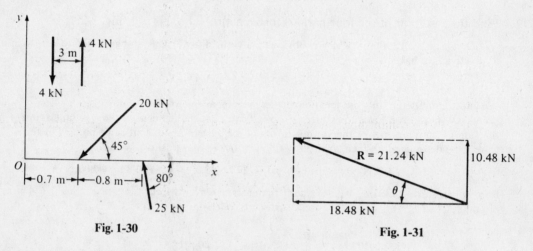

Fig. 1-30   **Fig. 1-31**

We must now locate the line of action of $\mathbf{R}$ within the coordinate system of Fig. 1-30. By Varignon's theorem, the moment of $\mathbf{R}$ about an arbitrary point, say O, must equal the sum of the moments of all the forces and couples in the original system about O; we shall use the theorem to write a moment equation. We first break the 20- and 25-kN forces into their x and y components, as indicated by the dashed arrows in Fig. 1-32, taking care to place the components of each force at the *same* point on the line of action of that force. We also assume a trial location for the resultant, as indicated by the solid vector $\mathbf{R}$ at the distance d from O.

Now, taking counterclockwise moments as positive, we obtain

$$21.24d = -(14.14 \text{ kN})(0.7 \text{ m}) + (24.62 \text{ kN})(1.5 \text{ m}) + 12 \text{ kN·m}$$

from which we find that $d = 1.838$ m. Because d turned out to be positive, we know that the assumed location of $\mathbf{R}$ is correct. If we had assumed the incorrect location shown in Fig. 1-33, the moment equation would have yielded a negative value for d.

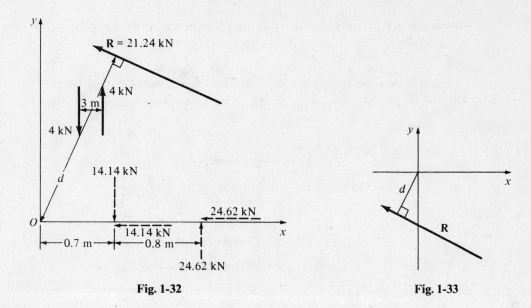

Fig. 1-32

Fig. 1-33

1.22   A building that is 60 m tall has essentially the rectangular configuration shown in Fig. 1-34. Horizontal wind loads will act on the building, exerting pressures on the vertical face that are expected to be uniform within each of three "layers" as shown. These pressures are:

Height above Ground, m	Design Wind Speed, m/s	Pressure, N/m^2
0–20	35.7	781
20–40	45.4	1264
40–60	49.9	1530

Determine the resultant horizontal wind force expected to act on the face of the structure.

We have

$$|\mathbf{P}_1| = (20 \text{ m})(50 \text{ m})(781 \text{ N/m}^2) = 781 \text{ kN}$$
$$|\mathbf{P}_2| = (20 \text{ m})(50 \text{ m})(1264 \text{ N/m}^2) = 1264 \text{ kN}$$
$$|\mathbf{P}_3| = (20 \text{ m})(50 \text{ m})(1530 \text{ N/m}^2) = 1530 \text{ kN}$$

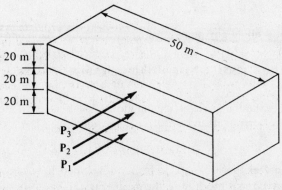

Fig. 1-34

These forces are taken to act at the midpoint of each layer and appear as shown in Fig. 1-35. Their resultant is

$$|\mathbf{R}| = 781 + 1264 + 1530 = 3575 \text{ N}$$

To locate its line of action, we use Varignon's theorem: The moment of $\mathbf{R}$ about any point, say O, is equal to the sum of the moments of the three forces about that same point. Thus, we have

$$781(10) + 1264(30) + 1530(50) = 3575d$$

from which $d = 34.19$ m.

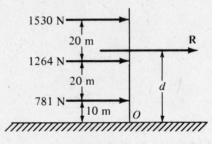

Fig. 1-35

1.23   The weight and water-pressure forces on a bulkhead are as shown in Fig. 1-36. Find the resultant $\mathbf{R}$ of the four given forces.

Summing forces vertically and horizontally yields

$$R_x = -7500 \text{ lb}$$
$$R_y = -3500 - 14,000 - 2200 = -19,700 \text{ lb}$$

so that

$$|\mathbf{R}| = \sqrt{(-7500)^2 + (-19,700)^2} = 21,080 \text{ lb}$$

and, from Fig. 1-37, $\theta = \arctan (19,700/7500) = 69.16°$.

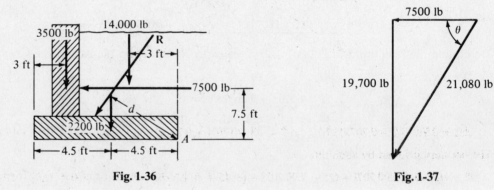

Fig. 1-36   **Fig. 1-37**

The moment of $\mathbf{R}$ about any point must equal the sum of the moments of the four given forces about that point. Selecting point A for convenience and taking counterclockwise moments as positive, we have

$$21,080d = (7500 \text{ lb})(7.5 \text{ ft}) + (14,000 \text{ lb})(3 \text{ ft}) + (3500 \text{ lb})(6 \text{ ft}) + (2200 \text{ lb})(4.5 \text{ ft})$$

or $d = 6.125$ ft.

The resultant is thus a force of magnitude 21,080 lb directed downward and to the left at an angle of 69.16° to the horizontal, and whose line of action lies 6.125 ft from A.

1.24   A three-dimensional expandable space frame developed for the U.S. space program consists of hinged elements. A typical module is shown in Fig. 1-38: Point A is located at the center of an imaginary cube outlining the module, and B, C, and D are situated at the midpoints of cube

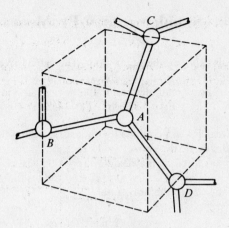

Fig. 1-38

edges.* If *AC* carries a tensile force of 25 kN, *AB* a tension of 40 kN, and *AD* a tension of 15 kN, find the resultant force acting at *A*.

The forces may be represented as in Fig. 1-39. They may be represented in component form as

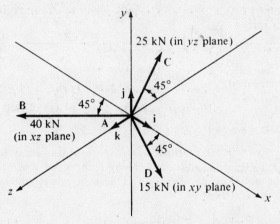

Fig. 1-39

$$\mathbf{AC} = 25(0.707\mathbf{j} - 0.707\mathbf{k})\,\text{kN} \qquad \mathbf{AB} = 40(-0.707\mathbf{i} + 0.707\mathbf{k})\,\text{kN} \qquad \mathbf{AD} = 15(0.707\mathbf{i} - 0.707\mathbf{j})\,\text{kN}$$

The resultant is found by addition:

$$\mathbf{R} = [(-40 + 15)0.707\mathbf{i} + (25 - 15)0.707\mathbf{j} + (-25 + 40)0.707\mathbf{k}]\,\text{kN} = (-17.68\mathbf{i} + 7.07\mathbf{j} + 10.6\mathbf{k})\,\text{kN}$$

Its magnitude is

$$|\mathbf{R}| = \sqrt{(-17.68)^2 + (7.07)^2 + (10.6)^2} = 21.78\,\text{kN}$$

The direction cosines of the resultant are

$$\cos\theta_x = \frac{-17.68}{21.78} = 0.812 \qquad \cos\theta_y = \frac{7.07}{21.78} = 0.325 \qquad \cos\theta_z = \frac{10.6}{21.78} = 0.487$$

The sum of the squares of the direction cosines should equal unity; hence we may check by computing $(0.812)^2 + (0.325)^2 + (0.487)^2 = 1.00$.

---

* Adapted from *Mechanical Engineering*, July 1975, p. 49.

Supplementary Problems

1.25   A ship lays communications cable on the ocean floor. The cable leaves a reel on the ship with a tension of 8000 lb, caused by the pull of cable that has already been unwound. If the cable comes off the ship at an angle of 35° down from the horizontal, determine the horizontal and vertical components of the force the cable exerts on the ship.   *Ans.* $F_H = 6553$ lb; $F_V = 4589$ lb

1.26   One of the lunar landing vehicles was equipped with a surface sampling system capable of digging into the lunar surface with a small shovel; the shovel could then be rotated to deposit the sample in a container (Fig. 1-40*). If the horizontal force in the flexible tape is 350 N and the torsion springs create a 100-N compressive force in the bar attached to the shovel, find the resultant force exerted by the linkage on the shovel.   *Ans.*   288 N, at 14.2° to the horizontal

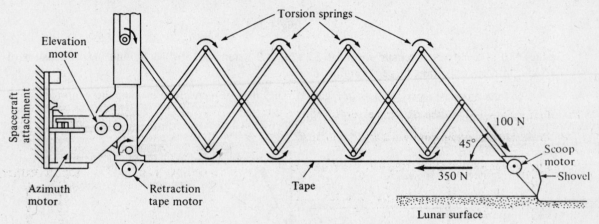

Fig. 1-40

1.27   In designing structures to withstand tornadoes, it is convenient to separate the so-called "moving velocity" of the wind (**C** in Fig. 1-41) into a tangential velocity **T** and a radial velocity **R**. If the tangential velocity is found to be 75 m/s, the radial velocity is 30 m/s, and the angle between these two vectors is 135°, determine the moving velocity **C**.   *Ans.*   98.5 m/s

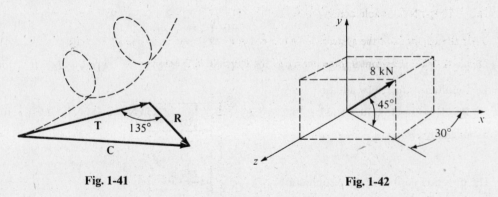

Fig. 1-41   **Fig. 1-42**

1.28   An 8-kN force is directed as shown in Fig. 1-42. Determine the x, y, and z components of this force.

   Ans. $F_x = 4.899$ N; $F_y = 5.657$ N; $F_z = 2.829$ N

---

* Adapted from *JPL Space Programs Summary 37-43*, vol. VI, p. 5. Provided through the courtesy of the Jet Propulsion Laboratory, California Institute of Technology, Pasadena, California.

1.29 In Problem 1.27 we considered a two-dimensional representation of a tornado. A more realistic approach is to include a vertical velocity (Fig. 1-43). In a particular tornado, at a distance of 100 ft from the "eye" of the tornado, the tangential velocity is 130 mi/h, the vertical velocity is 100 mi/h, and the radial velocity is 120 mi/h. What is the resultant velocity?

Ans.   203 mi/h ($\cos \theta_x = 0.640$, $\cos \theta_y = 0.492$, $\cos \theta_z = 0.5911$)

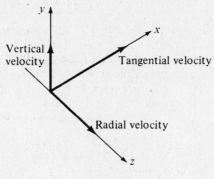

Fig. 1-43

1.30 Find the resultant of the six parallel forces acting on bar AB in Fig. 1-44.

Ans.   300 kN, acting downward at 15.83 m to the left of A

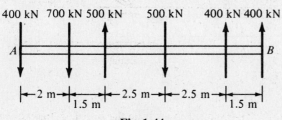

Fig. 1-44

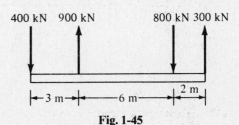

Fig. 1-45

1.31 Find the resultant of the four parallel forces acting on bar AB in Fig. 1-45.

Ans.   1200-kN·m couple acting clockwise

1.32 Find the resultant of the system of two forces and one couple shown in Fig. 1-46.

Ans.   A 440-lb horizontal force acting to the left at 3.36 ft below A

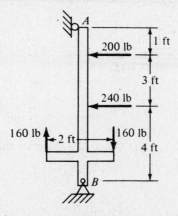

Fig. 1-46

1.33   Find **A** × **B** for the vectors **A** and **B** in Fig. 1-47.

Ans.   **A** × **B** = 15**j** − 10**k**; |**A** × **B**| = 18.03 with direction cosines 0, 0.832, −0.555

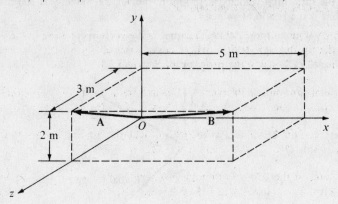

Fig. 1-47

1.34   A 24,000-lb force acts on a beam as shown in Fig. 1-48. Find the moment of this force about an axis through *A* and perpendicular to the plane of the page.   *Ans.*   233,100 lb·ft

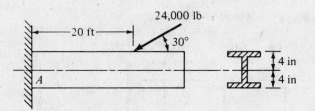

Fig. 1-48

1.35   Find the moment of the 160-kN force in Fig. 1-49 about *O*.

Ans.   **M**₀ = −19.4**i** + 84.8**j** + 99.4**k**; |**M**₀| = 132.1 kN·m

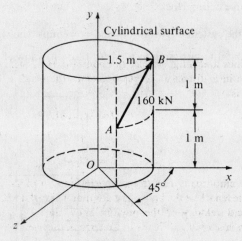

Fig. 1-49

1.36   In Problem 1.35, find the moment of the 160-kN force about the *x* axis.   *Ans.*   −179.4**i** kN·m

1.37   Guy cable ②in Problem 1.9 is tensioned with a force of 48,000 lb. (*a*) Determine the moment of this force about the tower base *O*.   (*b*) Determine the moment of this force about the axis *C-C* in Fig. 1-19.

Ans.   (*a*) 19,220,000**k** lb·ft; (*b*) 16,660,000 lb·ft

1.38   Consider a force of magnitude 150 kN. The tail of the vector representing the force passes through the point (2, 0, 3), and the tip through (0, 6, 0), where coordinates are in meters. Determine the moment of the force about the point (0, 6, 3), using the program of Problem 1.10.   *Ans.*   (385.7**i** + 128.6**j**) kN·m

1.39   Use the computer program of Problem 1.14 to find the moment of the 250-kN force in Problem 1.12 about the diagonal *DB*.   *Ans.* $M_x = -217.2$ kN·m; $M_y = 0$; $M_z = 54.3$ kN·m

1.40   Find the moment of the 250-kN force in Problem 1.12 about a line parallel to the *y* axis and passing through the midpoint of side *OE*.   *Ans.* $M_x = 0$; $M_y = -346.2$ kN·m; $M_z = 0$

1.41   Find the moment of the 250-kN force in Problem 1.12 about an axis passing through point *G* and the midpoint of line *CB*.   *Ans.* $M_x = 184.6$ kN·m; $M_y = 0$; $M_z = 92.3$ kN·m

1.42   The rigid block in Fig. 1-50 is acted upon by three couples as indicated. Find the resultant of the system.

Ans.   1591-N·m moment having direction cosines $\cos \theta_x = 0.503$, $\cos \theta_y = -0.864$, $\cos \theta_z = 0$

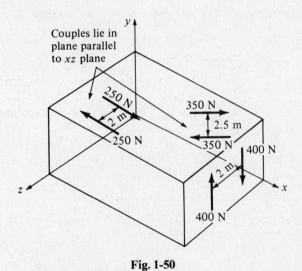

Fig. 1-50

1.43   Power transmission lines and long, slender horizontal bars of rectangular cross section may, when subject to wind loads, vibrate in a direction perpendicular to the wind. If the wind velocity is $\mathbf{V}_{rel}$, the resulting drag force on a body is

$$\mathbf{D} = \tfrac{1}{2} C_D \rho h L V_{rel}^2$$

and the lifting force is

$$\mathbf{L} = \tfrac{1}{2} C_L \rho h L V_{rel}^2$$

where C_D and C_L are empirically determined coefficients, ρ is the mass density of the air, h is the depth of the body, and L is the length of the body. The angle at which the wind strikes the body is $\alpha = \arctan(V_y/V)$, where V_y is the vertical velocity of the moving body, and V is the horizontal component of the wind velocity. The situation is shown in Fig. 1-51. Determine the force component F_y causing vertical vibration.

Ans. $F_y = \tfrac{1}{2} \rho h L V^2 (\sec^2 \alpha)(C_D \sin \alpha + C_L \cos \alpha)$

1.44   A rigid metal slab is subject to the three concentrated forces shown in Fig. 1-52. Find the resultant of this force system.   *Ans.*   A 125-kN force acting at $x = 0.213$ ft and $z = 0.408$ ft

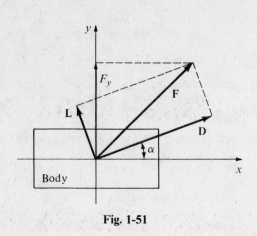

Fig. 1-51

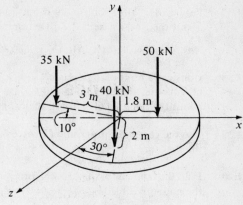

Fig. 1-52

Chapter 2

Statics: Equilibria of Rigid Bodies

FREE-BODY DIAGRAM

The free-body diagram of a structure or component consists of a drawing (approximately to scale) of the structure or component, together with vectors representing the effects of all forces and couples acting directly on it, due to bodies in contact with its surface (so-called *surface forces*) as well as to gravitational (weight), magnetic, and other volume-distributed effects (called *body forces*). Unknown forces (usually corresponding to reactions) must be designated by vectors applied at points of known support.

SUPPORT DESIGNATIONS

Roller Reaction

Because of the nature of a roller, there is only a single vertical reaction force $\mathbf{R}_A$ acting at the point of support A, as shown in Fig. 2-1. (See Problems 2.5 and 2.6.) This is often called a *smooth-surface reaction*.

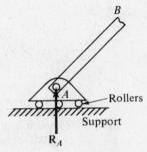

Fig. 2-1

Similarly, a tubular collar on a frictionless bar CD (Fig. 2-2) can transmit to the pinned member AB only a force $\mathbf{F}$ normal to CD.

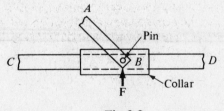

Fig. 2-2

Pin Reaction

A structural member AB that is joined to a supporting body by a frictionless pin (or hinge) capable of transmitting only a force (but no moment) from the support to the member is depicted as in Fig. 2-3.

27

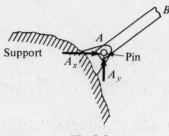

Fig. 2-3

The force transmitted to the member is often designated by its horizontal and vertical components. Thus, at the point of attachment A the structural member AB is subject to the force components A_x and A_y shown.

Rough-Surface Reaction

A structural member AB in contact with a rough surface is subject to two reaction components, A_x and A_y in Fig. 2-4, just as if it were pinned. These components are termed the *frictional* and *normal* components of the reaction, respectively, and are usually designated F and N.

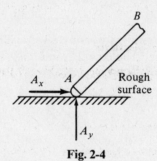

Fig. 2-4

Clamped (Fixed) Reaction

If a structural member CD, subject to couples and forces, is joined to a support in such a manner that both translation and rotation are prevented at the joint C between the two (e.g., by welding), the system is depicted as in Fig. 2-5. The effect of the support on member CD is indicated with horizontal and vertical force components C_x and C_y, together with a moment (couple) $\mathbf{M}_C$ that prevents rotation at the point of support C (Fig. 2-6).

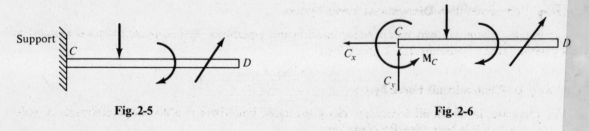

Fig. 2-5   Fig. 2-6

Elastic (Spring) Reaction

Occasionally a loaded structural member EF is in contact with a flexible member GH that permits some deformation of EF at the point of contact (Fig. 2-7). The effect of GH on EF is to exert a spring-type force $\mathbf{F}_{\text{spring}}$ at the point of contact. Thus, a free-body diagram of EF would be drawn as in Fig. 2-8. (See Problem 2.6.)

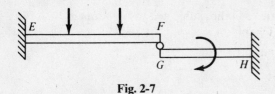

Fig. 2-7

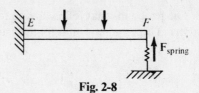

Fig. 2-8

REQUIRED NUMBER OF INDEPENDENT EQUILIBRIUM EQUATIONS

For a *general three-dimensional force system*,

$$\Sigma\, \mathbf{F} = 0 \quad \text{and} \quad \Sigma\, \mathbf{M}_0 = 0$$

Alternatively, in terms of components along the x, y, and z axes, these vector relations become

$$\Sigma\, F_x = 0 \qquad \Sigma\, F_y = 0 \qquad \Sigma\, F_z = 0$$

$$\Sigma\, M_x = 0 \qquad \Sigma\, M_y = 0 \qquad \Sigma\, M_z = 0$$

General Three-Dimensional Concurrent Force System

Such a system involves three independent equilibrium equations. These may be force equations, moment equations, or any combination of force and moment equations.

General Three-Dimensional Parallel Force System

Such a system again involves three independent scalar equations. Alternatively, a vector solution method may be utilized.

General Two-Dimensional Coplanar Force System

Three independent scalar equilibrium equations are available. A scalar solution method is often simplest and most direct. (See Problems 2.5 and 2.10 through 2.12.)

General Two-Dimensional Parallel Force System

In this case there are two independent equilibrium equations: one force equation and one moment equation or two moment equations. Scalar solution methods are usually most efficient. (See Problems 2.6 to 2.8.)

Coplanar, Concurrent Two-Dimensional Force System

Here again there are two independent equilibrium equations. The simplest solution method is a scalar method. (See Problems 2.2, 2.3, and 2.4.)

Collinear (One-Dimensional) Force System

For this case, in which all forces act along the same line, there is only one equilibrium equation. The scalar approach is best. (See Problem 2.9.)

Two-Force Member

A special case of the collinear force system is a body that is in equilibrium under the action of two forces, which then must be of equal magnitude and oppositely directed along the same line of action. Such a loaded body is termed a *two-force member*. (See Problems 2.1 and 2.4.)

The problems that follow are concerned with equilibria of bodies subjected to two-dimensional force systems. Three-dimensional force systems are treated in Chapter 4.

Solved Problems

2.1   A weight W is suspended from a fine wire AB and a very flexible wire BCD, which passes over a frictionless pulley at C (Fig. 2-9). The end of wire BCD is attached to a 10-kN weight, and the wires make the angles shown with the vertical. Determine the tension in wire AB and the weight W.

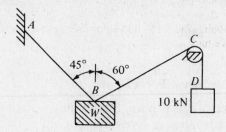

Fig. 2-9

We first draw the free-body diagram for the pulley (Fig. 2-10b), showing the effects of all bodies in contact with it. These include the horizontal and vertical components of the reactions at the pulley axle and the tension in wire BCD. Because the pulley is free of friction, the 10-kN force due to the weight passes unchanged over the pulley and appears as tension in wire BC, as shown.

Next, we draw the free-body diagram for the weight W (Fig. 2-10a). The 10-kN force in wire BC, the unknown tension $\mathbf{T}_{AB}$, and the gravitational attraction $\mathbf{W}$ act on it. (Although it is best to draw the pulley (part b) first, the bodies should be placed in proper position relative to each other.) Note the axes indicating the positive x and y directions.

For equilibrium at B (Fig. 2-10a),

$$\Sigma F_x = 10 \sin 60 - |\mathbf{T}_{AB}| \sin 45 = 0 \qquad \text{or} \qquad T_{AB} = 12.2 \text{ kN}$$

and

$$\Sigma F_y = 12.2 \cos 45 + 10 \cos 60 - |\mathbf{W}| = 0 \qquad \text{or} \qquad |\mathbf{W}| = 13.6 \text{ kN}$$

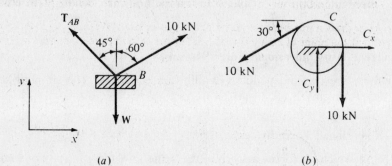

(a)   (b)

Fig. 2-10

2.2   A cylindrical liquid-storage tank weighing 2000 N is to be pushed over a change of elevation of 0.25 m by a horizontal force $\mathbf{F}$, as indicated in Fig. 2-11. Determine the magnitude of $\mathbf{F}$ required for the tank to just break contact with the ground at A.

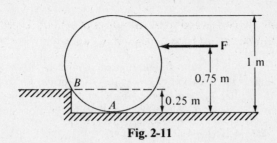

Fig. 2-11

The complete free-body diagram for the tank is shown in Fig. 2-12. Note that the tank is in equilibrium under the action of three nonparallel forces, including the reaction $\mathbf{R}_B$ at B. Hence, the lines of action of these forces must intersect at a common point in the plane of the forces. (Otherwise, the forces would give rise to an unbalanced moment and, hence, acceleration.) This establishes the direction of $\mathbf{R}_B$. Since we are not seeking the reaction at B, we can use point B as a moment center for our equilibrium equation. Denoting the sum of the moments about B as $\Sigma\, M_B$ and using the symbol $+\circlearrowright$ to indicate that we are taking clockwise moments to be positive, we have

$$+\circlearrowright \Sigma\, M_B = -0.50|\mathbf{F}| + 2000\,\frac{\sqrt{3}}{4} = 0$$

from which $|\mathbf{F}| = 1732\text{ N}.$

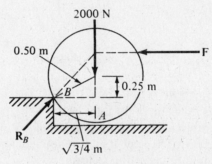

Fig. 2-12

2.3 Three identical solid metal cylinders, each of unit length, are stacked within a rigid bin as shown in Fig. 2-13. The weight of each cylinder is 400 N. Find the forces at the points where the cylinders touch one another and the walls of the bin. Assume that there is no friction at any contact surface.

First, let us draw a free-body diagram for the top cylinder. We let $\mathbf{R}_1$ denote the force (acting along the 45° line through the point of contact) that each of the lower cylinders exerts on the upper one (Fig. 2-14).

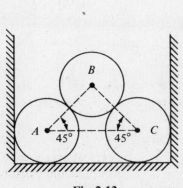

Fig. 2-13

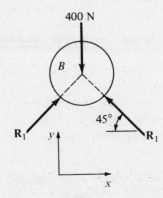

Fig. 2-14

Then, for equilibrium,

$$\Sigma F_y = 2|\mathbf{R}_1| \sin 45° - 400 = 0$$

from which $|\mathbf{R}_1| = 283$ N. Note that designating each force as $\mathbf{R}_1$, and thus taking advantage of the symmetry, effectively utilizes the equation of horizontal equilibrium for cylinder B.

We may now draw the free-body diagram for cylinder A at the lower left. This is done in Fig. 2-15, where $\mathbf{R}_2$ and $\mathbf{R}_3$ denote the forces the bin exerts on the cylinder. For equilibrium,

$$\Sigma F_y = |\mathbf{R}_3| - 400 - 283 \sin 45° = 0 \qquad \text{or} \qquad |\mathbf{R}_3| = 600 \text{ N}$$

$$\Sigma F_x = |\mathbf{R}_2| - 283 \cos 45° = 0 \qquad \text{or} \qquad |\mathbf{R}_2| = 200 \text{ N}$$

and similarly for cylinder C.

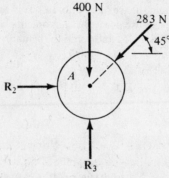

Fig. 2-15

2.4 The four-bar mechanism $ABCD$ in Fig. 2-16 is attached by a spring at its left end to a rigid wall and by a rigid bar at its right end to the right wall. The spring constant is 10.2 kN/m; that is, a force of 10.2 kN is required to stretch the spring 1 m. Initially, when $a = 0$, all bars are horizontal and the spring tension is 200 N. The load $\mathbf{P}$ is then applied, and the bars open to the position shown. Find the force $\mathbf{P}$ required to cause this deformation.

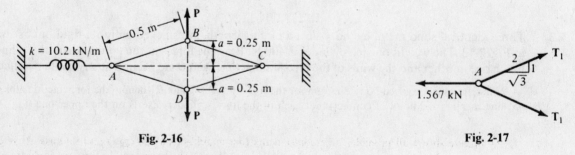

Fig. 2-16   **Fig. 2-17**

When $a = 0$, the spring is stretched beyond its unloaded length by

$$\frac{200 \text{ N}}{10,200 \text{ N/m}} = 0.0196 \text{ m}$$

with the frame pulled open to the position shown, the horizontal projections of bars AB and BC are, from the geometry, both equal to $\sqrt{(0.5)^2 - (0.25)^2} = 0.433$ m. Thus, the total stretch of the spring beyond its unloaded length is

$$0.0196 + 2(0.500 - 0.433) = 0.1536 \text{ m}$$

The spring tension corresponding to this total stretch is

$$T = (0.1536 \text{ m})(10.2 \text{ kN/m}) = 1.567 \text{ kN}$$

We may now draw a free-body diagram for the pin at A; this is done in Fig. 2-17, where $\mathbf{T}_1$ is the axial force in bars AB and AD. For equilibrium,

$$\Sigma F_x = -1.567 + 2|\mathbf{T}_1| \frac{\sqrt{3}}{2} = 0$$

so that $|\mathbf{T}_1| = 0.905$ kN.

Finally, we draw the free-body diagram for the pin at B (Fig. 2-18) and note that, for equilibrium,

$$\Sigma F_y = |\mathbf{P}| - 2(0.905)(\tfrac{1}{2}) = 0$$

from which $|\mathbf{P}| = 0.905$ kN.

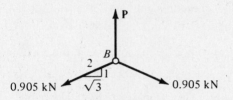

Fig. 2-18

2.5 The simple crane in Fig. 2-19, which is lifting a vertical load of 8000 lb, is rigidly attached to the horizontal base AB. The base is pinned at point A and rests on a smooth cylindrical roller at B. Neglecting the weight of the crane, find the reactions at points A and B.

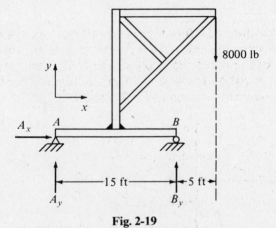

Fig. 2-19

The figure shows all possible force components that could act on the crane and its base. (It is good practice to show both force components at the pin A, even though the horizontal component is clearly zero.) For equilibrium, we have

$$+\!\curvearrowleft \Sigma M_A = 8000(20) - 15B_y = 0 \qquad \text{or} \qquad B_y = 10{,}670 \text{ lb}$$

and

$$\Sigma F_y = A_y + 10{,}670 - 8000 = 0 \qquad \text{or} \qquad A_y = -2670 \text{ lb}$$

Also,

$$\Sigma F_x = A_x = 0$$

2.6 The horizontal rigid bars AB and CD in Fig. 2-20 are subject to vertical forces of 2 kN and 1 kN as shown. Ends A and D are pinned, and bar CD rests on a smooth cylindrical roller located at E. Further, ends B and C interact through a second cylindrical roller as indicated. Determine the reaction at the right end of bar CD.

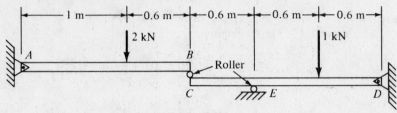

Fig. 2-20

The smooth rollers can exert only normal forces on the rigid bars. Since these forces are vertical and the applied loadings are vertical, the pin reactions at A and D must also be vertical only, although each of these pins has the capability of exerting both horizontal and vertical force components. Thus, the free-body diagrams for the two bars appear as in Fig. 2-21, where $\mathbf{R}_1$ represents the vertical force exerted by the roller interacting with the bars.

From the left-hand free-body diagram, we have, in the notation of (*1.10*),

$$+\circlearrowleft \Sigma M_A = (2 \text{ kN})(1 \text{ m}) - |\mathbf{R}_1|(1.6 \text{ m}) = 0$$

from which $|\mathbf{R}_1| = 1.25$ kN. Then, from the right-hand free-body diagram,

$$+\circlearrowleft \Sigma M_E = (1 \text{ kN})(0.6 \text{ m}) - |\mathbf{R}_D|(1.2 \text{ m}) - (1.25 \text{ kN})(0.6 \text{ m}) = 0$$

so that $|\mathbf{R}_D| = -0.125$ kN. That is, the reaction at D is downward.

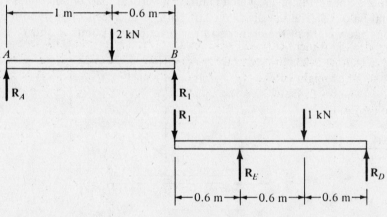

Fig. 2-21

2.7 A shipyard crane moves on rails that are 8 ft apart (Fig. 2-22) and is designed to be able to lift a load of $P = 30$ tons. The weight of the crane itself is 30 tons, and a massive counterbalance of unknown weight W is located at the left end of the crane (point A). The weight of the crane acts through the center of gravity of the system, which is located 1.5 ft to the right of wheel C. Assume that the reactions of the rails on wheels B and C involve only vertical components. The crane must not tip to the right when the full load of 30 tons is lifted, and it must not tip to the left when no load is being lifted. Use these two criteria to determine the magnitude and location of the counterweight.

When the load of 30 tons is being lifted and the crane is just on the verge of tipping about point C, there is no force acting between the track and the wheel at B. Then we have, for equilibrium,

$$+\circlearrowleft \Sigma M_C = 30(15) + 30(1.5) - |\mathbf{W}|(x + 8) = 0 \quad \text{or} \quad |\mathbf{W}|x + 8|\mathbf{W}| = 495 \tag{1}$$

When no load is being lifted and the crane is just on the verge of tipping about point B, there is no force acting between the track and the wheel at C. For equilibrium in this case we have

$$+\circlearrowleft \Sigma M_B = -|\mathbf{W}|x + 30(9.5) = 0 \quad \text{or} \quad |\mathbf{W}|x = 285 \tag{2}$$

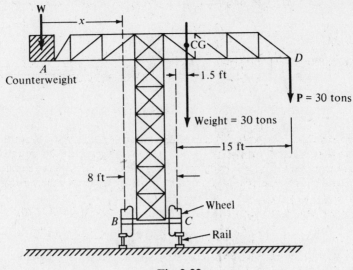

Fig. 2-22

Both these conditions must be satisfied simultaneously. Substituting (2) in (1) yields $|\mathbf{W}| = 26.25$ tons, and then substitution in (2) gives $x = 10.86$ ft.

2.8   Two rigid bars of identical cross section are welded together with their ends at an angle of 60°, as shown in Fig. 2-23. End A is suspended from a fine wire, and end C is subject to a vertical load $W/2$. The weight of bar AB is W, and its length is L; the corresponding quantities for bar BC are $2W$ and $2L$. Determine the angle θ between BC and the horizontal when the system is in equilibrium.

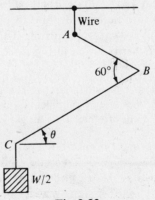

Fig. 2-23

Let us begin by making a relatively accurate sketch of the system in a plausible equilibrium configuration. In particular, let us assume that the angle θ is such that the weight of bar BC acting through the midpoint of BC has its line of action to the *left* of point A. Then we obtain Fig. 2-24 and, from the geometry, we have for equilibrium

$$+\circlearrowleft \Sigma\, M_A = W\frac{L}{2}\cos(60° - \theta) - 2W[L\cos\theta - L\cos(60° - \theta)] - \frac{W}{2}[2L\cos\theta - L\cos(60° - \theta)] = 0$$

Simplifying yields

$$\cos(60 - \theta) = \cos\theta$$

from which we find that $\theta = 30°$.

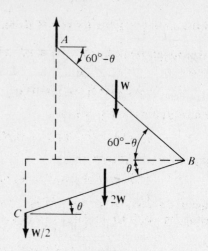

Fig. 2-24

Does this result depend upon our assumption that the line of action of the gravitational attraction 2**W** lies to the left of point *A*? To answer this question, we should draw a second free-body diagram showing the action line passing to the *right* of *A*. We would find that a summation of moments about *A* leads to the exact same solution. Thus, the result is independent of the assumption, provided care is taken in specifying the geometry of the moment arms.

2.9   An aerospace manufacturer is designing a hybrid balloon-helicopter system, called the "helicostat," to serve as a flying crane for transporting material in mountainous regions. The system consists of two cylindrical horizontal balloons, each 26 m long and 12 m in diameter, linked by a trusslike structure below which hangs a small cabin to accommodate one person. A cable below this cabin lifts loads as great as 20,000 N. Each balloon is filled with helium. The truss between the balloons supports two turbine engines, one to power a helicopter rotor for lifting, and the other to drive a propeller for forward propulsion. The weight of the two balloons, truss, engines, and operator is 27,300 N. Determine the lifting force that the helicopter rotor must exert to lift a 20,000-N load.

For a balloon filled with a lighter-than-air gas, the principle of Archimedes, familiar from physics, states that a lift L_G is produced because of the difference in the densities of air and gas. That is, displacing a volume of air with an equal volume of lighter-than-air gas gives rise to a net upward force. For the helicostat,

$$L_G = Q_{\text{air}} - Q_{\text{He}}$$

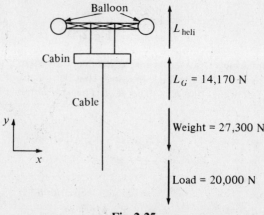

Fig. 2-25

where Q_{air} is the weight of the air displaced by the two balloons, and Q_{He} is the weight of the helium in both balloons.

From tables of physical constants we find that air weighs 4.16 N/m³ and helium weighs 1.75 N/m³. The volume of the two balloons is

$$2\pi(6 \text{ m})^2(26 \text{ m}) = 5880 \text{ m}^3$$

Thus, the weight of the air displaced by both balloons is

$$(5880 \text{ m}^3)(4.16 \text{ N/m}^3) = 24{,}460 \text{ N}$$

and the weight of the helium in the two balloons is

$$(5880 \text{ m}^3)(1.75 \text{ N/m}^3) = 10{,}290 \text{ N}$$

Consequently the lift L_G due to the balloons is $L_G = 24{,}460 - 10{,}290 = 14{,}170$ N.

We thus have the situation depicted in Fig. 2-25, where L_{heli} is the required helicopter rotor lift. Then

$$\Sigma F_y = L_{heli} + 14{,}170 - 27{,}300 - 20{,}000 = 0$$

and $L_{heli} = 33{,}130$ N.

2.10   A flight simulator for training aircraft pilots appears as shown in Fig. 2-26. The forward portion of an aircraft, weighing 2500 lb with the horizontal platform, is rigidly attached to the platform; they are raised or lowered as CD rotates about an axle at C. Additional movement is provided as plunger ED moves within cylinder CE. The lower cylinder-plunger device AFB rotates about an axle at A and is constrained to be in contact with CED by a bracket that can transmit to

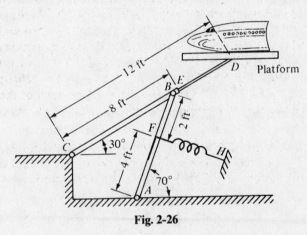

Fig. 2-26

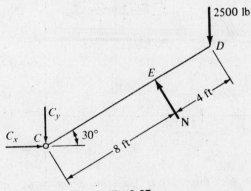

Fig. 2-27

CED only a force normal to *CED*. Stiffness is imparted to the system by spring *FH*. Determine the force the spring exerts on *AFB* in the position shown.

The free-body diagram for *CED* is shown in Fig. 2-27. For equilibrium,

$$+\circlearrowleft \Sigma M_C = 2500(12) \cos 30° - 8|\mathbf{N}| = 0$$

from which $|\mathbf{N}| = 3250$ lb. Now the free-body diagram for *AB* may be drawn, as in Fig. 2-28, where $\mathbf{N}_1$ is the required spring force. Again, for equilibrium,

$$+\circlearrowleft \Sigma M_A = (3250)(\cos 30°)(6 \cos 70°) + (3250)(\sin 30°)(6 \sin 70°) - 4|\mathbf{N}_1| = 0$$

from which $|\mathbf{N}_1| = 3735$ lb.

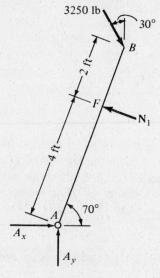

Fig. 2-28

2.11 Curved bars *AB* and *BC* in Fig. 2-29 are pinned at ends *A* and *C* and joined together by a pin at *B*. Such a system is called a *three-hinged arch*. The loading consists of the 36-kN vertical force shown. Determine the reactions at pins *A* and *C*.

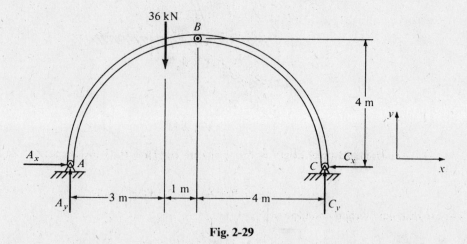

Fig. 2-29

Let us first work with the entire arch system, remembering that the pin forces at *B* are internal to the entire system and hence do not appear in the system free-body diagram. In that case, Fig. 2-29 serves as the free-body diagram, and we have

$$+\curvearrowleft \Sigma M_A = 36(3) - 8C_y = 0 \qquad \text{or} \qquad C_y = 13.5 \text{ N}$$

$$\Sigma F_y = A_y + 13.5 - 36 = 0 \qquad \text{or} \qquad A_y = 22.5 \text{ N}$$

$$\Sigma F_x = A_x - C_x = 0 \qquad \text{or} \qquad A_x = C_x$$

Next let us consider bar BC. (Although Fig. 2-30 shows the free-body diagrams for both AB and BC, we need only use that for BC.) For equilibrium for bar BC,

$$+\curvearrowleft \Sigma M_B = 4C_x - 13.5(4) = 0$$

from which $C_x = 13.5$ N and, therefore, $A_x = 13.5$ N. Note that, since A_x and C_x are found to be positive, they must act in the directions shown in Fig. 2-30.

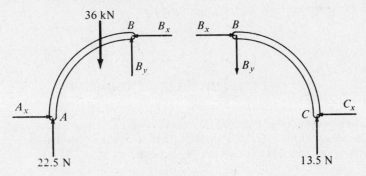

Fig. 2-30

2.12 The rigid bar BC in Fig. 2-31 is pinned at end C and supported by a spring at B. The spring constant (i.e., the force required to stretch the spring a unit length) is k. The spring is unstretched when $\theta = 45$. Then a load P is applied at the midpoint of BC. Neglecting the weights of BC and the spring, find the value of θ when the system reaches equilibrium.

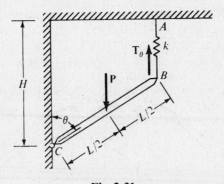

Fig. 2-31

Let the unstretched (free) length of the spring be L_0. Then from the geometry, $L_0 = H - L \cos 45°$ and

$$H = L_0 + L \cos 45° \tag{1}$$

For moment equilibrium about point C,

$$+\curvearrowleft \Sigma M_C = |\mathbf{P}| \frac{L}{2} \sin \theta - |\mathbf{T}_\theta| L \sin \theta = 0 \qquad \text{or} \qquad |\mathbf{T}_\theta| = \frac{|\mathbf{P}|}{2} \tag{2}$$

where $\mathbf{T}_\theta$ denotes the spring force when the system is at equilibrium.

From the definition of the spring constant,

$$|\mathbf{T}_\theta| = (H - L\cos\theta - L_0)k \qquad (3)$$

Substituting (1) in (3) yields

$$|\mathbf{T}_\theta| = Lk(\cos 45° - \cos\theta) \qquad (4)$$

Then (2) and (4) and the substitution $|\mathbf{P}| = P$ yield

$$\theta = \arccos\left(\frac{\sqrt{2}}{2} - \frac{P}{2Lk}\right) \qquad (5)$$

This analysis assumes that the spring force T_θ remains vertical. A more refined approach would take into account the rigid-body rotation of the spring about point A. However, even for relatively large angles of rotation of the spring, (5) is a good approximation.

Supplementary Problems

2.13   The solid circular cylinder in Fig. 2-32 is of unit length and rests in the trough as shown. All surfaces are smooth. The weight of the cylinder is 392.4 N. Determine the forces that the cylinder exerts on each of the contact surfaces per unit length.   *Ans.* $\mathbf{R}_A = 679.6$ N; $\mathbf{R}_B = 784.8$ N

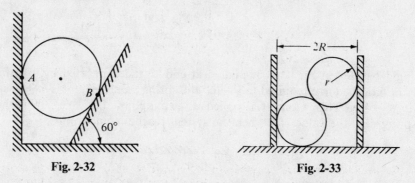

Fig. 2-32   Fig. 2-33

2.14   Figure 2-33 shows two solid cylinders of unit length, each of weight W and radius r. They are lying in a rigid rectangular box, also of unit length. Obviously, for the cylinders to occupy the positions shown, $2r > R$. Determine the force per unit length exerted by each of the cylinders upon the vertical walls of the box. The surfaces of the cylinders and box are smooth.   *Ans.* $W(R - r)/\sqrt{r^2 - (R - r)^2}$.

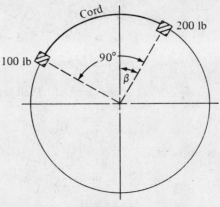

Fig. 2-34

2.15 Two small, smooth bodies rest on the curved surface of a smooth cylinder and are connected by a weightless flexible cord, as indicated in Fig. 2-34. There is no friction between the cord and the cylinder, and the weights of the bodies are as shown. Find the value of the angle β for equilibrium of the system.   *Ans.*   26.57°

2.16 The rigid bar AB in Fig. 2-35 is pinned at A and supported by a roller at B. It is subject to loads of 200 lb and 100 lb as indicated, and carries a movable weight $W = 150$ lb.   Determine the location of W so that the vertical reactions at A and B will be equal.   *Ans.* $x = 6.17$ ft

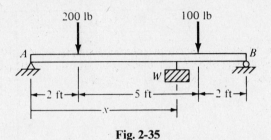

Fig. 2-35

2.17 The rigid bar AB in Fig. 2-36 is pinned at A and supported on a smooth roller at B. The loading consists of two forces and a couple, as shown. Determine the vertical reactions at ends A and B.

Ans. $\mathbf{R}_A = 1950$ lb; $\mathbf{R}_B = 750$ lb

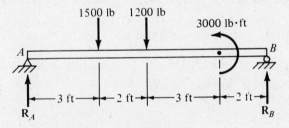

Fig. 2-36

2.18 A scale for weighing very small objects has a beam length of 0.6 m and a pointer of length 30 cm (Fig. 2-37). When a weight of 0.1 N is placed in the left pan of the balance, it causes a deflection of the pointer from its vertical position of $DE = 3$ mm.   Determine the distance x from the center of gravity of beam AB to the knife-edge C when the system is in equilibrium. The weight of the beam is 3 N.   *Ans.*   0.01 m

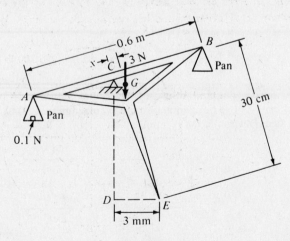

Fig. 2-37

2.19   A two-story building has the elevation shown in Fig. 2-38. The building's dead weight of 9 kips acts through its center of gravity. The Uniform Building Code specifies design wind forces of 4.12 and 1.90 kips acting at the top of the second and first stories, respectively. The code also specifies that a safety factor of 1.5 be applied to each wind load. Find the required tie-down force at A, assuming a pin reaction at B.

   Ans. $\mathbf{R}_A = 5$ kips

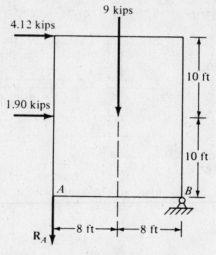

Fig. 2-38

2.20   A crane is supported by an overhead rail and has a weight of 12 kN, acting through its center of gravity as shown in Fig. 2-39. The crane must be able to lift a 3-kN load. The support consists of a pin at point A and a smooth-surface reaction at B. Determine the reactions at A and B.

   Ans. $\mathbf{R}_B = 15$ kN; $A_y = 30$ kN; $A_x = 0$

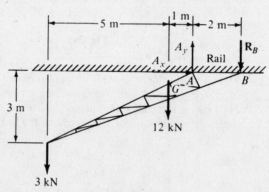

Fig. 2-39

2.21   The vertical four-sided metal plate shown in Fig. 2-40 is pinned at A and supported by a smooth roller at B. The loading consists of two horizontal forces, each of magnitude 60 N, together with a couple of magnitude 50 N·m as indicated. Determine the reaction at B.   *Ans.* $\mathbf{R}_B = 40$ N directed vertically upward

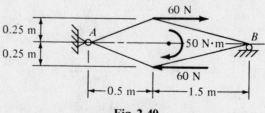

Fig. 2-40

2.22   Two vertical triangular plates ABC and CDE are joined by a smooth pin at C, as well as being supported by pins at A and E (Fig. 2-41). Loadings consist of a vertical force of 40 kN and a couple of magnitude 25 kN·m, applied as shown. Neglecting the weight of the plates, determine the pin reactions at A and E.

Ans. $A_x = 6.9$ N; $A_y = 26.9$ N; $E_x = -6.9$ N; $E_y = 13.1$ N

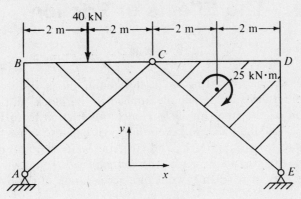

Fig. 2-41

Chapter 3

The Effects of Friction

DRY FRICTION

Consider a block of weight W resting on a horizontal plane. Both contact surfaces are dry (unlubricated). If a horizontal force **P** is gradually applied to the block, an oppositely directed force **F** arises to hold the block in equilibrium (Fig. 3-1). Hence this friction force **F** is a *developed* force. As the magnitude of **P** is increased, the block will eventually just begin to move (to the right in the figure), since the nature of the contact between the block and the plane limits the value of **F** that can be developed. The greatest frictional force that can arise is called the *limiting friction*, and when **F** has this value motion of the block is impending. Any increase in **P** will cause acceleration of the block to the right.

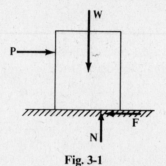

Fig. 3-1

The friction force always lies within and parallel to the contact surfaces and is directed so as to oppose relative motion of the two bodies having these contact surfaces. In the case of three or more bodies in contact (in pairs), it is necessary to understand that friction tends to prevent *relative motion* between any two bodies in contact, and that the direction of relative motion may sometimes be different from the direction of *absolute motion* (i.e., with respect to the earth as a fixed body).

For a block loaded as in Fig. 3-1, the law of dry friction states that the maximum possible value of the force **F** (the resistance to **P**) is proportional to the normal force **N**; the constant of proportionality is usually written μ. Thus,

$$|\mathbf{F}_{max}| = \mu|\mathbf{N}|$$

Experiments have shown that the relation between the friction force and time usually has the form given in Fig. 3-2. The straight-line region at the left corresponds to the static condition in which the force **P** gradually increases with time until **F** (also increasing) reaches a peak value, at which time motion

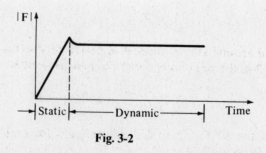

Fig. 3-2

of the block is *about to begin*. Until that instant the magnitude of **F** depends on the *coefficient of static friction*, denoted μ_S. Thus, we usually write $|\mathbf{F}_{max}| = \mu_S|\mathbf{N}|$.

When motion of the block actually begins, the resistance decreases slightly but remains essentially constant. During that phase the proportionality constant is called the *coefficient of kinetic friction* and denoted μ_K, so that $|\mathbf{F}| = \mu_K|\mathbf{N}|$.

In this book we are concerned only with the static case and hence only with μ_S which, for brevity, we shall denote as μ. The case $\mu = 0$ is that of the smooth surface assumed in Chapter 2. Typical experimentally determined values of μ for commonly encountered pairs of surfaces are

Mild steel on mild steel, 0.6	Metal on stone, 0.30 to 0.70
Copper on mild steel, 0.48	Stone on stone, 0.40 to 0.72
Rubber on metal, 0.45	Rubber on concrete, 0.40 to 0.92

When the maximum friction force has been developed, the angle θ between **N** and the resultant **R** of $\mathbf{F}_{max}$ and **N** (Fig. 3-3) is called the *angle of friction*. (See Problem 3.11.)

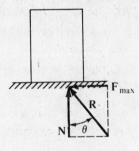

Fig. 3-3

PROBLEMS INVOLVING FRICTION

Problems involving friction and friction forces usually require more care than problems in which smooth surfaces are assumed. In Chapter 2, for example, we had to show, on free-body diagrams, the force and moment reactions appropriate to the various types of supports. But as long as we placed forces or force components along the proper lines of action, it did not matter whether we assumed their directions (senses) correctly or not. If we assumed a sense along a line of action incorrectly, the force turned out to have a negative magnitude, indicating the need to reverse the assumed direction. No harm was done.

Unfortunately, that is not true of friction forces. It is essential that the correct sense (along the line of action) of a friction force be shown, or else the nature of the problem is changed. Further, *the friction force must always be oriented so as to oppose relative motion*.

Great care must be taken to use the relation $|\mathbf{F}| = \mu|\mathbf{N}|$ only if it is certain that motion between adjacent surfaces is impending. If that is not the case, then **F** must be regarded as simply an unknown to be determined with the equations of static equilibrium.

BELT FRICTION

Flexible belts wrapped around curved surfaces are often used to transmit power or lift weights. For a system like that in Fig. 3-4, the relation between the belt tensions is

$$\frac{|\mathbf{T}_2|}{|\mathbf{T}_1|} = e^{\mu\alpha} \tag{3.1}$$

where $|\mathbf{T}_2| > |\mathbf{T}_1|$, μ is the coefficient of friction, and α is the central angle subtended by the belt, *measured in radians*. (See Problem 3.12.)

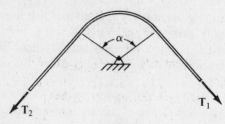

Fig. 3-4

Solved Problems

3.1   A 35-kg ladder of length L rests against a vertical wall and is inclined at 60° to the horizontal. The coefficient of friction between the ladder and the wall as well as between the ladder and the ground is 0.25. How far up the ladder can a 72-kg person climb before the ladder begins to slip?

   The free-body diagram for the ladder and person is shown in Fig. 3-5, where xL is the distance the person has climbed, so that $0 < x < L$. From the geometry of the problem it is clear that slipping impends simultaneously at A and B, at which time the friction forces are as shown. For equilibrium, we have

$$+\circlearrowleft \Sigma M_B = |\mathbf{N}_A|L \cos 60° - \frac{|\mathbf{N}_A|}{4}L \sin 60° - 706(L - xL)\cos 60° - 343\frac{L}{2}\cos 60° = 0$$

$$\Sigma F_x = \frac{|\mathbf{N}_A|}{4} - |\mathbf{N}_B| = 0$$

$$\Sigma F_y = |\mathbf{N}_A| - 343 - 706 + \frac{|\mathbf{N}_B|}{4} = 0$$

from which we find that $x = 0.45$.

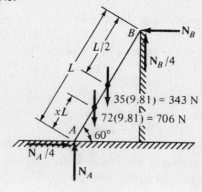

Fig. 3-5

3.2   Three rigid blocks, of masses 120, 160, and 200 kg, are arranged on top of a rough, rigid surface (Fig. 3-6). The top block is restrained against horizontal motion by a surrounding cap. Find the maximum value that the horizontal force $\mathbf{F}$ may have before motion begins.

   The weights of the three blocks are

$$(120 \text{ kg})(9.81 \text{ m/s}^2) = 1177 \text{ N}$$

$$(160 \text{ kg})(9.81 \text{ m/s}^2) = 1570 \text{ N}$$

and

$$(200 \text{ kg})(9.81 \text{ m/s}^2) = 1962 \text{ N}$$

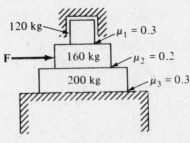

Fig. 3-6

When motion is impending, two possibilities exist. The first is that the middle block alone will begin to slip to the right, and the second is that the middle and lowest blocks will begin to move together (as one rigid body) to the right.

For the first possibility, the free-body diagram of the middle block is that of Fig. 3-7. Then, for equilibrium,

$$\Sigma F_y = |\mathbf{N}_2| - 1177 - 1570 = 0$$

$$\Sigma F_y = |\mathbf{F}_1| - 0.3(1177) - 0.2|\mathbf{N}_2| = 0$$

The first of these equations yields $|\mathbf{N}_2| = 2747$ N, and then the second gives $|\mathbf{F}_1| = 902$ N.

For the second possibility, the free-body diagram of the middle and lowest blocks (as one unit), again when motion is impending, is that of Fig. 3-8. Now, for equilibrium,

$$\Sigma F_y = -1177 - 1570 - 1962 + |\mathbf{N}_3| = 0$$

$$\Sigma F_x = |\mathbf{F}_2| - 0.3(1177) - 0.3|\mathbf{N}_3| = 0$$

The first of these equations yields $|\mathbf{N}_3| = 4709$ N, and the second yields $|\mathbf{F}_2| = 1766$ N.

Since $|\mathbf{F}_1| = 902$ N is smaller than $|\mathbf{F}_2|$, that is the force at which motion first impends.

Fig. 3-7　　　　　　　　　　　　　　　　　　**Fig. 3-8**

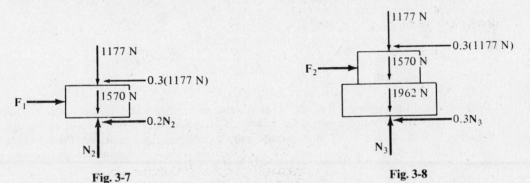

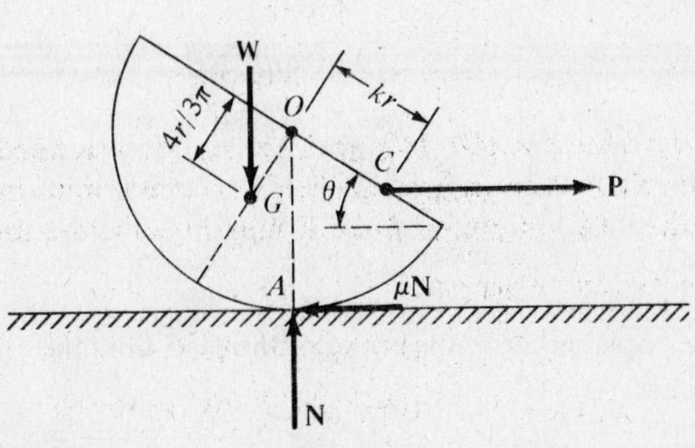

Fig. 3-9

3.3 A solid semicircular bar of weight W and radius r rests on a horizontal plane (Fig. 3-9) and is loaded by a horizontal force $\mathbf{P}$ acting at a point C on its flat surface; point C is located a distance kr (where $0 \leqslant k \leqslant 1$) from the center O of the semicircle. The coefficient of friction between the horizontal plane and the bar is μ. Find the angle θ that the flat surface of the bar will make with the horizontal when motion impends. (It is necessary to know that the weight of the bar acts through the center of gravity G of its cross section, which is located at a distance of $4r/3\pi$ from the center of the semicircle.)

It is important to realize that the normal reaction $\mathbf{N}$ at the point of contact A must be directed toward O. Then, for equilibrium, we have

$$\Sigma F_x = |\mathbf{P}| - \mu|\mathbf{N}| = 0$$

$$\Sigma F_y = |\mathbf{N}| - |\mathbf{W}| = 0$$

$$+\!\!\curvearrowleft \Sigma M_A = |\mathbf{P}|(r - kr \sin \theta) - |\mathbf{W}| \frac{4r}{3\pi} \sin \theta = 0$$

These equations yield the solution $\theta = \arcsin [3\pi\mu/(3\mu k\pi + 4)]$.

3.4 A solid circular shaft of radius r rotates at constant angular velocity ω in a bearing of slightly larger radius R (Fig. 3-10). The coefficient of friction between their surfaces is μ. Determine the location of the center O' of the shaft with respect to the center O of the bearing.

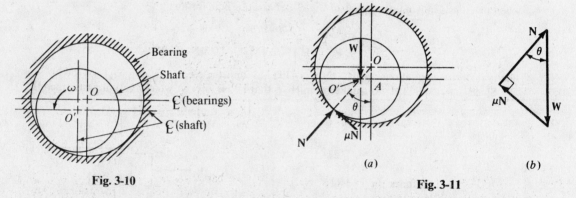

Fig. 3-10   Fig. 3-11

In drawing the free-body diagram of the rotating shaft (Fig. 3-11a), it is essential to realize that the normal force at the point of contact of the shaft and bearing acts along a line that passes through the centers of both. The friction force is of course perpendicular to the normal reaction and is thus tangential to both circles (shaft and bearing) at their point of contact. In the diagram, $\mathbf{W}$ denotes the gravitational reaction to the weight of the shaft.

Equilibrium of the shaft is represented by the closed force triangle in Fig. 3-11b. Since $OO' = R - r$, we have, from the force triangle,

$$|\mathbf{W}| = \sqrt{|\mathbf{N}|^2 + \mu^2|\mathbf{N}|^2} = |\mathbf{N}|\sqrt{1 + \mu^2}$$

$$\cos \theta = \frac{|\mathbf{N}|}{|\mathbf{W}|} = \frac{|\mathbf{N}|}{|\mathbf{N}|\sqrt{1 + \mu^2}} = \frac{1}{\sqrt{1 + \mu^2}}$$

$$\sin \theta = \frac{\mu|\mathbf{N}|}{|\mathbf{W}|} = \frac{\mu}{\sqrt{1 + \mu^2}}$$

The horizontal displacement of the center of the shaft from the center of the bearing is

$$O'A = OO' \sin \theta = \frac{\mu(R - r)}{\sqrt{1 + \mu^2}}$$

and its vertical displacement is

$$OA = OO' \cos \theta = \frac{R - r}{\sqrt{1 + \mu^2}}$$

3.5   A circular ring is held in a vertical plane, and a straight bar whose length is equal to the radius R of the ring is placed in the ring so that its ends rest on the rough inside surface of the ring (Fig. 3-12). The coefficient of friction between the ends of the bar and the inside of the ring is 0.5. Determine the inclination of the bar from the horizontal at which motion impends. Assume that the bar does not move out of the vertical plane of the ring.

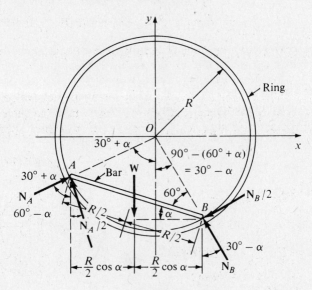

Fig. 3-12

Figure 3-12 includes the free-body diagram for the bar at the time of impending motion. (Note that angle ABO is 60° because triangle OAB is equilateral.) At equilibrium we have three equations for the three unknowns $\mathbf{N}_A$, $\mathbf{N}_B$, and the desired angle of inclination α:

$$+\circlearrowleft \Sigma M_O = \frac{|\mathbf{N}_A|}{2} R + \frac{|\mathbf{N}_B|}{2} R - |\mathbf{W}| \left[\frac{R}{2} \cos \alpha - R \sin (30° - \alpha) \right] = 0 \tag{1}$$

$$\Sigma F_x = -|\mathbf{N}_B| \sin (30° - \alpha) - \frac{|\mathbf{N}_B|}{2} \cos (30° - \alpha) + |\mathbf{N}_A| \sin (30° + \alpha) - \frac{|\mathbf{N}_A|}{2} \sin (60° - \alpha) = 0 \tag{2}$$

$$\Sigma F_y = -|\mathbf{W}| + |\mathbf{N}_A| \cos (30° + \alpha) + \frac{|\mathbf{N}_A|}{2} \cos (60° - \alpha) + |\mathbf{N}_B| \cos (30° - \alpha) - \frac{|\mathbf{N}_B|}{2} \sin (30° - \alpha) = 0 \tag{3}$$

From (2) we obtain

$$|\mathbf{N}_A| = |\mathbf{N}_B| \frac{\sin (30° - \alpha) - \frac{1}{2} \cos (30° - \alpha)}{\sin (30° + \alpha) - \frac{1}{2} \sin (60° - \alpha)} \equiv |\mathbf{N}_B| Q$$

Substituting this into (1) and (3) eventually yields an equation for the unknown angle α:

$$\frac{Q + 1}{Q \sin (30° + \alpha) + \frac{1}{2} Q \cos (60° - \alpha) + \cos (30° - \alpha) - \frac{1}{2} \sin (30° - \alpha)} = \cos \alpha - 2 \sin (30° - \alpha)$$

Trial-and-error solution yields the approximate value $\alpha = 10°$.

3.6 A two-body system consisting of a solid circular cylinder together with a triangular block rests on an inclined plane as shown in Fig. 3-13. The weight of the cylinder is W_C, and that of the block is W_B. Assume that the block does not tip and that the coefficient of friction μ is the same at all pairs of contact surfaces. Determine the minimum weight of the block so that the cylinder will not move down the plane.

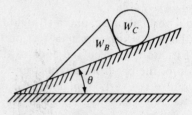

Fig. 3-13

It is necessary to be very careful in drawing the free-body diagrams for these bodies. The diagrams are shown in Fig. 3-14, but it is best to draw that for the cylinder first, showing the forces exerted on it by the inclined plane and the block. Since the cylinder is about to move down the plane, the frictional component μN of the force exerted by the block on the cylinder must have the direction indicated, so as to keep the cylinder from rolling down the plane. However, because the cylinder rolls about the point of contact between cylinder and inclined plane but does not slip, there is no justification for assuming that the maximum friction force, given by μN_C, is developed. Instead, we must solve for $\mathbf{F}_C$ as an unknown.

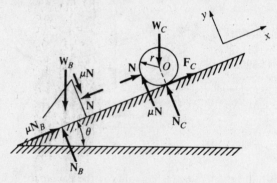

Fig. 3-14

Thus, there are five unknowns: $\mathbf{N}, \mathbf{N}_B, \mathbf{N}_C, \mathbf{F}_C$, and $\mathbf{W}_B$. We have two equilibrium equations for the block,

$$\Sigma F_x = -|\mathbf{N}| + \mu|\mathbf{N}_B| - |\mathbf{W}_B| \sin \theta = 0$$

$$\Sigma F_y = |\mathbf{N}_B| - \mu|\mathbf{N}| - |\mathbf{W}_B| \cos \theta = 0$$

and three for the cylinder,

$$\Sigma F_x = |\mathbf{N}| + |\mathbf{F}_C| - |\mathbf{W}_C| \sin \theta = 0$$

$$\Sigma F_y = |\mathbf{N}_C| + \mu|\mathbf{N}| - |\mathbf{W}_C| \cos \theta = 0$$

$$+\curvearrowleft \Sigma M_O = \mu|\mathbf{N}|r - |\mathbf{F}_C|r = 0$$

These five equations yield

$$W_B = \frac{(W_C \sin \theta)(1 - \mu)}{\mu \cos \theta - \sin \theta}$$

3.7 A 200-kg block is located atop a 100-kg block as indicated in Fig. 3-15. The top block is subject to a horizontal force of 400 N, and the lower block has a flexible cable attached to it which passes

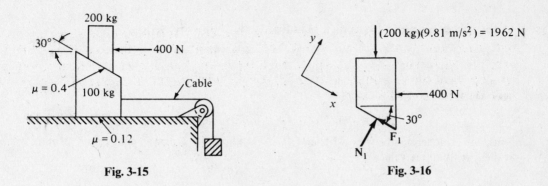

Fig. 3-15   **Fig. 3-16**

over a smooth pulley. A tension **T** develops in the cable because another block is attached at its other end. Determine the cable tension for equilibrium of the lower block. The coefficients of friction at the contact surfaces have the values indicated.

Here there is no assurance that equilibrium does indeed exist. Nonetheless, let us begin by drawing the free-body diagram for the top block, designating the normal and friction forces exerted on it by the lower block as N_1 and F_1, respectively. The diagram is shown in Fig. 3-16; note that we do *not*, at this stage, use the relation $F_1 = \mu N_1$, since we do not know that motion is impending.

If equilibrium exists, we have

$$\Sigma F_x = -|F_1| - 400 \cos 30° + 1962 \cos 60° = 0$$

$$\Sigma F_y = |N_1| - 400 \sin 30° - 1962 \sin 60° = 0$$

from which we find that $|F_1| = 635$ N and $|N_1| = 1899$ N. The coefficient of friction indicated by these results is $\mu = |F_1|/|N_1| = 0.334$. Since this is less than the actual value of 0.4 given for the block-to-block contact surfaces, the friction force with magnitude $|F_1| = 635$ N can indeed develop and equilibrium does exist.

Now we draw the free-body diagram for both blocks together, assuming that the impending motion of the system is to the right. We obtain Fig. 3-17a, from which, at equilibrium,

$$\Sigma F_x = |T| - 400 - |F_2| = 0$$

$$\Sigma F_y = |N_2| - 1962 - 981 = 0$$

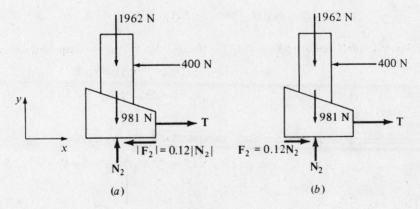

Fig. 3-17

These equations yield

$$|N_2| = 2943 \text{ N} \qquad |F_2| = 0.12|N_2| = 353 \text{ N} \qquad |T| = 753 \text{ N}$$

We must also consider the possibility that the impending motion is to the left, in which case the frictional force is directed to the right as in Fig. 3-17*b*. Then we have

$$\Sigma F_x = |\mathbf{T}| - 400 + |\mathbf{F}_2| = 0$$

$$\Sigma F_y = |\mathbf{N}_2| - 1962 - 981 = 0$$

from which

$$|\mathbf{N}_2| = 2943 \text{ N} \qquad |\mathbf{F}_2| = 0.12|\mathbf{N}_2| = 353 \text{ N} \qquad |\mathbf{T}| = 47 \text{ N}$$

Thus, any cable tension between 47 N and 753 N will hold the system in equilibrium. Motion will impend at these two limiting values.

3.8   The system in Fig. 3-18 consists of two identical ladders, each of weight W and length L, pinned together at the top (point B) and with lower ends A and C resting on a rough horizontal surface. When each of the ladders makes an angle of $30°$ with the vertical, a person of weight W is able to climb halfway up either ladder before slipping occurs at one of the lower ends. Determine the coefficient of friction between the ladders and the horizontal surface.

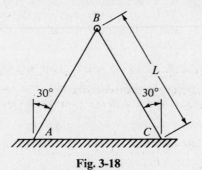

Fig. 3-18

Let us assume that the person climbs the left ladder, AB. It is not clear whether slipping first occurs at A or at C, but we shall assume that motion is impending at A. The free-body diagram for the system then appears as in Fig. 3-19, where the force $\mathbf{F}_C$ is an unknown to be found from the equations of equilibrium and is *not* necessarily given by $\mu \mathbf{N}_C$. For equilibrium,

$$+\!\curvearrowleft \Sigma M_C = |\mathbf{N}_A|L - |\mathbf{W}|\frac{L}{2}\sin 30° - 2|\mathbf{W}|\left(L\sin 30° + \frac{L}{2}\sin 30°\right) = 0$$

from which we find $|\mathbf{N}_A| = \frac{7}{4}|\mathbf{W}|$, and

$$\Sigma F_y = \frac{7}{4}|\mathbf{W}| + |\mathbf{N}_C| - 2|\mathbf{W}| - |\mathbf{W}| = 0$$

from which $|\mathbf{N}_C| = \frac{5}{4}|\mathbf{W}|$.

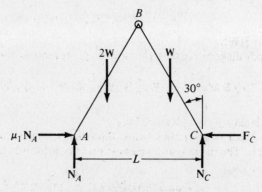

Fig. 3-19

Now we draw the free-body diagram for member AB (Fig. 3-20), in which B_x and B_y denote the components of the force that BC exerts on AB through the pin at B. For equilibrium,

$$+\!\!\downarrow\!\!\text{\Large$\circlearrowleft$}\ \Sigma\, M_B = \frac{7}{4}|\mathbf{W}|L \sin 30^\circ - \frac{7}{4}\mu_1|\mathbf{W}|L\cos 30^\circ - 2|\mathbf{W}|\frac{L}{2}\sin 30^\circ = 0$$

which we solve to obtain $\mu_1 = \sqrt{3}/7 = 0.247$.

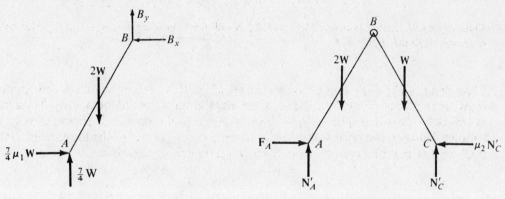

Fig. 3-20   **Fig. 3-21**

According to Fig. 3-19, horizontal equilibrium requires that $|\mathbf{F}_C| = \mu_1|\mathbf{N}_A|$. We must answer the following question: With the computed coefficient of friction $\mu_1 = \sqrt{3}/7$, can a horizontal force sufficient to maintain equilibrium develop at C? With this coefficient of friction, the maximum magnitude that $\mathbf{F}_C$ can have is

$$|\mathbf{F}_C|_{max} = \mu_1|\mathbf{N}_C| = \frac{\sqrt{3}}{7}\frac{5}{4}|\mathbf{W}| = 0.309|\mathbf{W}|$$

whereas at A we have

$$\mu_1|\mathbf{N}_A| = \frac{\sqrt{3}}{7}\frac{7}{4}|\mathbf{W}| = 0.433|\mathbf{W}|$$

Thus, since the maximum force that can arise at C is smaller than that required for horizontal equilibrium, our solution is not a physical possibility. System equilibrium cannot exist under the assumption that motion is impending at A.

Consequently, we must now investigate the case in which slipping is impending at C when the person is halfway up AB. The free-body diagram for the system now appears as in Fig. 3-21 and, for equilibrium,

$$+\!\!\downarrow\!\!\text{\Large$\circlearrowleft$}\ \Sigma\, M_C = |\mathbf{N}'_A|L - |\mathbf{W}|\frac{L}{2}\sin 30^\circ - 2|\mathbf{W}|\left(L\sin 30^\circ + \frac{L}{2}\sin 30^\circ\right) = 0$$

from which $|\mathbf{N}'_A| = \frac{7}{4}|\mathbf{W}|$, and

$$\Sigma\, F_y = \tfrac{7}{4}|\mathbf{W}| + |\mathbf{N}'_C| - 2|\mathbf{W}| - |\mathbf{W}| = 0$$

which yields $|\mathbf{N}'_C| = \frac{5}{4}|\mathbf{W}|$.

Now the free-body diagram for the right member BC appears as in Fig. 3-22, and for equilibrium we have

$$+\!\!\downarrow\!\!\text{\Large$\circlearrowleft$}\ \Sigma\, M_B = -\frac{5}{4}|\mathbf{W}|\frac{L}{2} + |\mathbf{W}|\frac{L}{2}\sin 30^\circ + \frac{5}{4}\mu_2|\mathbf{W}|L\cos 30^\circ = 0$$

which we solve to obtain $\mu_2 = \sqrt{3}/5 = 0.346$.

We should now check to ascertain whether this coefficient of friction permits a force at A large enough for system equilibrium. The maximum magnitude that the friction force at A can have is

$$|\mathbf{F}_A|_{max} = \mu_2|\mathbf{N}'_A| = \frac{\sqrt{3}}{5}\frac{7}{4}|\mathbf{W}| = 0.606|\mathbf{W}|$$

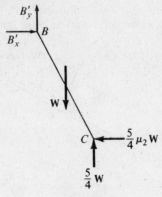

Fig. 3-22

while the frictional reaction at C is

$$\mu_2|\mathbf{N}_C'| = \frac{\sqrt{3}}{5}\frac{5}{4}|\mathbf{W}| = 0.433|\mathbf{W}|$$

Thus, the friction force required at A for equilibrium is smaller than the maximum possible friction force, so $\mu_2 = \sqrt{3}/5$ represents a physically possible solution.

3.9 A cylindrical bar of weight W rests between a rough vertical wall and an inclined hinged bar CD whose weight is negligible, as shown in Fig. 3-23. The coefficients of friction between contact surfaces have the values indicated. At the upper end of the bar, a force $\mathbf{P}$ is applied at 45° to the horizontal. Find the value of $\mathbf{P}$ such that motion of the cylindrical bar is impending upward.

We first draw the free-body diagram for the inclined bar CD (Fig. 3-24). Note that the friction force $\mathbf{F}_2$ could have either of the two indicated senses without entering into the equilibrium equation for moments about point C, which is

$$+\circlearrowleft \Sigma M_C = 8|\mathbf{N}_2| - (|\mathbf{P}|\cos 15°)(14) = 0 \quad \text{or} \quad |\mathbf{N}_2| = 1.69|\mathbf{P}| \tag{1}$$

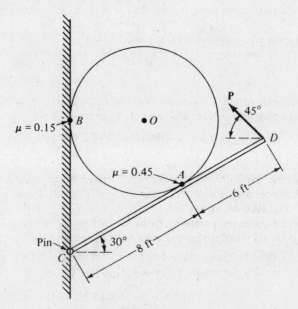

Fig. 3-23

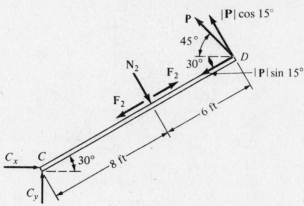

Fig. 3-24

Next we should draw the free-body diagram for the cylindrical bar. At this stage, it is not certain whether slipping is impending at point A or point B. In particular, there is no reason to assume that motion *simultaneously* impends at both A and B. Hence, let us first *assume* that motion is impending at A but not at B. In that case, the friction force at A is $0.45|\mathbf{N}|$, whereas the frictional reaction at B is merely an unknown force $\mathbf{F}$, to be found from the equilibrium equations. We should *not* set $\mathbf{F}_1 = 0.15\,|\mathbf{N}_1|$. The free-body diagram is that shown in Fig. 3-25. For equilibrium of the cylindrical bar, we have

$$+\!\!\circlearrowleft \Sigma\, M_O = 0.45|\mathbf{N}_2|r - |\mathbf{F}_1|r = 0 \qquad \text{or} \qquad |\mathbf{F}_1| = 0.45|\mathbf{N}_2|$$

$$\Sigma\, F_x = |\mathbf{N}_1| - |\mathbf{N}_2|\sin 30° - 0.45|\mathbf{N}_2|\cos 30° = 0$$

$$\Sigma\, F_y = |\mathbf{N}_2|\cos 30° - |\mathbf{F}_1| - 0.45|\mathbf{N}_2|\sin 30° - |\mathbf{W}| = 0$$

The last two equations yield $|\mathbf{N}_1| = 4.60|\mathbf{W}|$ and $|\mathbf{N}_2| = 5.17|\mathbf{W}|$.

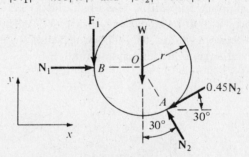

Fig. 3-25

We must now check to see if the value of $|\mathbf{F}_1|$ computed above can develop at B, given the friction coefficient of 0.15 existing there. From the computed values, we have

$$\frac{|\mathbf{F}_1|}{|\mathbf{N}_1|} = \frac{0.45|\mathbf{N}_2|}{|\mathbf{N}_1|} = \frac{0.45(5.17|\mathbf{W}|)}{4.60|\mathbf{W}|} = 0.505$$

which indicates that a friction coefficient of 0.505 would be required to develop the computed value of $|\mathbf{F}_1|$ at point B. Since this exceeds the given value of 0.15, the force $\mathbf{F}_1$ cannot possibly develop, and thus our assumption of slipping at A is incorrect.

We must now investigate impending motion at B, with no motion impending at A but with the frictional reaction at A being found simply from the equilibrium equations. In that case the free-body diagram for the cylindrical bar appears as in Fig. 3-26. For equilibrium now,

$$\Sigma\, F_x = |\mathbf{N}_3| - |\mathbf{N}_2|\sin 30° - |\mathbf{F}_2|\cos 30° = 0$$

$$\Sigma\, F_y = |\mathbf{N}_2|\cos 30° - 0.15|\mathbf{N}_3| - |\mathbf{W}| - |\mathbf{F}_2|\sin 30° = 0$$

$$+\!\!\circlearrowleft \Sigma\, M_O = |\mathbf{F}_2|r - 0.15|\mathbf{N}_3|r = 0$$

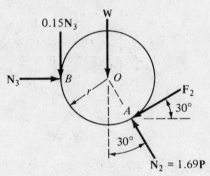

Fig. 3-26

from which we obtain $|\mathbf{F}_2| = 0.15|\mathbf{N}_3|$, $|\mathbf{N}_2| = 1.36|\mathbf{W}|$, $|\mathbf{N}_3| = 0.784|\mathbf{W}|$, and, from (*1*), $|\mathbf{P}| = 0.805|\mathbf{W}|$.

Lastly, we should check to ensure that the force $\mathbf{F}_2$ can develop at point A. From the above results, we have

$$\frac{|\mathbf{F}_2|}{|\mathbf{N}_2|} = \frac{0.15(0.785W)}{1.36W} = 0.086$$

as the minimum required value of μ. Hence our result is physically possible, since the given coefficient of friction at A is 0.45.

In summary, a force $|\mathbf{P}| = 0.805W$ causes motion of the cylindrical bar to impend upward with slipping at B (where the maximum possible friction force is developed) and with rolling at A (where a smaller than maximum friction force is developed).

3.10 A straight bar AB is supported in a frictionless ball-and-socket joint at its lower end A and rests against a rough vertical wall at its upper end B (Fig. 3-27). The weight of the bar is W, and the coefficient of friction between the bar and the vertical wall is μ. Determine the orientation of the bar, as measured by the angle θ, for impending motion.

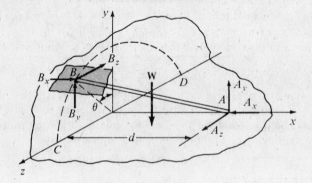

Fig. 3-27

End B could occupy any point on the dashed semicircle, which lies in the yz plane (and which we choose to coincide with the vertical wall). We seek the one orientation such that downward motion is impending. In drawing the free-body diagram for the bar, it is necessary to realize that the action of the wall on the bar at B must lie in a plane that is (1) normal to the yz plane and (2) simultaneously tangent to semicircle CD at B. We represent this action with three force components B_x, B_y, and B_z, parallel to the x, y, and z axes, respectively.

A view looking down the x axis toward the yz plane (Fig. 3-28) shows two of these components as well as the intersection (trace) of the plane tangent to the semicircle in the yz plane. From the force triangle for these two components (Fig. 3-28), together with the fact that the frictional component B_1, which obviously

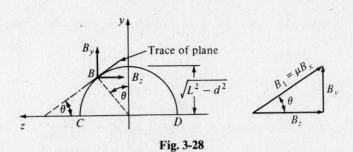

Fig. 3-28

lies in the yz plane, must also lie in the tangential plane and must be equal to μB_x, we have

$$B_y = \mu B_x \sin \theta \qquad B_z = \mu B_x \cos \theta$$

Thus, there are five unknowns: A_x, A_y, A_z, B_x, and θ. Since we seek only θ, we need write only two equilibrium equations:

$$\Sigma F_z = A_z - B_z = 0 \qquad \text{or} \qquad A_z = B_z = \mu B_x \cos \theta$$

$$+\!\circlearrowleft \Sigma M_y = B_x \sqrt{L^2 - d^2} \sin \theta - A_z d = 0$$

Substitution for A_z in the second equation eventually yields

$$\theta = \arctan \frac{\mu d}{\sqrt{L^2 - d^2}}$$

As an example, if $L = 3$ m, $d = 2.5$ m, and $\mu = 0.3$, then $\theta = \arctan [0.3(3)/\sqrt{3^2 - (2.5)^2}] = 14.3°$.

3.11   A problem that arises in mining and quarrying is the slipping of rock masses. Usually the slipping mass is of triangular cross section (shown shaded in Fig. 3-29), and the slipping failure initiates along a line inclined at the angle ψ to the horizontal. The slipping of the triangular mass is resisted by two mechanisms: (1) *cohesion*, a shear resistance between adjacent particles that is independent of the normal force pressing the particles together and exists even if the normal force is zero, and (2) *dry friction*. Their combined effect is best illustrated in a plot of shear force as a function of normal force (each per unit area), like that in Fig. 3-30. The total resistance to sliding for any given normal force is thus the sum of the resistance due to cohesion and that due to friction:

Shear force per unit area = cohesion + (normal force per unit area)(tan θ)

For a rock having a cohesion $c = 2000$ lb/ft^2, a unit weight of 160 lb/ft^3, and a friction angle $\theta = 20°$, determine the critical height H so that slipping of the triangular mass is impending on the plane $\psi = 50°$.

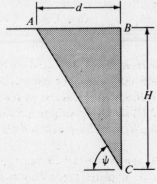

Fig. 3-29

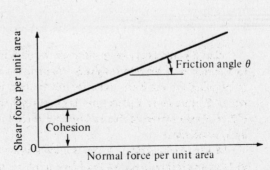

Fig. 3-30

We must first determine the weight of the triangular wedge, which we take to be of unit thickness perpendicular to the xy plane. From Fig. 3-29,

$$W = \tfrac{1}{2}dH(160 \text{ lb/ft}^3)$$

Because $d = H/\tan 50° = 0.844H$,   we have

$$W = \tfrac{1}{2}(0.84H)(H)(160) = 67.2H^2$$

Now, since $AC = H/\sin 50° = 1.30H$,   the cohesive force along AC has magnitude

$$|\mathbf{C}| = (2000 \text{ lb/ft}^2)(1 \text{ ft})(1.30H \text{ ft}) = 2600H$$

Using the concept of angle of friction θ as the angle between the normal force $\mathbf{N}$ and the resultant $\mathbf{R}$ of $\mathbf{N}$ and the friction force $\mathbf{F}$ (Fig. 3-31), we have

$$\frac{|\mathbf{F}|}{|\mathbf{N}|} = \tan 20°   \text{or} |\mathbf{F}| = 0.364\,\mathbf{N}$$

The free-body diagram for the triangular mass (Fig. 3-32) shows that, for equilibrium,

$$\Sigma F_x = |\mathbf{N}| \sin 50° - 2600H \cos 50° - 0.364|\mathbf{N}| \cos 50° = 0$$

$$\Sigma F_y = -67.2H^2 + |\mathbf{N}| \cos 50° + 2600H \sin 50° + 0.364|\mathbf{N}| \sin 50° = 0$$

These equations yield $H = 72.7$ ft.

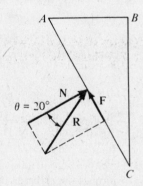

Fig. 3-31

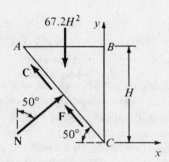

Fig. 3-32

3.12 Two pulleys are spaced 72 in apart, center to center, and power is transmitted from one to the other by a continuous belt (Fig. 3-33). The coefficient of friction between the belt and each pulley is 0.25. If the tension in the slack side of the belt is 160 lb, determine the tension in the tight side and the maximum torque that can be transmitted.

The *critical* (or *limiting*) *contact length* of the belt is the length of belt that is in contact with the smaller pulley, since the transmitted torque must be limited by the fact that less of the belt is in contact with the smaller pulley than with the larger pulley. The geometry of the situation is shown in Fig. 3-34, and we must find α to apply (*3.1*).

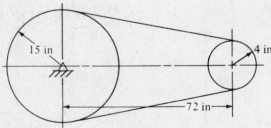

Fig. 3-33

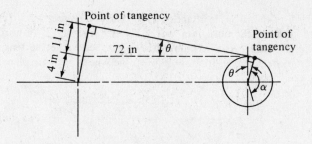

Fig. 3-34

Since $\sin\theta = \frac{11}{72}$,   we have $\theta = 8.80°$ or 0.154 rad. Then

$$\alpha = \pi - 2(0.154) = 2.834 \text{ rad}$$

The tension in the tight side of the belt is now found with (3.1):

$$|\mathbf{T}_2| = |\mathbf{T}_1|\, e^{\mu\alpha} = 160 e^{0.25(2.834)} = 325 \text{ lb}$$

The maximum torque that can be transmitted is then   (325 lb − 160 lb)(4 in) = 660 lb·in.

Supplementary Problems

3.13   A 24.46-kg ladder is 13 m in length. Its lower end rests on horizontal ground, and its top rests against a vertical wall. The ladder makes an angle of 50° with the horizontal, and the coefficient of friction for all pairs of surfaces is 0.3. The center of gravity of the ladder is located 5 m from its lower end. A 64-kg person starts up the ladder. Determine how far the person may climb up along the ladder before slipping impends.   *Ans.*   4.24 m

3.14   Two blocks rest upon a plane inclined at 25° to the horizontal. The lower block (block *A*) has a mass of 20 kg, and the upper block (*B*) has a mass of 80 kg. The coefficient of friction between block *A* and the inclined plane is 0.30, and that between block *B* and the plane is 0.75. These blocks are connected by a cord that is not in contact with the plane. Find the tension in this cord. (Be sure to check first to see if both bodies can slide down the plane.)   *Ans.* $|\mathbf{T}| = 29.7$ N

3.15   Two solid circular cylinders, both of radius 20 cm, are joined by a short axle of radius 10 cm, as shown in Fig. 3-35. The weight of the assembly is 450 N. The coefficient of friction between the cylinders and the horizontal plane is 0.25, and the vertical wall is smooth. A cord is wound around the axle, and a weight *W* is suspended from the cord. Determine the value of *W* for impending motion.   *Ans.*   450 N

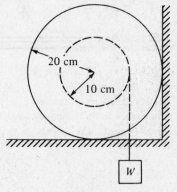

Fig. 3-35

3.16 A pair of wheels, both of radius $2r$, is attached to the ends of a short axle of radius r. The system is placed on a plane inclined at 30° to the horizontal and held in equilibrium by a horizontal cord as shown in Fig. 3-36. The total weight of the two wheels and axle is W. Determine the tension in the cord, and find the minimum value of the coefficient of friction between the wheels and the plane.   *Ans.*   0.366 W;   0.174

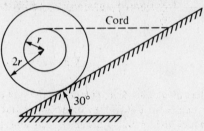

Fig. 3-36

3.17 Two straight bars AB and BC are pinned at B (Fig. 3-37). The upper end A is pinned to a vertical wall, and end C rests against the rough wall with coefficient of friction 0.60. The weight of bar AB is $2W$, and that of BC is W. Each bar is of length L. Find the maximum value of the angle θ for equilibrium.

Ans.   39.6°

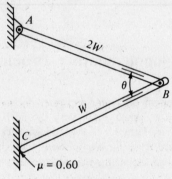

Fig. 3-37

3.18 A solid cylindrical bar of mass 30 kg rests in a trough formed by the two inclined planes (Fig. 3-38). Find the minimum vertical force **P** needed to cause impending rotary motion of the bar. The coefficient of friction is 0.2 between all pairs of surfaces.   *Ans.*   109 N

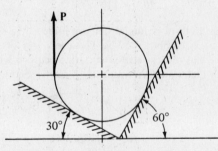

Fig. 3-38

3.19 In a simple mechanical system employed in certain fabrication processes, a relatively thin flat plate is pulled over a flat surface (Fig. 3-39). It is occasionally necessary to stop the process, and this is accomplished by introducing a cylindrical roller, whose weight may be neglected, as shown. The coefficient of friction between all pairs of surfaces is μ. Find the minimum value of μ so that the plate cannot be pulled through, no matter how great the tension **T**.

Ans. $\dfrac{\sin \alpha}{1 + \cos \alpha} = \tan \dfrac{\alpha}{2}$

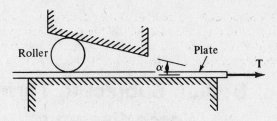

Fig. 3-39

3.20   Three solid circular cylinders of equal radii r and weights W rest on a horizontal surface, each cylinder being in contact with the other two (Fig. 3-40). The coefficient of friction is μ for all contact surfaces. Find the minimum value of μ for which the cylinders are in equilibrium in the position shown.   *Ans.*   0.268

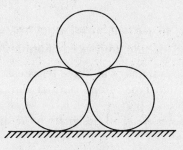

Fig. 3-40

3.21   Reconsider Problem 3.11: Determine the critical height H so that slipping of the triangular mass is impending on the plane $\psi = 35°$.   *Ans.*   111 ft

3.22   A cable passes over a cylindrical bar as shown in Fig. 3-41, with the coefficient of friction between the surfaces being 0.35. A force of 10,000 N is applied to one end of the cable. Determine the maximum and minimum masses M that such a force can hold in equilibrium.   *Ans.*   3058 kg;   340 kg

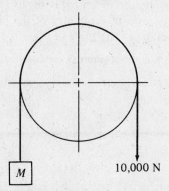

10,000 N

M

Fig. 3-41

Chapter 4

Equilibria of Bodies Subject to Three-Dimensional Force Systems

Three types of three-dimensional force systems may act on a solid body. These systems are:

1. A three-dimensional system of parallel forces, with three equations of static equilibrium (see Problems 4.1 through 4.4)
2. A three-dimensional system of concurrent forces, with three equilibrium equations (see Problem 4.5)
3. The general three-dimensional loading, with six equilibrium equations (see Problems 4.6 through 4.9)

In this chapter, we shall solve systems of all three types using, for the most part, a vector approach; for three-dimensional problems, that type of approach is almost always more efficient than the use of scalars.

For convenience, in this chapter we shall designate by F the magnitude of a vector $\mathbf{F}$ (rather than using $|\mathbf{F}|$).

Solved Problems

4.1 A thin metal plate ABC in the form of an isosceles triangle lies in the horizontal (xz) plane (Fig. 4-1). It is held in equilibrium by three vertical cords as shown. A downward vertical force of 800 N is applied at point E on the axis of symmetry of the plate. Find the tensile force in each of the three cords. Neglect the weight of the plate.

For equilibrium of moments about point D, we have

$$\Sigma \mathbf{M}_D = (-0.2\mathbf{k}) \times (-800\mathbf{j}) + (-0.3\sqrt{3}\mathbf{k}) \times (T_3\mathbf{j}) + (0.3\mathbf{i}) \times (T_2\mathbf{j}) + (-0.3\mathbf{i}) \times (T_1\mathbf{j}) = 0$$

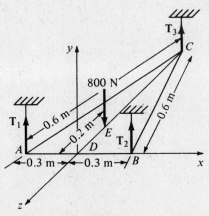

Fig. 4-1

Using (1.6), we get

$$-160\mathbf{i} + 0.3\sqrt{3}\,T_3\mathbf{i} + 0.3T_2\mathbf{k} - 0.3T_1\mathbf{k} = 0$$

Collecting the coefficients of $\mathbf{i}$ and $\mathbf{k}$ individually and realizing that the coefficient of each unit vector must vanish for equilibrium, we obtain the two equations

$$(-160 + 0.3\sqrt{3}\,T_3)\mathbf{i} = 0 \quad \text{and} \quad (0.3T_2 - 0.3T_1)\mathbf{k} = 0$$

from which we find that $T_3 = 308$ N and $T_1 = T_2$.

Finally, for vertical equilibrium of forces, we have

$$\Sigma \mathbf{F} = T_1\mathbf{j} + T_2\mathbf{j} + T_3\mathbf{j} - 800\mathbf{j} \doteq 0$$

For the computed values of the forces, this yields $T_1 = T_2 = 246$ N.

4.2 A flat circular plate lies in the horizontal (xz) plane and is supported at the three circumferential points shown in Fig. 4-2. The weight of the plate is W. Find the value of each of the three reactions.

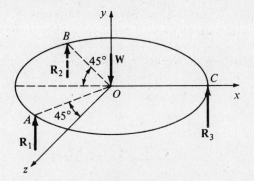

Fig. 4-2

Let the radius of the plate be a, as in the top view in Fig. 4-3. Then, for moment equilibrium about point O, we have

$$\Sigma \mathbf{M}_O = (\mathbf{r} \times \mathbf{F}) = \left(-\frac{a}{\sqrt{2}}\mathbf{i} + \frac{a}{\sqrt{2}}\mathbf{k}\right) \times (R_1\mathbf{j}) + \left(-\frac{a}{\sqrt{2}}\mathbf{i} - \frac{a}{\sqrt{2}}\mathbf{k}\right) \times (R_2\mathbf{j}) + (a\mathbf{i}) \times (R_3\mathbf{j}) = 0$$

Expanding and using (1.6) yields

$$\left(-\frac{a}{\sqrt{2}}R_1 + \frac{a}{\sqrt{2}}R_2\right)\mathbf{i} = 0 \quad \text{and} \quad \left(-\frac{a}{\sqrt{2}}R_1 - \frac{a}{\sqrt{2}}R_2 + aR_3\right)\mathbf{k} = 0$$

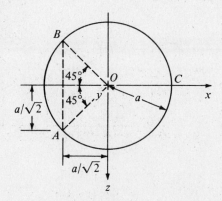

Fig. 4-3

from which $R_1 = R_2$ and $R_3 = \sqrt{2}R_1$.   Then, for force equilibrium,

$$\Sigma \mathbf{F} = R_1\mathbf{j} + R_2\mathbf{j} + R_3\mathbf{j} - W\mathbf{j} = 0$$

which yields $R_1 = R_2 = 0.292W$ and $R_3 = 0.414W$.

4.3 A mass of 400 kg is raised by means of a weightless flexible cord wound around a cylindrical drum of diameter 1 m (Fig. 4-4). The drum is concentrically mounted on a rigid axle that is supported in frictionless bearings at A and B. The crank BCD lies in the vertical (xy) plane and is loaded by a horizontal force $\mathbf{F}$ acting parallel to the z axis. The mass of the drum is 100 kg, and the mass of the axle and crank may be neglected. Determine the magnitude of $\mathbf{F}$ that will just hold the 400-kg mass in equilibrium, neglecting all friction effects.

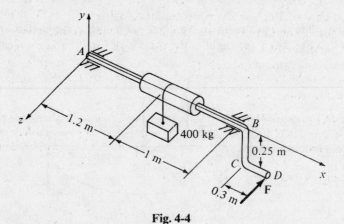

Fig. 4-4

The free-body diagram for the system consisting of axle, drum, and crank appears in Fig. 4-5. Since the bearings are frictionless, they may exert components of force on the axle in the y and z directions at A and B.

For moment equilibrium about point A, we have

$$\Sigma \mathbf{M}_A = (1.2\mathbf{i}) \times (-981\mathbf{j}) + (1.2\mathbf{i} + 0.5\mathbf{k}) \times (-3924\mathbf{j}) + (2.2\mathbf{i}) \times (B_z\mathbf{k}) + (2.2\mathbf{i}) \times (B_y\mathbf{j})$$
$$+ (2.5\mathbf{i} - 0.25\mathbf{j}) \times (-F\mathbf{k}) = 0$$

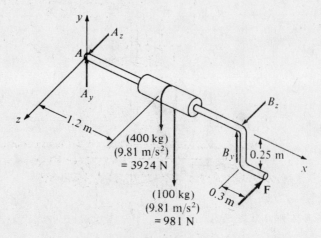

Fig. 4-5

After expanding and collecting coefficients of **i**, **j**, and **k**, we obtain

$$(1962 + 0.25F)\mathbf{i} = 0 \qquad (-2.2B_z + 2.5F)\mathbf{j} = 0 \qquad (-1177 - 4709 + 2.2B_y)\mathbf{k} = 0$$

The first of these equations yields $F = -7848$ N, indicating that **F** acts in the $+z$ direction, rather than as shown in Fig. 4-5.

4.4   In preparation for the first manned flight to the moon, it was necessary to transport the Saturn V rocket booster and its umbilical tower approximately 3.5 mi over relatively flat ground at Cape Kennedy, Florida. The rocket and its attached tower together weighed 6000 tons and had a height of 363 ft. The center of gravity of the booster and its tower was known to be located 140 ft above the base of the booster. A "crawler-transporter," designed to move the rocket and tower while both were vertical, consisted of a flat platform 131 ft long and 114 ft wide, supported on a 41-ft-long truck at each corner. Each truck consisted of a number of toothed wheels around which was wrapped a continuous flexible tread, much like a tank track. The weight of the crawler was 2750 tons. It was specified that the top of the rocket could move from its true vertical position no more than 0.5 ft horizontally, due to small wind pressures; this corresponds to a maximum angle from the vertical of 4 minutes. Determine the loads on the front and rear trucks when the inclination is 4 minutes.

The free-body diagram for the rocket and its tower, together with the crawler-transporter and its four trucks, is given in Fig. 4-6. It shows a simple three-dimensional parallel force system that we can treat as a two-dimensional problem. The reaction of the ground on each front truck is denoted $\mathbf{R}_A$, and that on each rear truck $\mathbf{R}_B$.

We must first convert the 4 minutes to radians:

$$4 \text{ minutes} \frac{1°}{60 \text{ minutes}} \frac{1 \text{ rad}}{57.3°} = 0.00116 \text{ rad}$$

From this, we find that the maximum horizontal movement of the center of gravity of the booster and tower is approximately

$$(140 \text{ ft})(0.00116 \text{ rad}) = 0.1624 \text{ ft}$$

Now, for equilibrium, we have

$$+\circlearrowright \Sigma M_A = (2750 \text{ tons})(65 \text{ ft}) + (6000 \text{ tons})(65 \text{ ft} + 0.1624 \text{ ft}) - 2|\mathbf{R}_B|(130 \text{ ft}) = 0$$

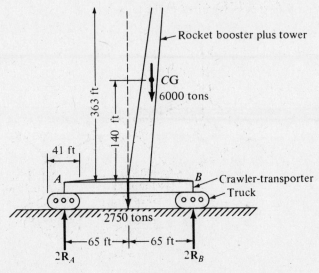

Fig. 4-6

from which $|\mathbf{R}_B| = 2191$ tons.   Then, for equilibrium of vertical forces, we have

$$\Sigma F_y = 2|\mathbf{R}_A| + 2(2191) - 2750 - 6000 = 0$$

from which $|\mathbf{R}_A| = 2184$ tons.

4.5   Bars *DA*, *DC*, and *DB* in Fig. 4-7 are joined in a ball-and-socket joint at *D*, and their lower ends rest in frictionless bearings so as to form a tripodlike structure. The system is subject to a horizontal force of 2000 N acting parallel to the *x* axis as shown. Determine the force in each of the three bars, neglecting the weight of the bars.

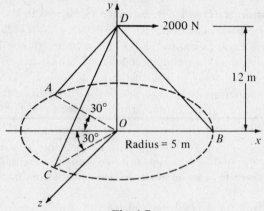

Fig. 4-7

Each bar is in equilibrium under the action of the forces acting at *D* and at its lower bearing. Hence, each bar is a two-force member, and the force acting within the bar must be directed along its centerline. If we cut through all three bars with any horizontal plane below *D* and above the *xz* plane, the bar forces appear as external forces, as in the free-body diagram in Fig. 4-8.

Since the length of *DB* is $\sqrt{5^2 + 12^2} = 13$ m,   the force in *DB* is

$$\mathbf{F}_{DB} = \frac{F_{DB}}{13}(5\mathbf{i} - 12\mathbf{j} + 0\mathbf{k})$$

where F_{DB} denotes the unknown magnitude of the force.

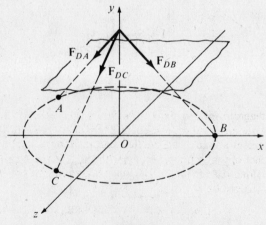

Fig. 4-8

Similarly, the forces in bars DC and DA are

$$\mathbf{F}_{DC} = \frac{F_{DC}}{13}[-5(\cos 30°)\mathbf{i} - 12\mathbf{j} + 5(\sin 30°)\mathbf{k}]$$

and

$$\mathbf{F}_{DA} = \frac{F_{DA}}{13}[-5(\cos 30°)\mathbf{i} - 12\mathbf{j} - 5(\sin 30°)\mathbf{k}]$$

For equilibrium of forces, we have

$$\Sigma \mathbf{F} = 2000\mathbf{i} + \frac{F_{DB}}{13}(5\mathbf{i} - 12\mathbf{j}) + \frac{F_{DC}}{13}\left(-\frac{5\sqrt{3}}{2}\mathbf{i} - 12\mathbf{j} + \frac{5}{2}\mathbf{k}\right) + \frac{F_{DA}}{13}\left(-\frac{5\sqrt{3}}{2}\mathbf{i} - 12\mathbf{j} - \frac{5}{2}\mathbf{k}\right) = 0$$

Next, collecting coefficients of $\mathbf{i}$, $\mathbf{j}$, and $\mathbf{k}$, we obtain the three equations

$$\left(2000 + \frac{5F_{DB}}{13} - \frac{5\sqrt{3}}{2}\frac{F_{DC}}{13} - \frac{5\sqrt{3}}{2}\frac{F_{DA}}{13}\right)\mathbf{i} = 0$$

$$\left(-\frac{12}{13}F_{DB} - \frac{12}{13}F_{DC} - \frac{12}{13}F_{DA}\right)\mathbf{j} = 0$$

$$\left(\frac{5}{2}\frac{F_{DC}}{13} - \frac{5}{2}\frac{F_{DA}}{13}\right)\mathbf{k} = 0$$

These yield $F_{DC} = F_{DA} = 1393$ N and $F_{DB} = -2786$ N. The minus sign on F_{DB} indicates that the assumed direction is incorrect, and the force in that bar is compressive, not tensile.

4.6   A hinged door $ABCD$ covers the opening to a bin. The door is held open by a cable EF secured to a vertical wall at F, as indicated in Fig. 4-9. The door has a mass of 200 kg, and the hinges at A and B are frictionless. Determine the tension in the cable.

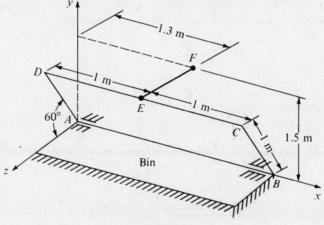

Fig. 4-9

The free-body diagram for the door is shown in Fig. 4-10. To eliminate the moments of the hinge reactions, we shall write an equation expressing the equilibrium of moments about *line AB*. According to (1.13), to find the moment about a line, we first find the moment about a point on the line, and then take the dot (scalar) product of that moment vector with the unit vector along the line (in this case AB).

The unit vector along AB is merely $\lambda_{AB} = \mathbf{i}$. Since only the gravity vector and the cable tension have moments about line AB, we have

$$\Sigma M_{AB} = \lambda_{AB} \cdot (\mathbf{r}_{E/A} \times \mathbf{T}) + \lambda_{AB} \cdot (\mathbf{r}_{G/A} \times \mathbf{W}) = 0 \tag{1}$$

where $\mathbf{r}_{E/A}$ denotes the vector from A to E (which locates one point on the line of action of the cable tension) and $\mathbf{r}_{G/A}$ denotes the vector from A to G (which locates one point on the line of action of the gravity

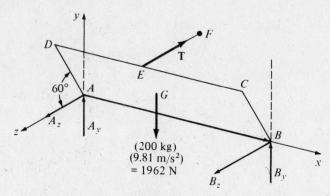

Fig. 4-10

vector). Note that any convenient point on either of these lines of action could be employed; the choice is made for simplicity, given the geometry of the situation.

The cross products in (1) correspond to the moments of the forces about A, and the dot products are their moments about the line AB. Since the hinge reactions at A and B pass through AB, they contribute nothing to the moment relation (1).

From the geometry, we have

$$\mathbf{r}_{E/A} = 1\mathbf{i} + 1(\sin 60°)\mathbf{j} + 1(\cos 60°)\mathbf{k} \tag{2}$$

$$\mathbf{r}_{G/A} = 0.5\mathbf{i} + 0.5(\sin 60°)\mathbf{j} + 0.5(\cos 60°)\mathbf{k} \tag{3}$$

$$\mathbf{EF} = 0.3\mathbf{i} + (1.5 - 1\sin 60°)\mathbf{j} + (-1)(\cos 60°)\mathbf{k} \tag{4}$$

The gravitational attraction vector is $-1962\mathbf{j}$, and the cable tension is

$$\mathbf{T} = \frac{T}{EF} = \frac{[0.3\mathbf{i} + (1.5 - \sin 60°)\mathbf{j} - (\cos 60°)\mathbf{k}]T}{\sqrt{(0.3)^2 + (0.634)^2 + (0.5)^2}}$$

$$= (0.398\mathbf{i} + 0.736\mathbf{j} - 0.581\mathbf{k})T \tag{5}$$

According to (1.12), the mixed triple product may be computed as

$$\mathbf{P} \cdot (\mathbf{Q} \times \mathbf{R}) = \begin{vmatrix} P_x & P_y & P_z \\ Q_x & Q_y & Q_z \\ R_x & R_y & R_z \end{vmatrix} \tag{6}$$

where $\mathbf{P}$ corresponds to λ_{AB} in (1), $\mathbf{Q}$ corresponds to $\mathbf{r}_{E/A}$ or $\mathbf{r}_{G/A}$, and $\mathbf{R}$ corresponds to $\mathbf{T}$ or the gravity vector. Thus, (1) becomes

$$\begin{vmatrix} 1 & 0 & 0 \\ 1 & 0.866 & 0.5 \\ 0.348 & 0.736 & -0.581 \end{vmatrix} T + \begin{vmatrix} 1 & 0 & 0 \\ 1 & 0.433 & 0.25 \\ 0 & -1962 & 0 \end{vmatrix} = 0$$

from which $T = 1126$ N.

4.7   A horizontal rigid boom OB is subject to a vertical load W and is supported by two cables attached to a vertical supporting wall, as shown in Fig. 4-11. The supported end of the boom, at the origin of the coordinate system, lies in a smooth ball-and-socket joint. Write a FORTRAN program for determining the forces in both cables.

We first express the forces in the cables in the vector form

$$\mathbf{T}_1 = |\mathbf{T}_1|\left(-\frac{FL}{CL_1}\mathbf{i} + \frac{y_1}{CL_1}\mathbf{j} + \frac{z_1}{CL_1}\mathbf{k} \right)$$

$$\mathbf{T}_2 = |\mathbf{T}_2|\left(-\frac{FL}{CL_2}\mathbf{i} + \frac{y_2}{CL_2}\mathbf{j} + \frac{z_2}{CL_2}\mathbf{k} \right)$$

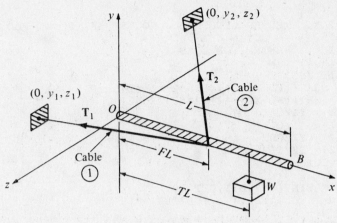

Fig. 4-11

where CL_1 and CL_2 are the lengths of cables ① and ②, respectively. Next, for equilibrium we have

$$\Sigma \mathbf{M}_O = (FL)\mathbf{i} \times |\mathbf{T}_1|\left(-\frac{FL}{CL_1}\mathbf{i} + \frac{y_1}{CL_1}\mathbf{j} + \frac{z_1}{CL_1}\mathbf{k}\right)$$

$$+ (FL)\mathbf{i} \times |\mathbf{T}_2|\left(-\frac{FL}{CL_2}\mathbf{i} + \frac{y_2}{CL_2}\mathbf{j} + \frac{z_2}{CL_2}\mathbf{k}\right) + (TL)\mathbf{i} \times (-W)\mathbf{j} = 0$$

Expanding and collecting the coefficients of $\mathbf{j}$ and $\mathbf{k}$ yield the scalar equations

$$\frac{(FL)y_1}{CL_1}T_1 - \frac{(FL)y_2}{CL_2}T_2 - (TL)W = 0$$

$$\frac{(FL)z_1}{CL_1}T_1 + \frac{(FL)z_2}{CL_2}T_2 = 0$$

These equations may be written symbolically as

$$A(1,1)T_1 - A(1,2)T_2 = W$$

$$A(2,1)T_1 + A(2,2)T_2 = 0$$

from which the cable tensions are readily found. A FORTRAN program that will do so is the following:

```
00010       PROGRAM CRANE1(INPUT,OUTPUT)
00020C
00030C      PROGRAM CRANE 1 ---- HORIZONTAL RIGID BOOM LOADED BY A VERTICAL
00040C      CONCENTRATED LOAD W AT AN ARBITRARY POINT AND SUSPENDED BY TWO
00050C      CABLES RUNNING FROM AN ARBITRARY POINT ON THE BOOM TO TWO ARBITRARY
00060C      POINTS ON THE VERTICAL WALL.  BOOM REST IN BALL-AND-SOCKET JOINT
00070C      AT ORIGIN OF COORDINATE SYSTEM AND RUNS ALONG X-AXIS.
00080C      L:  BOOM LENGTH
00090C      FL: DISTANCE FROM BALL-AND-SOCKET TO POINT OF ATTACHMENT OF CABLES
00100C      TL: DISTANCE FROM BALL-AND-SOCKET TO POINT OF VERTICAL LOAD
00110C      0,Y1,Z1: COORDINATES OF END OF CABLE 1 AT POINT OF ATTACHMENT
00120C               TO WALL
00130C      0,Y2,Z2: COORDINATES OF END OF CABLE 2 AT POINT OF ATTACHMENT
00140C               TO WALL
00150C
00160       DIMENSION A(10,10),B(10)
00170       PRINT *,'  ENTER THE COORDINATES OF THE END POINTS OF CABLES'
00180       PRINT *,'  CABLE 1 : X1, Y1, Z1 ;   CABLE 2 : X2, Y2, Z2'
00190       READ(*,*)          X1, Y1, Z1,          X2, Y2, Z2
00200       PRINT *,'  ENTER LENGTH BTW SOCKET AND POINT LOAD APPLIED'
```

```
00210        READ(*,*)    TL
00220        PRINT *,'   ENTER LENGTH BTW SOCKET AND POINT ROD ATTACHED'
00230        READ(*,*)    FL
00240        PRINT *,'   ENTER THE LOAD '
00250        READ(*,*)    W
00260        W1= (TL/FL)*W
00270        CL1= SQRT((FL-X1)**2+Y1**2+Z1**2)
00280        CL2= SQRT((FL-X2)**2+Y2**2+Z2**2)
00290        A(1,1)= Y1/CL1
00300        A(2,1)= Z1/CL1
00310        A(1,2)= Y2/CL2
00320        A(2,2)= Z2/CL2
00330        B(1)= W1
00340        B(2)= 0.
00350        CALL MATINV(A,2,B,1,DET,10)
00360        RX = (FL/CL1)*B(1) + (FL/CL2)*B(2)
00370        RY = W - W1
00380        DO 10 I= 1,2
00390     10 PRINT 100,I,B(I)
00400        PRINT 110
00410        PRINT 120
00420        PRINT 130, RX,RY,0
00430    100 FORMAT(/,10X,'THE TENSION IN CABLE ',I2,' IS',F10.2)
00440    110 FORMAT(//,10X,'THE REACTION AT BALL AND SOCKET ')
00450    120 FORMAT(/,10X,'COMPONENTS IN X, Y, Z DIRECTION')
00460    130 FORMAT(/,10X,'X :',F8.2,'   Y :',F8.2,'   Z :',F8.2)
00470        END
```

Although Fig. 4-11 shows the load at a point to the right of the point of attachment of the cables, the program is valid for any locations of these two points.

4.8   For the crane of Problem 4.7, let $y_1 = 15$ ft, $z_1 = 16$ ft, $y_2 = 12$ ft, and $z_2 = -13$ ft. Assume an 8000-lb load acts 20 ft from the ball-and-socket joint, and the cables are attached to OB 25 ft from this joint. Use the FORTRAN program to find the cable tensions.

We need only input the coordinates and the lengths FL and TL. The program provides the following output:

```
ENTER THE COORDINATES OF THE END POINTS OF CABLES
CABLE 1 : X1, Y1, Z1 ;   CABLE 2 : X2, Y2, Z2
?  0,15,16,0,12,-13
ENTER LENGTH BTW SOCKET AND POINT LOAD APPLIED
?  20
ENTER LENGTH BTW SOCKET AND POINT ROD ATTACHED
?  25
ENTER THE LOAD
?  8000

         THE TENSION IN CABLE  1  IS  7149.73

         THE TENSION IN CABLE  2  IS  8103.83
```

4.9   Rigid vertical bar OA in Fig. 4-12 supports rigid member FD, which is tied back to OA by a horizontal cable ED. There is a ball-and-socket joint at O. The plane FDE makes an angle of α radians with the xy plane. The upper end of the bar at A is anchored to the xz plane by two cables as indicated, and a vertical load P acts at the end of member FD. Write a FORTRAN program to determine the forces in cables ① and ②.

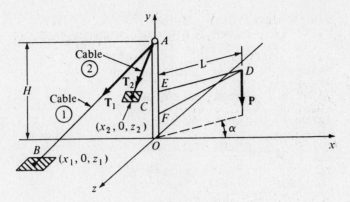

Fig. 4-12

We first express the forces in the cables in unit-vector form:

$$\mathbf{T}_1 = |\mathbf{T}_1|\left(\frac{x_1}{CL_1}\mathbf{i} - \frac{H}{CL_1}\mathbf{j} + \frac{z_1}{CL_1}\mathbf{k}\right)$$

$$\mathbf{T}_2 = |\mathbf{T}_2|\left(\frac{x_2}{CL_2}\mathbf{i} - \frac{H}{CL_2}\mathbf{j} + \frac{z_2}{CL_2}\mathbf{k}\right)$$

where CL_1 and CL_2 are the lengths of cables ① and ②, respectively. For equilibrium,

$$\Sigma\,\mathbf{M}_O = H\mathbf{j} \times |\mathbf{T}_1|\left(\frac{x_1}{CL_1}\mathbf{i} - \frac{H}{CL_1}\mathbf{j} + \frac{z_1}{CL_1}\mathbf{k}\right) + H\mathbf{j} \times |\mathbf{T}_2|\left(\frac{x_2}{CL_2}\mathbf{i} - \frac{H}{CL_2}\mathbf{j} + \frac{z_2}{CL_2}\mathbf{k}\right)$$

$$+\,[L(\cos\alpha)\mathbf{i} - L(\sin\alpha)\mathbf{k}] \times (-P\mathbf{j}) = 0$$

Expanding and collecting coefficients of **i** and **k** yield the scalar equations

$$\frac{Hz_1}{CL_1}T_1 + \frac{Hz_2}{CL_2}T_2 = PL\sin\alpha$$

$$\frac{Hx_1}{CL_1}T_1 + \frac{Hx_2}{CL_2}T_2 = -PL\cos\alpha$$

which may be written symbolically in the form

$$A(1,1)T_1 + A(1,2)T_2 = B(1)$$

$$A(2,1)T_1 + A(2,2)T_2 = B(2)$$

A FORTRAN program for finding T_1 and T_2 is the following:

```
00010        PROGRAM CRANE2(INPUT,OUPUT)
00020C
00030C       PROGRAM CRANE2 ---- VERTICAL RIGID MAST OF HEIGHT H ALONG
00040C       Y-AXIS WITH BASE IN BALL-AND-SOCKET JOINT AT ORIGIN OF XYZ
00050C       COORDINATE SYSTEM.  RIGID BOOM ATTACHED ABOVE ORIGIN WITH
00060C       HORIZONTAL PROJECTION L IS SUBJECTED TO VERTICAL FORCE P
00070C       AT EXTREMITY. MAST BRACED BY TWO CABLES FROM TOP OF MAST TO
00080C       TWO ARBITRARY POINT IN THE X-Z PLANE.
00090C              H: MAST HEIGHT
00100C              L: PROJECTION OF BOOM LENGTH ON X-Z PLANE
00110C          ALPHA: ANGLE OF PLANE OF BOOM AND MAST WITH X-AXIS
00120C       X1,0,Z1: COORDINATES OF END OF CABLE 1 AT POINT OF
00130C                ATTACHMENT TO XZ PLANE
00140C       X1,0,Z1: COORDINATES OF END OF CABLE 1 AT POINT OF
00150C                ATTACHMENT TO XZ PLANE
00160
```

```
00170        DIMENSION A(10,10),B(10)
00180        PRINT *,'   ENTER THE COORDINATES OF THE END POINTS OF CABLES'
00190        PRINT *,'   CABLE 1 : X1, Z1 ;   CABLE 2 : X2, Z2'
00200        READ(*,*)          X1, Z1,              X2, Z2
00210        PRINT *,'   ENTER LENGTH OF BAR'
00220        READ(*,*)   H
00230        PRINT *,'   ENTER LENGTH OF L'
00240        READ(*,*)   L
00250        PRINT *,'   ENTER THE ANGLE '
00260        READ(*,*)   ANG
00270        PRINT *,'   ENTER THE LOAD '
00280        READ(*,*)   P
00290        CL1= SQRT(X1**2+H**2+Z1**2)
00300        CL2= SQRT(X2**2+H**2+Z2**2)
00310        A(1,1)= Z1*H/CL1
00320        A(2,1)= X1*H/CL1
00330        A(1,2)= Z2*H/CL2
00340        A(2,2)= X2*H/CL2
00350        B(1)=  P*L*SIN(ANG)
00360        B(2)= -P*L*COS(ANG)
00370        CALL MATINV(A,2,B,1,DET,10)
00380        DO 10 I= 1,2
00390     10 PRINT 100,I,B(I)
00400    100 FORMAT(/,10X,'THE TENSION IN CABLE ',I2,' IS',F10.2)
00410        END
```

4.10 For the crane of Fig. 4-12, let $x_1 = -20$ ft, $z_1 = 18$ ft, $x_2 = -25$ ft, and $z_2 = -22$ ft. Assume the height of bar OA is 10 ft, member FD is 7.5 ft long, angle α is 0.25 rad, and the load acting at D is 12,000 lb. Use the FORTRAN program to find the forces in cables ① and ②.

In response to the prompting of the program, we input the given parameters to obtain the following:

```
      ENTER THE COORDINATES OF THE END POINTS OF CABLES
      CABLE 1 : X1, Z1 ; CABLE 2 : X2, Z2
?  -20,18,-25,-22
      ENTER LENGTH OF BAR
?  10
      ENTER LENGTH OF L
?  7.5
      ENTER THE ANGLE
?  0.25
      ENTER THE LOAD
?  12000

      THE TENSION IN CABLE  1  IS  7450.82

      THE TENSION IN CABLE  2  IS  4099.65
```

Supplementary Problems

4.11 A square plate $ACEF$, of weight W, lies in a horizontal plane (Fig. 4-13). It is suspended by wires at points D and G and is also supported by a short post at B. Find the forces in the wires and the post.

Ans. $T_D = T_G = 2W/3$; $T_B = W/3$

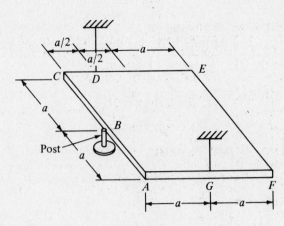

Fig. 4-13

4.12 The rigid shaft AD in Fig. 4-14 is supported in frictionless bearings at A and C. Pulleys are keyed to the shaft at B and D, and each pulley has a radius of 0.15 m. The belt pulls indicated consist of two forces parallel to the z axis at B and two forces parallel to the y axis at D. Neglecting the weights of shaft and pulleys, determine the bearing reactions and the magnitude of **P** necessary for equilibrium.

Ans. $|\mathbf{P}| = 875$ N; $A_z = 87.5$ N; $A_y = -612$ N; $C_z = -87.5$ N; $C_y = 1837$ N

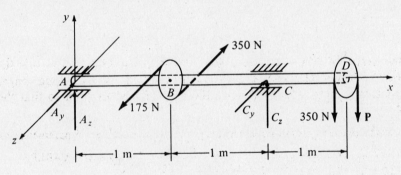

Fig. 4-14

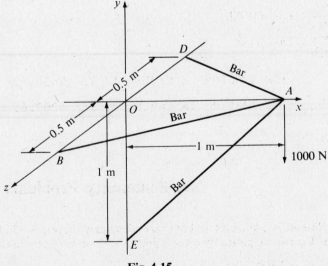

Fig. 4-15

4.13 For the tripodlike structure of Problem 4.5, let the applied loading at D be $\mathbf{F} = (800\mathbf{k} - 1200\mathbf{i})$ N.   Determine the force in each of the three bars, neglecting the weight of the bars.

     Ans. $F_{DC} = -2824$ N; $F_{DB} = 1488$ N; $F_{DA} = 1336$ N

4.14 The three-bar truss in Fig. 4-15 has elements AB, AD, and AE joined at a frictionless ball-and-socket joint at A, where a vertical load of 1000 N is applied. Bars AB and AD lie in the horizontal (xz) plane. Determine the force in each bar, neglecting the bar weights.   *Ans.* $F_{AB} = F_{AD} = 559$ N; $F_{AE} = -1414$ N

4.15 For the crane of Fig. 4-11, take the points of attachment of the cables to be located at (0, 14 ft, 28 ft) and (0, 23 ft, -25 ft). Assume that a load of 12,000 lb acts downward at a point 35 ft from the ball-and-socket joint, and the cables are attached 30 ft from that joint. Find the cable tensions using the computer program.

     Ans.   15,270 lb;   17,880 lb

4.16 For the crane of Problem 4.9, assume that the cables are anchored at the points $(-4.7$ m, 0, 5.9 m) and $(-5.2$ m, 0, -6.1 m); bar OA is 4.8 m tall; length L is 3.9 m; plane FDE makes an angle of 0.30 rad with the xy plane; and a vertical load of 80,000 N acts at point D. Use the computer program to determine the cable tensions.   *Ans.*   55,470 N;   33,430 N

Chapter 5

Trusses

A *truss* is a two- or three-dimensional collection of long, straight bars. If the bars are all in one plane, they are assumed to be joined by frictionless pins at their ends, which are called *nodes*. If the bars lie in three-dimensional space, they are joined by frictionless ball-and-socket joints. In elementary analysis we usually neglect the weight of the truss. Since each bar is loaded only at its ends, each bar is a two-force member and must be in a state of either tension (Fig. 5-1a) or compression (Fig. 5-1b). The tensile or compressive force acting at the ends is transmitted unchanged in magnitude and direction through the length of the bar. Bar forces are often labeled with the letters designating the endpoints of the bar, so force **P** in Fig. 5-1 could be labeled **AB**.

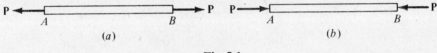

$$(a) \qquad\qquad (b)$$

Fig. 5-1

For a plane truss there are two simple, analytical methods for determining the bar forces once the external reactions have been found. These are

1. *The method of joints.* A node of the truss, in which no more than two intersecting bars have unknown bar forces, is selected for analysis. For such a concurrent force system, there are two independent equilibrium equations and thus the two unknown bar forces may be found. The procedure is repeated until all bar forces have been found. (See Problems 5.1 and 5.4.)

2. *The method of sections.* An imaginary plane is passed through the plane truss in such a manner as to intersect no more than three bars with unknown bar forces. Now there are three equations of equilibrium and thus the bar forces may be determined. (See Problems 5.2 and 5.3.)

For a three-dimensional truss, either method may be used (in slightly modified form). (See Problem 5.5.)

Tensile bar forces are almost always regarded as positive, and compressive forces as negative. In view of this sign convention, it is simplest to designate all unknown bar forces as tensile before solving for them. If a value is found to be positive, it is a tensile force; a value that is found to be negative is a compressive force. In addition, a tensile force of, say, 10 kN is usually written as 10 kN (T) and a compressive force of 18 kN as 18 kN (C).

For trusses with many members, the determination of all bar forces obviously involves long, tedious calculations. For this reason, computerized approaches are usually employed by designers. Most plane (two-dimensional) trusses involving modest numbers of bars may be handled by a simple program, usually written in FORTRAN. (See Problem 5.6.)

Solved Problems

5.1   The three-panel cantilever-type truss in Fig. 5-2 is pinned at E and tied to a vertical wall by a member DF. Determine the forces in the bars due to the vertical load **P** applied at A.

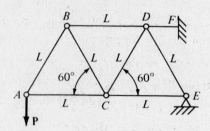

Fig. 5-2

Member DF is loaded only at its ends and is a two-force member, so the force must be directed along its length. Hence, the free-body diagram for the truss appears as in Fig. 5-3. For equilibrium of the entire truss, we have

$$+\circlearrowleft \Sigma M_E = |\mathbf{DF}|L\sin 60° - |\mathbf{P}|(2L) = 0 \qquad \text{or} \qquad |\mathbf{DF}| = 2.309|\mathbf{P}|\,(T)$$

$$\Sigma F_x = -E_x + |\mathbf{DF}| = 0 \qquad \text{or} \qquad E_x = 2.309|\mathbf{P}|$$

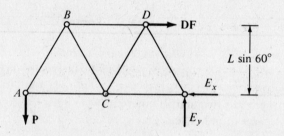

Fig. 5-3

Because the geometry is simple and all the bar forces are required, we employ the method of joints. We must start at node A because that is the only node at which there are only two unknown bar forces; all the others have three or more. The free-body diagram of node A appears in Fig. 5-4, where unknown bar forces are considered to be in tension. For equilibrium,

$$\Sigma F_y = |\mathbf{AB}|\sin 60° - |\mathbf{P}| = 0 \qquad \text{or} \qquad |\mathbf{AB}| = 1.155|\mathbf{P}|\,(T)$$

$$\Sigma F_x = |\mathbf{AC}| + |\mathbf{AB}|\cos 60° = 0 \qquad \text{or} \qquad |\mathbf{AC}| = -0.577|\mathbf{P}|\,(C)$$

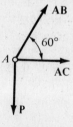

Fig. 5-4

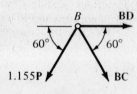

Fig. 5-5

These results tell us that **AB** acts in tension, and **AC** in compression.

We may now consider node B, since only two of the bar forces there are now unknown. The free-body diagram for node B is given in Fig. 5-5. For equilibrium,

$$\Sigma F_y = -1.155|\mathbf{P}|\sin 60° - |\mathbf{BC}|\sin 60° = 0 \qquad \text{or} \qquad |\mathbf{BC}| = -1.155|\mathbf{P}|\,(C)$$

$$\Sigma F_x = |\mathbf{BD}| + |\mathbf{BC}|\cos 60° - 1.155|\mathbf{P}|\cos 60° = 0 \qquad \text{or} \qquad |\mathbf{BD}| = 1.155|\mathbf{P}|\,(T)$$

Next, we analyze node C (Fig. 5-6). It is simplest to show the forces in bars BC and AC as compressive (as just determined). For equilibrium,

$$\Sigma F_y = -1.155|\mathbf{P}|\sin 60° + |\mathbf{CD}|\sin 60° = 0 \qquad \text{or} \qquad |\mathbf{CD}| = 1.155|\mathbf{P}|\,(\text{T})$$

$$\Sigma F_x = |\mathbf{CE}| + |\mathbf{CD}|\cos 60° + 1.155|\mathbf{P}|\cos 60° + 0.577|\mathbf{P}| = 0 \qquad \text{or} \qquad |\mathbf{CE}| = -1.732|\mathbf{P}|\,(\text{C})$$

Finally, the free-body diagram for node D is given in Fig. 5-7 and, for equilibrium,

$$\Sigma F_y = -1.155|\mathbf{P}|\sin 60° - |\mathbf{DE}|\sin 60° = 0 \qquad \text{or} \qquad |\mathbf{DE}| = -1.155|\mathbf{P}|\,(\text{C})$$

As a check on the computations, we should now consider node E. The bar forces already determined, together with the pin reactions there, should correspond to vertical and horizontal equilibrium of that node. This check will not, however, be shown.

Fig. 5-6   **Fig. 5-7**

5.2   The triangular truss in Fig. 5-8 is subject to three vertical loads as shown. Determine the forces in bars BD, CD, and CE.

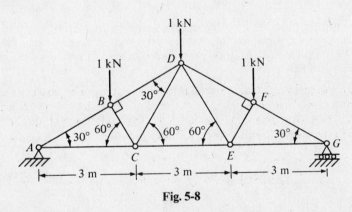

Fig. 5-8

From the symmetry, we note that each end reaction is a vertical force of 1.5 kN. We shall use the method of sections, passing a vertical section through the three bars of interest. The free-body diagram of the portion of the truss to the left of this section is shown in Fig. 5-9.

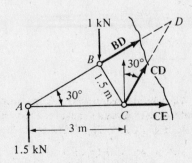

Fig. 5-9

It is convenient to begin with the sum of the moments about node C, since two of the unknown bar forces intersect there:

$$+\!\!\circlearrowleft \Sigma \, M_C = |\mathbf{BD}|(1.5 \text{ m}) - (1 \text{ kN})(1.5 \text{ m}) \cos 60° + (1.5 \text{ kN})(3 \text{ m}) = 0$$

from which we find $|\mathbf{BD}| = -2.5 \text{ kN (C)}$.

Next we take the sum of the moments about node A, since another pair of bar forces intersects there. Since the vertical component of $\mathbf{CD}$ is $|\mathbf{CD}| \cos 30°$,   we have

$$+\!\!\circlearrowleft \Sigma \, M_A = (1 \text{ kN})[(3 - 1.5 \cos 60°) \text{ m}] - |\mathbf{CD}|(\cos 30°)(3 \text{ m}) = 0$$

from which $|\mathbf{CD}| = 0.866 \text{ kN (T)}$.

Still another pair of bar forces intersects at node D. (We may write a moment equilibrium equation about such a point even though it is not part of the free body because, for equilibrium, the sum of the moments of all forces on the free body is zero about any point in the plane.) Thus, we have

$$+\!\!\circlearrowleft \Sigma \, M_D = (1.5 \text{ kN})(4.5 \text{ m}) - (1 \text{ kN})[(1.5 + 1.5 \cos 60°) \text{ m}] - |\mathbf{CE}|[(3 \sin 60°) \text{ m}] = 0$$

which yields $|\mathbf{CE}| = 1.73 \text{ kN (T)}$.

5.3   A square truss consists of nine bars arranged as shown in Fig. 5-10 and subject to the vertical load $\mathbf{P}$ applied at E. Determine the forces in bars CD, AB, and EF.

The vertical reactions at A and D are found from the equations

$$+\!\!\circlearrowleft \Sigma \, M_A = -|\mathbf{R}_D|L + |\mathbf{P}|(\tfrac{2}{3}L) = 0 \qquad \text{or} \qquad |\mathbf{R}_D| = \tfrac{2}{3}|\mathbf{P}|$$

$$\Sigma \, F_y = |\mathbf{R}_A| + \tfrac{2}{3}|\mathbf{P}| - |\mathbf{P}| = 0 \qquad \text{or} \qquad |\mathbf{R}_A| = \tfrac{1}{3}|\mathbf{P}|$$

Now we pass through the truss the section shown by the dashed curve in Fig. 5-10. Only three bars containing unknown bar forces are intersected by this section. (The fact that the section is not a plane is of no significance.) The free-body diagram for the portion of the truss above the section appears in Fig. 5-11. For equilibrium, we have

$$\Sigma \, F_x = -|\mathbf{EF}| = 0 \qquad\qquad \text{or} \qquad |\mathbf{EF}| = 0$$

$$+\!\!\circlearrowleft \Sigma \, M_B = |\mathbf{P}|(\tfrac{2}{3}L) + |\mathbf{CD}|(L) = 0 \qquad \text{or} \qquad |\mathbf{CD}| = -\tfrac{2}{3}|\mathbf{P}| \text{ (C)}$$

$$+\!\!\circlearrowleft \Sigma \, M_C = -|\mathbf{P}|(\tfrac{1}{3}L) - |\mathbf{BA}|(L) = 0 \qquad \text{or} \qquad |\mathbf{BA}| = -\tfrac{1}{3}|\mathbf{P}| \text{ (C)}$$

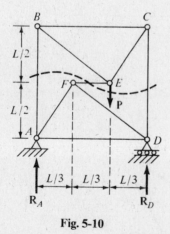

Fig. 5-10

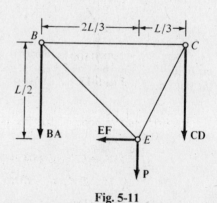

Fig. 5-11

5.4   The communications satellite RELAY consists of a central cylindrical core (housing electronic components) surrounded by six trusses oriented in uniformly spaced radial planes. Each of the trusses has the configuration indicated in Fig. 5-12 and, during launch, is subject to forces

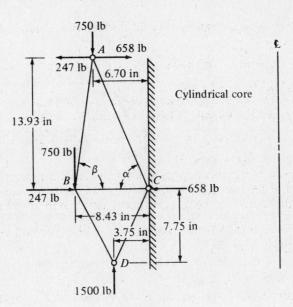

Fig. 5-12

corresponding to 30 times the usual gravitational attraction. These loads are indicated in the figure. Determine the forces in all bars of the truss.

Let us begin by applying the method of joints at node D. The free-body diagram appears in Fig. 5-13, where $\psi = \arctan(3.75/7.75) = 26.0°$ and $\theta = \arctan(4.68/7.75) = 31.2°$. For equilibrium,

$$\Sigma F_x = |DC| \sin \psi - |DB| \sin \theta = 0 \quad \text{or} \quad 0.438|DC| = 0.520|DB|$$

and

$$\Sigma F_y = |DC| \cos \psi + |DB| \cos \theta + 1500 = 0$$

from which $|DB| = -762 \text{ lb (C)}$ and $|DC| = -927 \text{ lb (C)}$.

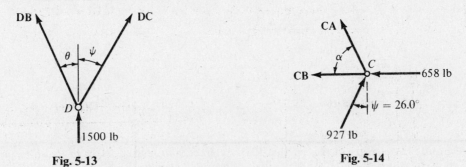

Fig. 5-13   **Fig. 5-14**

Next we analyze node C. The free-body diagram is given in Fig. 5-14, where $\alpha = \arctan(13.93/6.70) = 64.3°$. Then

$$\Sigma F_y = 927 \cos 26.0° + |CA| \sin 64.3° = 0 \quad \text{or} \quad |CA| = -925 \text{ lb (C)}$$

$$\Sigma F_x = -|CB| - 658 + 927 \sin 26.0° - |CA| \cos 64.3° = 0$$

so that $|CB| = 149 \text{ lb (T)}$.

Finally, to find bar force **AB** we consider node A. We have the free-body diagram in Fig. 5-15 and the equilibrium equation

$$\Sigma F_y = -750 + 925 \sin 64.3° - |AB| \sin \beta = 0$$

Since $\beta = \arctan(13.93/1.73)$, this yields $|AB| = 84 \text{ lb (T)}$.

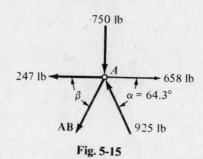

Fig. 5-15

5.5   The three-dimensional truss $ABCD$ in Fig. 5-16 is used for the ground-testing of a communications satellite model. Ends A, B, and C of the inclined bars (all of length L) lie in a horizontal (xz) plane, and bars AB, AC, and BC constitute an equilateral triangle. Ball-and-socket joints at A, B, and C transfer the weight W of the model to the xz plane. The vertical centerline of the model lies above the centroid of triangle ABC, and the horizontal plane is smooth. Find the force in each of the horizontal bars.

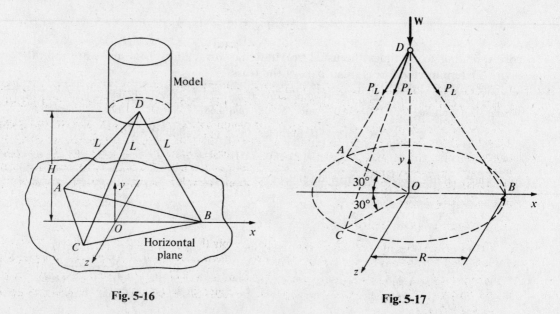

Fig. 5-16   **Fig. 5-17**

From the symmetry, it is clear that the magnitudes of the axial forces in the three inclined bars are identical; we denote them by P_L. If we pass a horizontal plane through these bars at some distance below D, we obtain for node D the free-body diagram shown in Fig. 5-17. Summing forces in the y direction then yields

$$\Sigma F_y = -W - 3P_L \frac{H}{\sqrt{H^2 + R^2}} = 0$$

where we have used the fact that $L^2 = H^2 + R^2$.   Solving, we obtain

$$P_L = \frac{-W\sqrt{H^2 + R^2}}{3H}$$

Next, we consider node B, which is subject to (1) the force P_L in bar DB, (2) the unknown forces in bars AB and BC, and (3) the vertical reaction of the smooth plane xz. Owing to the symmetry about the x axis, the forces in bars AB and BC must be of equal magnitude; we call that P and obtain the free-body diagram of Fig. 5-18. For equilibrium at node D, we have

$$\Sigma F_x = P_L \frac{R}{\sqrt{R^2 + H^2}} - 2P \cos 30° = 0 \qquad \text{or} \qquad P = \frac{WR\sqrt{3}}{9H}$$

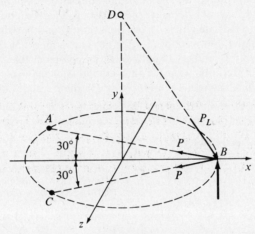

Fig. 5-18

5.6   Consider a pin-jointed truss in which all loads and reactions act only at the pins (nodes) of the system. Develop a FORTRAN computer program to determine the bar forces and reactions.

The most efficient approach is to write a program wherein the computer sets up two equilibrium equations at each node (based on the method of joints as applied in Problem 5.1) and then solves the resulting system of simultaneous linear algebraic equations to obtain both the bar forces and the components of reactions.* Such a program is given at the end of this problem. The program is also self-prompting; i.e., the terminal display questions the user about all geometric values and loads, and the user merely responds with appropriate input data.

The truss program is used as follows:

1.   Count the number of nodes in the truss, and multiply this by 2 to obtain the number of simultaneous equilibrium equations for the system. Enter this number in response to the prompt of line 00014.

2.   Assign a number, in order beginning with 1, to each bar, as indicated by the circled numbers in Problem 5.7. The ordering of the bars is of no significance. Enter the highest number in response to the prompt of line 00016.

3.   Introduce two numbered vectors at each node. One vector should extend horizontally to the right, the other vertically upward. (These are shown as vectors 1, 2, . . . , 11, 12 in Fig. 5-20.) The order in which vectors are numbered from node to node is immaterial.

4.   Enter the value of the applied load (excluding reactions) acting along each node vector of step 3, in response to the prompt of line 00018. Because of the particular subroutine used here for the solution of simultaneous linear algebraic equations (line 00042), it is necessary to designate downward loads and loads to the left as positive, in opposition to the conventional designations.

5.   Enter the coordinates of the tail of each vector, in response to the prompt of line 00023. Note that horizontal vectors, such as vector 3 in Fig. 5-20, are designated by only a horizontal coordinate, and vertical vectors, such as vector 4, by only a vertical coordinate (always of the tail).

6.   To designate which nodes are connected by bars, enter the four vector numbers corresponding to each bar (separated by commas), in response to the prompt of line 00029. The vector numbers for each node

---

* The procedure employed here is based upon that developed in A. Chajes, *Structural Analysis* (Englewood Cliffs, N.J.: Prentice-Hall, 1983).

should be entered in the order horizontal-vector number, vertical-vector number. Thus, in Problem 5.7, for bar ① the designation must be 1,2,3,4 or 3,4,1,2.

7. The program will next respond with a query regarding support reactions. It will number the reactions beginning with the numeral immediately following the number of members (line 00016) and continuing through to the numeral corresponding to the number of simultaneous equations (line 00014). The user must determine the type of external support existing at each support point and enter previously assigned vector numbers to indicate either a pin joint (vertical and horizontal) or roller (vertical only) reaction at each support point. For example, for the pin-joint support at the left of the truss in Problem 5.7, we would enter the vector numbers 1 and 2 to tell the computer that there are reaction components in both the x and y directions (a pin joint) at that support. For the roller support at the right, only the vector number 10 would be entered. The order in which these reaction designators are entered is immaterial.

8. Immediately after the data are entered, the computer will print out the magnitudes of all bar forces and reactions. Positive bar forces are tensile; negative forces are compressive.

The program is as follows:

```
00008C    ****               A = COEFFICIENT MATRIX (N * N)        ****
00009C    ****               P = KNOWN LOAD MATRIX   (N * 1)        ****
00010C    ****               C = COORDINATE MATRIX   (N)           ****
00011C    ****                                                     ****
00012 PROGRAM TRUSS(INPUT, OUTPUT)
00013 DIMENSION A(50, 50),  P(50, 1), C(50)
00014 PRINT*, 'ENTER THE NUMBER OF SIMULTANEOUS EQUATIONS;'
00015 READ*, N
00016 PRINT*, 'ENTER THE NUMBER OF MEMBERS:'
00017 READ*, NM
00018 PRINT*,'ENTER THE VALUES OF APPLIED LOAD:'
00019 DO 10 I = 1, N
00020     PRINT*,'JOINT',I,':'
00021     READ*, P(I, 1)
00022 10 CONTINUE
00023 PRINT*,'ENTER THE COORDINATES OF THE TAIL OF EACH VECTOR'
00024 DO 20 I = 1, N
00025     PRINT*,'JOINT',I,':'
00026     READ*, C(I)
00027 20 CONTINUE
00028 DO 30 M = 1, NM
00029     PRINT*,'ENTER THE VECTOR NUMBERS I, J, K, L FOR MEMBER ',M
00030     READ*, I, J, K, L
00031     ALENGTH = SQRT(((C(K) - C(I)) ** 2) + ((C(L) - C(J)) ** 2))
00032     A(I, M) = (C(K) - C(I)) / ALENGTH
00033     A(J, M) = (C(L) - C(J)) / ALENGTH
00034     A(K, M) = - (C(K) - C(I)) / ALENGTH
00035     A(L, M) = - (C(L) - C(J)) / ALENGTH
00036 30 CONTINUE
00037 DO 40 M = (NM + 1), N
00038     PRINT*,'ENTER THE VECTOR NUMBER FOR REACTION', M
00039     READ*, I
00040     A(I, M) = 1.0
00041 40 CONTINUE
00042 CALL MATINV(A, N, P, 1, DET, 50)
00043 PRINT*,'SOLUTION:'
00044 PRINT*,'*********'
00045 DO 50 I = 1, NM
00046     PRINT 70,'MEMBER', I, P(I, 1)
00047 50 CONTINUE
00048 DO 60 I = (NM + 1), N
00049     PRINT 70,'REACTION', I, P(I, 1)
00050 60 CONTINUE
00051 70 FORMAT (A, 1X, I2, F 8.2)
00052 END
```

READY.

5.7   The truss in Fig. 5-19 is subjected to three vertical forces as shown. Use the computer program developed in Problem 5.6 to determine all bar forces and support reactions.

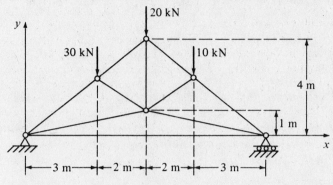

Fig. 5-19

There are six nodes and hence twelve simultaneous equations for step 1 of Problem 5.6. We introduce the bar numbers and vectors shown in Fig. 5-20 for steps 2 and 3.

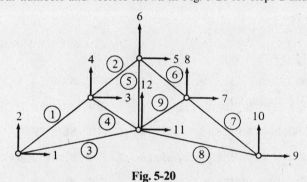

Fig. 5-20

The remaining steps of the procedure are evident in the following printout.

```
ENTER THE NUMBER OF SIMULTANEOUS EQUATIONS:
? 12
ENTER THE NUMBER OF MEMBERS:
? 9
ENTER THE VALUES OF APPLIED LOAD:
 JOINT1:
? 0
 JOINT2:
? 0
 JOINT3:
? 0
 JOINT4:
? 30
 JOINT5:
? 0
 JOINT6:
? 20
 JOINT7:
? 0
 JOINT8:
? 10
 JOINT9:
? 0
 JOINT10:
? 0
 JOINT11:
```

```
        JOINT12:
?   0
    ENTER THE COORDINATES OF THE TAIL OF EACH VECTOR
        JOINT1:
?   0
        JOINT2:
?   0
        JOINT3:
?   3
        JOINT4:
?   2.4
        JOINT5:
?   5
        JOINT6:
?   4
        JOINT7:
?   7
        JOINT8:
?   2.4
        JOINT9:
?   10
        JOINT10:
?   0
        JOINT11:
?   5
        JOINT12:
?   1
    ENTER THE VECTOR NUMBERS I, J, K, L FOR MEMBER 1
?   1,2,3,4
    ENTER THE VECTOR NUMBERS I, J, K, L FOR MEMBER 2
?   3,4,5,6
    ENTER THE VECTOR NUMBERS I, J, K, L FOR MEMBER 3
?   1,2,11,12
    ENTER THE VECTOR NUMBERS I, J, K, L FOR MEMBER 4
?   3,4,11,12
    ENTER THE VECTOR NUMBERS I, J, K, L FOR MEMBER 5
?   11,12,5,6
    ENTER THE VECTOR NUMBERS I, J, K, L FOR MEMBER 6
?   5,6,7,8
    ENTER THE VECTOR NUMBERS I, J, K, L FOR MEMBER 7
?   7,8,9,10
    ENTER THE VECTOR NUMBERS I, J, K, L FOR MEMBER 8
?   11,12,9,10
    ENTER THE VECTOR NUMBERS I, J, K, L FOR MEMBER 9
?   11,12,7,8
    ENTER THE VECTOR NUMBER FOR REACTION10
?   1
    ENTER THE VECTOR NUMBER FOR REACTION11
?   2
    ENTER THE VECTOR NUMBER FOR REACTION12
?   10
    SOLUTION:
    ********
MEMBER   1    -72.57
MEMBER   2    -46.96
MEMBER   3     57.79
MEMBER   4    -24.41
MEMBER   5     38.67
MEMBER   6    -46.96
MEMBER   7    -55.49
MEMBER   8     44.19
MEMBER   9     -8.14
REACTION 10      .00
REACTION 11    34.00
REACTION 12    26.00
```

Supplementary Problems

5.8   The truss in Fig. 5-21 is pinned at F and supported by a roller at A so that the reaction at A is normal to the 45° inclined surface. Determine the forces in bars AF, AB, and BE.

  Ans. $|AF| = -14.99$ kN (C); $|AB| = -14.99$ kN (C); $|BE| = -10$ kn (C)

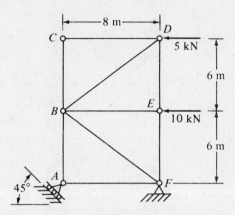

Fig. 5-21

5.9   The truss shown in Fig. 5-22 is subject to seven vertical loads. Determine the forces in bars DE, EK, and KJ.   *Ans.* $|DE| = -8|P|$ (C); $|EK| = -2|P|/\sqrt{2}$ (C); $|KJ| = 9|P|$ (T)

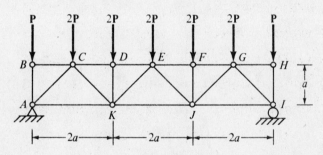

Fig. 5-22

5.10   For the three-dimensional truss and model in Figs. 5-16 and 5-17, assume that the model is loaded by a horizontal force **F** directed parallel to the x axis. Determine the magnitude of the forces in bars AB and BC due to **F** only; i.e., do not consider the weight W. Assume that the satellite is very small relative to the tower, so that **F** acts at point D at the top of the tower.   *Ans.* $2|F|\sqrt{3}/3$

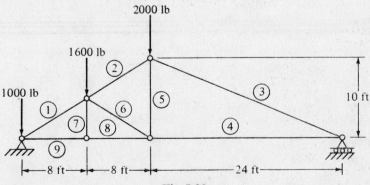

Fig. 5-23

5.11   The truss in Fig. 5-23 is subject to three vertical forces as shown. Use the computer program of Problem 5.6 to determine the bar forces and reactions for the indicated bar numbering system.

Ans.   ①, −4679.25;   ②, −3169.82;   ③, −2912.00;   ④, 2688.00;   ⑤, 800.00;   ⑥, −1509.44;   ⑦, 0;   ⑧, 3968.00;   ⑨, 3968.00;   reaction 10, 0;   reaction 11, 3480.00;   reaction 12, 1120.00

Chapter 6

Centroids, Moments of Inertia, and Distributed Loads

CENTROIDS AND FIRST MOMENTS

A line, an area, and a volume of finite size are shown in Fig. 6-1a, b, and c, respectively. The coordinates of the *centroid* of each of these figures are located with the following definitions:

$$\bar{x} = \frac{\int x\, dL}{L} \qquad \bar{y} = \frac{\int y\, dL}{L} \qquad \text{for a line of length } L$$

$$\bar{x} = \frac{\int x\, dA}{A} \qquad \bar{y} = \frac{\int y\, dA}{A} \qquad \text{for an area of magnitude } A$$

$$\bar{x} = \frac{\int x\, dV}{V} \qquad \bar{y} = \frac{\int y\, dV}{V} \qquad \bar{z} = \frac{\int \bar{z}\, dV}{V} \qquad \text{for a volume of magnitude } V$$

In each of these defining equations, the numerator on the right-hand side is termed the *first moment* (of the length, area, or volume) about the appropriate axis. If a finite length, area, or volume is made up of a number of subelements of simple geometry such as line segments, arcs, and triangles, then the integrals in these equations may be replaced with finite summations. (See Problems 6.1 to 6.8.)

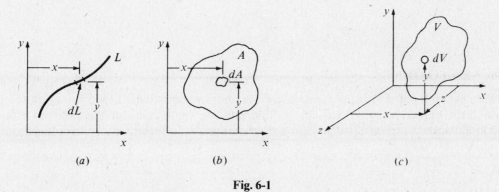

(a)   *(b)*   *(c)*

Fig. 6-1

The *center of gravity* of a body is that point on the body through which the weight of the body could be considered to be concentrated for all orientations of the body. For a body whose weight per unit volume is uniform, the center of gravity lies at its centroid.

87

SECOND MOMENT, OR MOMENT OF INERTIA, OF AN AREA

Analogous to the definitions of the first moment of a plane area, as given above, are the following definitions of the *second moment*, or *moment of inertia*, of an area about the x and y axes, respectively:

$$I_x = \int y^2 \, dA \qquad I_y = \int x^2 \, dA$$

The unit of the moment of inertia is the fourth power of length. (See Problems 6.9 to 6.12.)

PARALLEL-AXIS THEOREM FOR MOMENT OF INERTIA OF AN AREA

Consider the plane area A in Fig. 6-2. After the centroid G has been located, pass through G axes x_G and y_G parallel, respectively, to the x and y axes. Then I_x and I_y, the moments of inertia of A about the x and y axes, are related to I_{x_G} and I_{y_G}, the moments of inertia about x_G and y_G, by

$$I_x = I_{x_G} + A(y_1)^2 \qquad \text{and} \qquad I_y = I_{y_G} + A(x_1)^2$$

(See Problems 6.10 to 6.12.)

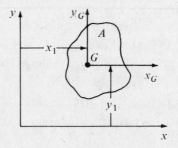

Fig. 6-2

RADIUS OF GYRATION

The *radius of gyration* of an area A about the x axis and that about the y axis are defined to be

$$r_x = \sqrt{\frac{I_x}{A}} \qquad \text{and} \qquad r_y = \sqrt{\frac{I_y}{A}}$$

DISTRIBUTED LOADINGS

Common examples of *distributed loadings* are the uniformly distributed load acting on the beam of Fig. 6-3a and the linearly varying load due to fluid pressure on the dam in Fig. 6-3b. At a distance y below the liquid surface in Fig. 6-3b, the liquid exerts a horizontal force per unit area (termed *pressure*)

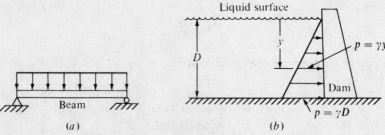

Fig. 6-3

on the dam given by $p = \gamma y$,   where γ is the specific weight of the liquid, i.e., the weight per unit volume. The total force exerted by the liquid on the dam is the mean pressure (over the submerged height D of the dam) multiplied by the area over which this pressure acts. This resultant liquid force acts through the centroid of the triangular pressure distribution diagram drawn in Fig. 6-3b, i.e., at $2D/3$ below the liquid surface.

The liquid forces acting on a submerged curved surface, such as AB in Fig. 6-4, are (1) a horizontal component F_H equal to the product of the pressure at the centroid of the vertical projection of the surface and the area of the vertical projection and (2) a vertical component F_v equal to the weight of liquid located vertically above the surface. (See Problem 6.21.)

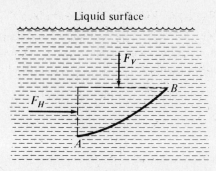

Fig. 6-4

Solved Problems

6.1   A thin wire lies in three-dimensional space and consists of a quadrant AB of a circle together with two straight regions BC and CD oriented parallel to the z and x axes, respectively, as shown in Fig. 6-5. Find the centroid of the wire.

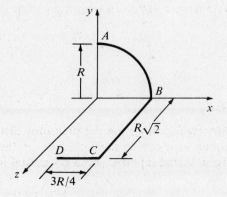

Fig. 6-5

The locations of the centroids of all three segments are known or easily found, so we use a summation. For $\bar{x}$ we have

$$\bar{x} = \frac{\sum_{i=1,2,3} \bar{x}_i (\Delta L)_i}{\sum_{i=1,2,3} (\Delta L)_i}$$

where $\bar{x}_i$ represents the distance from the yz plane to the centroid of each segment, $(\Delta L)_i$ represents the length of each segment, and we consider the segments AB, BC, and CD in that order. Then we have

$$\bar{x} = \frac{\dfrac{2R}{\pi}\dfrac{\pi R}{2} + R(R\sqrt{2}) + \dfrac{5}{8}R\left(\dfrac{3}{4}R\right)}{\dfrac{\pi R}{2} + R\sqrt{2} + \dfrac{3}{4}R} = 0.772R$$

$$\bar{y} = \frac{\sum_{i=1,2,3} y_i(\Delta L)_i}{\sum_{i=1,2,3}(\Delta L)_i} = \frac{\dfrac{2R}{\pi}\dfrac{\pi R}{2} + 0 + 0}{\dfrac{\pi R}{2} + R\sqrt{2} + \dfrac{3}{4}R} = 0.268R$$

and

$$\bar{z} = \frac{\sum_{i=1,2,3} z_i(\Delta L)_i}{\sum_{i=1,2,3}(\Delta L)_i} = \frac{0 + \dfrac{R\sqrt{2}}{2}R\sqrt{2} + R\sqrt{2}\left(\dfrac{3}{4}R\right)}{\dfrac{\pi R}{2} + R\sqrt{2} + \dfrac{3}{4}R} = 0.552R$$

6.2   Locate the centroid of a triangle.

We introduce the coordinate system of Fig. 6-6. Then the y coordinate of the centroid is

$$\bar{y} = \frac{\displaystyle\int y\,dA}{A}$$

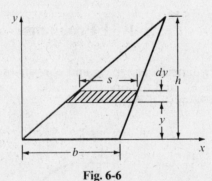

Fig. 6-6

It is simplest to choose an element such that y is the same for all points in the element. The horizontal shaded area satisfies this condition, and the area dA of the element is $s\,dy$. Thus,

$$\bar{y} = \frac{\displaystyle\int ys\,dy}{A}$$

The product $ys\,dy$ represents the first moment of the shaded element about the x axis.

From similar triangles, $s/b = (h - y)/h$. Substituting for s and A in the above integral then yields

$$\bar{y} = \frac{\displaystyle\int_0^h y\,\dfrac{b}{h}(h - y)\,dy}{\frac{1}{2}bh} = \frac{2}{h^2}\int_0^h (hy - y^2)\,dy$$

$$= \frac{2}{h^2}\left(h\left[\frac{y^2}{2}\right]_0^h - \left[\frac{y^3}{3}\right]_0^h\right) = \frac{2}{h^2}\left(\frac{h^3}{2} - \frac{h^3}{3}\right) = \frac{h}{3}$$

$\bar{x}$ may be found with an analogous procedure.

6.3   Locate the centroid of a semicircle.

The polar coordinate system shown in Fig. 6-7 is a logical choice for such an area. The shaded element of area is approximately a rectangle, and its area is given by $\rho\, d\theta\, d\rho$. The y coordinate of the centroid is given by

$$\bar{y} = \frac{\displaystyle\int y\, dA}{\displaystyle\int dA} = \frac{\displaystyle\int_0^\pi \int_0^r (\rho \sin\theta)(\rho\, d\theta\, d\rho)}{\displaystyle\int_0^\pi \int_0^r \rho\, d\theta\, d\rho} = \frac{\displaystyle\int_0^\pi \left[\frac{\rho^3}{3}\right]_0^r \sin\theta\, d\theta}{\displaystyle\int_0^\pi \left[\frac{\rho^2}{2}\right]_0^r d\theta}$$

$$= \frac{\dfrac{r^3}{3} \displaystyle\int_0^\pi \sin\theta\, d\theta}{\dfrac{r^2}{2} \displaystyle\int_0^\pi d\theta} = \frac{2r}{3\pi}[-\cos\theta]_0^\pi = \frac{4r}{3\pi}$$

By symmetry, $\bar{x} = 0$.

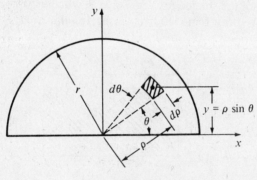

Fig. 6-7

The location of the centroid of a quadrant of a circle may be found by merely replacing the upper limit π with $\pi/2$. The result is $\bar{x} = \bar{y} = 4r/3\pi$.

6.4   Area OAB in Fig. 6-8 is bounded by the coordinate axes and the parabola $y = H(1 - x^2/K^2)$. Locate the x and y coordinates of the centroid of the area.

By definition, the y coordinate of the centroid is

$$\bar{y} = \frac{\displaystyle\int y\, dA}{A} \tag{1}$$

To evaluate the integral, we select a thin vertical element (shaded in Fig. 6-8) of height y and width dx; the centroid of this essentially rectangular element lies at the midpoint of its height, that is, a distance $y/2$

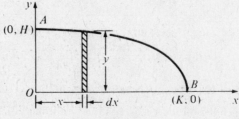

Fig. 6-8

above the x axis. The first moment of this element is then $(y/2)y\,dx$. The area A in the denominator of (1) is merely the sum (integral) of the areas of all such rectangular elements. Hence we have

$$\bar{y} = \frac{\displaystyle\int_0^K \frac{y}{2}\, y\, dx}{\displaystyle\int_0^K y\, dx} = \frac{\displaystyle\frac{1}{2}\int_0^K H^2\!\left(1 - \frac{2x^2}{K^2} + \frac{x^4}{K^4}\right) dx}{\displaystyle\int_0^K H\!\left(1 - \frac{x^2}{K^2}\right) dx} = \frac{2}{5} H$$

The x coordinate of the centroid is $\bar{x} = \int x\, dA/A$. We use the same rectangular element to find that

$$\bar{x} = \frac{\displaystyle\int_0^K xy\, dx}{\displaystyle\int_0^K y\, dx} = \frac{\displaystyle\int_0^K xH\!\left(1 - \frac{x^2}{K^2}\right) dx}{\displaystyle\int_0^K H\!\left(1 - \frac{x^2}{K^2}\right) dx} = \frac{3}{8} K$$

6.5   Locate the centroid of the shaded area in Fig. 6-9, which is the area that remains after one corner and a semicircle have been removed from a rectangular area.

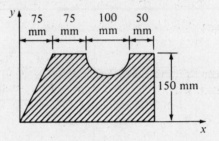

Fig. 6-9

The shaded area consists of (1) a 150 mm by 300 mm rectangle, minus (2) a 150 mm by 75 mm triangle, minus (3) a semicircular area. Since the centroids of (2) and (3) were determined in Problems 6.2 and 6.3, respectively, integration is not necessary and a finite summation may be used.

The y coordinate of the centroid is given by $\bar{y} = \int y\, dA/A$. The numerator, representing the first moment of the shaded area about the x axis, may be evaluated as the first moment of the rectangle, minus that of the triangle, minus that of the semicircle. Thus

$$\bar{y} = \frac{150(300)(75) - \dfrac{1}{2}(150)(75)(100) - \dfrac{1}{2}\pi(50)^2\left[150 - \dfrac{4(50)}{3\pi}\right]}{300(150) - \dfrac{1}{2}(75)(150) - \dfrac{1}{2}\pi(50)^2} = 65.08 \text{ mm}$$

Similarly, the x coordinate of the centroid is $\bar{x} = \int x\, dA/A$. The numerator here represents the first moment of the rectangle, minus that of the triangle, minus that of the semicircle about the y axis. Thus,

$$\bar{x} = \frac{150(300)(150) - \dfrac{1}{2}(150)(75)(25) - \dfrac{1}{2}\pi(50)^2(200)}{300(150) - \dfrac{1}{2}(75)(150) - \dfrac{1}{2}\pi(50)^2} = 164.3 \text{ mm}$$

6.6   Locate the centroid of the I beam shown in Fig. 6-10.

The centroid, which lies on the y axis, has the y coordinate $\bar{y} = \int y\, dA/A$.

The section of the I beam may be divided into five component rectangles as shown, and the numerator

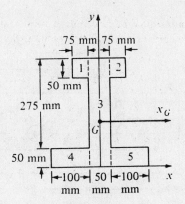

Fig. 6-10

of this expression may then be evaluated by numerical summation. Thus,

$$\bar{y} = \frac{75(50)(300) + 75(50)(300) + 50(325)(325/2) + 50(100)(25) + 50(100)(25)}{75(50) + 75(50) + 50(325) + 100(50) + 100(50)} = 152.3 \text{ mm}$$

The horizontal axis passing through the centroid is denoted by x_G in the figure.

6.7 Determine the x coordinate of the centroid of the shaded area in Fig. 6-11, which consists of one quadrant of a circle from which has been removed the smaller semicircle.

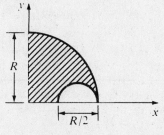

Fig. 6-11

The x coordinate of the centroid of the shaded area is given by $\bar{x} = \sum_{i=1,2} \bar{x}_i (\Delta A)_i / \sum_{i=1,2} (\Delta A)_i$.

The location of the centroid of the quadrant was found in Problem 6.3. The x coordinate of the centroid of the semicircle lies on its vertical axis of symmetry, i.e., at a distance $3R/4$ from the y axis. Thus, we have

$$\bar{x} = \frac{\dfrac{4R}{3\pi} \dfrac{\pi}{4} R^2 - \left(R - \dfrac{R}{4}\right)\left(\dfrac{\pi}{2}\right)\left(\dfrac{R}{2}\right)^2}{\dfrac{\pi}{4} R^2 - \dfrac{\pi}{2}\left(\dfrac{R}{2}\right)^2} = 0.099R$$

6.8 The solid in Fig. 6-12 consists of (1) a rectangular block, *plus* (2) a smaller rectangular block atop the larger block, *plus* (3) a triangular wedge at its right end, *less* (4) a hole of diameter 1 in is drilled through the larger block, *plus* (5) a solid circular disk is attached to the forward face of the block. Both the disk and the hole are centered on the height of the larger block, 2.5 in above the xz plane, as shown. Determine the location of the x coordinate of the centroid of the solid, given the dimensions shown in the figure.

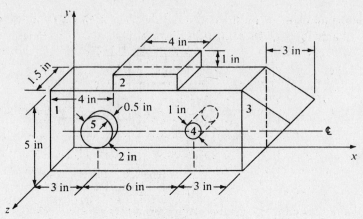

Fig. 6-12

The x coordinate of the centroid is given by

$$\bar{x} = \frac{\sum_{i=1,2,3} \bar{x}_i (\Delta V)_i}{\sum_{i=1,2,3} (\Delta V)_i}$$

The two summations are best performed in tabular form, as follows:

Volume	$\bar{x}_i$, in	$(\Delta V)_i$, in^3	$\bar{x}_i(\Delta V)_i$, in^4
1	6	$12(1.5)(5) = 90$	540
2	6	$4(1)(1.5) = 6$	36
3	13	$\frac{1}{2}(5)(3)(1.5) = 11.25$	146.3
4	9	$-\pi(0.5)^2(1.5) = -1.178$	-10.6
5	3	$\pi(1)^2(0.5) = 1.57$	4.71
Totals		107.6	716.4

Hence, $\bar{x} = 716.4/107.6 = 6.66$.

6.9   Find the moment of inertia of a rectangle about an axis coinciding with the base.

We use the coordinate system shown in Fig. 6-13. Since y is constant for all points in the shaded element, we have

$$I_x = \int y^2\, da = \int_0^h y^2 b\, dy = b\left[\frac{y^3}{3}\right]_0^h = \frac{1}{3} bh^3$$

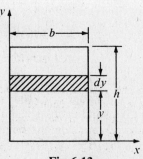

Fig. 6-13

6.10 Determine the moment of inertia and radius of gyration of the channel section in Fig. 6-14 about a horizontal axis through its centroid.

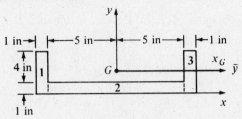

Fig. 6-14

The centroid lies on the y axis, and its y coordinate is given by $\bar{y} = (\int y\, dA)/A$.
We evaluate $\bar{y}$ by summation, using the numbered rectangles:

$$\bar{y} = \frac{1(5)(2.5) + 10(1)(0.5) + 1(5)(2.5)}{1(5) + 10(1) + 1(5)} = 1.5 \text{ in}$$

The horizontal axis passing through the centroid is denoted by x_G in the figure.

It is convenient to first determine the moment of inertia with respect to the x axis, and then apply the parallel-axis theorem. For each of the three component rectangles, the moment of inertia about an axis through its base was found in Problem 6.9 to be $I_x = bh^3/3$.   For the entire figure, then

$$I_x = \tfrac{1}{3}(1)(5)^3 + \tfrac{1}{3}(10)(1)^3 + \tfrac{1}{3}(1)(5)^3 = 86.6 \text{ in}^4$$

According to the parallel-axis theorem, $I_x = I_{x_G} + Ay_1^2$. Then

$$86.6 = I_{x_G} + 20(1.5)^2 \quad \text{or} \quad I_{x_G} = 41.6 \text{ in}^4$$

The radius of gyration with respect to the x_G axis is $r_{x_G} = \sqrt{I_{x_G}/A} = \sqrt{41.6/20} = 1.45 \text{ in}$.

6.11 Determine the second area moment and radius of gyration of the I section shown in Fig. 6-15 about a horizontal axis passing through its centroid.

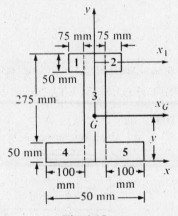

Fig. 6-15

The centroid, which lies on the y axis, was found in Problem 6.6 to be at $\bar{y} = 152.3$ mm.   The horizontal axis passing through the centroid is denoted x_G in the figure.

We shall first determine the second area moment with respect to the x axis. For rectangles 3, 4, and 5, the second moment about this axis is given by $I_x = bh^3/3$.   For rectangles 1 and 2, it is first necessary to determine the second moment $I_x = bh^3/12$ about a horizontal axis x_1 passing through their centroids, and then apply the parallel-axis theorem to transfer this result to the x axis.

For the entire figure, we thus have

$$I_x = \tfrac{1}{3}(100)(50)^3 + \tfrac{1}{3}(100)(50)^3 + \tfrac{1}{3}(50)(325)^3 + [\tfrac{1}{12}(75)(50)^3 + 75(50)(300)^2]2 = 12.6 \times 10^8 \text{ mm}^4$$

From the parallel-axis theorem, $I_x = I_{x_G} + Ay_1^2$,   we obtain

$$12.6 \times 10^8 = I_{x_G} + 33.75 \times 10^3(152.3)^2 \qquad \text{or} \qquad I_{x_G} = 4.8 \times 10^8 \text{ mm}^4$$

The radius of gyration with respect to the x_G axis is $r_{x_G} = \sqrt{I_{x_G}/A} = \sqrt{(4.8 \times 10^8)/(33.75 \times 10^3)} = $ 119.3 mm.

6.12   Determine the moment of inertia of the hollowed rectangular area of Fig. 6-16 about a horizontal axis through its centroid.

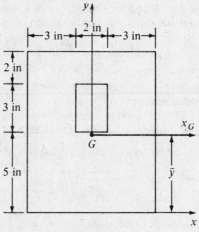

Fig. 6-16

The centroid lies on the y axis, and its location is given by $\bar{y} = (\int y \, dA)/A$.   The numerator may be evaluated as the first moment of the larger rectangle about the x axis, minus the first moment of the smaller rectangle. Thus,

$$\bar{y} = \frac{8(10)(5) - 2(3)(6.5)}{8(10) - 2(3)} = 4.88 \text{ in}$$

The horizontal axis through the centroid is denoted x_G in the figure.

We shall first compute the moment of inertia of the larger rectangle about the x_G axis. This is done by finding its moment of inertia about a horizontal axis through its centroid (assuming that the 2 in by 3 in hole is not present), and then transferring this result to the x_G axis. For the entire rectangle, this application of the parallel-axis theorem gives

$$I'_{x_G} = \tfrac{1}{12}(8)(10)^3 + 8(10)(5 - 4.88)^2 = 668 \text{ in}^4$$

Similarly, for the smaller rectangle that has been removed, its moment of inertia with respect to the x_G axis is found by computing its moment of inertia with respect to a horizontal axis through its centroid and then transferring this result to the x_G axis. This yields

$$I''_{x_G} = \tfrac{1}{12}(2)(3)^3 + 2(3)(6.5 - 4.88)^2 = 20.3 \text{ in}^4$$

Consequently, the moment of inertia of the hollowed rectangular area is

$$I_x = I'_{x_G} - I''_{x_G} = 668 - 20.3 = 647.7 \text{ in}^4$$

6.13   A very light vehicle for carrying instrumentation several hundred kilometers above the surface of the earth was designed at the Jet Propulsion Laboratory in California. It consisted of a very thin square membrane, 800 m on a side, coated to absorb solar radiation. The solar radiation pressure for the design altitude was known to be 4.66 N/km². This pressure was considered to be adequate to slowly propel the vehicle through the upper atmosphere, where there is virtually no atmospheric pressure to oppose solar pressure. Determine the force on the sail, assuming that solar pressure acts normal to the plane of the sail.

The force acting normal to the sail is given by the pressure (force per unit area) multiplied by the area of the sail. Thus,

$$F = (4.66 \text{ N/km}^2)(0.8 \text{ km})(0.8 \text{ km}) = 2.98 \text{ N}$$

6.14 The Hovercraft is an air-cushion vehicle used for daily passenger service across the English Channel. In operation, very large volumes of air are continuously directed downward into a plenum chamber formed by the bottom plating of the ship and a strong, flexible skirt surrounding the ship bottom, as indicated in Fig. 6-17. Due to the pressure, the air forms a "cushion" that supports the vehicle. The ship may be approximated as a rectangle 77 ft long and 45 ft wide. The total weight of the ship, passengers, and fuel is 96,000 lb. Determine the air pressure in the plenum chamber required to support the vehicle. Assume a uniform distribution of pressure over the rectangular area of the ship bottom.

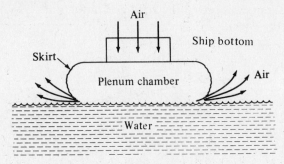

Fig. 6-17

The total force to be supported by the air is 96,000 lb, acting over a 77 ft by 45 ft rectangular area. Thus, the pressure, or force per unit area, is

$$p = \frac{96,000 \text{ lb}}{(77 \text{ ft})(45 \text{ ft})} = 27.71 \text{ lb/ft}^2 \quad \text{or} \quad 0.192 \text{ lb/in}^2$$

6.15 The simply supported beam in Fig. 6-18 is loaded by two linearly varying loadings as indicated. Determine the reactions at the ends of the beam.

The resultants of the distributed loads are shown as dashed vectors in Fig. 6-18. They are found as the areas of the triangular load diagrams: For beam segment AB, we have

$$\tfrac{1}{2}(2 \text{ m})(6000 \text{ N/m}) = 6000 \text{ N}$$

and for beam segment BC,

$$\tfrac{1}{2}(3 \text{ m})(4000 \text{ N/m}) = 6000 \text{ N}$$

Each resultant acts through the centroid of the load-diagram area, as shown.

Now, replacing the distributed loads with these resultants, we may write the equilibrium equations

$$+\curvearrowleft \Sigma M_A = \tfrac{2}{3}(6000) + 4(6000) - 5|\mathbf{R}_C| = 0 \qquad \text{or} \qquad |\mathbf{R}_C| = 5600 \text{ N}$$

$$+\curvearrowleft \Sigma M_C = -1(6000) - 4\tfrac{1}{3}(6000) + 5|\mathbf{R}_A| = 0 \qquad \text{or} \qquad |\mathbf{R}_A| = 6400 \text{ N}$$

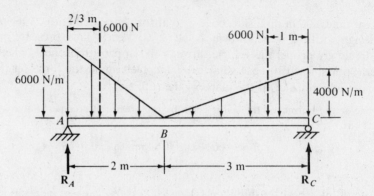

Fig. 6-18

6.16   A rigid slab rests on a flexible subgrade and carries a massive stamping machine; together, slab and machine weigh 300,000 lb. A portion of the subgrade begins to lose bearing strength, with the result that the slab tips through a 10° angle (Fig. 6-19). The subgrade is incapable of carrying tension, so the weight of the machine must be resisted by a triangular distribution of normal pressure together with a shear reaction, as indicated. Determine the maximum value w_0 of the normal pressure developed at the right end of the slab. Assume the slab and machine are of unit depth (into the page).

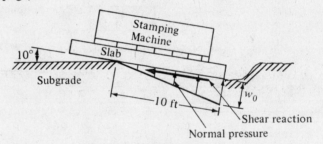

Fig. 6-19

The vertical load of 300,000 lb must be held in equilibrium by the combined action of the resultant **N** of the distributed normal pressure and the shear force $\mathbf{F}_S$ acting to the left along the bottom of the slab.

The force triangle for these forces is drawn in Fig. 6-20. It shows that the magnitude of **N** is 300,000 cos 10° = 295,400 lb.   Since this value must equal the area of the load diagram, we have, for a unit depth of the slab,

$$\tfrac{1}{2}(10)(w_0) = 295,400 \qquad \text{or} \qquad w_0 = 59,100 \text{ lb/ft}$$

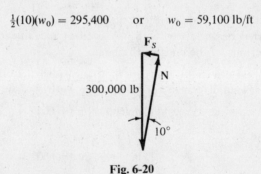

Fig. 6-20

6.17   The distribution of the load due to wind effects along the axis of an aircraft propeller is approximately parabolic, as indicated in Fig. 6-21. Determine the torque (moment) necessary to rotate the propeller at constant angular velocity.

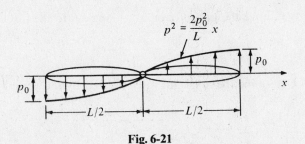

Fig. 6-21

It is necessary to find both the resultant of the distributed loading and the location of its line of action. For each half of the propeller, the magnitude of the resultant is given by the area of the load diagram, and that is found by considering the differential area $p\,dx$ (Fig. 6-22) and summing all such areas over that half of the propeller. For the right half, we have

$$\int p\,dx = \int_0^{L/2} \frac{\sqrt{2}}{\sqrt{L}}\, p_0 x^{1/2}\,dx = \sqrt{\frac{2}{L}}\, p_0 \left[\frac{x^{3/2}}{3/2}\right]_0^{L/2} = \frac{p_0 L}{3}$$

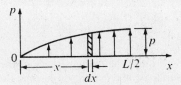

Fig. 6-22

This resultant acts through the centroid of the right half of the load diagram, which is located a distance $\bar{x}$ from the propeller shaft, where

$$\bar{x} = \frac{\displaystyle\int xp\,dx}{\displaystyle\int p\,dx} = \frac{\displaystyle\int_0^{L/2} \frac{\sqrt{2}}{\sqrt{L}}\, p_0 x^{3/2}\,dx}{\displaystyle\int_0^{L/2} \frac{\sqrt{2}}{\sqrt{L}}\, p_0 x^{1/2}\,dx} = \frac{3}{10}L$$

For the left half of the propeller, the resultant of the loading and its location may be surmised from the symmetry. Together, the resultant "halves" appear as in Fig. 6-23, where T_0 is the torque necessary to drive the propeller. For equilibrium of moments about the propeller shaft, we have

$$|\mathbf{T}_0| = 2\,\frac{3L}{10}\,\frac{p_0 L}{3} = \frac{p_0 L^2}{5}$$

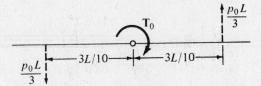

Fig. 6-23

6.18   A chimney in the form of a right circular cylindrical shell is subject to horizontal wind loading. Experimental evidence indicates that the loading creates a positive pressure on the side on which the wind impinges and a suction (negative pressure) on the opposite (downwind) side. Also, the pressure is known to vary linearly along the height of the chimney, so that the pressure at any point a distance z above the ground and at an angle θ to the direction of the wind is given by

$$p = p_0 (\cos \theta)\left(1 + \frac{z}{H}\right)$$

(see Fig. 6-24). Determine the resultant force exerted by the wind on the chimney.

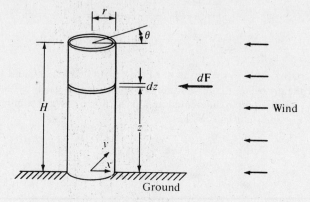

Fig. 6-24

The pressure distribution around the circumference of the chimney is given to be that in Fig. 6-25; p is everywhere normal to the surface of the chimney. For each pressure component p_y acting in the y direction at the point represented by the angle θ, there must be an oppositely directed pressure component $-p_y$ acting at the angle $-\theta$. Thus, all the y components of the pressure cancel one another, and the resultant of the wind loading consists only of x components. From the given pressure variation we have, at angle θ,

$$p_x = p \cos \theta = p_0(\cos^2 \theta)\left(1 + \frac{z}{H}\right)$$

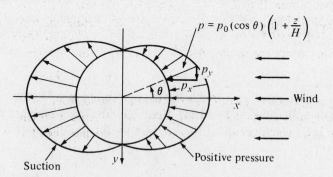

Fig. 6-25

Let $d\mathbf{F}$ be the horizontal wind force that acts on a ring-shaped section of the chimney, of height dz and at a distance z above the ground (see Fig. 6-24). Then the pressure p_x acts over a surface area $r\, d\theta\, dz$ and yields the magnitude

$$|d\mathbf{F}| = \int_{\theta=0}^{\theta=2\pi} p_0(\cos^2 \theta)\left(1 + \frac{z}{H}\right)r\, d\theta\, dz = p_0 r\left(1 + \frac{z}{H}\right)\pi\, dz$$

To find $\mathbf{F}$, we integrate this expression over the height of the chimney, thereby summing the wind forces on all such ring-shaped sections:

$$|\mathbf{F}| = \left|\int d\mathbf{F}\right| = \int_0^H p_0 r\left(1 + \frac{z}{H}\right)\pi\, dz = \frac{3}{2}p_0 \pi r H$$

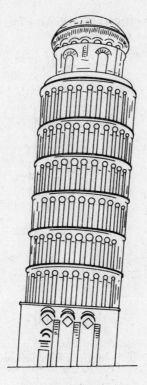

Fig. 6-26

6.19 The Leaning Tower of Pisa, Italy, built in 1350, is 58.2 m tall and has a circular base of diameter 19.6 m. For the past several centuries its longitudinal axis has been inclined by 5.6° toward the south from the vertical (Fig. 6-26). The weight of the tower is 144 MN. The diameter of its cross section changes slightly from bottom to top, and accordingly its center of gravity is approximately 27.1 m above the base. The pressure that the sandy, claylike soil exerts on the rigid, circular base slab of the tower may reasonably be approximated with the relation

$$p = A + Br^{0.625}\cos\theta \qquad N/m^2$$

where r and θ are polar coordinates (with θ measured from due south, as in Fig. 6-27) and A and B are constants to be determined. Find the maximum pressure exerted on the base of the tower by the soil (which occurs at the extreme south), and the minimum pressure exerted (at the extreme north).

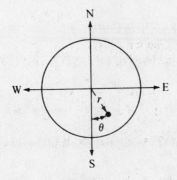

Fig. 6-27

Figure 6-28 is the elevation of the tower looking from west to east. The horizontal displacement δ of the center of gravity of the tower from the vertical is

$$\delta = (5.6°)\frac{1 \text{ rad}}{57.3°}(27.1 \text{ m}) = 2.65 \text{ m}$$

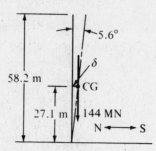

Fig. 6-28

The moment of the weight vector about the east–west axis in Fig. 6-27 then has the magnitude

$$M = (144 \text{ MN})(2.65 \text{ m}) = 381.6 \text{ MN} \cdot \text{m}$$

The shaded element of the base slab in Fig. 6-29 has area $dA = r \, dr \, d\theta$. The reaction of the soil on this area is $p \, dA$, and for vertical equilibrium with the tower weight of 144 MN, we have $\int_{\text{base}} p \, dA = 144$.

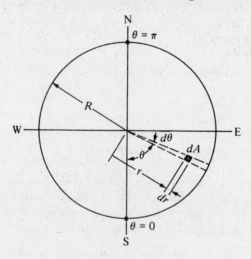

Fig. 6-29

Substituting the assumed pressure distribution for p gives us

$$2\int_{\theta=0}^{\pi}\int_{r=0}^{R}(A + Br^{0.625}\cos\theta)r \, dr \, d\theta = 144$$

or

$$2A\left[\frac{r^2}{2}\right]_0^R[\theta]_0^\pi + 2B\left[\frac{r^{2.625}}{2.625}\right]_0^R[\sin\theta]_0^\pi = 144$$

which yields $A = 144/\pi R^2$.

For moment equilibrium of the soil reaction and the weight of the tower about the east–west axis, we have

$$2\int_{\theta=0}^{\pi}\int_{r=0}^{R}(A + Br^{0.625}\cos\theta)(r\cos\theta)r \, dr \, d\theta = 381.6$$

or

$$2A\left[\frac{r^3}{3}\right]_0^R [\sin\theta]_0^\pi + 2B\left[\frac{r^{3.625}}{3.625}\right]_0^R \frac{\pi}{2} = 381.6$$

from which $B = (3.625)(381.6)/\pi R^{3.625}$.

The pressure distribution on the base is thus

$$p = \frac{144}{\pi R^2} + \frac{(3.625)(381.6)}{\pi R^{3.625}} r^{0.625} \cos\theta \qquad (1)$$

The peak pressure at the southern extremity of the base is found by setting $r = R = 9.8$ m and $\theta = 0$ in (1):

$$p_{max} = \frac{144}{\pi(9.8)^2} + \frac{(3.625)(381.6)}{\pi(9.8)^{3.625}} (9.8)^{0.625} \cos 0 = 0.945 \text{ MPa}$$

The minimum pressure at the northern extremity is found by setting $r = R$ and $\theta = \pi$ in (1):

$$p_{min} = \frac{144}{\pi(9.8)^2} + \frac{(3.625)(381.6)}{\pi(9.8)^{3.625}} (9.8)^{0.625} \cos\pi = 0.009 \text{ MPa}$$

6.20   A rectangular tank is filled with oil and has a gate in the shape of an isosceles trapezoid on one end. The trapezoid has bases of 18 ft and 12 ft, and an altitude of 4 ft, with the 18-ft base uppermost. Determine the magnitude and location of the resultant force acting against the gate. Consider the oil to have a specific weight of 56.2 lb/ft³.

Let us introduce the coordinate system shown in Fig. 6-30, in which the gate (shaded) is depicted as a portion of a triangle having its apex at the origin of the coordinate system. The oil pressure at any depth $12 - y$ below the surface of the oil is given by $p = (56.2 \text{ lb/ft}^3)[(12 - y) \text{ ft}]$, so that the horizontal force (acting perpendicular to the plane of the page) on an element of height dy and length $2x$ is

$$d\mathbf{F} = p\,da = (56.2)(12 - y)(2x)\,dy$$

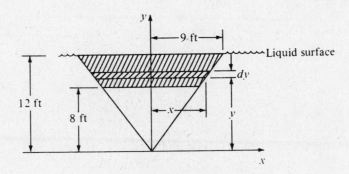

Fig. 6-30

The desired force is found by integrating such elemental forces over all horizontal elements running from $y = 8$ ft to $y = 12$ ft above the origin. From the geometry, we have $x = \frac{3}{4}y$. Thus,

$$F = \int d\mathbf{F} = \int_8^{12} (56.2)(12 - y)(2x)\,dy$$

$$= (56.2)(2)\int_8^{12} (12 - y)(\tfrac{3}{4}y)\,dy = 6320 \text{ lb}$$

To locate the vertical position $\bar{y}$ of this resultant force, we realize that the moment of **F** about any axis must be equal to the sum of the moments of all of its components. The x axis is a convenient axis to

use, so we write

$$6320\bar{y} = (56.2)(2)\int_{8}^{12}(12-y)(\tfrac{3}{4}y)(y)\,dy$$

from which we find that $\bar{y} = 9.43$ ft.   Owing to the symmetry, the resultant force acts through the y axis.

6.21 A reinforced-concrete dam has the cross section shown in Fig. 6-31. The upstream face is parabolic, with the vertex of the parabola at A. For a section of the dam 1 m thick perpendicular to the plane of the paper, determine the resultant force that the water exerts on the curved face AB. The water is seawater, with density 1.026×10^3 kg/m³.

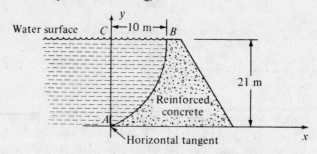

Fig. 6-31

With coordinate axes placed as in Fig. 6-32, the equation of the parabolic face must be of the form $y = Kx^2$ if it is to have a horizontal tangent at its vertex A. To find K we note that when $x = a$, then $y = b$; substitution yields

$$b = Ka^2 \qquad \text{or} \qquad K = \frac{b}{a^2}$$

so that the equation is $y = bx^2/a^2$.

Let us first find the x coordinate of the centroid of the area ABC. For this purpose we select the shaded element shown in Fig. 6-32, whose centroid lies at a distance $x/2$ from the y axis. Integration yields

$$\bar{x} = \frac{\displaystyle\int \frac{x}{2}x\,dy}{\displaystyle\int x\,dy} = \frac{\displaystyle\frac{1}{2}\int_0^b \frac{ya^2}{b}\,dy}{\displaystyle\int_0^b \left(\frac{ya^2}{b}\right)^{1/2}dy} = \frac{3}{8}a$$

The area ABC itself is equal to the denominator: $\int_0^b (ya^2/b)^{1/2}\,dy = \tfrac{2}{3}ab$.

The vertical force exerted by a volume of water of cross section ABC and 1 m thickness is

$$\tfrac{2}{3}(10\text{ m})(21\text{ m})(1.026 \times 10^3\text{ kg/m}^3)(9.81\text{ m/s}^2)(1\text{ m}) = 1410\text{ kN}$$

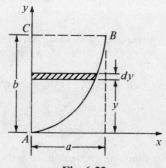

Fig. 6-32

The horizontal force arising from the water pressure on a 1-m thickness of the vertical plane AC may be found using the area of the triangular pressure distribution diagram in Fig. 6-33. It is

$$\tfrac{1}{2}(21 \text{ m})(1.026 \times 10^3 \text{ kg/m}^3)(9.81 \text{ m/s}^2)(21 \text{ m})(1 \text{ m}) = 2220 \text{ kN}$$

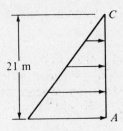

Fig. 6-33

Thus, the volume of water ABC of 1-m thickness has the free-body diagram shown in Fig. 6-34. $\mathbf{R}_D$ is the resultant force exerted by the dam on the volume of water ABC.

The three forces in Fig. 6-34 may be represented by the force triangle in Fig. 6-35. It yields

$$|\mathbf{R}_D|^2 = (1410)^2 + (2220)^2 \qquad \text{or} \qquad |\mathbf{R}_D| = 2630 \text{ kN}$$

$$\theta = \arctan \frac{1410}{2220} = 32.4°$$

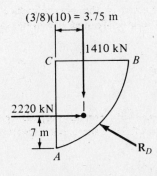

Fig. 6-34

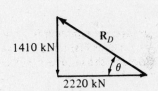

Fig. 6-35

The force exerted by the water on the dam is equal and opposite to $\mathbf{R}_D$ and is that shown in Fig. 6-36. We know the angle θ at which it acts, but not its intercept d on the x axis. To find that, we sum moments about A:

$$+\!\downarrow\!\circlearrowleft \Sigma M_A = 2220(7) + 1410(3.75) = (2630 \sin 32.4°) d \qquad \text{or} \qquad d = 14.78 \text{ m}$$

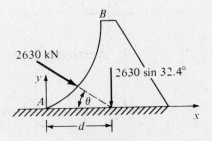

Fig. 6-36

Supplementary Problems

6.22   A thin wire in three-dimensional space consists of a quadrant of a circle AB in the yz plane, a linear portion BC parallel to the x axis and lying in the xy plane, and a linear portion CDE also lying in the xy plane but extending a distance $2R$ below the xz plane (Fig. 6-37). Determine the location of the y coordinate of the centroid of the wire.   *Ans.* $\bar{y} = 0.165R$

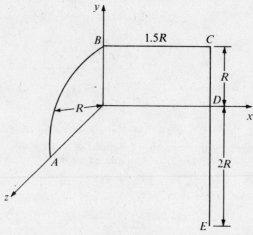

Fig. 6-37

6.23   Locate the y coordinate of the centroid of a plane parabolic area oriented as shown in Fig. 6-38.

   Ans. $\bar{y} = 2a/5$

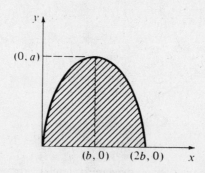

Fig. 6-38

6.24   Locate the centroid of the channel section in Fig. 6-39.   *Ans.* $\bar{y} = 4.1$ mm; $\bar{x} = 0$

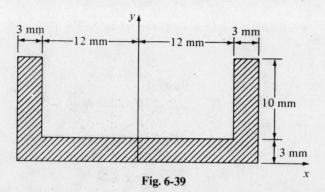

Fig. 6-39

6.25   Locate the centroid of the shaded area in Fig. 6-40, in which a rectangle has been removed from a semi-circle.   *Ans.* $\bar{x} = 0$; $\bar{y} = 70$ mm

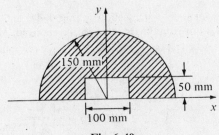

Fig. 6-40

6.26   Locate the centroid of the shaded area in Fig. 6-41, which remains after an equilateral triangle has been removed from a rectangle.   *Ans.* $\bar{x} = 0$; $\bar{y} = 102.5$ mm

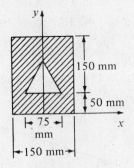

Fig. 6-41

6.27   Determine the y coordinate of the centroid of the shaded area in Fig. 6-11.   *Ans.* $\bar{y} = 0.637R$

6.28   A thin-walled right circular conical shell is oriented as indicated in Fig. 6-42. Determine the x coordinate of the centroid of its volume.   *Ans.* $\bar{x} = 2H/3$

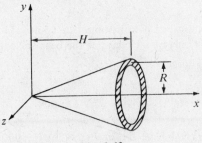

Fig. 6-42

6.29   Determine the y coordinate of the centroid of the volume in Fig. 6-12.   *Ans.* $\bar{y} = 2.67$ in

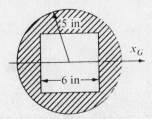

Fig. 6-43

6.30 Determine the moment of inertia about the x_G axis of the shaded area in Fig. 6-43, which remains after a square has been removed from a circle. The x_G axis is an axis of symmetry.   *Ans.* $I_{x_G} = 383 \text{ in}^4$

6.31 Locate the centroid of the channel-type section in Fig. 6-44, and determine the second moment of the cross-sectional area about a horizontal axis through the centroid.

Ans. $\bar{y} = 38.33$ mm; $I_{x_G} = 33 \times 10^6$ mm⁴

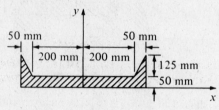

Fig. 6-44

6.32 An amphibious barge is designed like the Hovercraft described in Problem 6.14. It is rectangular, with dimensions 18.3 m by 9.75 m, and two fans develop an air-cushion pressure of 6.9 kN/m². Determine the maximum load (vehicle plus payload) that can be supported by this cushion pressure.   *Ans.* 1231 kN

6.33 The simply supported beam in Fig. 6-45 is subject to a vertical loading as indicated. Determine the beam reactions.   *Ans.* $|\mathbf{R}_A| = \frac{5}{24} w_0 L$; $|\mathbf{R}_B| = \frac{7}{24} w_0 L$

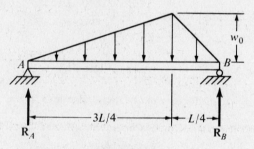

Fig. 6-45

6.34 The simply supported beam in Fig. 6-46 is subject to a vertical loading distributed parabolically according to the relation $y^2 = 54,000x$ N/m. Determine the beam reactions.

Ans. $|\mathbf{R}_A| = 322$ N; $|\mathbf{R}_B| = 483$ N

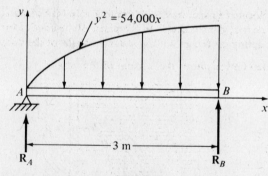

Fig. 6-46

6.35 A fully loaded and fueled Boeing 727 aircraft has a weight of approximately 142,000 lb. The lifting force (or lift) on each wing has a parabolic distribution that is symmetrical about a vertical line through the center of the cabin, as shown in Fig. 6-47. Each wing is approximately 68 ft long, measured from the outside of

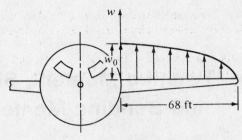

Fig. 6-47

the cabin. Determine the maximum value w_0 of the lift per unit length of wing, which occurs at the root of the wing, adjacent to the cabin. Neglect lift due to the circular fuselage as a first approximation.

Ans. $w_0 = 1566$ lb/ft

6.36   An "air bearing" is a device employed to move heavy loads over uneven surfaces. It consists of a housing into which high-pressure air is pumped and from which the air enters a manifold, which in turn distributes it to a number of small tubes. The air passes through these tubes to form an air cushion between the housing and the ground. If the housing in Fig. 6-48 is 10 in in diameter, and the air pressure is 85 lb/in², determine the maximum load it can carry.   *Ans.*   6700 lb

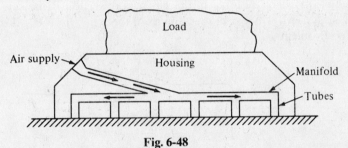

Fig. 6-48

6.37   A more accurate representation of the wind pressure on the chimney of Problem 6.18 is

$$p = p_0(\cos\theta)[1 + (z/H)^{0.25}]$$

Determine the resultant wind force on the chimney.   *Ans.* $|\mathbf{F}| = 7.2\, p_0 rH$

6.38   Reconsider the analysis of the soil pressure under the Leaning Tower of Pisa, in Problem 6.19. Determine what the angle of inclination of the tower from true vertical would have to be for the minimum soil pressure (at the northern extremity of the base) to be zero.   *Ans.*   5.71°

6.39   A rectangular gate is located in the lower portion of a side wall of a rectangular tank (Fig. 6-49). The gate is 2 m tall and 3 m wide (i.e., perpendicular to the plane of the page). Determine the magnitude and location of the resultant force acting on the gate if the specific weight of the water is 9.81 kN/m³.

Ans.   298.4 kN, located 0.94 m above the bottom of the tank

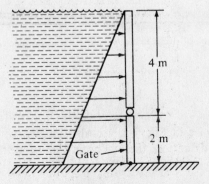

Fig. 6-49

Chapter 7

Axial Force, Twisting Moment, Shearing Force, and Bending Moment

Here we are concerned with means for expressing the variation of loadings along the length of a straight bar. The loadings of concern are axial forces in the direction of the bar, twisting moments (about the longitudinal axis), and transverse loadings (across the longitudinal axis) leading to shearing forces and bending moments.

AXIAL FORCE

For axial loads, a single coordinate extending along the length of the bar is used to specify location (Fig. 7-1). By definition, the axial force in the bar at any section is the sum of the forces to the left of that section. Thus, in Fig. 7-1 if $x < a$, then the axial force at x is $-\mathbf{P}_1$. If $a < x < b$, the axial force at x is $\mathbf{P}_2 - \mathbf{P}_1$. (See Problem 7.1.)

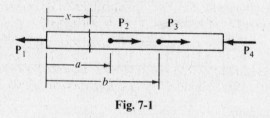

Fig. 7-1

TWISTING MOMENT

For a bar subject to twisting moments (couples) as in Fig. 7-2, the same type of coordinate system is used as for axial force. Again by definition, the twisting moment in the bar at any section is the sum of the twisting moments to the left of that section. The choice of which direction (clockwise or counterclockwise) to take as positive is arbitrary. Thus, in Fig. 7-2 if $x < a$, then the twisting moment at x is $\mathbf{M}_1$. If $a < x < L$, the twisting moment at x is $\mathbf{M}_1 - \mathbf{M}_2$. (See Problems 7.2 and 7.3.) A bar subject to twisting moments is usually called a *shaft*.

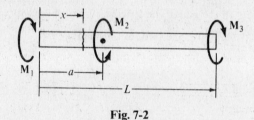

Fig. 7-2

SHEARING FORCE

Transverse forces, like those in Fig. 7-3, are also located with a single-coordinate system, usually with x as the coordinate. By definition, the algebraic sum of all the vertical forces to one side (say, the

110

left side) of the cross section denoted by any value of x is called the *shearing force* (or, sometimes, *shear force*) at that section. Usually it is denoted by **V**. Thus, in Fig. 7-3 we would write, at x_1,

$$V = R_1 - P_1 - P_2$$

A bar subject to transverse loads and/or moments in the plane of the bar is called a *beam*. Equations may be written to express the shearing force at every point along the length of the beam; a plot of such an equation is called a *shearing force* (or *shear*) *diagram*. (For applications see Problems 7.4 and 7.5.)

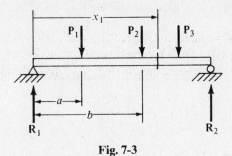

Fig. 7-3

BENDING MOMENT

By definition, the algebraic sum of the moments of the external forces to one side (say, the left side) of a cross section of a beam about an axis that lies in the section and is perpendicular to the vertical forces is called the *bending moment* at that cross section. It is usually denoted by **M**. Thus, at x_1 in Fig. 7-3,

$$M = R_1 x_1 - P_1(x_1 - a) - P_2(x_1 - b)$$

As is true for shearing force, equations can be written to express the bending moment at every point along a beam, and such equations can be plotted as *bending moment diagrams*. (See Problems 7.4 and 7.5.)

SIGN CONVENTIONS

The customary sign conventions for shearing force and bending moment are indicated in Fig. 7-4. A force that tends to bend the beam so that it is concave upward is said to produce a positive bending moment. A force that tends to shear the left portion of the beam upward with respect to the right portion is said to produce a positive shearing force.

An easier method for determining the algebraic sign of the bending moment at any section is to note that upward external forces produce positive bending moments, downward forces yield negative bending moments.

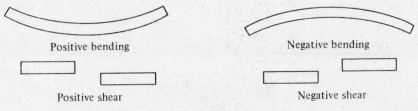

Positive bending   Negative bending

Positive shear   Negative shear

Fig. 7-4

RELATIONS AMONG LOAD INTENSITY, SHEARING FORCE, AND BENDING MOMENT

A simple beam with a varying load specified by $\mathbf{w}(x)$ is shown in Fig. 7-5. The coordinate system has its origin at the left end A, and distances to various sections in the beam are denoted by values of the variable x.

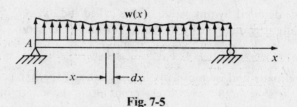

Fig. 7-5

For any value of x, the relationship between the load $\mathbf{w}(x)$ and the shearing force $\mathbf{V}$ is

$$w = \frac{dV}{dx} \tag{7.1}$$

The relationship between the shearing force and the bending moment $\mathbf{M}$ is

$$V = \frac{dM}{dx} \tag{7.2}$$

(See Problem 7.4.)

SINGULARITY FUNCTIONS

For ease in treating problems involving concentrated forces and concentrated moments, we introduce the *singularity* or *half-range* function

$$f_n(x) = \langle x - a \rangle^n$$

where for $n > 0$ the quantity in pointed brackets is zero if $x < a$ and is the usual $(x - a)$ if $x > a$. Thus if the argument $x - a$ is positive, the pointed brackets function just as ordinary parentheses. From this definition, it is obvious that algebraic operations, differentiation, and integration involving singularity functions follow all the usual rules. (See Problem 7.6.)

COMPUTER SOLUTION

Problems involving the determination of shearing forces and bending moments along the length of a beam are well suited to computer solution. Simple programs for determining V and M may be written in either BASIC or FORTRAN; a BASIC program is developed in Problem 7.7 and applied in Problem 7.8.

Solved Problems

7.1   The uniform bar AF in Fig. 7-6 is subject to three concentrated forces, together with a shear force acting only over the region BD and varying linearly from zero at D to a peak value P/L per unit length at B. Write equations for, and draw a diagram describing, the axial force along the bar.

We place the origin of our coordinate system at F, with positive values to the left. At any section denoted by a value of x, the axial force is the algebraic sum of all forces to the right of that section. Hence, in FE we have $N_{FE} = -P$,   and in ED the axial force is $N_{ED} = -P + 3P = 2P$.

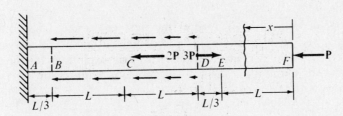

Fig. 7-6

To find the axial force at sections to the left of D, we first draw the shear load diagram shown in Fig. 7-7. From that diagram we can write, for any section x lying in DC,

$$N_{DC} = -P + 3P - \left[\frac{x - 4L/3}{2L} \frac{P}{L}\right]\left(\frac{1}{2}\right)\left(x - \frac{4L}{3}\right) = 2P - \frac{P}{4L^2}\left(x - \frac{4L}{3}\right)^2$$

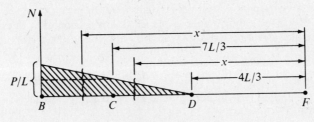

Fig. 7-7

where the quantity in brackets is the magnitude of the varying shearing force at section x. With this equation, we can evaluate the axial forces at D and C, which are

$$N_D = 2P \quad \text{and} \quad N_C = 2P - \frac{P}{4L^2}\left(\frac{7L}{3} - \frac{4L}{3}\right)^2 = \frac{7P}{4}$$

For any section x lying in part CB of the bar, Fig. 7-7 yields, for the sum of the forces to the right of that section,

$$N_{CB} = -P + 3P - 2P - \left[\frac{x - 4L/3}{2L} \frac{P}{L}\right]\left(\frac{1}{2}\right)\left(x - \frac{4L}{3}\right) = -\frac{P}{4L^2}\left(x - \frac{4L}{3}\right)^2$$

This equation yields, for the axial force at C (actually, very slightly to the left of C), $N_C = -P/4$. Also, at B, $N_B = -P$.

The area of the load diagram in Fig. 7-7 is $\frac{1}{2}(P/L)(2L) = P$; hence the varying shearing force acts as a compressive load $-P$ on sections to the left of B, and

$$N_{BA} = -P + 3P - 2P - P = -P$$

Our five equations lead to the plot in Fig. 7-8.

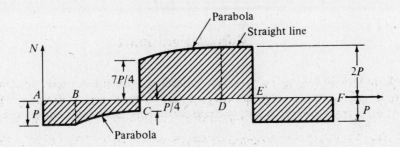

Fig. 7-8

7.2   The straight bar in Fig. 7-9 is clamped at the right end and subject to a uniformly distributed twisting moment m_T per unit length of the shaft in the region AB, as well as two concentrated twisting moments applied at O and B as shown. Write equations for the twisting moment along the length of the shaft, and draw the twisting moment diagram for the bar.

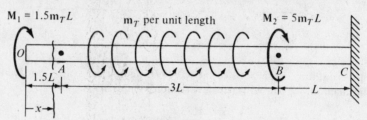

Fig. 7-9

We introduce a coordinate system with origin at O. In part OA of the bar, the twisting moment is simply M_1, since that is the only moment to the left of any section at x. In part AB, for any value of x the twisting moment is the algebraic sum of M_1 and the portion of the distributed moment that is to the left of x. Hence,

In AB: $M_T = 1.5 m_T L - m_T(x - 1.5L)$

Finally, between B and C, the algebraic sum of all twisting moments to the left of any section is $M_1 + M_2 - m_T(3L)$:

In BC: $M_T = 1.5 m_T L + 5 m_T L - 3 m_T L = 3.5 m_T L$

These equations yield the twisting moment diagram in Fig. 7-10.

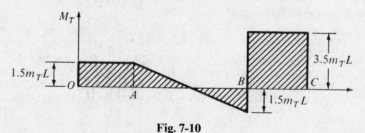

Fig. 7-10

7.3   The straight shaft OA in Fig. 7-11 is clamped at A and loaded by a uniformly varying twisting moment that increases in intensity linearly from zero at O to m_{T_A} per unit length of shaft at A. Write an equation for the twisting moment along the length of the shaft, and draw the twisting moment diagram.

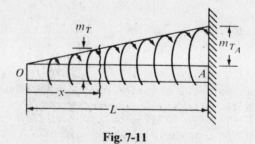

Fig. 7-11

At any section at a distance x from the left end, the intensity of the twisting moment is found from similar triangles to be

$$m_T = \frac{x}{L} m_{T_A}$$

The sum of all the twisting moments to the left of the section at x is the area of the triangular load diagram to the left of x:

$$M_T = \tfrac{1}{2}xm_T = \frac{x^2}{2L}\, m_{T_A}$$

A plot of this equation provides the twisting moment diagram in Fig. 7-12.

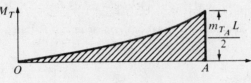

Fig. 7-12

7.4   The simply supported beam in Fig. 7-13 carries a vertical load that increases uniformly from zero at the left end to a maximum value of 9 kN/m at the right end. Draw the shearing force and bending moment diagrams for the beam.

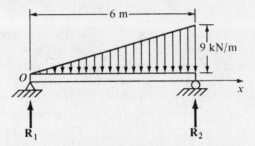

Fig. 7-13

For the purpose of determining the reactions $\mathbf{R}_1$ and $\mathbf{R}_2$ the entire distributed load may be replaced by its resultant, which acts through the centroid of the triangular loading diagram. This resultant is obtained as the area of the load diagram: $(1/2)(6\text{ m})(9\text{ kN/m}) = 27\text{ kN}$, and it is applied 4 m to the right of the left support, as shown in Fig. 7-14a. By summing moments at both ends of the beam, we find $\mathbf{R}_1 = 9\text{ kN}$ and $\mathbf{R}_2 = 18\text{ kN}$.

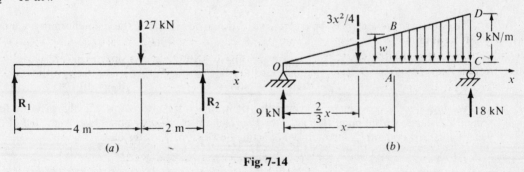

Fig. 7-14

This resultant cannot be used for the purpose of drawing shear and moment diagrams. We must instead consider the distributed load and determine the shear and moment at a section a distance x from the left end, as shown in Fig. 7-14b. At this section x, the load intensity w is found from the similar triangles OAB and OCD to be $3x/2$ kN/m. The total load acting to the left of x (the area of triangle OAB) is then $(1/2)(3x/2)(x)$. It acts through the centroid of triangle OAB, i.e., through a point located a distance $\tfrac{2}{3}x$ from O (dashed vector in Fig. 7-14b).

The shearing force and bending moment at A are now readily found to be

$$V = 9 - \frac{3x}{4}x = 9 - 0.75x^2 \text{ kN} \qquad \text{and} \qquad M = 9x - \frac{3x^2}{4}\frac{x}{3} = 9x - 0.25x^3 \text{ kN·m}$$

These equations hold along the entire length of the beam. The shearing force thus is plotted as a parabola having the value 9 kN when $x = 0$, and -18 kN when $x = 6$ m. The bending moment is a third-degree polynomial. It vanishes at the ends of the beam and assumes a maximum value where the shear is zero. (Because $V = dM/dx$, the point of zero shear must be the point where the tangent to the moment diagram is horizontal.) This point of zero shear may be found by setting $V = 0$ above, to obtain $x = 3.46$ m. The bending moment at this point is found by substituting in the expression given above:

$$M_{x=3.46} = 9(3.46) - 0.25(3.46)^3 = 20.75 \text{ kN·m}$$

The plots of the shear and moment equations appear in Fig. 7-15.

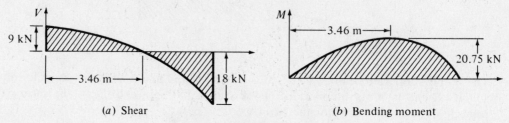

(a) Shear   (b) Bending moment

Fig. 7-15

7.5 Beam AE in Fig. 7-16 is simply supported at B and D and overhangs both ends. It is subject to a uniformly distributed load of 4 kN/m, as well as a couple of magnitude 8 kN·m applied at C. Draw the shearing force diagram and bending moment diagram for the beam.

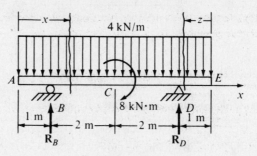

Fig. 7-16

The support reactions may be determined with the equations of static equilibrium for moments at B and vertical forces:

$$+\zeta \ \Sigma M_B = 4|\mathbf{R}_D| - 8 - 4(6)(2) = 0 \qquad \text{or} \qquad |\mathbf{R}_D| = 14 \text{ kN}$$

$$\Sigma F_v = |\mathbf{R}_B| + 14 - 4(6) = 0 \qquad \text{or} \qquad |\mathbf{R}_B| = 10 \text{ kN}$$

We introduce a coordinate system with origin at point A. In region AB, the shearing force at any section a distance x from point A is given by the resultant of the distributed load to the left of this section. This resultant is evidently a force of $4x$ kN acting downward. Thus we have

$$V = -4x \text{ kN} \qquad \text{for } 0 < x < 1 \text{ m} \tag{1}$$

For $x = 1$ m, this equation yields a shearing force of -4 kN. The shear at $x = 0$ is, of course, zero.

As soon as we pass to the right of B, the reaction $\mathbf{R}_B$ appears in the shearing force equation. For any section a distance x from A the shearing force in region BD is obtained by summing the applied forces to the left of this section. This sum is given by

$$V = -4x + 10 \text{ kN} \qquad \text{for } 1 \text{ m} < x < 5 \text{ m} \tag{2}$$

The couple at C does not enter the equations for shearing force because the couple does not have any force effect in any direction. It does, however, enter the equation indirectly since it influences the values of the reactions $\mathbf{R}_B$ and $\mathbf{R}_D$. Substituting $x = 1$ m and $x = 5$ m in (2) yields $V_{x=1} = 6$ kN and $V_{x=5} = -10$ kN.

For values of x greater than 5 m, the reaction $\mathbf{R}_D$ must be included in the equation for shearing force. Summing forces to the left of a section x in region DE, we find

$$V = -4x + 10 + 14 \text{ kN} \qquad \text{for } 5 \text{ m} < x < 6 \text{ m} \qquad (3)$$

Substituting $x = 5$ m and $x = 6$ m in (3), we find $V_{x=5} = 4$ kN and $V_{x=6} = 0$ kN.

The shearing force at any point along the bar is defined by one of the three equations (1), (2), and (3). Since V is a first-degree function of x in each of these equations, the shearing force diagram is a straight line in each region. The values of the ordinates at the endpoints of these regions have already been obtained by substitution. These values are plotted and connected by straight lines to obtain the shearing force diagram of Fig. 7-17.

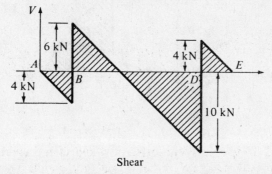

Shear

Fig. 7-17

To write equations for the bending moments along the beam, we begin at the left once again. At any section in region AB at a distance x from A, we have a downward distributed load $-4x$ that leads to the bending moment

$$M = -4x\frac{x}{2} = -2x^2 \qquad \text{for } 0 < x < 1 \text{ m}$$

In region BC, as soon as we pass to the right of the 10-kN reaction, the bending moment becomes

$$M = -4x\frac{x}{2} + 10(x - 1) = -2x^2 + 10x - 10 \qquad \text{for } 1 \text{ m} < x < 3 \text{ m}$$

In particular, at point C (where $x = 3$ m), $M_{x=3} = 2$ kN·m.

In region CD, for any section a distance x from the origin A, we again calculate the bending moment as the sum of the moments of all loads to the left of x. This sum must include the downward uniformly distributed load, the upward 10-kN reaction, and the applied couple of 8 kN·m. To determine the correct algebraic sign for this couple, we consider its effect if it were acting alone on the portion of the beam to the right of C (since we are working from left to right). It would then produce bending like that in Fig. 7-18.

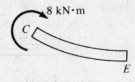

Fig. 7-18

For such bending the couple must be considered as positive, so that the bending moment in region CD is

$$M = -4x\frac{x}{2} + 10(x - 1) + 8 = -2x^2 + 10x - 2 \qquad \text{for } 3 \text{ m} < x < 5 \text{ m}$$

Just to the right of C, this equation yields $M_{x=3} = 10$ kN·m.

Finally, to determine the bending moment equation for region DE, it is simplest to introduce a new coordinate z having its origin at E and positive values to the left. Since the uniformly distributed load is the only force acting between E and a section at z, we have

$$M = -4z\frac{z}{2} = -2z^2 \qquad \text{for } 0 < z < 1 \text{ m}$$

Each of these equations is of the second degree, and it is easy to show that the curvature in each region is negative; i.e., the curve is concave downward. Thus, the bending moment diagram is that of Fig. 7-19. The abrupt jump of 8 kN·m at C corresponds to the applied couple of that magnitude acting at C.

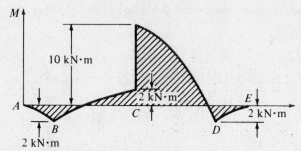

Bending moment

Fig. 7-19

7.6   The simply supported beam in Fig. 7-20*a* is subject to a uniform load over only 2 m of its length. Use singularity functions to write a single equation for the bending moment at any point along the beam.

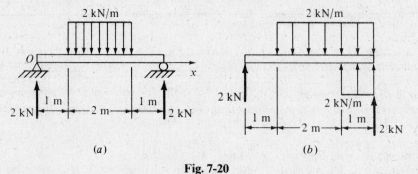

(*a*)   (*b*)

Fig. 7-20

From the symmetry, the support reactions are obviously both 2 kN. We introduce a coordinate system with origin at O and positive values to the right. Then at any section x of the beam, the bending moment due to the left reaction is represented by $2x$.

At any section x lying between the endpoints of the distributed load, the moment due to the portion of the distributed load that is to the left of x is

$$-2\langle x - 1\rangle \frac{\langle x - 1\rangle}{2}$$

This expression implies that the distributed load extends to the right end of the beam, but in fact that load ends at a point 3 m from the left support. As an artifice, we therefore must introduce a compensating uniform *upward* load of intensity 2 kN/m in the unloaded region at the right end (Fig. 7-20*b*) to "cancel" the extraneous downward load of 2 kN/m in this same region. This upward load has the moment

$$2\langle x - 3\rangle \frac{\langle x - 3\rangle}{2}$$

Putting these results together, we obtain a single equation for the bending moment at any position along the beam:

$$M = 2x - \langle x - 1\rangle^2 + \langle x - 3\rangle^2$$

7.7   Consider a straight beam, simply supported at two points that are not necessarily its endpoints (so that one or both ends may overhang the supports). The beam is subject to the simultaneous action of concentrated lateral forces, concentrated bending moments acting about axes perpendicular to its depth (to the plane of the page in Fig. 7-21), and distributed loads that may either be uniform over a given length of the beam or vary linearly in intensity from one point of the beam to another. Develop a computer program in the BASIC language to determine the shearing force and bending moment at every point along the length of the beam.

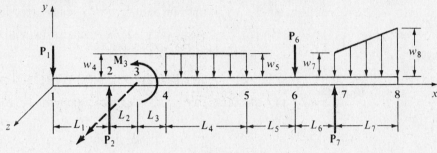

Fig. 7-21

The beam diagram must be supplemented as shown in Fig. 7-21. An xyz coordinate system must be added, with positive directions as shown. Then concentrated (point) loads and distributed loads are to be taken as positive in the direction of the positive y axis, i.e., upward. Double-headed vectors representing applied moments (such as that for M_3) are to be taken as positive in the direction of the positive z axis. All negative loadings must be so indicated when they are entered into the computer. The support reactions (here, P_2 and P_7) should be determined with the methods of earlier chapters.

The points of application of concentrated forces and moments and the endpoints of distributed loads must be numbered in order from 1, as shown in Fig. 7-21. It is then a good idea to number the loads, moments, and load intensities with these same numbers, as is done in the figure. Hence we have, for example, negative load P_1, positive (by the right-hand rule) moment M_3, and negative load intensity w_8. Finally, the lengths of the beam segments between numbered points ($L_1, L_2, \ldots, L_7$ in the figure) must be known. The pertinent information is then in proper form for use with the following BASIC program:

```
10 OPTION BASE 1
20 DIM SEGMENTLENGTH(20), POINTLOAD(21), EXTERMOM    (21),    DISTRULOAD(20, 2)
30 DIM SHEAR(21, 2), MOMENT(21, 2)
40 PRINT "PROGRAM SHEAR AND MOMENT"
50 PRINT "------------------------"
60 PRINT
70 INPUT "PLEASE ENTER THE NUMBER OF SEGMENTS: ", NUMSEG
80 PRINT
90 PRINT "PLEASE ENTER THE LENGTH OF EACH SEGMENT FROM LEFT TO RIGHT."
100 FOR I = 1 TO NUMSEG
110    INPUT  SEGMENTLENGTH(I)
120 NEXT I
130 PRINT
140 INPUT "PLEASE ENTER THE NUMBER OF POINT LOADS:", NUMPOINT
150 PRINT
160 FOR I = 1 TO NUMPOINT
170    INPUT "LOCATION AND LOAD :",  INSIDE, POINTLOAD(INSIDE)
180 NEXT I
190 PRINT
200 INPUT "PLEASE ENTER THE NUMBER OF EXTERNAL MOMENTS: ", NUMMOMENT
210 PRINT
220 FOR I = 1 TO NUMMOMENT
230    INPUT "LOCATION AND MOMENT: ", LOCATION, EXTERMOM(LOCATION)
240 NEXT I
250 PRINT
260 INPUT "PLEASE ENTER THE NUMBER OF LOADED SEGMENTS: ", NUMSEGLOAD
270 PRINT
```

```
280 FOR I = 1 TO NUMSEGLOAD
290   INPUT "SEGMENT NUMBER, LOADLEFT, LOADRIGHT :", NUM, DISTRULOAD(NUM, 1), DI
STRULOAD(NUM, 2)
300 NEXT I
310 PRINT
320 SHEAR(1, 2) = POINTLOAD(1)
330 MOMENT(1, 2)= -EXTERMOM(1)
340 FOR I = 1 TO NUMSEG
350   SHEAR(I + 1, 1) = SHEAR(I, 2) + (DISTRULOAD(I, 1) + DISTRULOAD(I, 2)) * S
EGMENTLENGTH(I) / 2
360   SHEAR(I + 1, 2) = SHEAR(I + 1, 1) + POINTLOAD (I + 1)
370   TEMP = ((2 * DISTRULOAD(I, 1) + DISTRULOAD(I, 2)) * SEGMENTLENGTH(I) ^ 2)
/ 6
380   MOMENT(I + 1, 1) = MOMENT(I ,2) + SHEAR(I, 2) * SEGMENTLENGTH(I) + TEMP
390   MOMENT(I + 1, 2) = MOMENT(I + 1, 1) - EXTERMOM(I + 1)
400 NEXT I
410 PRINT
420 LRPRINT "LOCATION", "SHEARLEFT", "SHEARRIGHT","MOMENTLEFT","MOMENTRIGHT"
430 FOR I = 1 TO NUMSEG + 1
440   LPRINT I, SHEAR (I, 1), SHEAR(I, 2), MOMENT(I, 1), MOMENT(I, 2)
450 NEXT I
460 END
```

This program is written in the 100/GW version of BASIC. Other versions may require minor changes in input format. For example, this program accepts the input data only in vertical column form; programs in other versions of BASIC will require the use of horizontal rows. The computer printout lists the shearing force and bending moment immediately to the left and immediately to the right of each numbered point. Hence, if the values of V and M at any particular point are required, it need only be numbered in sequence. Shearing force and bending moment diagrams are readily plotted from the output data; or, alternatively, an additional short program will permit the use of a computerized plotter.

Any consistent system of physical units may be utilized in the program.

7.8   Rework Problem 7.5 using the BASIC program of Problem 7.7.

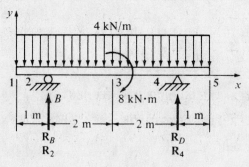

Fig. 7-22

The figure for Problem 7.5 (Fig. 7-16) is shown in Fig. 7-22 with the required modifications. The data that are entered in response to the program prompts are:

Number of segments: 4

Length of each segment: 1
                          2
                          2
                          1

Number of point loads: 2

Location and load: 2, 10
                     4, 14

Number of external moments: 1

Location and moment: 3, −8

Number of loaded segments: 4

Segment number, load left, load right: 1, −4, −4
                                          2, −4, −4
                                          3, −4, −4
                                          4, −4, −4

The computer printout is:

LOCATION	SHEARLEFT	SHEARRIGHT	MOMENTLEFT	MOMENTRIGHT
1	0	0	0	0
2	−4	6	−2	−2
3	−2	−2	2	10
4	−10	4	−2	−2
5	0	0	0	0

These data produce the diagrams required by Problem 7.5.

Supplementary Problems

7.9 The uniform bar in Fig. 7-23 is clamped at its left end and loaded by a shear force that varies linearly from zero at A to a peak value of **q** per unit length of bar at B. Write an equation for the axial force along the length of the bar, and draw its force diagram.   *Ans.* $N = qL/2 - qx^2/2L$;   Fig. 7-24

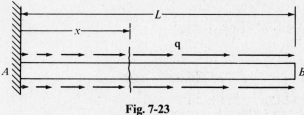

Fig. 7-23

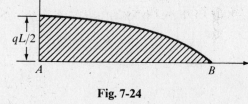

Fig. 7-24

7.10 The uniform bar in Fig. 7-25 is loaded by three concentrated forces and a shear force of magnitude 1.5 kN/m along its length. Write equations for axial force along the length of the bar, and draw its force diagram.

Ans.   In AB, $N = -7 - 1.5x$;   in BC, $N = -3 - 1.5x$;   in CD, $N = -11 - 1.5x$;   Fig. 7-26

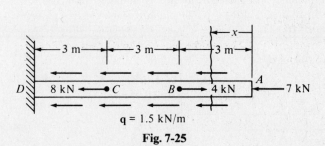

Fig. 7-25

Fig. 7-26

7.11 The straight shaft in Fig. 7-27 is supported in two frictionless bearings and subjected to five twisting moments as shown. Write equations for the twisting moment in the four regions of the shaft, and draw the twisting moment diagram.

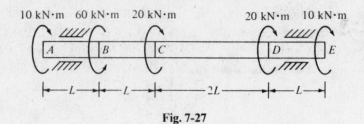

Fig. 7-27

Ans. In AB, $M_T = 10$ kN·m; in BC, $M_T = -50$ kN·m; in CD, $M_T = -30$ kN·m; in DE, $M_T = -10$ kN·m; Fig. 7-28

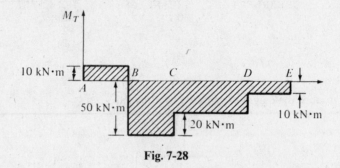

Fig. 7-28

7.12 Shaft AC in Fig. 7-29 is clamped at its right end and subject to twisting moments that are uniformly distributed over regions AB and BC as shown; their intensity is $\mathbf{m}_T$ per unit length of the shaft. Write equations for the twisting moment along the shaft, and draw the twisting moment diagram.

Ans. In AB, $M_T = m_T x$; in BC, $M_T = m_T L - m_T(x - L)$; Fig. 7-30

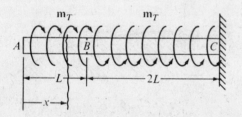

Fig. 7-29

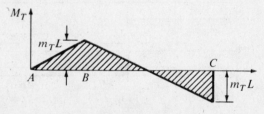

Fig. 7-30

7.13 Shaft AB in Fig. 7-31 is clamped at its right end and loaded by a concentrated twisting moment of 40 kN·m at O, together with a uniformly varying twisting moment that increases linearly in intensity from zero at A to 60 kN·m/m at B. Write equations for the twisting moment along the shaft, and draw the twisting moment diagram.   *Ans.* In OA, $M = -40$ kN·m; in AB, $M = [-40 + \frac{15}{4}(x - 2)^2]$ kN·m/m; Fig. 7-32

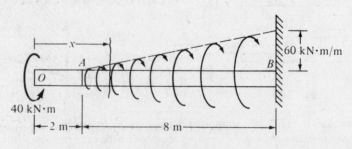

Fig. 7-31

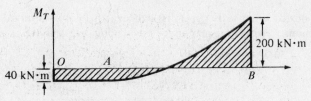

Fig. 7-32

7.14 The simply supported beam in Fig. 7-33 is loaded by a couple, a concentrated force, and a distributed load as shown. Write equations for the shearing force and bending moment along the length of the beam, and plot these relations.

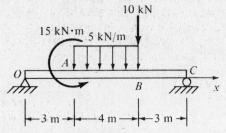

Fig. 7-33

Ans. For $0 < x < 3$, $V = 14.5$ and $M = 14.5x$; for $3 < x < 7$, $V = 14.5 - 5(x - 3)$ and $M = 14.5x - 15 - 2.5(x - 3)^2$; for $7 < x < 10$, $V = -15.5$ and $M = 14.5x - 15 - 2.5(x - 3)^2 - 10(x - 7)$; Fig. 7-34

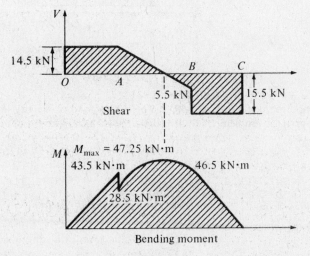

Shear

Bending moment

Fig. 7-34

7.15 The simply supported beam in Fig. 7-35 is subject to a downward force and a couple. Use singularity functions to write an equation for the bending moment along the length of the beam.

Ans. $M = 2.857 + 10\langle x - 2 \rangle^0 - 15\langle x - 5 \rangle$

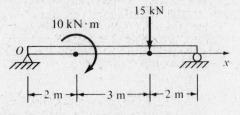

Fig. 7-35

7.16 The simply supported beam in Fig. 7-36 is loaded with two uniformly distributed loads as shown. Use singularity functions to write an equation for the bending moment at any point along the beam.

Ans. $M = 500x - 50\langle x \rangle^2 - 50\langle x - 4 \rangle^2$

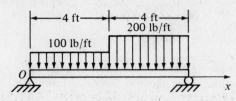

Fig. 7-36

7.17 Use the BASIC program of Problem 7.7 to determine the shearing forces and bending moments at the numbered locations on the beam of Fig. 7-37.

Ans.

LOCATION	SHEARLEFT	SHEARRIGHT	MOMENTLEFT	MOMENTRIGHT
1	0	36.36	0	0
2	-23.64	-23.64	25.44	25.44
3	-23.64	-23.64	13.62	23.62
4	-23.64	0	-1.999664E-02	-1.999664E-02

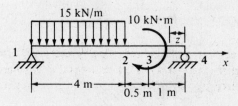

Fig. 7-37

7.18 The simply supported beam in Fig. 7-38 is subject to a load of linearly increasing intensity as shown. Use the BASIC program of Problem 7.7 to determine the shearing forces and bending moments at the numbered locations.

Ans.

LOCATION	SHEARLEFT	SHEARRIGHT	MOMENTLEFT	MOMENTRIGHT
1	0	-1.5	0	0
2	-1.5	-1.5	-4.5	-4.5
3	-3.75	6.75	-11.25	-11.25
4	0	0	0	0

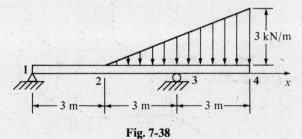

Fig. 7-38

PART II: *Mechanics of Deformable Bodies*

Chapter 8

Stress and Strain Analysis

NORMAL STRESS

If a plane cuts through a body subject to external loading, and the portion of the body to one side of the plane is removed, then a free-body diagram of the remaining portion must show a force acting on the cutting plane; this force represents the action of the portion of the body that has been removed. The component of this force perpendicular to the plane is called the *normal component* or *normal force*. Dividing the magnitude of the normal force by the area over which it acts yields the *normal stress* σ. (See Problem 8.1.)

SHEARING STRESS

The force acting on the cutting plane as defined above usually also has a component in the direction of the plane itself (i.e., lying in the plane). This component is called the *shearing force*. Dividing the magnitude of the shearing force by the area over which it acts yields the *shearing stress* τ. (See Problem 8.1.)

GENERAL STATE OF STRESS AT A POINT

If a three-dimensional rectangular block of very small size is considered to be removed from a body subject to external loads, there will be one normal stress and two shearing stresses on each of its six faces, as shown in Fig. 8-1. However, these stresses have only six distinct values at the point represented by this block. (See Problem 8.1.)

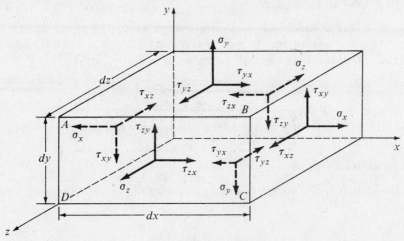

Fig. 8-1

125

Note, in Fig. 8-1, that by convention stresses are shown as heavy arrows but are not labeled as vectors (in bold type).

PRINCIPAL STRESSES

The block in Fig. 8-1 shows only the stresses acting on planes parallel to the xy, xz, and yz planes. In addition, normal and shearing stresses act on all other planes within the block, at all orientations—with one exception: On one set of mutually perpendicular planes, the shearing stresses are zero. Those planes are called the *principal planes*, and the normal stresses on those planes are called the *principal stresses*. Among the principal stresses are the greatest and smallest normal stresses occurring on all possible planes through a point.

At a point, let σ be a principal stress that acts on a plane whose normal has direction cosines l, m, and n with respect to the x, y, and z axes. Then the three principal stresses at that point are the roots of

$$\sigma^3 - I_1\sigma^2 + I_2\sigma - I_3 = 0 \tag{8.1}$$

where

$$I_1 = \sigma_x + \sigma_y + \sigma_z$$
$$I_2 = \sigma_x\sigma_y + \sigma_x\sigma_z + \sigma_y\sigma_z - \tau_{xy}^2 - \tau_{xz}^2 - \tau_{yz}^2 \tag{8.2}$$
$$I_3 = \sigma_x\sigma_y\sigma_z + 2\tau_{xy}\tau_{yz}\tau_{zx} - \sigma_x\tau_{yz}^2 - \sigma_y\tau_{zx}^2 - \sigma_z\tau_{xy}^2$$

For each of these roots (each principal stress), the direction cosines l, m, n can be found with

$$\sigma l = \sigma_x l + \tau_{xy}m + \tau_{xz}n$$
$$\sigma m = \tau_{xy}l + \tau_y m + \tau_{yz}n \tag{8.3}$$
$$\sigma n = \tau_{xz}l + \tau_{yz}m + \sigma_z n$$

and

$$l^2 + m^2 + n^2 = 1 \tag{8.4}$$

In two dimensions, at a point with normal stresses σ_x and σ_y and shearing stress τ_{xy}, the principal stresses are the solutions of

$$\sigma = \frac{\sigma_x + \sigma_y}{2} \pm \sqrt{\left(\frac{\sigma_x - \sigma_y}{2}\right)^2 + \tau_{xy}^2} \tag{8.5}$$

(See Problems 8.4 and 8.8.)

DIRECTIONS OF PRINCIPAL STRESS

For any point in a loaded solid body, the directions in which the principal stresses act are called the directions of principal stress, or simply the *principal directions*. For the two-dimensional case, the angle θ_p between the x axis and the principal directions is given by

$$\tan 2\theta_p = \frac{\tau_{xy}}{(\sigma_x - \sigma_y)/2} \tag{8.6}$$

This equation has multiple roots, of which only the first two are of interest. (See Problem 8.8.)

MAXIMUM SHEARING STRESS

With respect to the principal planes, the direction cosines of the normals to the planes of maximum shearing stress are

$$\pm\frac{1}{\sqrt{2}} \qquad 0 \qquad \pm\frac{1}{\sqrt{2}} \tag{8.7}$$

The values of τ corresponding to these directions are, respectively,

$$\tau = \pm\tfrac{1}{2}(\sigma_1 - \sigma_2) \qquad \tau = \pm\tfrac{1}{2}(\sigma_2 - \sigma_3) \qquad \tau = \pm\tfrac{1}{2}(\sigma_3 - \sigma_1) \tag{8.8}$$

The maximum value of the shearing stress is always half the difference between the largest and smallest principal stresses,

$$\tau_{\max} = \pm\tfrac{1}{2}(\sigma_{\max} - \sigma_{\min}) \tag{8.9}$$

and it occurs on a plane that bisects the angle between the principal planes associated with $\sigma_{\max}$ and $\sigma_{\min}$.

NORMAL STRAIN

The loading on a body results in deformation of the body. The change in length per unit length of a bar that is loaded in tension or compression is called the *normal strain* ε. It is computed as the change in length divided by the original length and is a dimensionless quantity.

SHEARING STRAIN

Suppose a right angle is marked at a point on the surface of a body that is free of external loading. The change in the angle that occurs after loading has been applied is termed the *shearing strain* γ at that point. The angle must be expressed in radians; hence the shearing strain is dimensionless.

STRAINS ON INCLINED PLANES

As is true of stresses, strains occur not only on planes parallel to the coordinate planes, but also on all possible planes through a point. Consider the rectangular element $OABC$ in Fig. 8-2, loaded in tension in the x and y directions and by shearing forces at its boundaries. Along an arbitrary x' axis, at an angle θ to the x axis, this loading produces a normal strain

$$\varepsilon_{x'} = \frac{\varepsilon_x + \varepsilon_y}{2} + \frac{\varepsilon_x - \varepsilon_y}{2}\cos 2\theta + \frac{\gamma_{xy}}{2}\sin 2\theta \tag{8.10}$$

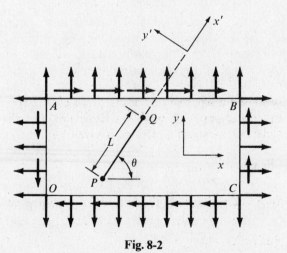

Fig. 8-2

With reference to the x' and y' axes shown, it produces a shearing strain

$$\gamma_{x'y'} = -(\varepsilon_x - \varepsilon_y)\sin 2\theta + \gamma_{xy}\cos 2\theta \tag{8.11}$$

(See Problem 8.13.)

PRINCIPAL STRAINS

The greatest and least of all the normal strains occurring on all possible planes through a point are called the *principal strains* at the point. In two dimensions, with normal strains ε_x and ε_y and shearing strain γ_{xy}, the principal strains are given by

$$\varepsilon = \frac{\varepsilon_x + \varepsilon_y}{2} \pm \sqrt{\left(\frac{\varepsilon_x - \varepsilon_y}{2}\right)^2 + \left(\frac{\gamma_{xy}}{2}\right)^2} \qquad (8.12)$$

The directions in which the principal strains act are called the *directions of principal strain*. The angles θ_p between these directions and the x axis are given by the first two roots of

$$\tan 2\theta_p = \frac{\gamma_{xy}}{\varepsilon_x - \varepsilon_y} \qquad (8.13)$$

(See Problem 8.17.)

STRESS-STRAIN CURVE

Consider a bar subject to increasing tensile loading. Corresponding values of the resulting normal stress and normal strain may be plotted as the *stress-strain curve* for the material. For some common engineering materials, including especially metallic substances, this curve has an initial linear portion, as in Fig. 8-3.

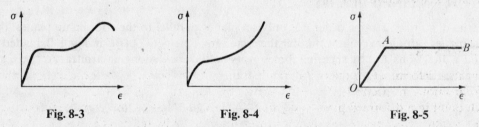

Fig. 8-3   Fig. 8-4   Fig. 8-5

Polymeric materials like synthetic rubber exhibit the stress-strain behavior shown in Fig. 8-4.

For many types of steel, the stress-strain curve may be approximated, as in Fig. 8-5, by a linear region followed by a region of *yielding*, i.e., of increasing strain with no corresponding increase in stress. Region OA is termed the *elastic range* for the material, and region AB is called the *plastic* or *yield range*. The value of the stress σ at yielding is called the *yield point* of the material.

For a body loaded in shear, a similar *shearing stress-strain curve* may be plotted.

MODULUS OF ELASTICITY

The *modulus of elasticity* or *Young's modulus* E for a material is the slope of the linear portion of its stress-strain curve (see Figs. 8-3 and 8-5). Because strain is dimensionless, E has the units of stress, newtons per square meter (pascals) or pounds per square inch, for example.

PROPORTIONAL LIMIT

The maximum tensile stress that may be developed in a material such that stress is a linear function of strain is called the *proportional limit* of the material. Not all materials have a proportional limit.

ELASTIC LIMIT

The maximum tensile stress that may be developed in a material such that there is no residual deformation when the load is removed is called the *elastic limit* of the material. For many metallic materials, the elastic and proportional limits are nearly identical. For materials in which they are different, the elastic limit is usually greater than the proportional limit.

ISOTROPIC AND ANISOTROPIC MATERIALS

A material having the same elastic properties in all directions at any point is said to be *isotropic*. This property is common to many metals.

A material having different elastic properties in various directions at a point is *anisotropic*. This behavior is typical of modern composite materials.

HOMOGENEOUS AND NONHOMOGENEOUS MATERIALS

A material having the same elastic properties at all points within the material is said to be *homogeneous*.

A material having different elastic properties at different points within it is *nonhomogeneous*. Sandwich-type materials composed of two thin metallic faces separated by a core (usually of hexagonal cells) are nonhomogeneous.

For a homogeneous, isotropic material, the directions of principal stress are identical with the directions of principal strain. (See Problem 8.17.)

DISPLACEMENTS

A point in a deformed (due to loading) solid body will be displaced by distances u, v, and w in the x, y, and z directions, respectively. These displacements have the units of length.

At each point in a deformed body under two-dimensional loading, the normal strains ε_x and ε_y and the shearing strain γ_{xy} are related to the displacements u and v by the equations

$$\varepsilon_x = \frac{\partial u}{\partial x} \qquad \varepsilon_y = \frac{\partial v}{\partial y} \qquad \gamma_{xy} = \frac{\partial u}{\partial y} + \frac{\partial v}{\partial x} \tag{8.14}$$

(See Problem 8.12.)

EQUATION OF COMPATIBILITY

For deformations under two-dimensional loading, the normal and shearing strains at a point are not independent, but are linked by the *compatibility equation*

$$\frac{\partial^2 \varepsilon_x}{\partial y^2} + \frac{\partial^2 \varepsilon_y}{\partial x^2} = \frac{\partial^2 \gamma_{xy}}{\partial x \, \partial y} \tag{8.15}$$

POISSON'S RATIO

When a bar is subject to simple tensile loading, the length of the bar (in the direction of the load) increases, but the lateral dimensions (perpendicular to the load) decrease. The ratio of the lateral strain to that in the axial direction is called *Poisson's ratio*. It is denoted in this book by μ. For most metals it lies in the range from 0.25 to 0.34. (See Problems 8.14 to 8.16.)

HOOKE'S LAW

For a bar loaded in tension within its elastic range, we have Hooke's law, $\sigma = E\varepsilon$, since E denotes the slope of the stress-strain curve. For three-dimensional loadings the effect of lateral contraction must be considered; hence, the general three-dimensional form of Hooke's law is

$$\varepsilon_x = \frac{1}{E}\left[\sigma_x - \mu(\sigma_y + \sigma_z)\right]$$

$$\varepsilon_y = \frac{1}{E}\left[\sigma_y - \mu(\sigma_x + \sigma_z)\right] \qquad (8.16)$$

$$\varepsilon_z = \frac{1}{E}\left[\sigma_z - \mu(\sigma_x + \sigma_y)\right]$$

COEFFICIENT OF LINEAR THERMAL EXPANSION

A body normally expands when it is heated and contracts when it is cooled. The change in the length of a bar per unit length when it is subject to a one-degree change in temperature is called the *coefficient of linear thermal expansion* (or contraction) α of its material. The value of this parameter is independent of the unit of length, but does depend upon the temperature scale. It has the unit per degree Celsius or per degree Fahrenheit.

DILATATION

The change in volume per unit volume of a solid body subject to external loads is called its *dilatation* e. This parameter is dimensionless and is usually approximated as $e = \varepsilon_x + \varepsilon_y + \varepsilon_z$. (See Problem 8.15.)

Using e, we may rewrite Hooke's law (8.16) to give stresses in terms of strains:

$$\sigma_x = \frac{\mu E}{(1 + \mu)(1 - 2\mu)}e + \frac{E}{1 + \mu}\varepsilon_x$$

$$\sigma_y = \frac{\mu E}{(1 + \mu)(1 - 2\mu)}e + \frac{E}{1 + \mu}\varepsilon_y \qquad (8.17)$$

$$\sigma_z = \frac{\mu E}{(1 + \mu)(1 - 2\mu)}e + \frac{E}{1 + \mu}\varepsilon_z$$

BULK MODULUS

If a solid body is subject to a uniform hydrostatic pressure p, then $\sigma_x = \sigma_y = \sigma_z = -p$. The corresponding normal strains are, from Hooke's law,

$$\varepsilon_x = \varepsilon_y = \varepsilon_z = -\frac{p}{E}(1 - 2\mu) \qquad (8.18)$$

Now, letting $e = \varepsilon_x + \varepsilon_y + \varepsilon_z$ and solving for $-p/e$ yield

$$-\frac{p}{e} = \frac{E}{3(1 - 2\mu)} \equiv K \qquad (8.19)$$

where the minus sign indicates that the volume decreases as the pressure increases. This equation defines the *bulk modulus K* as the negative of the ratio of the hydrostatic pressure to the volumetric strain it produces, which we may write as $K = -p/(\Delta V/V)$.

The units of the bulk modulus are the same as the units of pressure. (See Problem 8.18.)

DIFFERENTIAL EQUATIONS OF EQUILIBRIUM

The normal and shearing stresses on a differential element of a loaded body are related to the forces exerted on the body, including gravitational attraction, magnetic forces, and such. If the magnitudes of these body forces per unit volume in the directions of the x and y axes (for a two-dimensional problem) are X and Y, the relationships are

$$\frac{\partial \sigma_x}{\partial x} + \frac{\partial \tau_{xy}}{\partial y} + X = 0 \quad \text{and} \quad \frac{\partial \sigma_y}{\partial y} + \frac{\partial \tau_{xy}}{\partial x} + Y = 0 \tag{8.20}$$

(See Problems 8.20 and 8.21.) Corresponding relations exist for the three-dimensional case but are not discussed in this book.

In certain types of engineering problems, it is acceptable to neglect the variation in the normal and shearing stresses between two points of a solid body that are a differential distance dx, dy, dz apart. This is the *mechanics* or *strength of materials* approach, and it is very much employed in engineering. However, some complex problems require a *theory of elasticity* approach, in which this variation is considered.

Solved Problems

8.1   Describe the general state of stress at a point in a three-dimensional solid body.

Consider a solid body of arbitrary shape, with a loading that consists of a number of *external* concentrated forces, distributed loads, and couples as indicated in Fig. 8-6. To determine the *internal* effects of these external loads, we pass a plane through the body as indicated in Fig. 8-7, removing the right-hand portion but recognizing that we must include a resultant **F** to represent the action of the right portion on the left portion. We may then denote as ΔF the force acting on a very small area ΔA of the cutting plane.

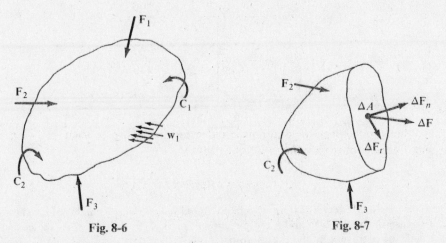

Fig. 8-6   Fig. 8-7

In general, ΔF does not act perpendicular to the cutting plane; thus, it can be resolved into two components, ΔF_n normal to the cutting plane and ΔF_t lying in that plane. If the magnitudes of ΔF_n and ΔF_t are each divided by the area ΔA, we obtain the relations

$$\sigma = \frac{\Delta F_n}{\Delta A} \quad \text{and} \quad \tau = \frac{\Delta F_t}{\Delta A}$$

where the magnitudes of the vectors are denoted by light type. We define σ as the normal stress acting at the point of application of $\Delta \mathbf{F}$, and τ as the shearing stress acting at the same point.

Next, let us pass three pairs of mutually perpendicular cutting planes through the body of Fig. 8-6, so as to remove a solid rectangular element of dimensions dx, dy, and dz. The stresses acting on the six faces of the element are those shown in Fig. 8-1. The directions indicated are the positive directions for these stresses; i.e., as usual, tension is taken to be positive and compression negative. For shearing stresses, a double subscript is necessary. The first letter denotes the direction of the normal to the plane on which the shear acts, and the second denotes the direction of the shearing stress.

Each of the normal and shearing stresses in Fig. 8-1 is a vector, and the matrix

$$\begin{pmatrix} \sigma_x & \tau_{xy} & \tau_{xz} \\ \tau_{yx} & \sigma_y & \tau_{yz} \\ \tau_{zx} & \tau_{zy} & \sigma_z \end{pmatrix}$$

is called the *stress matrix* at the point being considered. Although it appears that there are nine distinct stress components at each point, there are in fact only six. To see that this is so, consider a summation of moments of forces (determined by multiplying stress by area by distance) about an axis parallel to the x axis and extending along the stress vector σ_x in Fig. 8-1. We obtain

$$+\circlearrowleft \Sigma M_{\sigma x} = 2\tau_{zy}\, dx\, dy\, \frac{dz}{2} - 2\tau_{yz}\, dx\, dz\, \frac{dy}{2} = 0$$

from which we find that $\tau_{zy} = \tau_{yz}$. Two similar summations yield $\tau_{yx} = \tau_{xy}$ and $\tau_{zx} = \tau_{xz}$. Thus, at any point in a stressed body, there are six (not nine) independent stress components, namely σ_x, σ_y, σ_z, τ_{xy}, τ_{xz}, and τ_{yz}.

8.2   Determine the state of stress on a plane inclined to the x, y, and z axes, given the stresses acting parallel to those axes.

We assume that the inclined plane (*ABC* in Fig. 8-8) cuts off a very small tetrahedron *OABC* as shown. (Think of it as a corner of the block in Fig. 8-1.) We also assume that the six stresses σ_x, σ_y, σ_z, $\tau_{xy} = \tau_{yx}$, $\tau_{xz} = \tau_{zx}$, and $\tau_{yz} = \tau_{zy}$ are known, and that each is constant over each of the four triangular faces of the tetrahedron. Then the force acting on each face is merely the corresponding stress multiplied by the area of the face.

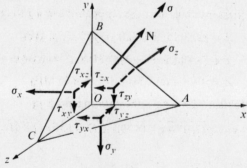

Fig. 8-8

Let us construct a vector **N** normal to face *ABC* as shown. This normal is directed away from the origin *O*. Let us also denote by l, m, and n the direction cosines of **N**; they are then the cosines of the angles **N** makes with the positive x, y, and z axes, respectively. Thus,

$$\mathbf{N} = l\mathbf{i} + m\mathbf{j} + n\mathbf{k} \tag{1}$$

where $\mathbf{i}$, $\mathbf{j}$, and $\mathbf{k}$ are unit vectors along the x, y, and z axes, respectively. We now denote by da the area of face ABC; then the area of face OBC is $l\,da$, that of OAC is $m\,da$, and that of OAB is $n\,da$. Finally, we take the x, y, and z components of the stress acting on ABC to be X, Y, and Z, respectively.

Equilibrium of the forces acting on the tetrahedron in the x direction leads to the equation

$$\Sigma\,F_x = X\,da - \sigma_x l\,da - \tau_{yx}m\,da - \tau_{zx}n\,da = 0$$

This equation and the corresponding equations in the y and z directions yield

$$X = \sigma_x l + \tau_{xy}m + \tau_{xz}n$$
$$Y = \tau_{xy}l + \sigma_y m + \tau_{yz}n \qquad (2)$$
$$Z = \tau_{xz}l + \tau_{yz}m + \sigma_z n$$

These three equations constitute a description of the state of stress on the inclined plane whose normal is denoted by (1). In both (1) and (2) we have, from analytic geometry,

$$l^2 + m^2 + n^2 = 1 \qquad (3)$$

If we denote by σ the normal stress on plane ABC in the direction of $\mathbf{N}$, we have

$$\sigma = lX + mY + nZ \qquad (4)$$

Substituting (2) in (4) yields

$$\sigma = l^2\sigma_x + m^2\sigma_y + n^2\sigma_z + 2lm\tau_{xy} + 2ln\tau_{xz} + 2mn\tau_{yz} \qquad (5)$$

A shearing stress τ also acts on plane ABC. The resultant of the normal stress σ and this shearing stress is simply $\sqrt{X^2 + Y^2 + Z^2}$, where X, Y, and Z are given by (2). Since σ and τ are perpendicular, we have

$$\tau = \sqrt{X^2 + Y^2 + Z^2 - \sigma^2} \qquad (6)$$

8.3   At a certain point in a loaded elastic solid, the stresses are

$$\sigma_x = 30\text{ MPa} \qquad \sigma_y = -20\text{ MPa} \qquad \sigma_z = 0 \qquad \tau_{xy} = 10\text{ MPa} \qquad \tau_{xz} = 0 \qquad \tau_{yz} = -15\text{ MPa}$$

Determine the normal and shearing stresses on a plane through the point, if the normal to the plane has direction cosines 0.15, 0.31, and 0.939 with respect to the x, y, and z axes.

Here $l = 0.15$, $m = 0.31$, and $n = 0.939$. The normal stress is given by (5) of Problem 8.2:

$$\sigma = (0.15)^2(30) + (0.31)^2(-20) + 0 + 2(0.15)(0.31)(10) + 2(0.15)(0.939)(0) + 2(0.31)(0.939)(-15)$$
$$= -9.05\text{ MPa}$$

To find the shearing stress, we must first use (2) of Problem 8.2 to find

$$X = (30)(0.15) + (10)(0.31) + 0 = 7.6\text{ MPa}$$
$$Y = (10)(0.15) + (-20)(0.31) + (-15)(0.939) = -18.79\text{ MPa}$$
$$Z = 0 + (-15)(0.31) + 0 = -4.65\text{ MPa}$$

Finally, from (6) of Problem 8.2 we have the shearing stress as

$$\tau = \sqrt{(7.6)^2 + (-18.79)^2 + (-4.65)^2 - (-9.05)^2} = 18.72\text{ MPa}$$

8.4   For the three-dimensional state of stress described by

$$\sigma_x = 110\text{ MPa} \qquad \sigma_y = 70\text{ MPa} \qquad \sigma_z = 80\text{ MPa}$$
$$\tau_{xy} = -50\text{ MPa} \qquad \tau_{yz} = 60\text{ MPa} \qquad \tau_{zx} = -65\text{ MPa}$$

determine the principal stresses and their directions.

From (8.2) we first calculate

$$I_1 = 110 + 70 + 80 = 260$$

$$I_2 = (110)(70) + (110)(80) + (70)(80) - (-50)^2 - (60)^2 - (-65)^2 = 11,775$$

$$I_3 = (110)(70)(80) + 2(-50)(60)(-65) - (110)(60)^2 - (70)(-65)^2 - (80)(-50)^2 = 114,250$$

Then (8.1) becomes

$$\sigma^3 - 260\sigma^2 + 11,775\sigma - 114,250 = 0 \qquad\qquad (1)$$

Although it is possible to solve this cubic equation in closed form, it is simpler to solve it by trial and error, with the aid of a pocket calculator. For this, we set

$$\sigma^3 - 260\sigma^2 + 11,775\sigma - 114,250 = R$$

and try various values of σ, seeking those for which the error R is zero. After several trials, we have the following:

σ	R
175	$-656,750$
190	$-499,000$
200	$-159,200$
210	$+153,500$

From the last two values, it is apparent that $\sigma = 205$ will make the error very nearly zero. Hence, 205 is one root of (1).

Let us now find the direction cosines for the stress vector corresponding to $\sigma_1 = 205$ MPa. If we substitute this value in the first two equations of (8.3) and rearrange, we get

$$(205 - 110)l_1 - (-50)m_1 - (-65)n_1 = 0$$

$$-(-50)l_1 + (205 - 70)m_1 - (60)n_1 = 0$$

After simplifying and arbitrarily setting $l_1 = 1$ in these two equations, we have

$$95 + 50m_1' + 65n_1' = 0$$

$$50 + 135m_1' - 60n_1' = 0$$

where the primes indicate values based on the arbitrary $l_1 = 1$. These equations are readily solved to yield

$$m_1' = -0.760 \qquad \text{and} \qquad n_1' = -0.877 \qquad\qquad (2)$$

Substituting these values into (8.4) yields

$$l_1^2 + (-0.760)^2 + (-0.877)^2 = 1 \qquad\qquad (3)$$

With $l_1 = 1$, the left-hand side of (3) becomes $1 + 0.5776 + 0.7691 = 2.3467$, whereas it should exactly equal unity. Thus, we conclude that the true value of l_1 must be

$$l_1 = \frac{1}{\sqrt{2.3467}} = \frac{1}{1.53} = 0.653$$

The values (2) must be scaled similarly, and we obtain

$$m_1 = \frac{-0.760}{1.53} = -0.497 \qquad \text{and} \qquad n_1 = -\frac{0.877}{1.53} = -0.573$$

Given the definition of direction cosines, it is obvious that all three algebraic signs may be reversed if desired.

The remaining two roots of (*l*) are found by the same trial-and-error process to be approximately 13 and 41. Thus, the three principal stresses are 205 MPa, 13 MPa, and 41 MPa. The direction cosines for the latter two stresses may be found by the procedure we used for the first principal stress. The details are omitted here, because this same problem is solved with a more efficient method in Problem 8.6.

8.5   Develop a FORTRAN program for determining the three principal stresses and their directions in terms of the normal and shear stresses indicated in Fig. 8-1.

The principal stresses must be found with (*8.1*) and (*8.2*). The iterative approach used in Problem 8.4 is ideal for FORTRAN implementation; in the program that follows, the iteration begins with the largest of the given normal stresses σ_x, σ_y, and σ_z. The direction cosines also are determined essentially as in Problem 8.4.

```
00001*****************************************************************
00002          `            PROGRAM THREEDE (INPUT,OUTPUT)
00003*****************************************************************
00004*
00005*        AUTHOR: KATHLEEN DERWIN
00006*        DATE  : JANUARY 25,1988
00007*
00008*    BRIEF DESCRIPTION:
00009*       THIS PROGRAM DETERMINES THE THREE-DIMENSIONAL PRINCIPAL
00010*    STRESSES AND THE DIRECTION COSINES FOR A PARTICULAR STATE
00012*    OF NORMAL AND SHEAR STRESS.
00014*
00015*    INPUT:
00017*       THE USER IS PROMPTED FOR THE STATE OF STRESS AT A POINT.
00018*    NAMELY, THE THREE ORTHOGONAL COMPONENTS OF THE NORMAL STRESS,
00020*    AND THE THREE COMPONENTS OF SHEAR STRESS ARE ENTERED. (SEE
00022*    TEXT FOR THE COORDINATE SYSTEM AND SIGN CONVENTION FOLLOWED.)
00025*
00026*    OUTPUT:
00030*       THE THREE PRINCIPAL STRESSES AT THE POINT ARE PRINTED AS
00032*    WELL AS THE DIRECTION COSINES FOR EACH PRINCIPAL STRESS.
00035*
00040*    VARIABLES:
00042*       SIGX,SIGY,SIGZ     --- THE COMPONENTS OF NORMAL STRESS
00043*                              AT A PARTICULAR POINT.
00044*       TAUXY,TAUYZ,TAUXZ --- THE COMPONENTS OF SHEARING STRESS
00045*                              AT A PARTICULAR POINT.
00046*       X1                 --- GUESS AT SMALLEST POS. ROOT TO CUBIC.
00047*       Y,Y1               --- VALUES OF CUBIC EQN AT EACH INCREMENT OF X1
00048*       DX                 --- THE SIZE OF INCREMENT IN THE ROOT SEARCH.
00049*       I1,I2,I3           --- CONSTANTS OF THE CUBIC STRESS EQN.
00050*       R1,R2,R3           --- ROOTS OF CUBIC STRESS EQUATION.
00052*       SIG(3)             --- THREE PRINCIPAL STRESSES (R1,R2,R3).
00054*       BQ,CQ              --- CONSTANTS OF THE QUADRATIC EQN.
00056*       DISC               --- DISCRIMINATE OF QUADRATIC EQUATION.
00058*       L(3),M(3),N(3)     --- DIRECTION COSINES FOR EACH PRIN.STRESS.
00060*       A,B,C,D,E,F,G,H,K  --- TEMPORARY VARIABLES TO AID IN SOLVING
00062*                              THE SIMULTANEOUS EQUATIONS FOR DIRECTION
00064*                              COSINES.
00065*
00070*****************************************************************
00072*****************************************************************
00074*                         MAIN PROGRAM
00078*****************************************************************
00078*****************************************************************
00080*
00082*    VARIABLE DECLARATIONS
00084*
00200     REAL SIGX,SIGY,SIGZ,TAUXY,TAUXZ,TAUYZ,I1,I2,I3A,I3B,I3C
```

```
00205        REAL I3,DX,X1,Y,Y1,R1,R2,R3,BQ,CQ,DISC
00210        REAL SIG(3),L(3),M(3),N(3),NSQRD,A,B,C,D,E,F,G,H,K
00215        INTEGER I,J
00220*
00225*    USER INPUT OF SHEAR AND NORMAL STRESS COMPONENTS
00230*
00300        PRINT*,'DETERMINATION OF 3-D PRINCIPAL STRESSES...'
00310        PRINT*,' '
00315        PRINT*,'ENTER THE STATE OF STRESS AT THE POINT DESIRED;'
00320        PRINT*,'INPUT SIGX, SIGY, SIGZ :'
00325        READ*, SIGX,SIGY,SIGZ
00330        PRINT*,'INPUT TAUXY, TAUYZ, TAUXZ :'
00335        READ*,TAUXY,TAUYZ,TAUXZ
00340*
00345*     CALCULATING THE CONSTANTS FOR THE CUBIC STRESS EQUATION
00350*
00400        I1= SIGX+SIGY+SIGZ
00405        I2=SIGX*SIGY+SIGX*SIGZ+SIGY*SIGZ-TAUXY**2-TAUXZ**2-TAUYZ**2
00410        I3A= SIGX*((SIGY*SIGZ)-(TAUYZ**2))
00415        I3B= TAUXY*((TAUXY*SIGZ)-(TAUYZ*TAUXZ))
00420        I3C= TAUXZ*((TAUXY*TAUYZ)-(SIGY*TAUXZ))
00425        I3=I3A-I3B+I3C
00430*
00435*    FINDING THE SMALLEST POSITIVE ROOT OF THE CUBIC STRESS EQUATION
00440*
00500        DX=.005
00505        X1=0
00510 10     Y=(X1**3)- (I1*(X1**2))+(I2*X1)-I3
00520        Y1=((X1+DX)**3)-(I1*((X1+DX)**2))+(I2*(X1+DX))-I3
00530        IF(Y.EQ.0.0) THEN
00540           R1=X1
00550           GOTO 30
00560        ELSE
00570           IF((Y*Y1).GT.0.0) THEN
00575              X1=X1+DX
00580              GOTO 10
00585           ELSE
00590              R1=X1+DX/2
00595              GOTO 30
00600           ENDIF
00605        ENDIF
00608*
00610*     NOW, SOLVING THE REMAINING QUADRATIC EQN. FOR THE OTHER TWO ROOTS
00615*
00620 30     BQ=R1-I1
00625        CQ=I3/R1
00630        DISC = SQRT((BQ**2)-(4*CQ))
00640        R2=(-BQ+DISC)/2
00650        R3=(-BQ-DISC)/2
00652*
00655*     ASSIGNING THE ROOTS TO THE PRINCIPAL STRESS ARRAY
00658*
00660        SIG(1)=R2
00670        SIG(2)=R1
00680        SIG(3)=R3
00685*
00690*     SOLVING FOR THE DIRECTION COSINES FROM THE KNOWN SIMULTANEOUS
00692*     EQUATION RELATIONSHIPS.
00695*
00700        DO 50 I=1,3
00705           A=TAUXY/(SIGY-SIG(I))
00710           B=TAUXY/(SIGX-SIG(I))
00715           C=TAUYZ/(SIGY-SIG(I))
00720           D=TAUXZ/(SIGX-SIG(I))
00725           E=(-A/(2*B*C))+(1/(2*B*D))
00730           F=((-1-(A**2))/(2*A*B*C))+((1+(B**2))/(2*B*D))
```

```
00735          G=((A*D)-C)/(1-(A*B))
00740          H=((C**2) - (A**2) -(2*A*C*D))/(2*A*B*C)
00745          K=(1+(D**2))/(2*B*D)
00760          NSQRD= E/((F*(G**2))+H+K)
00770          N(I)= SQRT(NSQRD)
00780          IF(G.LT.0.0) THEN
00785              N(I)=N(I)*(-1)
00790          ENDIF
00795          M(I)=G*N(I)
00800          L(I)=(-B*M(I))+(-D*N(I))
00805 50 CONTINUE
00810*
00815*     PRINTING OUTPUT
00820*
00835     PRINT*,'   '
00840     PRINT 56,'SIGX','SIGY','SIGZ','TAUXY','TAUXZ','TAUYZ'
00845     PRINT 57,SIGX,SIGY,SIGZ,TAUXY,TAUXZ,TAUYZ
00848     PRINT*,'FOR THE STATE OF STRESS SHOWN, THE THREE PRINCIPAL'
00849     PRINT*,'STRESSES AND THEIR DIRECTION COSINES ARE AS FOLLOWS...'
00850     PRINT 58,'NO.','SIG(I)','L(I)','M(I)','N(I)'
00860     DO 55 J=1,3
00865         PRINT 60,J,SIG(J),L(J),M(J),N(J)
00870 55 CONTINUE
00871*
00872*     FORMAT STATEMENTS
00873*
00874 56 FORMAT(/,2X,6(A5,8X))
00875 57 FORMAT(2X,3(F7.2,5X),2(F8.2,5X),F8.2,/)
00880 58 FORMAT(/,2X,A3,7X,A6,8X,3(A4,9X))
00890 60 FORMAT(2X,I2,5X,F8.2,5X,3(F8.4,5X))
00900*
01000     END
```

8.6 Repeat Problem 8.4 using the FORTRAN program of Problem 8.5.

     The program prompts and inputs are shown on the first six lines below; the input data are summarized on the next two lines; and the solution is given in the remainder of the computer output. The principal stresses are displayed in the column marked SIG(I), and the corresponding direction cosines are printed in the three columns to its right.

```
DETERMINATION OF 3-D PRINCIPAL STRESSES...

ENTER THE STATE OF STRESS AT THE POINT DESIRED;
INPUT SIGX, SIGY, SIGZ :
? 110,70,80
INPUT TAUXY, TAUYZ, TAUXZ :
? -50,60,-65
```

SIGX	SIGY	SIGZ	TAUXY	TAUXZ	TAUYZ
110.00	70.00	80.00	-50.00	-65.00	60.00

```
FOR THE STATE OF STRESS SHOWN, THE THREE PRINCIPAL
STRESSES AND THEIR DIRECTION COSINES ARE AS FOLLOWS...
```

NO.	SIG(I)	L(I)	M(I)	N(I)
1	205.38	-.6514	.4953	.5748
2	13.54	-.1698	.6432	-.7467
3	41.08	.7393	.5845	.3344

8.7   For a two-dimensional state of stress in which we know σ_x, σ_y, and τ_{xy}, with $\sigma_z = \tau_{xz} = \tau_{yz} = 0$, find the maximum shearing stress and the directions of the planes on which it acts.

By substituting (8.5) into (8.9), we obtain

$$\tau_{max} = \pm \tfrac{1}{2}(\sigma_{max} - \sigma_{min})$$

$$= \pm \frac{1}{2} \left\{ \left[\frac{\sigma_x + \sigma_y}{2} + \sqrt{\left(\frac{\sigma_x - \sigma_y}{2} \right)^2 + \tau_{xy}^2} \right] - \left[\frac{\sigma_x - \sigma_y}{2} - \sqrt{\left(\frac{\sigma_x - \sigma_y}{2} \right)^2 + \tau_{xy}^2} \right] \right\}$$

$$= \pm \sqrt{\left(\frac{\sigma_x - \sigma_y}{2} \right)^2 + \tau_{xy}^2} \tag{1}$$

As is evident from (8.7), the planes of peak shearing stress are oriented at $\pm 45°$ to the principal planes.

Normal stresses σ_N also act on these planes of peak shearing stress. We find their magnitudes by using (5) of Problem 8.2 with direction cosines corresponding to planes that are at $+45°$ and $-45°$ to the principal directions as computed with (8.6). These magnitudes turn out to be equal and to have the value

$$\sigma_N = \frac{\sigma_x + \sigma_y}{2} \tag{2}$$

where σ_x and σ_y are the normal stresses parallel to the x and y axes.

8.8   Consider an element subject to the two-dimensional stresses indicated in Fig. 8-9. Determine the principal stresses and directions.

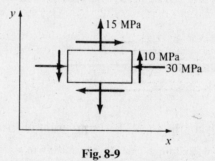

Fig. 8-9

From (8.5) with $\sigma_x = -30$ MPa, $\sigma_y = 15$ MPa, and $\tau_{xy} = 10$ MPa, we have

$$\sigma = \frac{-30 + 15}{2} \pm \sqrt{\left(\frac{-30 - 15}{2} \right)^2 + (10)^2} = -7.50 \pm 24.62$$

so that $\sigma_1 = 17.12$ MPa   and $\sigma_2 = -32.12$ MPa

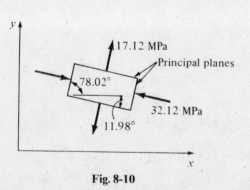

Fig. 8-10

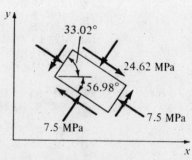

Fig. 8-11

The principal directions are given by (8.6):

$$\tan 2\theta_p = \frac{10}{(-30-15)/2} = -0.444$$

Then $2\theta_p = -23.95°$ or $156.04°$, and $\theta_p = -11.98°$ or $78.02°$.

The element subject to the principal stresses thus appears as in Fig. 8-10. Note that there are no shearing stresses on the principal planes. Note also that, by convention, the element is drawn as if it were bordered by the principal planes or (as in Figs. 8-9 and 8-11) the planes that are of interest in a particular discussion.

8.9   For the element of Problem 8.8, determine the peak shearing stress and its directions.

From Problem 8.7, the peak shearing stress is given by

$$\tau_{max} = \pm\sqrt{\left(\frac{-30-15}{2}\right)^2 + (10)^2} = \pm24.62 \text{ MPa}$$

This shearing stress occurs on planes oriented at $\pm45°$ to the principal planes found in Problem 8.8; they are shown in Fig. 8-11.

The normal stresses on the planes of peak shearing stress are of equal intensity; as indicated by (2) of Problem 8.7, their magnitude may be found as the mean of σ_x and σ_y, or $\sigma_N = (-30 + 15)/2 = -7.5 \text{ MPa}$, and they act as shown in Fig. 8-11.

8.10   Develop a program in the BASIC computer language for determining the principal stresses and directions for the two-dimensional loading described in Problem 8.7.

The principal stresses are given by (8.5), and the principal directions by (8.6). These simple expressions are utilized in the following program, which produces the angle θ_p in *degrees*:

```
00100 REM      THIS PROGRAM IS DEVELOPED TO EVALUATE THE PRINCIPAL STRESSES
00110 REM      AND THE ROTATING ANGLE IN 2-D PROBLEMS
00120 DIM      X(30),Y(30),S(30),P1(30),P2(30),T(30)
00130 REM      X, Y ARE THE NORMAL STRESSES IN THE X, Y DIRECTIONS
00140 REM      S IS THE SHEAR STRESS IN X-Y PLANE
00150 REM      P1, P2 ARE THE PRINCIPAL STRESSES
00160 REM      T IS THE ROTATING ANGLE
00170 PRINT    " PLEASE ENTER NO. OF STRESSES SET : "
00180 INPUT    N
00190 FOR      I=1 TO N
00200 PRINT    " PLEASE ENTER THE NORMAL STRESSES IN X, Y DIRECTIONS"
00210 PRINT    " AND SHEAR STRESS : "
00220 INPUT    X(I), Y(I), S(I)
00230 LET      A=(X(I)-Y(I))*(X(I)-Y(I))/4.0
00240 LET      B=SQR(A+S(I)*S(I))
00250 LET      C=(X(I)+Y(I))/2.0
00260 LET      P1(I)=C+B
00270 LET      P2(I)=C-B
00280 IF       X(I)=Y(I) THEN GOTO 320
00290 LET      A1=2.0*S(I)/(X(I)-Y(I))
00300 LET      T(I)=180*ATN(A1)/6.2831852
00310 GOTO     330
00320 LET      T(I)=45
00330 NEXT     I
00340 PRINT    "NO.","SIGXX","SIGYY","SIGXY","SIG(1)","SIG(2)","THETA"
00350 FOR      I=1 TO N
00360 PRINT    I,X(I),Y(I),S(I),P1(I),P2(I),T(I)
00370 NEXT     I
00380 END
```

8.11 For the element of Problem 8.8, determine the principal stresses and directions using the BASIC program of Problem 8.10.

In the first prompt below, the program requests the number of stress sets (sets of three stresses σ_x, σ_y, τ_{xy}) for which computations are required. In the second prompt, it requests the values of the stresses. The principal stresses are then displayed as SIG(1) and SIG(2), and the angle θ_p as THETA.

```
PLEASE ENTER THE NORMAL STRESSES IN X, Y DIRECTIONS
AND SHEAR STRESS :
? -30,15,10
NO.             SIGXX           SIGYY           SIGXY           SIG(1)
SIG(2)          THETA
 1              -30             15              10              17.1221
-32.1221        -11.9812
```

These values agree with the results of Problem 8.8.

8.12 Consider the functions $\varepsilon_x = axy$, $\varepsilon_y = by^3$, and $\gamma_{xy} = c - dy^2$, where a, b, c, and d are arbitrary constants. Can these functions describe a physically realizable state of plane strain in an elastic medium?

The compatibility equation (8.15) must be satisfied by any set of specified strains. For the given functions, we have

$$\frac{\partial^2 \varepsilon_x}{\partial y^2} = 0 \qquad \frac{\partial^2 \varepsilon_y}{\partial x^2} = 0 \qquad \frac{\partial^2 \gamma_{xy}}{\partial x \, \partial y} = 0$$

Substitution of these values into (8.15) shows that the compatibility equation is identically satisfied for all values of x and y. So the given functions do indeed describe a physically possible state of strain.

8.13 For the plane element of Fig. 8-2, let $\varepsilon_x = 200 \times 10^{-6}$, $\varepsilon_y = -110 \times 10^{-6}$, and $\gamma_{xy} = 100 \times 10^{-6}$. Determine the normal strain in the x' direction as well as the shearing strain $\gamma_{x'y'}$ for $\theta = 30°$.

From (8.10) we have the normal strain in the x' direction as

$$\varepsilon_{x'} = \left(\frac{200 - 110}{2} + \frac{200 + 110}{2} \cos 60° + \frac{100}{2} \sin 60°\right) \times 10^{-6} = 165.8 \times 10^{-6}$$

From (8.11) we obtain

$$\gamma_{x'y'} = [-(200 + 110) \sin 60° + 100 \cos 60°] \times 10^{-6} = -218.5 \times 10^{-6}$$

8.14 A square steel bar, 4 cm on a side and 1 m in length, is subject to an axial tensile force of 250,000 N. Determine the decrease in the lateral dimension due to this load.

We assume that the bar, shown in Fig. 8-12, extends along the x axis. The stress in the x direction is then

$$\sigma_x = \frac{250,000 \text{ N}}{(0.04 \text{ m})^2} = 1.56 \times 10^8 \text{ N/m}^2 = 156 \text{ MPa} \qquad (1)$$

Steel, like many other metals, exhibits an initial linear relation between the normal stress and the normal strain (Fig. 8-5) for loading in one direction only, as is the case here. This linear relationship is

$$\frac{\sigma_x}{\varepsilon_x} = E \qquad (2)$$

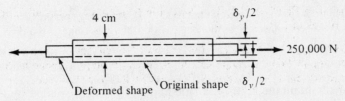

Fig. 8-12

where E is the modulus of elasticity of the material. For steel, E is usually about 200×10^9 N/m², or 200 GPa. For σ_x as computed in (1), then, the strain in the direction of the load is

$$\varepsilon_x = \frac{1.56 \times 10^8 \text{ N/m}^2}{200 \times 10^9 \text{ N/m}^2} = 0.00078 \tag{3}$$

This strain ε_x is accompanied by a lateral contraction δ_y, as shown in Fig. 8-12, and a corresponding lateral normal strain. Moreover, the ratio of lateral strain to axial strain is defined to be Poisson's ratio μ, for example,

$$\mu = \frac{\text{lateral strain}}{\text{axial strain}} = \frac{\varepsilon_y}{\varepsilon_x} \tag{4}$$

For most metals this ratio varies from about 0.25 to 0.35. If we use $\mu = 0.3$, we have, from (3) and (4),

$$\varepsilon_y = \mu\varepsilon_x = (0.3)(0.00078) = 0.000234$$

Since normal strain is computed as a change in length divided by the initial length, we can compute the decrease δ_y in the lateral dimension as

$$\delta_y = (\varepsilon_y)(40 \text{ mm}) = 0.00936 \text{ mm}$$

There is an equal decrease in the side of the bar that is perpendicular to the plane of Fig. 8-12.

8.15   Consider an elemental block subject to uniaxial tension (Fig. 8-13). Derive an approximate expression for the change of volume per unit volume due to this loading.

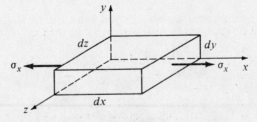

Fig. 8-13

The strain in the direction of the load may be denoted by ε_x. The strains in the other two orthogonal directions are then each $-\mu\varepsilon_x$. Consequently, if the initial dimensions of the element are dx, dy, and dz, then the final dimensions are

$$(1 + \varepsilon_x)\,dx \qquad (1 - \mu\varepsilon_x)\,dy \qquad (1 - \mu\varepsilon_x)\,dz$$

and the volume after deformation is

$$V' = (1 + \varepsilon_x)\,dx(1 - \mu\varepsilon_x)\,dy(1 - \mu\varepsilon_x)\,dz = (1 + \varepsilon_x)(1 - 2\mu\varepsilon_x)\,dx\,dy\,dz$$
$$= (1 - 2\mu\varepsilon_x + \varepsilon_x)\,dx\,dy\,dz$$

since the deformations are so small that the *squares* and *products* of strains may be neglected.
Since the initial volume was $dx\,dy\,dz$, the change of volume per unit volume is

$$\Delta V/V = (1 - 2\mu)\varepsilon_x$$

Hence, for a tensile force the volume increases slightly, and for a compressive force it decreases.

Also, the cross-sectional area of the element in a plane normal to the direction of the applied force is given approximately by $A = (1 - \mu\varepsilon_x)^2\, dy\, dz = (1 - 2\mu\varepsilon_x)\, dy\, dz$.

8.16 A square bar of aluminum, 2 in on a side and 10 in long, is loaded by axial tensile forces at the ends. Experimentally, it is found that the strain in the direction of the load is 0.001 in/in. Determine the volume of the bar when the load is acting. Take $\mu = 0.33$.

From Problem 8.15, the change of volume per unit volume is given by

$$\Delta V/V = \varepsilon_x(1 - 2\mu) = 0.001(1 - 0.66) = 0.00034$$

Consequently, the change of volume of the entire bar is $\Delta V = 2(2)(10)(0.00034) = 0.0136 \text{ in}^3$.

The original volume of the bar in the unstrained state is 40 in^3. Since a tensile force increases the volume, the final volume under load is 40.0136 in^3. Modern methods of measurement, employing laser beams, permit measurements having the accuracy implied here.

8.17 Strain measurements are often made with electric resistance gages, which consist essentially of fine wires cemented to the material being strained. One commercially available gage has three wires oriented at 60° to one another, as shown in Fig. 8-14. If $\varepsilon_0 = 220 \times 10^{-6}$, $\varepsilon_{60} = 120 \times 10^{-6}$, and $\varepsilon_{120} = -180 \times 10^{-6}$, determine the principal stresses and directions. The material under load is steel, for which $E = 200\,\text{GPa}$ and $\mu = 0.3$.

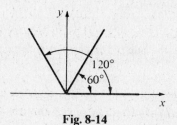

Fig. 8-14

We apply (8.10), which gives the normal strain at an angle θ to the x axis, in each of the directions of measured strain:

$$\varepsilon_0 = \varepsilon_x = 220 \times 10^{-6}$$

$$\varepsilon_{60} = \frac{\varepsilon_x + \varepsilon_y}{2} + \frac{\varepsilon_x - \varepsilon_y}{2}\cos 120° + \frac{\gamma_{xy}}{2}\sin 120° = 120 \times 10^{-6}$$

$$\varepsilon_{120} = \frac{\varepsilon_x + \varepsilon_y}{2} + \frac{\varepsilon_x - \varepsilon_y}{2}\cos 240° + \frac{\gamma_{xy}}{2}\sin 240° = -180 \times 10^{-6}$$

These three equations contain the three unknowns ε_x, ε_y, and γ_{xy}. Direct solution yields

$$\varepsilon_x = 220 \times 10^{-6} \qquad \varepsilon_y = -113 \times 10^{-6} \qquad \gamma_{xy} = 346 \times 10^{-6}$$

The principal strains are now found with (8.12):

$$\varepsilon_{1,2} = \left[\frac{220 - 113}{2} \pm \sqrt{\left(\frac{220 + 113}{2}\right)^2 + \left(\frac{346}{2}\right)^2}\right] \times 10^{-6}$$

from which $\varepsilon_1 = 293.5 \times 10^{-6}$ and $\varepsilon_2 = -186.5 \times 10^{-6}$.

The two-dimensional form of Hooke's law (8.17) is

$$\sigma_1 = \frac{E}{1 - \mu^2}(\varepsilon_1 + \mu\varepsilon_2) \qquad \sigma_2 = \frac{E}{1 - \mu^2}(\varepsilon_2 + \mu\varepsilon_1)$$

If we now substitute the principal strains in these relations, we get the principal stresses,

$$\sigma_1 = \frac{200 \times 10^9}{1 - (0.3)^2} \left[293.5 \times 10^{-6} + (0.3)(-186.5 \times 10^{-6}) \right] = 52.1 \text{ MPa}$$

$$\sigma_2 = \frac{200 \times 10^9}{1 - (0.3)^2} \left[-186.5 \times 10^{-6} + (0.3)(293.5 \times 10^{-6}) \right] = -21.6 \text{ MPa}$$

The directions of the principal stresses are given by (8.13):

$$\tan 2\theta_p = \frac{\gamma_{xy}}{\varepsilon_x - \varepsilon_y} = \frac{346}{220 + 113} = 1.039$$

so that $2\theta_p = 46.09°$ and $\theta_p = 23.05°$ and $113.05°$.

8.18   A solid steel sphere that is part of a deep-submergence system is subject to a hydrostatic pressure of 50 MPa. The sphere is 200 mm in diameter, $E = 210 \text{ GPa}$, and $\mu = 0.3$. Determine the decrease in the volume of the sphere at pressure.

Using (8.19) we obtain, for the bulk modulus,

$$K = \frac{E}{3(1 - 2\mu)} = \frac{210 \times 10^9 \text{ N/m}^2}{3(1 - 0.6)} = 175 \times 10^9 \text{ N/m}^2$$

Now, again from (8.19), the change of volume per unit volume is

$$e = -p/K = -\frac{50 \times 10^6 \text{ N/m}^2}{175 \times 10^9 \text{ N/m}^2} = -0.2857 \times 10^{-3}$$

The volume of the sphere prior to loading is $\frac{4}{3}\pi(0.1 \text{ m})^3 = 0.004189 \text{ m}^3$.   The total change of volume is thus

$$\Delta V = (-0.2857 \times 10^{-3})(0.004189 \text{ m}^3) = 1.196 \times 10^{-6} \text{ m}^3 = -1196 \text{ mm}^3$$

8.19   An element is in a state of stress such that a stress σ_x is exerted in the x direction, while lateral contraction is free to occur in the z direction but is completely restrained in the y direction. Find the ratio of the stress in the x direction to the strain in that direction. Also find the ratio of the strain in the z direction to that in the x direction.

Let us examine the general statement of Hooke's law, (8.16). If in those equations we set $\sigma_z = 0$ and $\varepsilon_y = 0$ to satisfy the conditions of the problem, then we obtain

$$\varepsilon_x = \frac{1}{E}(\sigma_x - \mu\sigma_y) \qquad \varepsilon_y = \frac{1}{E}(\sigma_y - \mu\sigma_x) = 0 \qquad \varepsilon_z = \frac{1}{E}\left[-\mu(\sigma_x + \sigma_y) \right]$$

From the second of these equations,

$$\sigma_y = \mu\sigma_x$$

Substituting in the first, we obtain

$$\varepsilon_x = \frac{1}{E}(\sigma_x - \mu^2\sigma_x) = \frac{1 - \mu^2}{E}\sigma_x$$

Solving this for σ_x as a function of ε_x and substituting in the third equation above, we have

$$\varepsilon_z = -\frac{\mu}{E}(\sigma_x + \mu\sigma_x) = -\frac{\mu(1 + \mu)}{E}\frac{\varepsilon_x E}{1 - \mu^2} = -\frac{\mu\varepsilon_x}{1 - \mu}$$

We may now form the ratios

$$\frac{\sigma_x}{\varepsilon_x} = \frac{E}{1 - \mu^2} \qquad \text{and} \qquad -\frac{\varepsilon_z}{\varepsilon_x} = \frac{\mu}{1 - \mu}$$

The first quantity, $E/(1 - \mu^2)$, is usually denoted as the *effective modulus of elasticity* and is useful in the theory of thin plates and shells. The second ratio, $\mu/(1 - \mu)$, is called the *effective value of Poisson's ratio*.

8.20 Find one type of solution of the two-dimensional equilibrium equations (8.20) that also satisfies the compatibility equation (8.15).

Let us neglect the body forces X and Y in the equilibrium equations (8.20), so that they become

$$\frac{\partial \sigma_x}{\partial x} + \frac{\partial \tau_{xy}}{\partial y} = 0 \qquad \frac{\partial \sigma_y}{\partial y} + \frac{\partial \tau_{xy}}{\partial x} = 0 \tag{1}$$

The two-dimensional form of Hooke's law (8.16) is

$$\varepsilon_x = \frac{1}{E}(\sigma_x - \mu\sigma_y) \qquad \varepsilon_y = \frac{1}{E}(\sigma_y - \mu\sigma_x) \tag{2}$$

We now introduce the function $\Phi(x, y)$, known as *Airy's stress function* and defined by the following three equations:

$$\sigma_x = \frac{\partial^2 \Phi}{\partial y^2} \qquad \sigma_y = \frac{\partial^2 \Phi}{\partial x^2} \qquad \tau_{xy} = -\frac{\partial^2 \Phi}{\partial x\, \partial y} \tag{3}$$

It is readily seen that the stresses (3) satisfy the equilibrium equations (1).

If we next introduce (3) into (2) and substitute the resulting strain expressions into the compatibility equation (8.15), we get

$$\frac{\partial^4 \Phi}{\partial x^4} + 2\frac{\partial^4 \Phi}{\partial x^2\, \partial y^2} + \frac{\partial^4 \Phi}{\partial y^4} = 0 \tag{4}$$

The quantity ∇^4, called the *biharmonic operator*, is defined as

$$\nabla^4 = \frac{\partial^4}{\partial x^4} + 2\frac{\partial^4}{\partial x^2\, \partial y^2} + \frac{\partial^4}{\partial y^4} \tag{5}$$

and the quantity ∇^2, the *Laplacian operator*, is defined as

$$\nabla^2 = \frac{\partial^2}{\partial x^2} + \frac{\partial^2}{\partial y^2} \tag{6}$$

Thus, (4) becomes

$$\nabla^4 \Phi = 0 \tag{7}$$

This last equation is a concise formulation of the problem. Any solution $\Phi(x, y)$ that satisfies (7) automatically satisfies the equations of equilibrium for the element as well as the compatibility equation. Solutions may be found either by using complex-variables techniques or by trial and error.

As an example, the polynomial

$$\Phi_2 = A_2 x^2 + B_2 xy + C_2 y^2 \tag{8}$$

can readily be shown to satisfy (7) for all values of A_2, B_2, and C_2. The polynomial

$$\Phi_3 = A_3 x^3 + B_3 x^2 y + C_3 xy^2 + D_3 y^3 \tag{9}$$

can readily be shown to satisfy (7) for all values of the constants A_3, B_3, C_3, and D_3. On the other hand, the polynomial

$$\Phi_4 = A_4 x^4 + B_4 x^3 y + C_4 x^2 y^2 + D_4 xy^3 + E_4 y^4 \tag{10}$$

satisfies (7) only if $E_4 = -A_4 - \frac{1}{6}C_4$. Many engineering problems can be solved by applying (8), (9), and (10), as you will see in following chapters.

8.21   Can the stress function $\Phi = Bx^3y^2$ describe a state of plane stress for the case of zero body forces?

> We need to determine whether the given function satisfies (7) of Problem 8.20. Applying the biharmonic operator, we obtain
>
> $$\nabla^4(Bx^3y^2) = \frac{\partial^4}{\partial x^4}(Bx^3y^2) + 2\frac{\partial^4}{\partial x^2\,\partial y^2}(Bx^3y^2) + \frac{\partial^4}{\partial y^4}(Bx^3y^2) = 0 + 24Bx + 0$$
>
> Because $\nabla^4\Phi$ does not vanish for all values of x and y, (7) is not satisfied and $\Phi = Bx^3y^2$ cannot describe a state of plane stress.

Supplementary Problems

8.22   At a point in a loaded elastic solid the stresses are

$$\sigma_x = -40\ \text{MPa} \qquad \sigma_y = 100\ \text{MPa} \qquad \sigma_z = 30\ \text{MPa}$$

$$\tau_{xy} = 30\ \text{MPa} \qquad \tau_{xz} = -15\ \text{MPa} \qquad \tau_{yz} = 25\ \text{MPa}$$

Find the normal and shearing stresses on a plane through the point whose normal has direction cosines $l_1 = 0.5$, $m_1 = 0.25$,   and $n_1 = 0.829$ with respect to the x, y, and z axes.

Ans. $\sigma = 23.1\ \text{MPa};\quad \tau = 65.8\ \text{MPa}$

8.23   For the three-dimensional state of stress described by

$$\sigma_x = -18\ \text{MPa} \qquad \sigma_y = -30\ \text{MPa} \qquad \sigma_z = 12\ \text{MPa}$$

$$\tau_{xy} = 7\ \text{MPa} \qquad \tau_{yz} = 11\ \text{MPa} \qquad \tau_{xz} = -3\ \text{MPa}$$

determine the principal stresses and their directions analytically.

Ans. $\sigma_1 = -15\ \text{MPa}, l_1 = 0.92, m_1 = 0.39, n_1 = -0.05;\quad \sigma_2 = 15\ \text{MPa}, l_2 = -0.04, m_2 = 0.23, n_2 = 0.97;$
$\sigma_3 = -36\ \text{MPa}, l_3 = -0.39, m_3 = 0.89, n_3 = -0.23$

8.24   Use the FORTRAN program of Problem 8.5 to determine the principal stresses and directions for an element subject to the following three-dimensional state of stress:

$$\sigma_x = -60\ \text{MPa} \qquad \sigma_y = 50\ \text{MPa} \qquad \sigma_z = -30\ \text{MPa}$$

$$\tau_{xy} = -35\ \text{MPa} \qquad \tau_{yz} = 110\ \text{MPa} \qquad \tau_{zx} = 70\ \text{MPa}$$

Ans.

```
DETERMINATION OF 3-D PRINCIPAL STRESSES...

ENTER THE STATE OF STRESS AT THE POINT DESIRED;
INPUT SIGX, SIGY, SIGZ :
? -60,50,-30
INPUT TAUXY, TAUYZ, TAUXZ :
? -35,110,70


   SIGX        SIGY        SIGZ        TAUXY       TAUXZ       TAUYZ
  -60.00      50.00      -30.00      -35.00       70.00      110.00

FOR THE STATE OF STRESS SHOWN, THE THREE PRINCIPAL
STRESSES AND THEIR DIRECTION COSINES ARE AS FOLLOWS...

  NO.      SIG(I)       L(I)        M(I)         N(I)
   1        -3.27      -.7996      .3999       -.4481
   2       127.86       .0706      .8034        .5912
   3      -164.60       .5964      .4410       -.6707
```

8.25   A plane element in a body is subject to the stresses shown in Fig. 8-15. Determine analytically (*a*) the principal stresses and their directions and (*b*) the maximum shearing stresses and the directions of the planes on which they occur.

Ans.   (*a*) $\sigma_{max} = 21.6$ MPa at $144°13'$, $\sigma_{min} = -41.6$ MPa at $54°13'$;   (*b*) $\tau_{max} = 31.6$ MPa at $9°13'$

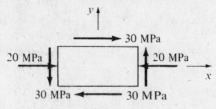

Fig. 8-15

8.26   For the element treated in Problem 8.25, determine the normal and shearing stresses acting on a plane inclined at 30° to the *x* axis.   *Ans.* $\sigma = -30$ MPa; $\tau = -24.4$ MPa

8.27   A plane element is subject to the stresses $\sigma_x = 8000$ lb/in^2 and $\sigma_y = 8000$ lb/in^2.   Determine analytically the maximum shearing stress existing in the element.   *Ans.*   0

8.28   A plane element is subject to the stresses shown in Fig. 8-16. Determine analytically (*a*) the principal stresses and their directions and (*b*) the maximum shearing stresses and the directions of the planes on which they act.   *Ans.*   (*a*) $\sigma_{max} = 181$ MPa at $121°45'$, $\sigma_{min} = 69$ MPa at $31°45'$;   (*b*) $\tau_{max} = 56$ MPa at $76°45'$

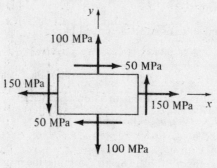

Fig. 8-16

8.29   A plane element is subject to the stresses shown in Fig. 8-17. Determine analytically (*a*) the principal stresses and their directions and (*b*) the maximum shearing stresses and the directions of the planes on which they act.

Ans.   (*a*) $\sigma_{max} = 200$ lb/in^2 at $50°40'$, $\sigma_{min} = -20,200$ lb/in^2 at $140°40'$;   (*b*) $\tau_{max} = 10,200$ lb/in^2 at $5°40'$

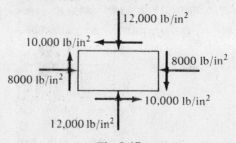

Fig. 8-17

8.30   Use the BASIC program of Problem 8.10 to determine the principal stresses and directions for the element shown in Fig. 8-18.

Ans.   SIG(1) = 58,027.8;   SIG(2) = 21,972.2;   THETA = -28.155

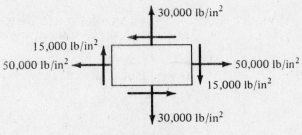

Fig. 8-18

8.31   Use the BASIC program developed in Problem 8.10 to determine the principal stresses and directions for the element in Fig. 8-19.   *Ans.*   SIG(1) = 114.34;   SIG(2) = −74.3398;   THETA = −16.0027

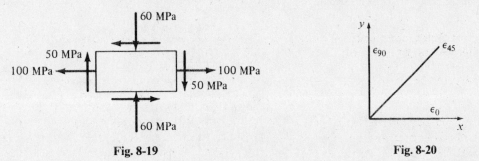

Fig. 8-19   **Fig. 8-20**

8.32   An electric strain gage with three wires oriented at 45° to one another as shown in Fig. 8-20 measures the following strains: $\varepsilon_0 = 175 \times 10^{-6}$, $\varepsilon_{45} = -100 \times 10^{-6}$,   and $\varepsilon_{90} = 125 \times 10^{-6}$.   The material under load is an aluminum alloy for which $E = 12 \times 10^6$ lb/in^2 and $\mu = 0.3$.   Determine the principal stresses and directions.   *Ans.*   4890 lb/in^2 and 250 lb/in^2;   −42.15° and 47.86°

8.33   A plane element has a measured strain in the x direction of -150×10^{-6}, a strain in the y direction of 100×10^{-6}, and a corresponding shear strain of 40×10^6. Determine the normal strain in a direction making an angle of 30° with the x axis.   *Ans.* -70.2×10^{-6}

8.34   A square aluminum plate is subject to the biaxial loading shown in Fig. 8-21. For this material, $E = 75$ GPa   and $\mu = 0.3$.   Find the change in the length of the diagonal OB due to the loading.

Ans.   2.259 mm

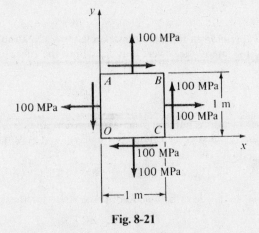

Fig. 8-21

8.35   A thin steel plate has the dimensions shown in Fig. 8-22 and is 1 cm thick. It is loaded by a force of 900 kN in the x direction and has a circle of diameter 0.1 m scribed at the center of the plate. Find the change in the diameter of this circle in the y direction due to the loading.   *Ans.* -0.045 mm

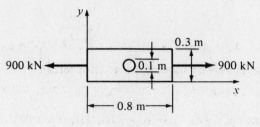

Fig. 8-22

8.36 A rectangular steel plate, 2 ft by 3 ft by 0.4 in thick, is subject to the biaxial loading shown in Fig. 8-23. For $E = 30 \times 10^6$ lb/in^2 and $\mu = 0.3$, determine the change in the thickness of the plate due to the loading.   *Ans.* -0.0003 in

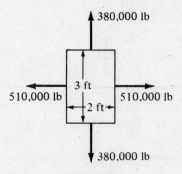

Fig. 8-23

8.37 A solid aluminum right circular cylinder is subject to a hydrostatic pressure of 300 lb/in^2. The cylinder has a radius of 2 in and a length of 10 in. For the aluminum, $E = 10 \times 10^6$ lb/in^2 and $\mu = 0.3$. Find the change in the volume of the cylinder due to the pressure.   *Ans.* -0.045 in^3

8.38 Consider an element in which a stress σ_x is exerted in one direction and lateral contraction is completely restrained in the other two directions. Find the effective modulus of elasticity and the effective value of Poisson's ratio.

   Ans. $E_{\text{eff}} = \dfrac{E(1 - \mu)}{(1 - 2\mu)(1 + \mu)}; \quad \mu_{\text{eff}} = 0$

8.39 A bar is subject to compression in the axial direction. Lateral expansion is restrained to half the amount it would ordinarily be if the lateral faces were load-free. Find the effective modulus of elasticity.

   Ans. $E_{\text{eff}} = \dfrac{E(1 - \mu)}{1 - \mu - \mu^2}$

8.40 A bar of uniform cross section is subject to uniaxial tension and develops a strain in the direction of the force of 1/800. Calculate the change of volume per unit volume. Assume $\mu = \frac{1}{3}$.

   Ans.   1/2400 (increase)

8.41 Can the function $\Phi = Ax^2y$ describe a state of plane stress for the case of zero body forces?

   Ans.   Yes

8.42 Can the function $\Phi = A(x^4y)$ describe a state of plane stress for the case of zero body forces?

   Ans.   No

8.43   Can the function

$$\Phi_5 = A_5 x^5 + B_5 x^4 y + C_5 x^3 y^2 + D_5 x^2 y^3 + E_5 x y^4 + F_5 y^5$$

describe a state of plane stress for the case of zero body forces?

Ans.   Yes, for the special case $E_5 = -5A_5 - C_5$, $F_5 = -\frac{1}{5}(B_5 + D_5)$

8.44   Consider the functions $\varepsilon_x = 4y^3$, $\varepsilon_y = 3x^2 y$,   and $\gamma_{xy} = -3x^2 y^2$.   Do these functions describe a physically possible state of strain in a body subject to two-dimensional loading?   *Ans.*   No

Chapter 9

Uniform Tension, Compression, and Shear

UNIFORM TENSION OR COMPRESSION

If we set $A_2 = B_2 = 0$ in (8) of Problem 8.20, that equation becomes $\Phi_2 = C_2 y^2$. If we now apply (3) of Problem 8.20 to Φ_2, we obtain

$$\sigma_x = \frac{\partial^2 \Phi_2}{\partial y^2} = 2C_2 = \text{constant} \qquad \sigma_y = \tau_{xy} = 0$$

Thus, for loading within the linear portion of the stress-strain curve (which is where these equations apply), the stress function Φ_2 describes the case of a bar lying along the x axis and loaded in uniform tension or compression. This is a special case of Problem 8.1 wherein only σ_x is different from zero.

AXIALLY LOADED CONSTANT-CROSS-SECTION BAR

For a bar of uniform cross section along its length L, of cross-sectional area A, and of modulus of elasticity E, subject to a load **P** acting along the axis of the bar and through the centroid of the cross section, the change Δ in the length of the bar due to the loading is

$$\Delta = \frac{PL}{AE}$$

where $P = |\mathbf{P}|$. If the bar is loaded in tension, it elongates by an amount Δ. If it is loaded in compression, it contracts by this amount. (See Problems 9.1 through 9.3.)

AXIALLY LOADED VARIABLE-CROSS-SECTION BAR

If the loaded bar has varying cross sections along its length, as in Fig. 9-1a, a computerized solution for the change in its length is appropriate. If the bar is in the form of a flat slab (Fig. 9-1b) or has a circular cross section all along its length (Fig. 9-1c), the change in length is readily found with the FORTRAN program of Problem 9.4. (See also Problem 9.5.)

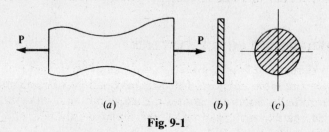

(a)   *(b)*   *(c)*

Fig. 9-1

EQUATIONS OF STATICS

The statics equations discussed earlier in this book apply to a single bar or system of bars that is in equilibrium. These equations are valid whether or not the material of the bar is within its elastic range.

150

GEOMETRY OF DEFORMATION

In this chapter we consider many systems of pinned bars subject to external loads applied only at the pinned joints, or nodes. We assume that the original (overall) geometry of the bar system is not changed significantly during deformation under such loading. Each bar may stretch or contract and, in addition, may rotate as a rigid body about either of its pinned ends. However, there is no bending of any bar, and only small normal strains are developed. These strains give rise to displacements that are linear functions of the applied loads. All such displacements are small compared to some characteristic dimension of the bar, e.g., its length. (See Problem 9.6.)

There are also exceptional structures in which each bar of the system behaves as a linear spring element while the entire system undergoes a deformation that is *nonlinear* with respect to the applied load. These systems are characterized by significant changes of the original geometry during the loading process. One example is discussed in Problem 9.7.

For every bar system subject to loading at its nodes, *compatibility* of displacements at joints must be enforced. (See Problem 9.9.)

THERMAL EFFECTS

Some or all of the bars of a pinned bar system may undergo changes of temperature (which are assumed to be constant along the length of any one bar). Such temperature changes induce forces in and displacements of bars, since the entire system of bars is usually fully or partially constrained by external bodies. Both mechanical and thermal effects on the bar system must be considered, and joint compatibility must be enforced. (See Problem 9.8.)

MANUFACTURING ERRORS, MISALIGNMENT

Occasionally, bar members are accidentally fabricated slightly longer or shorter than the specified design length. Even very small fabrication errors of this type may induce significant initial (locked-in) stresses prior to the application of external forces or temperature changes. (See Problem 9.16.)

STATICALLY DETERMINATE FORCE SYSTEMS

If the values of all the external forces that act on a body can be determined from the equations of static equilibrium alone, then the force system is statically determinate *externally*. Further, if all the bar forces can be found from statics alone, then the system is statically determinate *internally*. A system may be determinate externally, yet indeterminate internally. (See Problems 9.9 and 9.10.)

STATICALLY INDETERMINATE FORCE SYSTEMS

In many cases the external forces acting on a body cannot be determined from the equations of statics alone, because there are more unknown forces than equations of equilibrium. The system is then statically *indeterminate* externally. Solution requires the use of not only the equations of statics but also equations based upon compatible deformations of the nodal points. These equations are all solved simultaneously. (See Problems 9.11 to 9.15.)

UNIFORM SHEARING STRESS

If we set $A_2 = C_2 = 0$ in (8) of Problem 8.20, then that equation becomes $\Phi_2 = B_2 xy$. For loading within the elastic range for shearing, this corresponds to a constant shearing stress over the cross section of a bar. Shearing stresses arise in virtually all mechanical systems subject to applied forces and/or thermal effects. Excessive shearing stresses on the thin filamentary reinforcements in modern composite materials may lead to separation of the filament from the epoxy matrix and subsequent sudden collapse of the system. (See Problems 9.18 and 9.19.)

ANALYSIS FOR ULTIMATE STRENGTH (LIMIT DESIGN)

We assume that the stress-strain curves for the materials of concern here are of the form indicated in Fig. 9-2, i.e., characterizing an extremely ductile material such as structural steel. This representation implies that the material is incapable of developing stresses greater than that at the yield point.

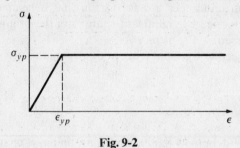

Fig. 9-2

In a statically indeterminate system, any inelastic behavior changes the conditions of constraint. Under these altered conditions, the loading that the system can carry usually increases over that predicted on the basis of completely elastic behavior. In one design method, termed *limit design* when applied to statically indeterminate structures, the *ultimate load*, under which some or all portions of the structure would reach the yield point and cause "collapse" of the system, is found and then divided by some factor of safety to determine a safe *working load*. (For applications, see Problems 9.20 and 9.21.)

Solved Problems

Elastic Analysis: Uniform Normal Stresses

9.1   A tensile load **P** acts on the ends of an initially straight bar of length L, constant cross-sectional area A, and modulus of elasticity E. Show that the total elongation due to the load is $\Delta = PL/AE$.

   The situation is shown in Fig. 9-3. From (*8*) of Problem 8.20 with $A_2 = B_2 = 0$ and (*3*) of the same problem, we have

$$\Phi_2 = C_2 y^2 \qquad \text{and} \qquad \sigma_x = \frac{\partial^2 \Phi_2}{\partial y^2} = 2C_2$$

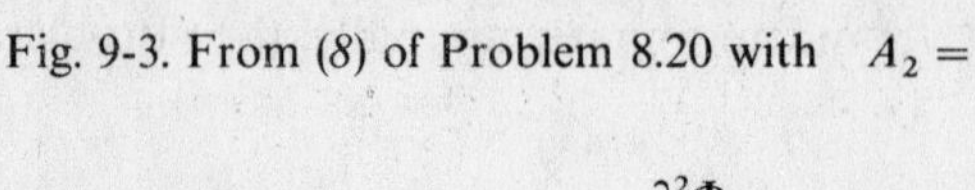

Fig. 9-3

The stress in the axial direction is thus $2C_2$, which is constant over the bar. By definition, the normal stress is given by P/A. Thus, $\sigma_x = 2C_2 = P/A$.

   Now, from (*2*) of Problem 8.20, the strain in the x direction is

$$\varepsilon_x = \frac{1}{E}(\sigma_x - \mu\sigma_y) = \frac{1}{E}\left(\frac{P}{A} - 0\right) = \frac{P}{AE}$$

Because this strain is independent of x, it is constant along the length L. And, since strain is defined to be change in length per unit length, the change in the total length L is $\Delta = PL/AE$.

9.2   A weightless bar of length 7 m is supported at its left end A as shown in Fig. 9-4 and subject to the forces shown at B, C, and D. The bar has a constant cross section of 10 cm^2 and is of steel for which $E = 200$ GPa.   Determine the total change in the length of the bar due to the loading.

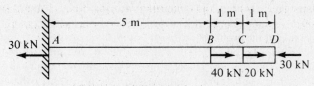

Fig. 9-4

Each of the three regions of the bar is in equilibrium. The free-body diagram of region AB is constructed by realizing that the resultant force acting on either side of any section cut through the bar in that region is a tensile force of 30 kN. In region BC, the resultant force on either side of any section is a compressive force of 10 kN. (On the left we have $30 - 40 = -10$ kN,   and on the right $20 - 30 = -10$ kN.) In region CD, a compressive force of 30 kN acts on every section. Thus, the free-body diagrams of the three regions appear as in Fig. 9-5.

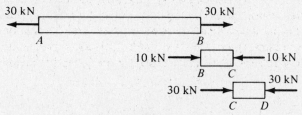

Fig. 9-5

In each portion of the bar, the length changes by PL/AE, where P denotes the magnitude of the axial force (tensile or compressive) acting in that portion. Thus, for the entire bar we have

$$\Delta = \frac{(30{,}000 \text{ N})(5 \text{ m})}{AE} + \frac{(-10{,}000 \text{ N})(1 \text{ m})}{AE} + \frac{(-30{,}000 \text{ N})(1 \text{ m})}{AE}$$

$$= \frac{110{,}000 \text{ N·m}}{(10 \text{ cm}^2)\left(\dfrac{1 \text{ m}}{100 \text{ cm}}\right)^2 (200 \times 10^9 \text{ N/m}^2)} = 5.5 \times 10^{-4} \text{ m} = 0.55 \text{ mm}$$

9.3   Modern composite materials are often composed of epoxy reinforced with filaments of extremely small diameter. One common reinforcement material is aluminum oxide, which in filamentary form has $E = 350 \times 10^6$ lb/in^2 and a tensile (breaking) strength of 4×10^6 lb/in^2. For a fiber of diameter 0.001 in and length 0.5 in, find the axial load corresponding to a normal stress of 3×10^6 lb/in^2 as well as the elongation of the fiber at that load.

By definition, $\sigma = P/A$. Hence, we have

$$P = \sigma A = (3 \times 10^6 \text{ lb/in}^2)(\pi/4)(0.001 \text{ in})^2 = 2.356 \text{ lb}$$

The elongation produced by this axial load is

$$\Delta = \frac{PL}{AE} = \frac{(2.356 \text{ lb})(0.5 \text{ in})}{(\pi/4)(0.001 \text{ in})^2(350 \times 10^6 \text{ lb/in}^2)} = 0.0043 \text{ in}$$

9.4   Consider an elastic bar of variable cross section, loaded in tension or compression at its ends, like that in Fig. 9-1. The variation of its cross section along its length may be known analytically, or in the form of measurements taken at a number of locations along its axis. Develop a FORTRAN program that determines the change in the length of the bar due to the loading for the cases in which (a) the bar is a slab of uniform thickness t (Fig. 9-1b) and (b) every cross section of the bar is circular (Fig. 9-1c).

The equation $\Delta = PL/AE$ cannot be applied to the entire length L of the bar, since it is derived under the assumption that the bar is of constant cross section. However, we may divide the length of the bar into a number of segments, in each of which the cross section is regarded as constant. If we have an equation $y = f(x)$ for the profile of the bar in Fig. 9-1, we can divide the length of the bar into infinitesimal segments each of length dx, take the cross section to be constant within each segment, and then use the calculus to apply $\Delta = PL/AE$ to all the segments and sum the results. If the bar consists of a finite number of segments whose dimensions have been measured, we can employ these measurements to find and sum the elongations (or contractions) for all the segments.

This approach is represented by the FORTRAN program that follows. The program is applicable to any bar of irregular cross section subject to axial tension or compression and covered under cases (a) and (b) as given above. Tensile loadings are, as usual, regarded as positive, so that positive axial deformations represent elongations and negative deformations represent compressions.

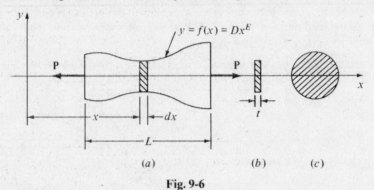

Fig. 9-6

The various quantities involved in the program are shown in Fig. 9-6. Note that in the equation $y = Dx^E$ describing the profile of the bar, E is an exponent and not the elastic modulus. The bar is, further, assumed to be symmetrical about its longitudinal axis. If the profile is given as a set of measurements, those measurements must have been taken at equal intervals along the bar.

```
00100********************************************************************
00110              PROGRAM SLBTEN1(INPUT,OUTPUT)
00120********************************************************************
00130*
00140*      AUTHOR: KATHLEEN DERWIN
00150*      DATE  : JANUARY 15,1988
00160*
00170*  BRIEF DESCRIPTION:
00180*    THIS PROGRAM DETERMINES THE CHANGE OF LENGTH OF A BAR DUE
00190*  TO AXIAL TENSION OR COMPRESSION. THE BAR MAY BE A CONSTANT
00200*  THICKNESS, VARIABLE WIDTH RECTANGULAR SLAB, OR A SOLID CIRCULAR
00210*  ROD WITH VARIABLE DIAMETER. IN EITHER CASE THE SHAFT IS CENTRALLY
00220*  LOADED BY AN AXIAL FORCE.
00230*    THE VARYING WIDTH (OF THE SLAB) OR DIAMETER (OF THE ROD) MAY
00240*  BE DESCRIBED EITHER ANALYTICALLY AS  Y = D*(X**E) WHERE X IS THE
00250*  GEOMETRIC AXIS OF THE BAR, OR NUMERICALLY USING THE MAGNITUDE OF
00260*  Y AT EACH END OF  N SEGMENTS, MEANING N+1 VALUES.
00270*
00280*  INPUT:
00290*    THE USER IS PROMPTED FOR THE TOTAL BAR LENGTH, THE ELASTIC
00300*  MODULUS, AND THE AXIAL LOAD. THE USER IS THEN ASKED IF THE
00310*  BAR IS BOUNDED BY A KNOWN FUNCTION, AS WELL AS THE SHAPE OF ITS
```

```
00320*     X-SECTION. FOR THE CASE OF THE SLAB, THE UNIFORM THICKNESS IS
00330*     ALSO ASKED FOR... IF THE FUNCTION IS KNOWN, THE CONSTANTS ARE
00340*     THEN PROMPTED AND THE ENDPOINTS OF THE BAR ON THE X-AXIS INPUTTED;
00350*     ALTERNATELY, THE NUMBER OF SEGMENTS AND MEASURED HEIGHTS/DIAMETERS
00360*     MUST BE ENTERED.
00370*
00380*     OUTPUT:
00390*         THE TOTAL ELONGATION OF THE BAR IS DETERMINED AND PRINTED.
00400*
00410*     VARIABLES:
00420*         L,T,EM      ---   LENGTH,THICKNESS,ELASTIC MODULUS OF BAR
00430*         D,E         ---   CONSTANTS OF Y = D*(X**E) GOVERNING BAR BOUNDARY
00440*         X0,XN       ---   ENDPOINTS OF SHAFT ON X-AXIS
00450*         P           ---   CENTRALLY APPLIED AXIAL LOAD
00460*         A(100)      ---   INDIVIDUAL SEGMENT HEIGHTS/DIAMETERS
00470*         AREA        ---   X-SECTIONAL AREA OF OF EACH SMALL INCREMENT
00480*         ANS         ---   DETERMINE IF USER HAS A KNOWN FUNCTION
00490*         TYPE        ---   DETERMINE BAR X-SECTION
00500*         DELTA       ---   UNIFORM BAR ELONGATION
00510*         LEN         ---   LENGTH OF INCREMENTAL ELEMENT
00520*
00530*******************************************************************************
00540*******************************************************************************
00550*                       MAIN PROGRAM
00560*******************************************************************************
00570*******************************************************************************
00580*
00590*     VARIABLE DECLARATION
00600*
00610       REAL I,T,L,EM,D,E,X0,XN,P,DELTA,A(100),AREA,LEN
00620       INTEGER ANS,TYPE,NUM,J
00630*
00640*         USER INPUT PROMPTS
00650*
00660       PRINT*,'ENTER THE TOTAL LENGTH OF THE BAR (IN M OR INCHES):'
00670       READ*,L
00680       PRINT*,'ENTER THE ELASTIC MODULUS (IN PASCALS OR PSI) :'
00690       READ*,EM
00700       PRINT*,'ENTER THE UNIFORM AXIAL LOAD (IN NEWTONS OR LBS) :'
00710       READ*,P
00720       PRINT*,'PLEASE DENOTE THE BAR X-SECTIONAL SHAPE:'
00730       PRINT*,'ENTER  1--SLAB  ;   2--CIRCULAR ROD'
00740       READ*,TYPE
00750*
00760*         IF A SLAB, PROMPT FOR ITS THICKNESS
00770*
00780       IF (TYPE.EQ.1) THEN
00790          PRINT*,'ENTER THE THICKNESS OF THE SLAB (IN M OR INCHES):'
00800          READ*,T
00810       ENDIF
00820       PRINT*,'DO YOU KNOW THE FUNCTION DESCRIBING THE BAR?'
00830       PRINT*,'ENTER  1--YES  ;   2--NO'
00840       READ*,ANS
00850*
00860*         IF ANS EQUALS ONE, THE USER KNOWS FUNCTION. PROMPT
00870*         FOR CONSTANTS AND ENDPOINTS.
00880*
00890       IF (ANS.EQ.1) THEN
00900          PRINT*,'F(X) = D * (X**E)'
00910          PRINT*,'ENTER D,E:'
00920          READ*,D,E
00930          PRINT*,'ENTER THE X-COORDINATE FOR BOTH ENDS OF THE BAR:'
00940          PRINT*,'(IN M OR INCHES):'
00950          READ*,X0,XN
00960*
```

```
00970      AREA = 0
00980      L=XN-X0
00990      LEN=L/50
01000      DO 20 I = X0,XN,LEN
01010          Y1=(D*(I**E))*2
01020          Y2=(D*((I+LEN)**E))*2
01030          Y=(Y1+Y2)/2
01040          IF(TYPE.EQ.1) THEN
01050              AREA=1/(Y*T) + AREA
01060          ELSE
01070              AREA=4/(3.14159*(Y**2)) + AREA
01080          ENDIF
01090 20 CONTINUE
01100*
01110*          IF ANS EQUALS TWO, THE USER DOES NOT KNOW FUNCTION.
01120*          PROMPT FOR NUMBER OF SEGMENTS AND MEASURED HEIGHTS/DIAMETERS.
01130*
01140      ELSE
01150          PRINT*,'ENTER THE NUMBER OF SECTIONS TO BE CALCULATED:'
01160          READ*,NUM
01170          IF(TYPE.EQ.1) THEN
01180              PRINT*,'ENTER THE HEIGHTS OF THE ENDS FOR SECTIONS 1 TO N:'
01190              PRINT*,'(IN M OR INCHES):'
01200          ELSE
01210              PRINT*,'ENTER THE DIAMETERS OF THE ENDS FOR SECTIONS 1 TO N:'
01220              PRINT*,'(IN M OR INCHES):'
01230          ENDIF
01240*
01250*          INPUT MEASURED HEIGHTS/DIAMETERS
01260*
01270          DO 30 J=1,NUM+1
01280              READ*,A(J)
01290 30      CONTINUE
01300*
01310          AREA = 0
01320          LEN = L/NUM
01330          DO 40 J = 1,NUM+1
01340              Y=(A(J)+A(J+1))/2
01350              IF(TYPE.EQ.1) THEN
01360                  AREA = 1/(Y*T) + AREA
01370              ELSE
01380                  AREA = 4/(3.14159*(Y**2)) + AREA
01390              ENDIF
01400 40      CONTINUE
01410      ENDIF
01420*
01430*          DETERMINING THE ELONGATION OF THE LOADED BAR
01440*
01450      DELTA=(P*LEN*AREA)/EM
01460*
01470      PRINT 50,DELTA
01480*
01490 50 FORMAT(2X,'THE DEFORMATION OF THE BAR IS:',F8.5,' (M OR IN.)')
01500*
01510      STOP
01520      END
```

9.5 A slab that has rectangular cross sections of thickness 15 mm is bounded by the curve $y = 0.1x^{1/2}$ from $x = 1$ m to $x = 1.5$ m, as is shown in Fig. 9-7. The slab is subject to a tensile loading of 1800 kN and has $E = 110$ GPa. Use the FORTRAN program of Problem 9.4 to find the elongation due to the loading.

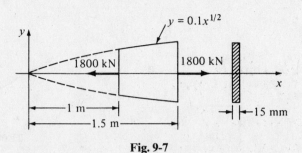

Fig. 9-7

For input data for the program we have a thickness t of 0.015 m; end coordinates of 1 m and 1.5 m; a load of 1800 kN; an elastic modulus of 110×10^9 N/m^2; and, for the parameters of the equation describing the profile of the bar, $D = 0.1$ and $E = 0.5$. The computer run, including responses to prompts, is then as follows:

```
ENTER THE TOTAL LENGTH OF THE BAR (IN M OR INCHES):
? 0.5
ENTER THE ELASTIC MODULUS (IN PASCALS OR PSI) :
? 110E+9
ENTER THE UNIFORM AXIAL LOAD (IN NEWTONS OR LBS) :
? 1800E+3
PLEASE DENOTE THE BAR X-SECTIONAL SHAPE:
ENTER  1--SLAB  ;   2--CIRCULAR ROD
? 1
ENTER THE THICKNESS OF THE SLAB (IN M OR INCHES):
? 0.015
DO YOU KNOW THE FUNCTION DESCRIBING THE BAR?
ENTER  1--YES  ;   2--NO
? 1
F(X) = D * (X**E)
ENTER D,E:
? 0.1,0.5
ENTER THE X-COORDINATE FOR BOTH ENDS OF THE BAR:
(IN M OR INCHES):
? 1,1.5
THE DEFORMATION OF THE BAR IS:  .00250 (M OR IN.)
```

The elongation is thus 2.5 mm.

9.6   Bars AB and BC in Fig. 9-8 are pinned at their ends and support a vertical load of 25,000 lb. Both bars are steel, for which $E = 30 \times 10^6$ lb/in^2. Determine the horizontal and vertical components of the displacement of point B.

If we let F_1 and F_2 represent the bar forces (Fig. 9-9), then we have

$$\Sigma F_x = \frac{1}{\sqrt{2}} F_2 - \frac{\sqrt{3}}{2} F_1 = 0$$

$$\Sigma F_y = \frac{1}{2} F_1 + \frac{1}{\sqrt{2}} F_2 - 25{,}000 = 0$$

from which we find that $F_1 = 18{,}300$ lb and $F_2 = 22{,}400$ lb. The corresponding stresses are

$$\sigma_1 = \frac{F_1}{A_1} = \frac{18{,}300}{0.45} = 40{,}700 \text{ lb/in}^2$$

$$\sigma_2 = \frac{F_2}{A_2} = \frac{22{,}400}{0.75} = 29{,}900 \text{ lb/in}^2$$

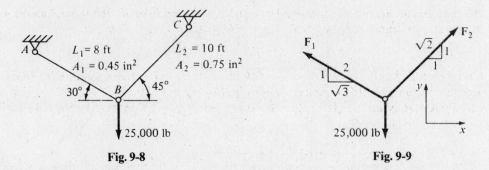

Fig. 9-8   **Fig. 9-9**

These stresses are well within the elastic limits of most types of steel. (It was necessary to determine the stresses before computing the deformations to ensure that the system is acting in the elastic range.)

We now can consider the deformations. If the bars were unlocked (separated) at B, then due to the tensile forces $\mathbf{F}_1$ and $\mathbf{F}_2$ they would elongate by amounts

$$\Delta_1 = \frac{F_1 L_1}{A_1 E} = \frac{(18,300 \text{ lb})(96 \text{ in})}{(0.45 \text{ in}^2)(30 \times 10^6 \text{ lb/in}^2)} = 0.1301 \text{ in}$$

and

$$\Delta_2 = \frac{F_2 L_2}{A_2 E} = \frac{(22,400 \text{ lb})(120 \text{ in})}{(0.75 \text{ in}^2)(30 \times 10^6 \text{ lb/in}^2)} = 0.1196 \text{ in}$$

As is shown in Fig. 9-10, the unlocked bar AB would elongate until B reached P. Bar AB would then rotate as a rigid body about pin A with P moving along the line ef perpendicular to AB. Similarly, the unlocked bar CB would elongate until B reached R. Bar CB would then rotate about pin C with R moving along the line gh perpendicular to CB. (Actually, both these rigid-body movements are along circular arcs, but for the very small rotations involved, the arcs may be approximated as the straight lines ef and gh.) These lines intersect at B', which is the final and correct location of B.

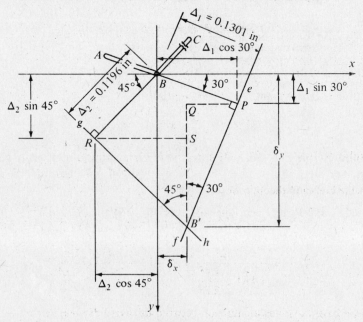

Fig. 9-10

From the geometry of this deformation diagram (with the introduction of auxiliary triangles $B'PQ$ and $B'RS$), we have the relations

$$\tan 30° = \frac{\Delta_1 \cos 30° - \delta_x}{\delta_y - \Delta_1 \sin 30°} \qquad \tan 45° = \frac{\delta_y - \Delta_2 \sin 45°}{\Delta_2 \cos 45° + \delta_x}$$

Since Δ_1 and Δ_2 are already known, these equations can be solved for the two unknowns δ_x and δ_y. The results are the desired displacements $\delta_x = 0.034$ in   and $\delta_y = 0.202$ in.

9.7   The two thin bars in Fig. 9-11a are pinned at A, B, and C and are initially horizontal and of length L when no load is applied. The weight of the bars is negligible. A force $\mathbf{Q}$ is then applied (gradually) at point B. Determine the magnitude of $\mathbf{Q}$ so as to produce a prescribed vertical deflection δ of point B.

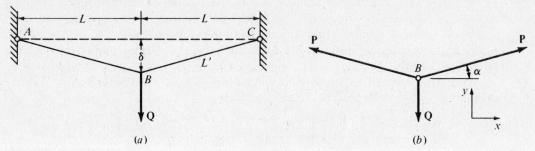

(a)   (b)

Fig. 9-11

This is a system in which the elongations of all the individual members satisfy Hooke's law and yet, for geometric reasons, deflection is *not* proportional to force. Each bar obeys the relation $\Delta = PL/AE$.   Each is initially of length L, and of length L' after the entire load $\mathbf{Q}$ has been applied. Thus,

$$L' - L = \frac{PL}{AE} \tag{1}$$

The free-body diagram of the pin at B is shown in Fig. 9-11b. For equilibrium,

$$\Sigma F_y = 2P \sin \alpha - Q = \theta \qquad \text{or} \qquad Q = 2P \frac{\delta}{L'}$$

Substituting for P from (1) yields

$$Q = 2 \frac{(L' - L)AE}{L} \frac{\delta}{L'} = \frac{2\delta AE}{L} \left(1 - \frac{L}{L'}\right) \tag{2}$$

But $$(L')^2 = L^2 + \delta^2 \tag{3}$$

Consequently, $$Q = \frac{2\delta AE}{L} \left(1 - \frac{L}{\sqrt{L^2 + \delta^2}}\right) \tag{4}$$

Also, from the binomial theorem we have

$$\sqrt{L^2 + \delta^2} = L\left(1 + \frac{\delta^2}{L^2}\right)^{1/2} = L\left(1 + \frac{1}{2}\frac{\delta^2}{L^2} + \cdots\right) \tag{5}$$

and thus $$1 - \frac{L}{L\left(1 + \frac{1}{2}\frac{\delta^2}{L^2}\right)} \approx 1 - \left(1 - \frac{1}{2}\frac{\delta^2}{L^2}\right) = \frac{1}{2}\frac{\delta^2}{L^2} \tag{6}$$

From this we have the following relation between force and displacement:

$$Q \approx \frac{2AE\delta}{L} \frac{\delta^2}{2L^2} = \frac{AE\delta^3}{L^3} \tag{7}$$

Thus the displacement δ is *not* proportional to the force $\mathbf{Q}$ even though Hooke's law holds for each bar individually. $\mathbf{Q}$ and δ do become more nearly proportional as δ becomes larger (assuming that Hooke's law still holds for the elongation of the bars). In this example, moreover, superposition does *not* hold. A characteristic of this system is that the action of the external forces is *appreciably* affected by the small deformations which take place. Then the stresses and displacements are not linear functions of the applied loads, and superposition does not apply.

9.8   The central span of the Golden Gate bridge is 4200 ft long and is supported by a cable from two towers having the geometry shown in Fig. 9-12. These towers are tied back to ground by additional cables as shown. As an approximation, assume that the towers undergo no horizontal deformation, i.e., that they are rigid. For a temperature increase of 40°F, determine the resulting vertical displacement of the midpoint of the cable, which corresponds to the downward vertical displacement of the center point of the bridge deck. The cables are steel, with $E = 30 \times 10^6$ lb/in^2 and coefficient of thermal expansion $\alpha = 6.5 \times 10^{-6}$ (°F)$^{-1}$. Neglect elongations of the vertical supporting cables.

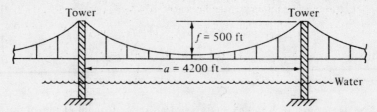

Fig. 9-12

A suspension cable hangs in an arc that is reasonably approximated as parabolic. The cable length, measured along the arc, is given approximately by*

$$L = a\left[1 + \frac{8}{3}\left(\frac{f}{a}\right)^2 - \frac{32}{5}\left(\frac{f}{a}\right)^4\right] \tag{1}$$

where f is the central cable sag, and a the span. Thus, prior to the temperature change the true cable length is

$$L_0 = 4200\left[1 + \frac{8}{3}\left(\frac{500}{4200}\right)^2 - \frac{32}{5}\left(\frac{500}{4200}\right)^4\right] = 4353.3336 \text{ ft}$$

A temperature rise of 40°F lengthens the cable by an amount

$$\Delta L_0 = (4353.33 \text{ ft})[6.5 \times 10^{-6} \text{ (°F)}^{-1}](40°F) = 1.1319 \text{ ft}$$

We now apply (*1*) again, after the temperature change, to find the central sag f_1:

$$L_0 + \Delta L_0 = 4354.46 = 4200\left[1 + \frac{8}{3}\left(\frac{f_1}{4200}\right)^2 - \frac{32}{5}\left(\frac{f_1}{4200}\right)^4\right]$$

This yields the quadratic equation

$$\frac{32}{5}\left(\frac{f_1}{4200}\right)^4 - \frac{8}{3}\left(\frac{f_1}{4200}\right)^2 + 0.0367775 = 0$$

which may be solved by trial and error with a hand calculator to yield $f_1 = 502.28$ ft. The vertical displacement due to the temperature rise is thus $502.28 - 500 = 2.28$ ft.

9.9   The rigid bar in Fig. 9-13 is suspended horizontally by two wires AB and CD. The wires are initially free of stress, until a load of 0.5 kN is hung on the bar. Find the position x of the load,

---

* See W. G. McLean and E. W. Nelson, *Engineering Mechanics*, 4th ed., Schaum's Outline Series (New York: McGraw-Hill, 1988).

as well as the force in each wire, such that the bar remains horizontal. Neglect the weight of the bar and the wires.

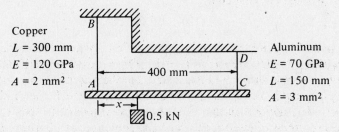

Fig. 9-13

Let P_{Cu} and P_{Al} denote the magnitudes of the forces in the copper and aluminum wires after the 0.5-kN load is applied. For static equilibrium we have (see Fig. 9-14)

$$\Sigma F_y = P_{Cu} + P_{Al} - 500 \text{ N} = 0$$

$$+\circlearrowleft \Sigma M_A = -P_{Al}(0.4) + (500 \text{ N})x = 0$$

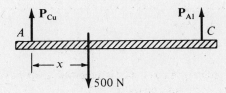

Fig. 9-14

Since the bar is to remain horizontal, the elongations of the wires must be equal. Applying $\Delta = PL/AE$, we thus have

$$\frac{P_{Cu}(0.3 \text{ m})}{(2 \text{ mm}^2)\left(\dfrac{1 \text{ m}}{10^3 \text{ mm}}\right)^2 (120 \times 10^9 \text{ N/m}^2)} = \frac{P_{Al}(0.15 \text{ m})}{(3 \text{ mm}^2)\left(\dfrac{1 \text{ m}}{10^3 \text{ mm}}\right)^2 (70 \times 10^9 \text{ N/m}^2)}$$

This equation, together with the two equilibrium equations, may be solved to yield

$$x = 0.254 \text{ m} \qquad P_{Cu} = 182 \text{ N} \qquad P_{Al} = 318 \text{ N}$$

9.10   Assume that the rigid bar of Problem 9.9 is now loaded by a downward vertical force of 7.5 kN, applied 0.18 m from point A. Determine the vertical displacement of the midpoint of the bar.

If we let P'_{Cu} and P'_{Al} denote the magnitudes of the axial forces in the wires, then the free-body diagram for the bar is that of Fig. 9-15. Then, for static equilibrium,

$$+\circlearrowleft \Sigma M_A = (0.18 \text{ m})(7.5 \text{ kN}) - (0.4 \text{ m})P'_{Al} = 0$$

from which $P'_{Al} = 3.375 \text{ kN}$;   hence, also, $P'_{Cu} = 4.125 \text{ kN}$.

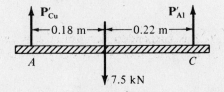

Fig. 9-15

The elongations of the copper and aluminum bars due to these axial forces are

$$\Delta_{Cu} = \frac{(4125 \text{ N})(0.3 \text{ m})}{(2 \text{ mm}^2)\left(\dfrac{1 \text{ m}}{10^3 \text{ mm}}\right)^2 (120 \times 10^9 \text{ N/m}^2)} = 5.156 \times 10^{-3} \text{ m or } 5.156 \text{ mm}$$

$$\Delta_{Al} = \frac{(3375 \text{ N})(0.15 \text{ m})}{(3 \text{ mm}^2)\left(\dfrac{1 \text{ m}}{10^3 \text{ mm}}\right)^2 (70 \times 10^9 \text{ N/m}^2)} = 2.411 \times 10^{-3} \text{ m or } 2.411 \text{ mm}$$

Since these elongations are unequal, the rigid bar AC has rotated about some point whose location is unknown. In Fig. 9-16 the original horizontal configuration of AC is shown by a solid line, and the final configuration by a dashed line. The point of rotation F is at some unknown distance d from C. From the geometry we have

$$\frac{2.411}{d} = \frac{5.156}{0.4 + d} \qquad \text{or} \qquad d = 0.351 \ m$$

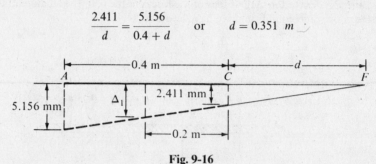

Fig. 9-16

The vertical displacement Δ_1 of the midpoint of bar AC is also found by using similar triangles:

$$\frac{\Delta_1}{0.2 + 0.351} = \frac{2.411}{0.351} \qquad \text{or} \qquad \Delta_1 = 3.78 \text{ mm}$$

9.11   The composite bar in Fig. 9-17a is rigidly attached to the two supports. The left portion of the bar is copper, of uniform cross-sectional area 12 in^2 and length 12 in. The right portion is aluminum, of uniform cross-sectional area 3 in^2 and length 8 in. At a temperature of 80°F the entire assembly is free of stress. The temperature of the structure drops, however, causing the right support to yield 0.001 in in the direction of the contracting metal. Determine the minimum temperature to which the assembly may be subjected in order that the stress in the aluminum does not exceed 24,000 lb/in^2. For copper $E = 16 \times 10^6 \text{ lb/in}^2$ and $\alpha = 9.3 \times 10^{-6} \, (°\text{F})^{-1}$; for aluminum $E = 10 \times 10^6 \text{ lb/in}^2$ and $\alpha = 12.8 \times 10^{-6} \, (°\text{F})^{-1}$.

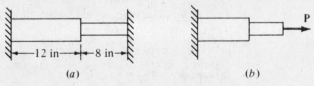

Fig. 9-17

It is perhaps simplest to consider that the bar is cut just to the left of the right supporting wall and is then free to contract due to the temperature drop ΔT. Then the total shortening of the composite bar is

$$(9.3 \times 10^{-6})(12)\Delta T + (12.8 \times 10^{-6})(8)\Delta T \qquad \text{in} \qquad\qquad (1)$$

We must still take into account the action of the support at the right. We do so by assuming it exerts an axial force **P** on the bar, as shown in Fig. 9-17b. For equilibrium, the resultant force acting over any section of either the copper or the aluminum must be equal to **P**. The application of the force **P** stretches the composite bar by an amount

$$\frac{P(12)}{12(16 \times 10^6)} + \frac{P(8)}{3(10 \times 10^6)} \quad \text{in}$$

If the right support were unyielding, we would equate this expression to (*1*). But, since the right support yields 0.001 in, we write

$$\frac{P(12)}{12(16 \times 10^6)} + \frac{P(8)}{3(10 \times 10^6)} = (9.3 \times 10^{-6})(12)\Delta T + (12.8 \times 10^{-6})(8)\Delta T - 0.001 \qquad (2)$$

The stress in the aluminum is not to exceed 24,000 lb/in²; since $\sigma = P/A$, the maximum permissible force is $P = A\sigma = 3(24,0000) = 72,000$ lb. Substituting this value of P in (*2*), we find $\Delta T = 115°F$. Therefore, the temperature may drop 115°F from the original 80°F to a final temperature of $-35°F$.

9.12   The 1.2-m-long steel bar shown in Fig. 9-18 has a circular cross section of area 15 cm² and is attached to an immovable wall at its left end. The wall at the right can move slightly to the left or right, and under the action of a 500-MN force it will move horizontally 1 m; that is, the "spring constant" of the wall is 500 MN/m. Determine the stress in the bar when the temperature of the bar is raised by 55°C. Take $E = 200 \, \text{GPa}$ and $\alpha = 12.5 \times 10^{-6} \, (°C)^{-1}$.

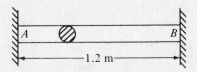

Fig. 9-18

Let us temporarily remove the right-hand restraining wall. The bar then may freely expand to, say, AB' in Fig. 9-19, due to the temperature rise ΔT. This free expansion Δ is given by $\Delta = \alpha L \Delta T$.

However, the true final position of the right end of the bar is B'', which is not necessarily midway between B and B', because the spring force **F** of the wall will push the right end of the bar to the left. That is, the bar is compressed an amount $\Delta_2 = FL/AE$.

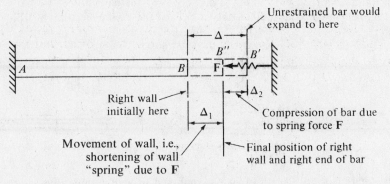

Fig. 9-19

Since the right wall started at position B and has moved to B'', it has moved to the right an amount Δ_1, which we may consider as a shortening of the wall's "spring." Then, as for any linear spring, we may write $F = kx$, or $\Delta_1 = F/k$.

From the geometry, we now have $\Delta_1 + \Delta_2 = \Delta$, or

$$\frac{F}{k} + \frac{FL}{AE} = \alpha L \Delta T \qquad (1)$$

Substituting known values yields

$$\frac{F}{500 \times 10^6 \text{ N/m}} + \frac{F(1.2 \text{ m})}{\left[(15 \text{ cm}^2)\left(\frac{1 \text{ m}}{100 \text{ cm}}\right)^2\right](200 \times 10^9 \text{ N/m}^2)} = [12.5 \times 10^{-6} \, (^\circ\text{C})^{-1}](1.2 \text{ m})(55^\circ\text{C}) \quad (2)$$

from which we get $F = 137,500$ N.   The axial stress is then

$$\sigma = \frac{F}{A} = \frac{137,500 \text{ N}}{15 \text{ cm}^2\left(\frac{1 \text{ m}}{100 \text{ cm}}\right)^2} = 91.7 \text{ MPa}$$

If the right wall is immovable (as well as the left), then its "spring constant" is infinite and the first term on the left side of (*1*) and (*2*) vanishes.

9.13 The rigid bar *AD* in Fig. 9-20 is pinned at *A* and attached to bars *BC* and *ED* as shown. The entire system is initially stressfree, and the weights of all bars are negligible. The temperature of bar *BC* is lowered by 50°F, and that of bar *ED* is raised by 50°F. Neglecting any possible lateral buckling, find the normal stresses in *BC* and *ED*. For *BC*, which is brass, assume $E = 14 \times 10^6$ lb/in² and $\alpha = 10.4 \times 10^{-6} \, (^\circ\text{F})^{-1}$; for *ED*, which is steel, take $E = 30 \times 10^6$ lb/in² and $\alpha = 6.5 \times 10^{-6} \, (^\circ\text{F})^{-1}$. The cross-sectional area of *BC* is 1 in²; that of *ED* is 0.5 in².

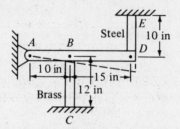

Fig. 9-20

Let us denote the forces acting on *AD* by $\mathbf{P}_{st}$ and $\mathbf{P}_{br}$, as in the free-body diagram of Fig. 9-21. Since *AD* will rotate as a rigid body about *A* (as shown by the dashed line), we have $\Delta_{br}/10 = \Delta_{st}/25$,   where Δ_{br} and Δ_{st} denote the axial compression of *BC* and the axial elongation of *DE*, respectively.

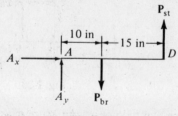

Fig. 9-21

The total change of length of *BC* is composed of a shortening due to the temperature drop and a lengthening due to the axial force $\mathbf{P}_{br}$. The total change of length of *DE* is composed of a lengthening due to the temperature rise and a lengthening due to the force $\mathbf{P}_{st}$. Hence we have

$$\frac{2}{5}\left[(6.5 \times 10^{-6})(10)(50) + \frac{P_{st}(10)}{0.5(30 \times 10^6)}\right] = -(10.4 \times 10^{-6})(12)(50) + \frac{P_{br}(12)}{1(14 \times 10^6)}$$

or

$$0.856P_{br} - 0.267P_{st} = 7750 \qquad (1)$$

For equilibrium, $+\!\!\curvearrowright \Sigma M_A = 10P_{br} - 25P_{st} = 0 \qquad (2)$

Solving (1) and (2) simultaneously yields $P_{st} = 4030$ lb and $P_{br} = 10,100$ lb. Then, using $\sigma = P/A$ for each bar, we obtain $\sigma_{st} = 8060$ lb/in^2 and $\sigma_{br} = 10,100$ lb/in^2.

9.14 Bars AB and BC, each of area $A_1 = 5$ cm^2, and bars AE and CE, each of area $A_2 = 7$ cm^2, support a curved rigid arch AC that is loaded by a central vertical force of 15 kN (Fig. 9-22). All joints of the system are pinned. Find the stress in each of the bars.

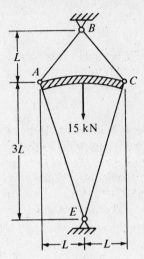

Fig. 9-22

Evidently, the upper bars are in tension, and the lower bars in compression. Thus, the free-body diagram of rigid arch AC appears as shown in Fig. 9-23. For vertical equilibrium, we have

$$\Sigma F_y = 2F_1\left(\frac{1}{\sqrt{2}}\right) + 2F_2\left(\frac{3}{\sqrt{10}}\right) - 15 = 0 \tag{1}$$

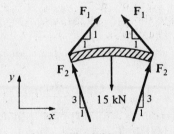

Fig. 9-23

This single equation contains two unknowns and hence must be supplemented by an equation stemming from the deformations of the system. Consideration of the symmetry indicates that the displacements of points A and C are equal, and both must be vertically downward. Let the final position of point A be denoted by A'.

The deformations of bars AB and AE are analyzed in Figs. 9-24 and 9-25. In Fig. 9-24 we "unlock" bar AB at A so that it is free to extend an amount Δ_1, after which it may rotate as a rigid body about point B. The final position of end A is at A', which gives a vertical displacement ΔA as shown. Then we have, from $\Delta = \dfrac{PL}{AE}$,

$$\Delta_1 = \frac{F_1(L\sqrt{2})}{A_1 E} \quad \text{and} \quad \Delta A = \sqrt{2}\Delta_1 = \frac{2F_1 L}{A_1 E} \tag{2}$$

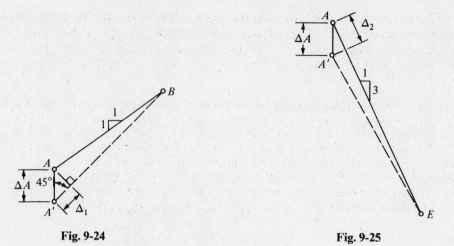

Fig. 9-24   **Fig. 9-25**

Similarly, when we "unlock" bar AE, it first shortens an amount Δ_2 and then rotates about pin E as a rigid body, with end A moving to A' (Fig. 9-25). For this bar we have

$$\Delta_2 = \frac{F_2(L\sqrt{10})}{A_2E} \quad \text{and} \quad \Delta A = \frac{\sqrt{10}}{3}\Delta_2 = \frac{10F_2L}{3A_2E} \tag{3}$$

Equating the expressions for ΔA in (2) and (3) yields

$$F_1 = \frac{5}{3}\frac{A_1}{A_2}F_2 \tag{4}$$

Then, substituting (4) in (1) yields

$$F_2 = \frac{15}{\dfrac{10}{3\sqrt{2}}\dfrac{A_1}{A_2} + \dfrac{6}{\sqrt{10}}}$$

For $A_1 = 5\,\text{cm}^2$ and $A_2 = 7\,\text{cm}^2$, this yields $F_2 = 4.188\,\text{kN}$ and $F_1 = 4.986\,\text{kN}$. These values yield the stresses in AB and AE:

$$\sigma_1 = \frac{F_1}{A_1} = \frac{4.986\,\text{kN}}{5\,\text{cm}^2} = 9.97\,\text{MPa} \qquad \sigma_2 = \frac{F_2}{A_2} = \frac{4.188\,\text{kN}}{7\,\text{cm}^2} = 5.98\,\text{MPa}$$

Owing to the symmetry, the stresses in BC and CE are equal to σ_1 and σ_2, respectively.

9.15   A hollow steel cylinder surrounds a solid copper cylinder (Fig. 9-26a), and the assembly is subject to an axial loading of 50,000 lb. The cross-sectional area of the steel is 3 in², while that of the

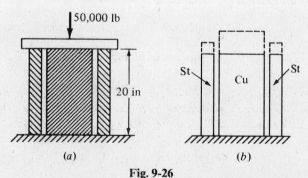

(a)   (b)

Fig. 9-26

copper is 10 in^2. The cylinders are the same height before the load·is applied. Determine the temperature rise (for the entire system) that is required to place the entire load on the copper cylinder. The cover plate at the top of the assembly is rigid. For copper, $E = 16 \times 10^6 \text{ lb/in}^2$ and $\alpha = 9.3 \times 10^{-6} \text{ (°F)}^{-1}$; for steel, $E = 30 \times 10^6 \text{ lb/in}^2$ and $\alpha = 6.5 \times 10^{-6} \text{ (°F)}^{-1}$.

One way to analyze this problem is to assume that the load and cover plate are removed and that the system is allowed to expand freely in response to a temperature rise ΔT. In that event the upper ends of the cylinders would assume the positions shown by the dashed lines in Fig. 9-26b.

The copper cylinder would expand upward more than the steel cylinder because the coefficient of linear expansion of copper is greater than that of steel. The upward expansion of the steel cylinder, in inches, would be $(6.5 \times 10^{-6})(20)\Delta T$; that of the copper, $(9.3 \times 10^{-6})(20)\Delta T$.

This is not, of course, the true situation because the load of 50,000 lb has not yet been considered. If all of this axial load is carried by the copper, then only the copper will be compressed, by an amount

$$\Delta_{Cu} = \frac{PL}{AE} = \frac{50,000(20)}{10(16 \times 10^6)}$$

We want the temperature rise ΔT that is just sufficient for all the load to be carried by the copper. In other words, we need to find ΔT such that the net expansion of the copper (heat expansion less load contraction) is just equal to the heat expansion of the steel. Consequently we write

$$(9.3 \times 10^{-6})(20)\Delta T - \frac{50,000(20)}{10(16 \times 10^6)} = (6.5 \times 10^{-6})(20)\Delta T$$

from which $\Delta T = 111°\text{F}$.

9.16   A trusslike system was to be built over the rigid block $ADECB$ in Fig. 9-27a, with two inclined bars from A and C being pinned at O and this pin joined by a vertical bar to point B. However, the vertical bar BO'' was accidentally cut 0.06 in short so that it had to be stretched, and bars AO and CO compressed, to be joined by the pin. All bars are steel, for which $E = 30 \times 10^6 \text{ lb/in}^2$. A_1 is the area of the vertical bar, and $1.5A_1$ is the area of each inclined bar. Find the axial stress in each of the three bars.

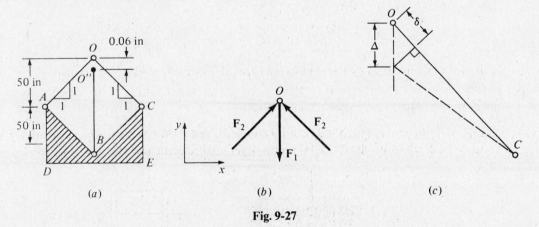

Fig. 9-27

Figure 9-27b shows the free-body diagram at O after the bars have been joined by the pin; we denote the compressive force in each inclined bar by $\mathbf{F}_2$, and the tensile force in the vertical bar by $\mathbf{F}_1$. The forces in the inclined bars are equal because of the symmetry, and for vertical equilibrium we have the relation

$$\Sigma F_y = 2F_2 \frac{1}{\sqrt{2}} - F_1 = 0 \qquad \text{or} \qquad F_2 = \frac{\sqrt{2}}{2} F_1 \qquad (1)$$

Consideration of the deformations indicates that bar CO can be considered to rotate as a rigid body about C, and then to compress by an amount δ in the direction of CO, or by Δ in the y direction, as shown in Fig. 9-27c. Bar BO'' stretches by an amount $F_1(100)/A_1E$, and this and Δ must sum to 0.06 in:

$$\frac{F_1(100)}{A_1E} + \frac{F_2(50\sqrt{2})}{1.5A_1E}\frac{1}{\cos 45°} = 0.06 \tag{2}$$

Solving (1) and (2) with $E = 30 \times 10^6$ lb/in^2, we obtain

$$\sigma_1 = \frac{F_1}{A_1} = 12{,}200 \text{ lb/in}^2 \text{ (T)} \qquad \sigma_2 = \frac{F_2}{1.5A_1} = 5800 \text{ lb/in}^2 \text{ (C)}$$

The final position of the pin is *not* midway between points O and O'', as may be seen by calculating the value of the term $F_1(100)/A_1E$ in (2) for $\sigma_1 = 12{,}200$ lb/in^2.

Elastic Analysis: Uniform Shearing Stresses

9.17　Show how the approach of Problem 8.20 can be used to describe a state of uniform shearing stress on any plane.

If we set $A_2 = C_2 = 0$ in (8) of Problem 8.20, that equation becomes $\Phi_2 = B_2xy$. Then (3) of that problem yields

$$\sigma_x = \sigma_y = 0 \qquad \tau_{xy} = -B_2 = \text{constant}$$

Thus, the simple stress function $\Phi_2 = B_2xy$ may be used to describe a state of uniform two-dimensional shear. The shear stresses so described lie in a plane that is normal to the x axis and cuts through the body. They are consequently parallel to the yz plane, as shown in Fig. 9-28.

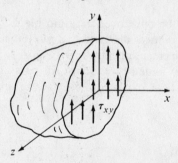

Fig. 9-28

9.18　A common type of vibration-reduction system consists of a synthetic rubber core bonded to two metallic face plates. In one particular application (Fig. 9-29), the lower extremity of the rubber is

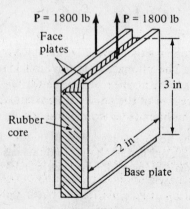

Fig. 9-29

bonded to a base plate, and a load **P** acts in the plane of each face plate. Determine the average shearing stress transmitted to the rubber core.

A free-body diagram of the right face plate indicates downward directed shearing stresses that we assume are uniformly distributed over the 2 in by 3 in contact surface. These are shown by the dashed vectors in Fig. 9-30.

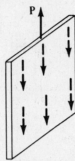

Fig. 9-30

Shearing stresses that are equal and opposite to those are exerted by the right face plate on the forward face of the rubber core; they are shown as solid vectors in Fig. 9-31. Similar stresses exerted by the left face plate on the rear face of the core are shown as dashed vectors.

For equilibrium of the right face plate, we have

$$\Sigma F_y = P - \tau_{xy}(3 \text{ in})(2 \text{ in}) = 0$$

which yields $\tau_{xy} = 300 \text{ lb/in}^2$.

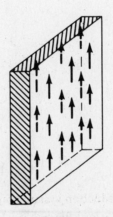

Fig. 9-31

Ultimate Strength (Limit Design)

In each of the following problems the material is assumed to behave according to the idealized stress-strain curve of Fig. 9-2. The ultimate load, or limit load, determined in each problem is then the maximum load that can be applied under the further assumption that the material has infinite ductility, i.e., the flat region of the curve extends indefinitely to the right. Although Fig. 9-2 implies the possibility of unbounded deformation, no structure can be allowed to deform excessively in practice.

Note that there is no unique strain that corresponds to the yield-point stress; hence, it is not possible, with the techniques given here, to find the deformations of the system. Further, solutions of ultimate-strength problems based upon inelastic action cannot be found as special cases of Problem 8.20, since the derivation of its equations is based upon the linear relationship between stress and strain that exists below the yield point.

9.19 A certain slab of composite material consists of a resin matrix reinforced by filamentary strands that extend in the direction of loading. A typical section of the system carries a load of 4000 N and is reinforced by four strands, each being of diameter 0.1 mm (see Fig. 9-32). Determine the shearing stress on each strand.

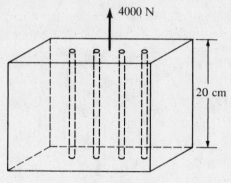

Fig. 9-32

The free-body diagram of a single strand is shown in Fig. 9-33. It indicates that the axial load of 1000 N must be resisted by shearing stresses that we assume to be uniformly distributed over the cylinderlike surface of the filament. For vertical equilibrium, we have

$$\Sigma F_y = 1000 - \tau_{xy}(0.2 \text{ m})(\pi)(0.1 \text{ mm})\left(\frac{1 \text{ m}}{10^3 \text{ mm}}\right) = 0$$

from which $\tau_{xy} = 15.9$ MPa.

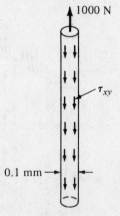

Fig. 9-33

9.20 A rigid horizontal bar is supported by four symmetrically placed inclined wires, as shown in Fig. 9-34a. Each wire is of cross-sectional area A, and the material has a yield point of σ_{yp}. Determine the ultimate vertical load $\mathbf{P}_u$ that can be carried by the system.

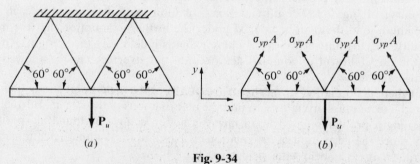

Fig. 9-34

Because of the symmetry, all four bars yield simultaneously. Thus, the free-body diagram at yielding is that of Fig. 9-34b. For static equilibrium,

$$\Sigma F_y = 4\sigma_{yp}A \sin 60° - P_u = 0$$

from which $P_u = 3.46\sigma_{yp}A$.

A working load would be obtained for the system by dividing P_u by an appropriate safety factor. The deformations need not be considered in this analysis; in fact, it is not possible to determine the vertical displacements because, as Fig. 9-2 shows, there is no unique strain corresponding to the yield stress σ_{yp}.

9.21   Bars AB and BC in Fig. 9-35a are pinned at their ends and support an ultimate vertical load of 5 kN at B. The material is steel, for which $\sigma_{yp} = 240$ MPa.   Determine the minimum area for each bar.

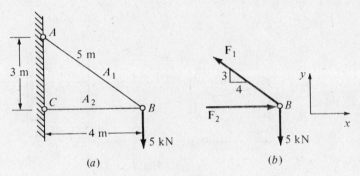

(a)   (b)

Fig. 9-35

The free-body diagram for the pin at B is shown in Fig. 9-35b. For static equilibrium, we must have

$$\Sigma F_y = \tfrac{3}{5}F_1 - 5 = 0 \qquad \text{or} \qquad F_1 = \tfrac{25}{3} \text{ kN}$$

$$\Sigma F_x = F_2 - \tfrac{4}{5}F_1 = 0 \qquad \text{or} \qquad F_2 = \tfrac{20}{3} \text{ kN}$$

For minimal cross-sectional area, yielding (and hence σ_{yp}) should be achieved simultaneously in the two bars. For that,

$$F_1 = \sigma_{yp}A_1 \qquad \text{or} \qquad \tfrac{25}{3} 1000 \text{ N} = (240 \times 10^6 \text{ N/m}^2)A_1$$

from which $A_1 = 34.7 \times 10^{-6}$ m^2 or 34.70 mm^2, and

$$F_2 = \sigma_{yp}A_2 \qquad \text{or} \qquad \tfrac{20}{3} 1000 \text{ N} = (240 \times 10^6 \text{ N/m}^2)A_2$$

from which $A_2 = 27.78 \times 10^{-6}$ m^2 or 27.78 mm^2.

These computed areas should, of course, be increased by some safety factor for acceptable design. Note that it is not possible to determine the displacement of point B, again because there is no unique strain corresponding to the yield point in Fig. 9-2.

Supplementary Problems

9.22   The rod in Fig. 9-36 is clamped at its left end and is subject to the axial forces shown. The uniform cross-sectional area of portion AB is 2600 mm^2, and that of BD is 1300 mm^2. Determine the maximum axial stress, neglecting the weight of the rod.   *Ans.*   152 MPa

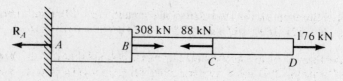

Fig. 9-36

9.23 Filamentary glass for use in composite materials has a tensile strength of 500,000 lb/in² and an elastic modulus of 50×10^6 lb/in². By how much does a 0.75-in-long strand of diameter 0.0001 in elongate under a tensile stress of 450,000 lb/in²? *Ans.* 0.00675 in

9.24 A steel bar in the form of a flat slab 20 mm thick is bounded by the curve $y = 0.1x^{1/2}$ from $x = 0.8$ m to $x = 2.0$ m, as shown in Fig. 9-37, and is subject to an axially applied tensile load of 1 MN. The material is steel, with elastic modulus 210 GPa. Determine the elongation of the bar, using the FORTRAN program of Problem 9.4. *Ans.* 2.52 mm

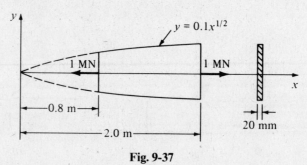

Fig. 9-37

9.25 In Problem 9.10, determine the vertical displacement under the point of application of the 7.5-kN load. *Ans.* 3.92 mm

9.26 Bars AC and BC in Fig. 9-38 are pinned at all points and loaded as shown. Determine the horizontal and vertical components of the displacement of point C due to the load **P**. Bar BC has cross-sectional area A_1, and bar AC has area $2A_1$. *Ans.* $\Delta_x = 0.267PL/A_1E$; $\Delta_y = 0.7125PL/A_1E$

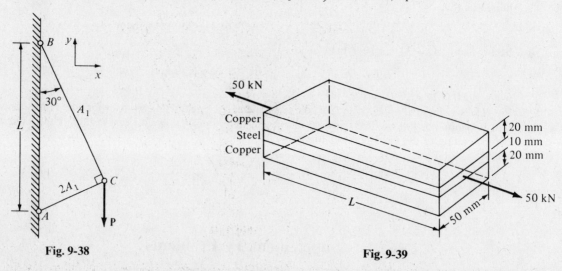

Fig. 9-38   **Fig. 9-39**

9.27 A flat steel slab is 10 mm thick and lies between two copper slabs that are each 20 mm thick (Fig. 9-39). The three are joined to rigid cover plates (not shown) at both ends. The entire system is heated uniformly while simultaneously a central axial force of 50 kN is applied as shown. Find the temperature rise required to place the entire load on the steel slab. For the steel, $E = 210\,\text{GPa}$ and $\alpha = 12 \times 10^{-6}\,(°C)^{-1}$; for the copper, $E = 105\,\text{GPa}$ and $\alpha = 17.5 \times 10^{-6}\,(°C)^{-1}$. *Ans.* 86.6°C

9.28   The system of three wires in Fig. 9-40, each of cross-sectional area 0.25 in², lies in a vertical plane and carries the load of 1000 lb. The wires are stressfree prior to application of the load. For steel, $E = 30 \times 10^6\,\text{lb/in}^2$ and $\alpha = 6.5 \times 10^{-6}\,(°F)^{-1}$; for copper, $E = 15 \times 10^6\,\text{lb/in}^2$ and $\alpha = 9.3 \times 10^{-6}\,(°F)^{-1}$. (a) Find the stress in each wire with the load acting. (b) Find the stress in each wire if the temperature of the entire system drops 20°F with the load still acting.

Ans.   (a) $\sigma_{st} = 1740\,\text{lb/in}^2$, $\sigma_{Cu} = 1300\,\text{lb/in}^2$;   (b) $\sigma_{st} = 850\,\text{lb/in}^2$, $\sigma_{Cu} = 1820\,\text{lb/in}^2$

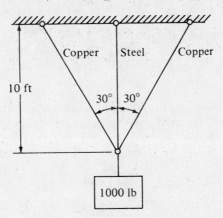

Fig. 9-40

9.29   The five-bar assembly of Fig. 9-41 was found to be slightly defective in that points A and C, which ought to have coincided, failed to coincide by a distance Δ. After these points had been forced to coincide, the joint at that point was pinned. Determine the forces existing in each bar. All bars have the same cross-sectional area.

Ans. $F_1 = F_2 = F_3 = \left(\dfrac{\sqrt{3}}{2 + 3\sqrt{3}}\right)\dfrac{\Delta AE}{L}$; $F_4 = F_5 = -\left(\dfrac{1}{2 + 3\sqrt{3}}\right)\dfrac{\Delta AE}{L}$

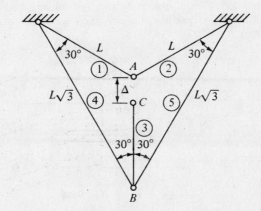

Fig. 9-41

9.30   The two bars of circular cross section in Fig. 9-42 are clamped to rigid walls but fail to meet by 2 mm at a certain reference temperature. Each bar is 50 mm in diameter. For brass, $E = 100\,\text{GPa}$ and $\alpha = 19.1 \times 10^{-6}\,(°C)^{-1}$. For aluminum, $E = 70\,\text{GPa}$ and $\alpha = 23 \times 10^{-6}\,(°C)^{-1}$. Neglecting the weight of the bars, determine the stress in each bar if the temperature is increased by 100°C.   *Ans.* 90.9 MPa

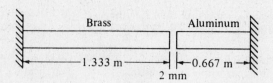

Fig. 9-42

9.31 In Problem 9.12, assume that both walls have a spring constant of 500 MN/m. Determine the axial stress in the bar. (*Hint*: Because of the symmetry about the midpoint of the bar, it is only necessary to consider one half of the bar and the corresponding forces and deformations.)   *Ans.* 68.75 MPa

9.32 A common composite material is glass-reinforced epoxy. Consider a single cylindrical strand of *E*-glass that has a 0.0001-in diameter and is 1.5 in long. For axial loading, the tensile strength of such a strand is 500,000 lb/in^2. Compute the shearing stresses acting on the curved sides of the strand under this maximum tensile stress.   *Ans.* 82 lb/in^2

9.33 The rigid bar *AB* is supported by the four rods shown in Fig. 9-43. The rods are all circular in cross section and of 50 mm diameter. They have a yield point of 300 MPa. Using limit design, determine the maximum weight of bar *AB*. Assume that the weight of *AB* is uniformly distributed along its length.

Ans.   1.38 MN

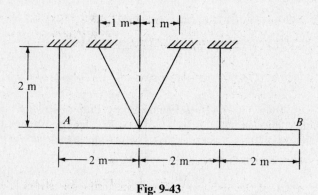

Fig. 9-43

9.34 The rigid bar *AB* in Fig. 9-44 is supported by two vertical rods and is pinned at *A*. The yield point of the steel in the rods is 40,000 lb/in^2, and they have the cross-sectional areas shown. Determine the ultimate load that may be applied at *B*.   *Ans.* 15,100 lb

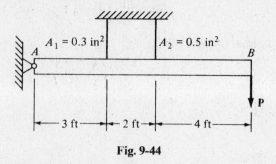

Fig. 9-44

9.35 A bar of uniform cross section *A* is rigidly fastened between two fixed walls. The material is aluminum with $E = 75$ GPa, $\sigma_{yp} = 140$ MPa, and $\alpha = 23.2 \times 10^{-6}\,(^\circ\text{C})^{-1}$. The temperature of the bar drops from 20°C to −80°C. Determine the stress in the bar after the temperature drop, assuming it is stressfree at 20°C.   *Ans.*   140 MPa

Chapter 10

Thin Rings and Shells of Revolution

An important application involving solid bodies subject to external loads that produce normal stresses is the axisymmetric loading of thin rings and shells of revolution (such as hollow cylinders and spheres) by internal or external uniform normal pressure. The simple theories discussed in this chapter are valid only when the thickness of the ring, cylinder, or sphere is no more than approximately 10 percent of the radius of the system. Also, in the case of uniform external pressure, it is assumed that the structure does not buckle and thus that design is based only upon stress criteria.

CYLINDRICAL SHELLS

For a cylindrical shell having closed ends, wall thickness h, internal radius r, and length L and subject to a uniform internal (normal) pressure p, the normal circumferential stress within the material of the shell is

$$\sigma_c = \frac{pr}{h} \tag{10.1}$$

and the normal longitudinal stress is

$$\sigma_L = \frac{pr}{2h} \tag{10.2}$$

(except at the closed ends of the cylinder). These are principal stresses, and no shearing stresses act in these directions. (See Problems 10.1 and 10.2.)

The increase in the radius of a cylinder due to this internal pressure (acting both radially and longitudinally) is

$$\Delta r = \frac{pr^2}{Eh}\left(1 - \frac{\mu}{2}\right) \tag{10.3}$$

and the increase in the volume of the cylinder is

$$\Delta V = \frac{p\pi r^3 L}{Eh}\left(\frac{5}{2} - 2\mu\right) \tag{10.4}$$

(See Problems 10.3 through 10.5.)

SPHERICAL SHELLS

For a spherical shell of wall thickness h and internal radius r, subject to uniform internal (normal) pressure p, the normal stress in the wall at any point is

$$\sigma = \frac{pr}{2h} \tag{10.5}$$

Because of the pointwise symmetry of the pressure about the center of the sphere, every direction in the midthickness of the wall of the sphere is a principal direction. The increase in the radius of the sphere due to this internal pressure is

$$\Delta r = \frac{pr^2}{2Eh}(1 - \mu) \qquad (10.6)$$

and the increase in the volume of the sphere is

$$\Delta V = \frac{2p\pi r^4}{Eh}(1 - \mu) \qquad (10.7)$$

(See Problems 10.6 and 10.7.)

SHELLS OF REVOLUTION

The shell of revolution shown in Fig. 10-1a is formed by rotating a plane curve (the *meridian*) about an axis lying in the plane of the curve. The radius of curvature of the meridian, denoted by r_1 and shown for an infinitesimal element in Fig. 10-1b, varies along the length of the meridian. This radius of curvature is defined by two lines perpendicular to the shell and passing through points B and C of Fig. 10-1b. Another parameter, r_2, denotes the radius of curvature of the shell surface in a direction perpendicular to the meridian. This radius of curvature is defined by perpendiculars to the shell through points A and B. The center of curvature corresponding to r_2 must lie on the axis of symmetry of the shell, although the center for r_1 in general does not lie there. An internal pressure p acting normal to the curved surface of the shell gives rise to *meridional stresses* σ_ϕ and *hoop stresses* σ_θ as indicated in the figure. These stresses are orthogonal to one another and act in the plane of the shell wall.

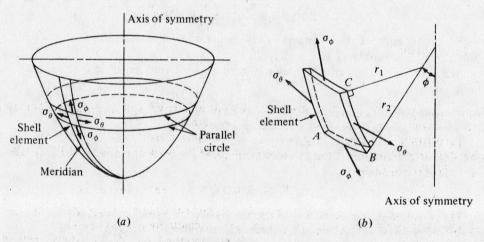

Fig. 10-1

From Equation (8.20) it can be shown that, for uniformly distributed meridional and hoop stresses,

$$\frac{\sigma_\phi}{r_1} + \frac{\sigma_\theta}{r_2} = \frac{p}{h} \qquad (10.8)$$

where h denotes the shell thickness. A second equation may be obtained by considering the vertical equilibrium of the entire shell above or below some convenient "parallel" circle. (See Problems 10.9 and 10.10.)

Solved Problems

10.1 A thin-walled cylinder is closed at both ends by cover plates and subject to a uniform internal pressure p. The wall thickness is h, and the inner radius r. Neglecting the restraining effects of the end plates, calculate the longitudinal (meridional) and circumferential (hoop) normal stresses existing in the cylinder walls due to this loading.

   To determine the circumferential stress σ_c, let us consider a section of the cylinder of length L to be removed from the vessel. The free-body diagram of half of this section appears in Fig. 10-2a.

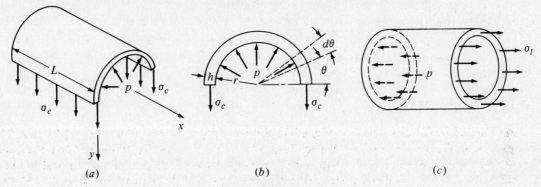

Fig. 10-2

   Note that the body has been cut in such a way that the originally *internal* effect (σ_c) now appears as a force *external* to this free body.

   Figure 10-2b shows the forces acting on a cross section of the half cylinder. The horizontal components of the radial pressures cancel one another by virtue of symmetry about the vertical centerline. In the vertical direction we have the equilibrium equation

$$\Sigma F_{\text{vert}} = -2\sigma_c hL + \int_0^\pi pr\, d\theta(\sin\theta)L = 0$$

Integrating yields

$$2\sigma_c hL = -prL[\cos\theta]_0^\pi \qquad \text{or} \qquad \sigma_c = \frac{pr}{h}$$

The resultant vertical force due to the pressure p could also have been obtained by multiplying the pressure by the horizontal *projected area* upon which the pressure acts.

   To determine the longitudinal stress σ_l, we consider a section to be passed through the cylinder normal to its geometric axis. The free-body diagram of the remaining portion of the cylinder is shown in Fig. 10-2c. For equilibrium,

$$\Sigma F_{\text{horiz}} = -p\pi r^2 + 2\pi rh\sigma_l = 0 \qquad \text{or} \qquad \sigma_l = pr/2h$$

The circumferential stress is thus twice the longitudinal stress. Consequently, if the water in a closed pipe freezes, the pipe will rupture in a line running longitudinally along the cylinder.

   Let us take the x axis to coincide with the geometric axis of the cylinder and the y axis to run tangentially, as shown in Fig. 10-2a, and set $B_2 = 0$ in (8) of Problem 8.20. Then from (3) of that same problem, we have

$$\sigma_x = \frac{\partial^2 \Phi_2}{\partial y^2} = 2C_2 = \text{constant}$$

$$\sigma_y = \frac{\partial^2 \Phi_2}{\partial x^2} = 2A_2 = \text{constant}$$

$$\tau_{xy} = 0$$

It thus is evident that the state of stress in the closed-end, internally pressurized cylindrical shell may be found from the stress function

$$\Phi_2 = \frac{pr}{2h}x^2 + \frac{pr}{4h}y^2$$

10.2   A vertical steel standpipe, i.e., a cylindrical tank open at the top and having a vertical axis, is 3 m in inside diameter and 25 m high. The tank is filled with oil having a weight density of 0.90×10^4 N/m^3. The material is structural steel having a yield point of 240 MPa, and a safety factor of 2 is to be used. What thickness of steel plate is necessary at the bottom of the tank if the welded longitudinal seam is presumed to be as strong as the solid metal? What thickness is required if the seam is only 75 percent as strong as the solid metal?

The pressure p (in any direction) at the base of the standpipe is given by the formula $p = \gamma h$, where γ represents the weight of the liquid per unit volume and h denotes the height of the column of oil above the base. This formula is immediately evident if we consider that the pressure on a square meter of the base numerically equals the weight of a column of oil 1 m^2 in cross section and h m high. Hence the pressure at the base is

$$p = (0.90 \times 10^4 \text{ N/m}^3)(25 \text{ m}) = 22.5 \times 10^4 \text{ N/m}^2 = 0.225 \text{ MPa}$$

Since this pressure is hydrostatic, it acts in all directions with the same magnitude; in particular, it acts radially against the inside wall of the standpipe as shown in Fig. 10-3. As may be seen from the equation $p = \gamma h$, the radial pressure decreases toward the top of the tank as shown in the sketch, but the maximum value occurs at the base and, consequently, that is the region that must be considered for design purposes.

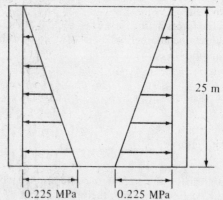

Fig. 10-3

Since the top of the tank is open, there is no longitudinal stress. From Problem 10.1 we know that the circumferential stress at any point in the standpipe is given by $\sigma_c = pr/h$. At the base of the tank, this equation becomes, for $\sigma_{yp} = 240$ MPa and a safety factor of 2,

$$\frac{240 \text{ MPa}}{2} = \frac{(0.225 \text{ MPa})(1.5 \text{ m})}{h}$$

from which $h = 0.0028$ m or 2.8 mm, assuming the longitudinal seams are as strong as the solid metal.

If the longitudinal seams are only 75 percent as strong as the solid metal, the thickness should be increased to $h = \frac{4}{3}(2.8 \text{ mm}) = 3.73$ mm.

10.3   Find the increase in volume per unit volume for a thin-walled circular cylindrical shell subject to a uniform internal pressure p, assuming that the radial expansion due to the pressure is constant along the length L of the cylinder. The ends of the cylinder are closed by circular plates.

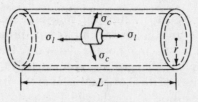

Fig. 10-4

The shell and a typical element are shown in Fig. 10-4, along with the principal stresses σ_c and σ_l on the element. It is customary to employ the two-dimensional form of Hooke's law (8.16) so that the circumferential and longitudinal strains ε_c and ε_l are given by

$$\varepsilon_c = \frac{1}{E}(\sigma_c - \mu\sigma_l) = \frac{1}{E}\left(\frac{pr}{h} - \mu\frac{pr}{2h}\right)$$

$$\varepsilon_l = \frac{1}{E}(\sigma_l - \mu\sigma_c) = \frac{1}{E}\left(\frac{pr}{2h} - \mu\frac{pr}{h}\right)$$

The increase in the circumference due to ε_c is thus

$$2\pi r\varepsilon_c = \frac{2\pi pr^2}{Eh}\left(1 - \frac{\mu}{2}\right)$$

and the expanded radius is

$$r' = \frac{\text{final circumference}}{2\pi} = \frac{2\pi r + \dfrac{2\pi pr^2}{Eh}\left(1 - \dfrac{\mu}{2}\right)}{2\pi} = r + \frac{pr^2}{Eh}\left(1 - \frac{\mu}{2}\right)$$

The change in the length of the cylinder is simply

$$L\varepsilon_l = \frac{prL}{Eh}\left(\frac{1}{2} - \mu\right)$$

so that the expanded length is

$$L' = L + \frac{prL}{Eh}\left(\frac{1}{2} - \mu\right)$$

The volume of the expanded cylindrical shell is then

$$\pi(r')^2 L' = \pi\left[r + \frac{pr^2}{Eh}\left(1 - \frac{\mu}{2}\right)\right]^2\left[L + \frac{prL}{Eh}\left(\frac{1}{2} - \mu\right)\right]$$

Expanding, dropping terms involving powers of p/E, and subtracting out the original volume yield, for the increase of volume,

$$\Delta V = \frac{p\pi r^3 L}{Eh}\left(\frac{5}{2} - 2\mu\right)$$

Thus, the change in volume per unit volume is

$$\frac{\Delta V}{V} = \frac{\dfrac{p\pi r^3 L}{Eh}\left(\dfrac{5}{2} - 2\mu\right)}{\pi r^2 L} = \frac{pr}{Eh}\left(\frac{5}{2} - 2\mu\right)$$

10.4 Prior to processing, grain is usually stored in silos that are, in essence, vertical circular cylinders (Fig. 10-5). Heat from the sun combines with moisture present in the grain to cause expansion of the stored grain, resulting in straining of the silo wall. Measurements indicate that the radius of the lower portion of the silo is changed by approximately 0.25 percent (higher up, the volumetric expansion of the grain causes vertical displacement of the grain). It is reasonable to neglect friction between the grain and the inside wall of the silo. For a silo having a radius of 3 m, a wall thickness of 10 mm, and $E = 200\,\text{GPa}$, find the hoop stress due to the expansion.

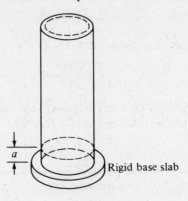

a

Rigid base slab

Fig. 10-5

As an approximation, let us consider only the lowest cylindrical disk of grain, of height a as shown in Fig. 10-5. Neglecting friction we have, approximately, $\varepsilon_l = 0$, so that the hoop strain in this lower disk is

$$\varepsilon_c = \frac{1}{E}(\sigma_c - \mu\sigma_l) = \frac{1}{E}\frac{pr}{h}$$

where p is the radial pressure of the grain on the inside wall of the silo. The elongation of the circumference of this lower disk is then $2\pi r(pr/Eh)$, and the elongated circumference is $2\pi r + 2\pi r(pr/Eh)$.

The expanded radius is thus

$$r + \frac{pr^2}{Eh}$$

But that is 1.0025 times the original radius, so we may write

$$1.0025r = r + \frac{pr^2}{(200 \times 10^9\,\text{N/m}^2)(0.010\,\text{m})}$$

For $r = 3\,\text{m}$, this yields $p = 1.67\,\text{MPa}$. The circumferential stress near the bottom of the silo is then

$$\sigma = \frac{pr}{h} = \frac{(1.67 \times 10^6\,\text{N/m}^2)(3\,\text{m})}{(0.010\,\text{m})} = 500\,\text{MPa}$$

Only relatively high-strength steels have this high a yield point, which explains why silos occasionally fail due to moisture-induced grain expansion.

10.5 A thin steel ring was to be slipped over a rigid circular shaft. The diameter of the shaft is 16 in, but the inside diameter of the ring was accidentally made 0.002 in smaller than that. The ring was heated, slipped over the shaft, and then allowed to cool, to produce a shrink fit. The ring has a thickness of 0.1 in and a specific weight γ of $0.283\,\text{lb/in}^3$, and $E = 30 \times 10^6\,\text{lb/in}^2$. The shaft now rotates in end bearings. Find the angular velocity of the shaft at which the ring just begins to break contact with the shaft.

Figure 10-6 shows the thin ring as well as the inertia force acting on an element of the ring subtending a

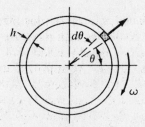

Fig. 10-6

central angle $d\theta$. The inertia force on the element is of the form

$$\frac{W}{g}r\omega^2$$

where W is the weight of the element, g is the gravitational constant, r is the ring's inner radius, and ω is its angular velocity in radian units. If the ring is of length L into the page, this becomes

$$\frac{(\gamma r\, d\theta\, hL)r\omega^2}{g}$$

The force per unit contact area between the ring and the shaft is then

$$\frac{(\gamma r\, d\theta\, hL)r\omega^2}{g(r\, d\theta\, L)} = \frac{\gamma h r\omega^2}{g}$$

which has the units of pressure, as it should.

From Problem 10.4, the increase in the radius of the ring due to an outwardly directed pressure p in the absence of longitudinal forces is $\Delta r = pr^2/Eh$. Here, p is the inertia force per unit contact area, and we need $\Delta r = 0.001$ in for the ring to begin to slip. Hence, we write

$$0.001 \text{ in} = \frac{\dfrac{\gamma h r\omega^2}{g}r^2}{Eh} = \frac{\dfrac{(0.283 \text{ lb/in}^3)(0.1 \text{ in})(8 \text{ in})\omega^2}{(386 \text{ in/s}^2)}(8 \text{ in})^2}{(30 \times 10^6 \text{ lb/in}^2)(0.1 \text{ in})}$$

which yields $\omega = 283$ rad/s or 2700 rpm.

10.6 A closed, thin-walled, spherical shell is subject to a uniform internal pressure p. The inside radius of the shell is r, and its wall thickness is h. Derive an expression for the tensile stress existing in the wall.

Let us consider one half of the sphere. This body is acted upon by the applied internal pressure p as well as the forces that the other half of the sphere exerts upon it. Because of the symmetry of loading and deformation, these forces may be represented by circumferential tensile stresses σ_c as shown in the free-body diagram of Fig. 10-7.

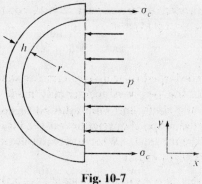

Fig. 10-7

This diagram represents the forces acting on the hemisphere, but shows only a projection of the hemisphere on a vertical plane. Actually, the pressure p acts over the entire inside surface of the hemisphere and in a direction perpendicular to the surface at every point. However, as mentioned in Problem 10.1, its resultant can be found by multiplying p by the *projection* of this surface, which is a circular area of radius r. The tensile stress σ_c acts only on a "ring" of inner radius r and width h. Hence, for equilibrium,

$$\Sigma F_x = \sigma_c 2\pi rh - p\pi r^2 = 0 \qquad \text{or} \qquad \sigma_c = \frac{pr}{2h}$$

From symmetry this circumferential stress is the same in all directions at any point in the wall of the sphere.

If we cut through the spherical shell with two mutually perpendicular diametral planes, we expose an element such as that shown shaded in Fig. 10-8. Because of the pointwise symmetry of the spherical system, we may call both perpendicular normal stresses σ_x (as they are labeled). If we now set $A_2 = B_2 = 0$ in (8) of Problem 8.20, then (3) of that problem yields

$$\sigma_x = \frac{\partial^2 \Phi_2}{\partial y^2} = 2C_2 = \text{constant}$$

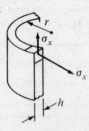

Fig. 10-8

and it is evident that the state of stress in an internally pressurized spherical shell may be found from the stress function

$$\Phi_2 = \frac{pr}{4h} y^2$$

10.7   A thin-walled, spherical steel shell has an inside radius of 1.5 m. The material has a working normal stress of 125 MPa, $E = 200$ GPa, and $\mu = 0.3$. The shell is subject to a uniform internal pressure of 3.5 MPa. Find the minimum required wall thickness. If the pressurization is achieved by first completely filling the shell with unpressurized water and then introducing additional water until the pressure of 3.5 MPa is attained, find the volume of additional water that must be introduced. The bulk modulus of water is 2100 MPa.

The normal stress in any direction at any point within the shell was found in Problem 10.6 to be $\sigma_c = pr/2h$. Here,

$$\sigma_c = 125 \times 10^6 \text{ N/m}^2 = \frac{(3.5 \times 10^6 \text{ N/m}^2)(1.5 \text{ m})}{2h}$$

from which we get $h = 0.021$ m $= 21$ mm as the required wall thickness.

Owing to the 3.5-MPa pressure, the metal shell increases in volume by the amount

$$\Delta V = \frac{2\pi pr^4}{Eh}(1 - \mu) = \frac{2\pi(3.5 \times 10^6 \text{ N/m}^2)(1.5 \text{ m})^4(0.7)}{(200 \times 10^9 \text{ N/m}^2)(0.021 \text{ m})} = 0.01854 \text{ m}^3$$

The compressibility of the water must also be considered. From (8.19) we have, as the bulk modulus, $K = -p/e$; that is, the bulk modulus is defined as the negative of the ratio of the hydrostatic pressure to the change in volume per unit volume. We may write this as

$$K = -\frac{p}{\Delta V/V} \qquad \text{or as} \qquad 2100 \times 10^6 \text{ N/m}^2 = -\frac{3.5 \times 10^6 \text{ N/m}^2}{\Delta V/V}$$

from which we find that

$$\frac{\Delta V}{V} = -0.00166 \qquad (1)$$

Thus, the decrease in the volume of the water due to the pressurization is

$$\Delta V = -0.00166 \tfrac{4}{3}\pi(1.5 \text{ m})^3 = -0.02347 \text{ m}^3$$

At this point we must be very careful. It might appear that one simply should add

$$0.01854 + 0.02347 = 0.0420 \text{ m}^3$$

to find the additional volume of water that must be pumped in. True, a cavity of this magnitude does exist. However, it must be filled with *pressurized* water. And to obtain $V = 0.0420 \text{ m}^3$ of water at 3.5 MPa, we use (*1*) to find that we must start with

$$V + (-\Delta V) = V(1 + 0.00166) = 0.04207 \text{ m}^3$$

of unpressurized water.

For these particular numerical values, it is true that the last correction is very small, approximately 0.16 percent of the uncorrected value. However, for the solution to be logically consistent, it should be so corrected.

10.8   A laminated pressure vessel is composed of two thin coaxial cylinders, as shown in Fig. 10-9a. Prior to assembly, there was a slight "interference" between the shells; i.e., the inner one was too large to slide into the outer one. The outer cylinder was heated, placed on the inner cylinder, and allowed to cool, thus providing a shrink fit. If both cylinders are steel, the mean diameter of the assembly is 100 mm, and the initial interference (of diameters) was 0.25 mm, find the tangential stresses in each shell arising from the shrinking. The thickness of the inner shell is 2.5 mm, and that of the outer shell is 2 mm. Take $E = 200$ GPa.

(*a*) Laminated pressure vessel   (*b*) Outer cylinder   (*c*) Inner cylinder

Fig. 10-9

There is evidently an interfacial pressure p acting between the adjacent faces of the two shells, even though there are no external applied loads. The pressure p may be considered to increase the diameter of the outer shell and decrease the diameter of the inner one, so that the inner shell fits inside the outer.

The radial expansion of a cylinder due to radial pressure alone was found in Problem 10.3 to be pr^2/Eh. Here, the increase in the radius of the outer shell due to p, plus the decrease in the radius of the inner one due to p, must equal the initial interference between radii, or 0.25/2 mm. Thus, we have

$$\frac{p(50^2)}{(200 \times 10^9 \times 10^{-6})(2.5)} + \frac{p(50)^2}{(200 \times 10^9 \times 10^{-6})(2)} = 0.125 \qquad \text{or} \qquad p = 11.1 \text{ MPa}$$

This pressure, illustrated in Fig. 10-9b and c, acts between the cylinders after the outer one has been shrunk onto the inner one. It gives rise to circumferential stresses

$$\sigma_c = \frac{pr}{h} = \frac{(11.1 \times 10^6)(50)}{2.5} = -222 \text{ MPa} \qquad \text{and} \qquad \sigma_c' = \frac{pr}{h} = \frac{(11.1 \times 10^6)(50)}{2} = 277 \text{ MPa}$$

in the inner and outer cylinders, respectively.

If, as an example, the laminated shell were subject to a uniform internal pressure, then these "shrink fit" stresses would be added algebraically to the stresses found by use of the simple formulas of Problem 10.1.

10.9 An oil storage tank in the form of a truncated right circular conical shell is rigidly attached to a base slab and completely filled with oil having a weight density of $0.9 \times 10^4 \text{ N/m}^3$. For the geometry shown in Fig. 10-10a, determine the meridional and hoop stresses at a point 1 m below the top of the tank, which has a wall thickness of 0.3 mm.

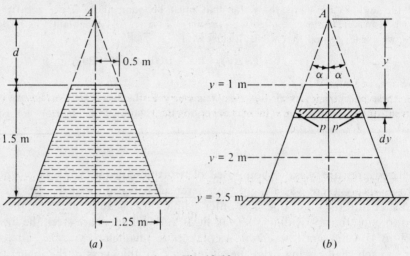

Fig. 10-10

The (imaginary) apex of the cone is located a distance d above the tank top. From similar triangles,

$$\frac{d + 1.5}{1.25} = \frac{d}{0.5} \quad \text{so} \quad d = 1 \text{ m}$$

Thus, we seek the stresses at a distance $y = 2 \text{ m}$ from the apex.

The oil exerts a pressure everywhere normal to the inside surface of the tank, as indicated in Fig. 10-10b. At an arbitrary depth y below the apex A, we consider a ring-shaped element of vertical depth dy subject to pressure p. Since such an element has a slant height of $dy\sqrt{5}/2$, and the force due to p is perpendicular to that slant height, the vertical component of the total force on this ring element is

$$p\left[\frac{1}{\sqrt{5}} \frac{\sqrt{5}\,dy}{2}\left(2\pi \frac{y}{2}\right)\right] \quad \text{or} \quad \frac{p\pi y}{2}\,dy$$

From hydrostatics, $p = w(y - 1)$, where w is the weight density of the oil.

If we now sum the upward forces on all rings in the part of the tank from $y = 1 \text{ m}$ to $y = 2 \text{ m}$, we will have the total upward vertical force due to the pressure of the oil in that part of the tank. We get

$$\int_{y=1}^{y=2} \frac{\pi w}{2}\, y(y - 1)\, dy = 1.310w = 11,790 \text{ N}$$

The free-body diagram of the portion of the tank between the top $(y = 1 \text{ m})$ and the location where the stresses are sought $(y = 2 \text{ m})$ is shown in Fig. 10-11, where σ_ϕ is the meridional stress. For vertical equilibrium,

$$11,790 \text{ N} - \sigma_\phi (2\pi)(1 \text{ m})(0.0003 \text{ m})\frac{2}{\sqrt{5}} = 0 \quad \text{or} \quad \sigma_\phi = 7.00 \text{ MPa}$$

The radius of curvature r_2 in (10.8) is the length of a normal between the surface of revolution and the axis of symmetry of the shell, as shown in Fig. 10-11. We also define r_0 as the projection

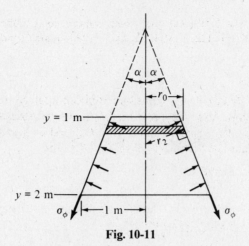

Fig. 10-11

of r_2 on a plane perpendicular to the axis of symmetry. For the conical tank (Fig. 10-11) we have $r_0/r_2 =$ $\cos \alpha$ and $\tan \alpha = r_0/y$.   Combining these two equations yields, at $y = 2$ m,

$$r_2 = \frac{y \tan \alpha}{\cos \alpha} = \frac{(2 \text{ m})(1/2)}{2/\sqrt{5}} = 1.118 \text{ m}$$

Because the generator of the cone is a straight line, the meridional radius of curvature r_1 goes to infinity. Then from (10.8) with, for the oil,

$$p = w(y - 1) = (0.9 \times 10^4 \text{ N/m}^3)(1 \text{ m}) = 0.9 \times 10^4 \text{ N/m}^2$$

we have

$$\frac{\sigma_\phi}{\infty} + \frac{\sigma_\theta}{1.118} = \frac{0.9 \times 10^4 \text{ N/m}^2}{0.0003 \text{ m}}$$

from which $\sigma_\theta = 33.6$ MPa.

10.10 The Tokamak Fusion Test Reactor, for use in experiments with power generation by plasma fusion, has the shape of a toroidal shell (Fig. 10-12). A near-vacuum exists inside the toroidal chamber, and the outside is subject to atmospheric pressure. If the material is steel having a yield point of 48,500 lb/in^2 and a safety factor of 4.5 is required, determine the required wall thickness.

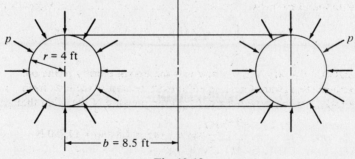

Fig. 10-12

A section cut through the torus (Fig. 10-13) indicates the unknown meridional and hoop stresses, σ_ϕ and σ_θ. For the analysis, we regard these unknowns as positive, corresponding to tension.

We first consider the vertical equilibrium of the entire shell below some convenient "parallel" circle, represented by the angle ϕ in Fig. 10-14. The atmospheric pressure, taken to be positive, is represented by the vectors p acting everywhere perpendicular to the external surface. The unknown meridional stress is σ_ϕ, defined in Fig. 10-1b and shown in Fig. 10-13. In Problem 10.6 we found that the resultant vertical force

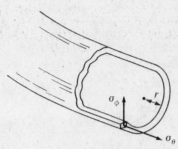

Fig. 10-13

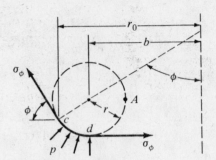

Fig. 10-14

due to the pressure p acting on the section cd may be obtained by multiplying the pressure by the horizontal projection of the area on which it acts. Thus, for equilibrium of the toroidal segment cd, we have

$$2\pi r_0 h\sigma_\phi \sin \phi + p\pi(r_0^2 - b^2) = 0$$

From the geometry, $\sin \phi = (r_0 - b)/r$,   so that

$$\sigma_\phi = -\frac{pr(r_0 + b)}{2r_0 h} \tag{1}$$

It is evident that the peak value of this stress occurs at the innermost points A where $r_0 = b - r$ and

$$\sigma_{\phi(max)} = -\frac{pr}{2h}\frac{2b - r}{b - r} \tag{2}$$

If σ_ϕ as given by (1) is substituted in (10.8) along with $r_0 = b + r \sin \phi$, $r_1 = r$, and $r_2 = (b + r \sin \phi)/\sin \phi$, we obtain

$$\sigma_\theta = -\frac{pr}{2h}$$

which holds at all points in the toroidal shell. Evidently the peak value of σ_ϕ as given by (2) exceeds the value of σ_θ and, hence, the maximum value of σ_ϕ controls the design.

To find h for the maximum value of σ_ϕ, we substitute the given values, along with $p = 14.7$ lb/in^2,   in (2) to obtain

$$-\frac{48,500 \text{ lb/in}^2}{4.5} = -\frac{(14.7 \text{ lb/in}^2)(48 \text{ in})[(17 - 4) \text{ ft}]}{2h[(8.5 - 4) \text{ ft}]}$$

which yields $h = 0.0946$ in ≈ 0.1 in.

Supplementary Problems

10.11 The deep submersible research vessel *Aluminaut* has a cylindrical pressure hull of outside diameter 2.5 m and a wall thickness of 150 mm. It is constructed of an aluminum alloy having a yield point of 450 MPa. Determine the circumferential stress in the cylindrical portion of the pressure hull when the vehicle is at its operating depth of 5000 m below the surface of the sea. Use the mean diameter of the shell in calculations, and consider seawater to have a weight density of 10^4 N/m^3.   *Ans.*   392 MPa

10.12 The undersea research vehicle *Alvin* has a spherical pressure hull of radius 39.64 in and of shell thickness 1.33 in. The pressure hull is HY-100 steel having a yield point of 100,000 lb/in^2. Determine the depth of submergence that would set up the yield-point stress in the spherical shell. Consider seawater to weigh 64.0 lb/ft^3.   *Ans.*   15,100 ft

10.13   The Deep Submergence Rescue Vehicle for assisting submarines in distress has a pressure hull consisting of three interconnected spherical shells, as indicated in Fig. 10-15. The shells have an outside diameter of 7.5 ft and a wall thickness of 0.75 in. The yield point of the material is 130,000 lb/in². Determine the circumferential stress in the spherical shells at the operating depth of 3500 ft below the surface of the sea. Neglect the effects of stress concentrations where the spheres are joined and the possibility of buckling due to hydrostatic pressure. Consider seawater to weigh 64.0 lb/ft³.   *Ans.*   46,700 lb/in²

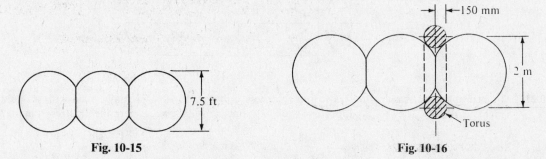

Fig. 10-15   **Fig. 10-16**

10.14   The Deep Submergence Rescue Vehicle of Problem 10.13 has a compressed-air storage tank in the form of a toroidal shell which surrounds two of the interconnected spherical shells (Fig. 10-16). The toroidal tank is made of steel having a 1000-MPa ultimate tensile strength. Determine the wall thickness of the torus required to withstand an internal air pressure of 30 MPa if a safety factor of 3 is used.   *Ans.*   14.7 mm

10.15   A thin-walled right circular cylindrical shell is subject to a uniform internal pressure of 0.6 MPa. The cylinder has a diameter of 0.8 m, a length of 7 m, and a wall thickness of 5 mm. The material is steel, for which $E = 200\,\text{GPa}$ and $\mu = 0.3$.   Calculate the increase in the volume of the shell due to the pressurization.   *Ans.*   0.00160 m³

10.16   In Problem 10.12 concerning *Alvin*, determine the decrease in the interior volume of the spherical pressure hull at the yield-point depth of 15,100 ft. Take $E = 30 \times 10^6\,\text{lb/in}^2$ and $\mu = 0.3$.   *Ans.*   1829 in³

10.17   A thin copper ring of internal diameter 199.50 mm and radial thickness 2 mm is heated and placed over a rigid circular shaft of 200 mm diameter. Determine the circumferential stress in the ring when the assembly is cooled to room temperature. For the ring, $E = 100\,\text{GPa}$.   *Ans.*   250 MPa

10.18   A storage tank in the form of a vertical right circular cylinder is 30 ft in radius and is filled to a depth of 60 ft with diesel fluid having a specific gravity of 0.82. The yield point of the steel shell plating is 40,000 lb/in², and a safety factor of 3 is required. Determine the minimum required wall thickness at the bottom of the tank, neglecting any localized bending effects there.   *Ans.*   0.575 in

10.19   A thin conical shell is suspended from its top and half filled with mercury, of specific gravity 13.6 (Fig. 10-17). Find the meridional and hoop stresses at a point 0.25 m below the point of attachment. The thickness of the shell wall is 1 mm.   *Ans.* $\sigma_\phi = 2.52\,\text{MPa}$; $\sigma_\theta = 0$

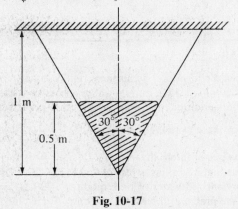

Fig. 10-17

10.20   A thin, elastic toroidal shell has the geometry shown in Fig. 10-18 and has a wall thickness of 2 mm. It is subject to an internal gas pressure of 0.05 MPa. Determine the maximum meridional and hoop stresses in the shell.   *Ans.* $\sigma_\phi = 2.81$ MPa; $\sigma_\theta = 1.25$ MPa

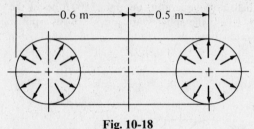

Fig. 10-18

10.21   The hemispherical vessel of radius R and thickness h in Fig. 10-19 is partially filled with a liquid whose weight density is γ. The shell is supported around its upper rim as shown. Determine the stresses in the shell.

Ans.   For $\alpha < 45°$, $\sigma_\phi = -\sigma_\theta = \dfrac{\gamma R^2}{h} \dfrac{0.0382}{\cos^2 \alpha}$;   for $45° < \alpha < 90°$, $\sigma_\phi = \dfrac{\gamma R^2}{h} \left[\dfrac{1 + \sin \alpha + \sin^2 \alpha}{3(1 + \sin \alpha)} - 0.355 \right]$ and

$\sigma_\theta = \dfrac{\gamma R^2}{h}(\sin \alpha - 0.707) - \sigma_\phi$

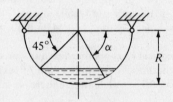

Fig. 10-19

10.22   A partial spherical shell is shown in Fig. 10-20. The only loading is its own dead weight, symbolized as q per unit area of the shell midsurface. The internal radius of the shell is r, and the lower edge of the shell is supported on rollers that can transmit no bending effects. Find the meridional and hoop stresses in the shell. (*Hint*: Use the angle ϕ to denote the location of any point on the shell.)

Ans. $\sigma_\phi = \dfrac{-qr}{h(1 + \cos \phi)}$; $\sigma_\theta = \dfrac{qr}{h} \left(\dfrac{1}{1 + \cos \phi} - \cos \phi \right)$

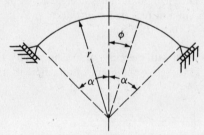

Fig. 10-20

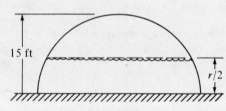

Fig. 10-21

10.23   A water storage tank has the form of a hemisphere rigidly attached to a base slab, as shown in Fig. 10-21. The internal radius of the tank is 15 ft, and its wall thickness is 0.05 in. The tank is filled with water to the depth $r/2$. Determine the meridional and hoop stresses at a point whose distance above the slab is $r/4$.

Ans. $\sigma_\phi = 4014$ lb/in^2; $\sigma_\theta = 1840$ lb/in^2

10.24   A cylindrical pressure vessel of internal radius 1 m, length 5 m, and wall thickness $h = 20$ mm is made of high-strength steel having a working stress of 250 MPa, $E = 210$ GPa, and $\mu = 0.3$. The vessel is initially filled with unpressurized water of bulk modulus 2100 MPa. How much additional water must be pumped in to increase the pressure to 5 MPa?   *Ans.*   0.0561 m^3

10.25 Suppose the hemispherical vessel of Problem 10.21 is filled with the liquid (Fig. 10-22). Determine the stresses in the shell due to this loading.

Ans. $\sigma_\phi = \dfrac{\gamma R^2}{3h}\left(\dfrac{1 - \cos^3 \phi}{\sin^2 \phi}\right)$; $\sigma_\theta = \dfrac{\gamma R^2}{3h}\left(3\cos\phi - \dfrac{1 - \cos^3\phi}{\sin^2\phi}\right)$

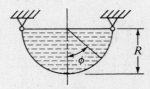

Fig. 10-22

Chapter 11

Torsion

If a bar is twisted in opposite directions at its ends by twisting moments (torques) **T** applied in planes perpendicular to the axis of the bar (Fig. 11-1a or b), it is said to be in *torsion*. We usually speak of the bar as being subject to *a* twisting moment **T**.

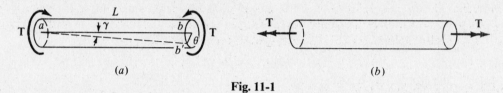

(a)   (b)

Fig. 11-1

TORSIONAL SHEARING STRESSES

For either a solid or a hollow circular shaft subject to a twisting moment **T**, the torsional shearing stress τ at a radial distance ρ from the axis of the shaft is

$$\tau = \frac{T\rho}{J} \tag{11.1}$$

where $T = |\mathbf{T}|$, and J is a parameter called the polar moment of inertia and defined below. It is found by applying the differential equations of equilibrium to the element shown in Fig. 8-1, together with suitable geometric relations resulting from the assumption that originally plane sections of the bar remain plane after they are loaded in torsion.

The stress τ in (11.1) varies linearly from zero at the center of the shaft (if it is solid) to a maximum at the outer fibers, as shown in Fig. 11-2a; the stress distribution for a hollow shaft is shown in Fig. 11-2b. Both parts of Fig. 11-2 assume action in the elastic range for the material. The most common units for shearing stress are megapascals in the SI system and pounds per square inch in the USCS system.

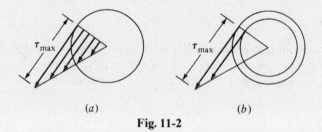

(a)   (b)

Fig. 11-2

POLAR MOMENT OF INERTIA

For a hollow circular shaft of outer diameter D_o and inner diameter D_i, the *polar moment of inertia* J of the cross-sectional area is given by

$$J = \frac{\pi}{32}(D_o^4 - D_i^4) \tag{11.2}$$

190

The polar moment of inertia of a solid circular shaft of diameter D is found by setting $D_i = 0$ to obtain

$$J = \frac{\pi D^4}{32} \tag{11.3}$$

The unit of J is a length to the fourth power, and the length is usually the meter in the SI system or the inch in the USCS system.

SHEARING STRAIN

If a generator a-b is marked on the surface of an untwisted bar as in Fig. 11-1a, then after a twisting moment $\mathbf{T}$ has been applied this line moves to a-b'. The angle γ (measured in radians) between the final and initial positions of the generator is defined as the *shearing strain* due to $\mathbf{T}$ at the surface of the bar. Comparable definitions hold for all interior generators of the bar.

MODULUS OF ELASTICITY IN SHEAR

The ratio of the shearing stress τ to the shearing strain γ is called the *modulus of elasticity in shear* G; that is, $G = \tau/\gamma$. The units of G are the same as those of shearing stress, since shearing strain is dimensionless.

ANGLE OF TWIST

If a shaft of length L is subject to a constant twisting moment $\mathbf{T}$ along its entire length, the angle θ through which one end of the bar will twist relative to the other is

$$\theta = \frac{TL}{GJ} \tag{11.4}$$

The unit of θ is radians.

The angle of twist per unit length of the shaft is

$$\phi = \frac{\theta}{L} = \frac{T}{GJ} \tag{11.5}$$

POWER TRANSMISSION

A shaft rotating with constant angular velocity ω (radians per second) is being acted on by a twisting moment $\mathbf{T}$ and hence transmits a power $P = T\omega$. Alternatively, in terms of the number of revolutions per second f, the power transmitted is $P = 2\pi f T$. (See Problems 11.6 to 11.8.)

COMPUTER SOLUTION

For a bar of circular cross section and variable diameter, the angle of twist θ is determined by dividing the bar into a number of segments along its length, such that in each segment the diameter may be taken to be constant. This procedure is well suited to computer implementation, and a FORTRAN program for implementing it is given in Problem 11.9. (See also Problem 11.10.)

ELASTOPLASTIC TORSION OF CIRCULAR BARS

As the twisting moment acting on either a solid or hollow circular bar is increased, it eventually reaches a magnitude for which the extreme fibers of the bar are at the *yield point in shear* of the material.

This is the maximum possible elastic twisting moment that the bar can withstand, and it is denoted T_e.

A further increase in the magnitude of the twisting moment puts interior fibers at the yield point, with yielding progressing from the outer fibers inward. The limiting case occurs when all fibers are stressed to the yield point in shear; the twisting moment at that point is the *fully plastic twisting moment*, denoted T_p. Provided we do not consider stresses greater than the yield point in shear, this is the maximum possible twisting moment the bar can carry. For a solid circular bar subject to torsion, it is shown in Problem 11.11 that $T_p = 4T_e/3$. (See also Problem 11.12.)

Solved Problems

11.1 So-called "torsion bars" are often used in high-performance cars to improve steering and handling characteristics. One end of the bar is usually attached by a bracket to the chassis frame, and the other end to the front wheel suspension. Both ends of the bar are splined, but the splines are purposely misaligned so that stresses are introduced into the bar when it is installed. In one particular case, to install the bar it is necessary to twist one end through 15° relative to the other end. The bar is 52 in long, has a solid circular cross section of diameter 1.25 in, and is made of steel with $G = 12 \times 10^6 \text{ lb/in}^2$. Find the maximum torsional shear stress that is induced in the bar.

From (*11.3*), the polar moment of inertia of the cross section is

$$J = \frac{\pi}{32}(1.25 \text{ in})^4 = 0.239 \text{ in}^4$$

Then, from (*11.4*) we have

$$(15°)\frac{1 \text{ rad}}{57.3°} = \frac{T(52 \text{ in})}{(12 \times 10^6 \text{ lb/in}^2)(0.239 \text{ in}^4)}$$

from which $T = 14,400 \text{ lb·in}$.

The shearing stress at the outer fibers of the shaft is found with (*11.1*):

$$\tau = \frac{T\rho}{J} = \frac{(14,400 \text{ lb·in})(0.625 \text{ in})}{0.239 \text{ in}^4} = 37,700 \text{ lb/in}^2$$

11.2 A bar of circular cross section (Fig. 11-3) is clamped at one end, free at the other, and loaded by a twisting moment that is uniformly distributed along the length L of the bar. The torsional rigidity of the bar is GJ (that is, the bar has polar moment J and modulus G). Determine the angle of twist of the free end of the bar.

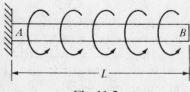

Fig. 11-3

Let the twisting moment be of intensity **t** per unit length of the bar. We introduce a coordinate x with its origin at the right end of the bar and positive values to the left. The free-body diagram of the portion of the bar to the right of some element dx of the bar is shown in Fig. 11-4. The twisting moment in this

Fig. 11-4

cross section is tx, so that, by (*11.4*), the angle of twist $d\theta$ across the length dx is

$$d\theta = \frac{tx\,dx}{GJ}$$

The total rotation of end B of the bar with respect to end A is found by integrating along the entire length L:

$$\theta_{B/A} = \int_{x=0}^{x=L} \frac{tx\,dx}{GJ} = \frac{tL^2}{2GJ} \tag{1}$$

11.3 The solid bar ABC in Fig. 11-5 has a circular cross section. It is loaded over the left 300 mm of its length by a uniformly distributed twisting moment, and at the free end C by a concentrated twisting moment of 80 N·m. The bar is steel for which $G = 84$ GPa, and its diameter is 15 mm. Find the angle of twist of end C and the maximum torsional shearing stress in the bar.

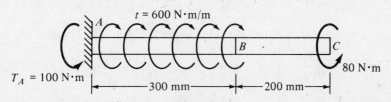

Fig. 11-5

The reactive torque at the fixed end is immediately found from statics to be 100 N·m, as shown in Fig. 11-5. A torque diagram, indicating the variation of the twisting moment along the length of the bar, then appears as in Fig. 11-6, where torques that are clockwise when viewed down the axis of the bar from C to A are taken to be positive.

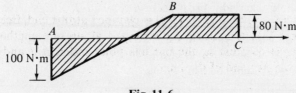

Fig. 11-6

Using (*1*) of Problem 11.2, we have

$$\theta_{B/A} = \frac{(600 \text{ N·m/m})(0.3 \text{ m})^2}{2GJ} = \frac{27}{GJ}$$

Hence, owing to the distributed torque, the portion BC of the bar rotates through the angle $27/GJ$ as a rigid body.

The effect of the concentrated 80 N·m torque is to produce an angle of twist at C given by

$$\theta_{C/A} = \frac{TL}{GJ} = \frac{(80 \text{ N·m})(0.5 \text{ m})}{GJ} = -\frac{40}{GJ}$$

The net rotation at C is thus $(27 - 40)/GJ$ or $-13/GJ$, where the minus sign indicates counter-clockwise rotation. For $G = 84\,\text{GPa}$ and J as given in (11.3), we have

$$\theta_C = \frac{-13}{GJ} = -\frac{13\ \text{N·m}^2}{(84 \times 10^9\ \text{N/m}^2)(\pi/32)(0.015\ \text{m})^4} = -0.031\ \text{rad} \quad \text{or} \quad -1.78°$$

From Fig. 11-6 it is evident that the peak torque occurs at the fixed end A and is $100\,\text{N·m}$. In the outer fibers of the bar at A, the peak torsional shearing stress is given by

$$\tau_{\text{max}} = \frac{T\rho}{J} = \frac{(100\ \text{N·m})(0.0075\ \text{m})}{(\pi/32)(0.015\ \text{m})^4} = 150.9 \times 10^6\ \text{N/m}^2 = 150.9\ \text{MPa}$$

11.4   A composite shaft is made of a 2-in-diameter solid aluminum rod with $G = 4 \times 10^6\,\text{lb/in}^2$, surrounded by a hollow circular steel cylinder of outside diameter 2.5 in and inside diameter 2 in with $G = 12 \times 10^6\,\text{lb/in}^2$. The two metals are rigidly connected where they join. If the composite shaft is loaded by a twisting moment of 14,000 lb·in, calculate the shearing stress at the outer fibers of the steel and at the extreme fibers of the aluminum. The action is within the elastic ranges of both materials.

Let T_1 be the torque carried by the aluminum shaft, and T_2 the torque carried by the steel. For static equilibrium of moments about the axis of the shaft, we have

$$T_1 + T_2 = 14,000\ \text{lb·in}$$

This is the only equation from statics available in this problem. Since it contains two unknowns, T_1 and T_2, it must be supplemented with an additional equation based on the deformations of the shaft.

Such an equation is easily found: Since the two materials are rigidly joined, their angles of twist must be equal. In a length L of the shaft we have, using the formula $\theta = TL/GJ$,

$$\frac{T_1 L}{(4 \times 10^6)(\pi/32)(2)^4} = \frac{T_2 L}{(12 \times 10^6)(\pi/32)[(2.5)^4 - (2)^4]} \quad \text{or} \quad T_1 = 0.231 T_2$$

This equation may be solved simultaneously with the statics equation to yield $T_1 = 2600\ \text{lb·in}$ and $T_2 = 11,400\ \text{lb·in}$.

The shearing stresses at the extreme fibers of the steel and the aluminum are, respectively, by (11.1),

$$\tau_2 = \frac{11,400(1.25)}{(\pi/32)[(2.5)^4 - (2)^4]} = 6300\ \text{lb/in}^2 \quad \text{and} \quad \tau_1 = \frac{2600(1)}{(\pi/32)(2)^4} = 1650\ \text{lb/in}^2$$

11.5   A stepped solid shaft of circular cross section (Fig. 11-7) is rigidly clamped at ends A and D and loaded by twisting moments $T_1 = 1000\,\text{N·m}$ and $T_2 = 1500\,\text{N·m}$ at points B and C. The material is steel for which $G = 84 \times 10^9\,\text{N/m}^2$,   the length L of the shaft is 500 mm, and the diameters of AB and CD are both 30 mm while that of BC is 50 mm. Determine the angle of twist at C and the peak torsional shearing stress.

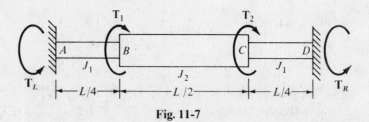

Fig. 11-7

The torque reactions at the left and right ends of the shaft, designated T_L and T_R respectively in the figure, are assumed to act in the directions indicated. A torque diagram showing the variation of the twisting

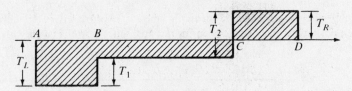

Fig. 11-8

moment along the length of the shaft then appears as in Fig. 11-8, for which torques that are clockwise when viewed from D to A have been taken to be positive.

For static equilibrium of torques about the longitudinal axis of the shaft, we have

$$T_1 + T_2 - T_L - T_R = 0 \tag{1}$$

This is the only available statics equation, and it contains two unknowns T_L and T_R. The system is thus statically indeterminate, and we must supplement the statics equation with another based on deformations. One such equation makes use of the relation $\theta = TL/GJ$, computed for the various portions of the bar:

$$\theta_{B/A} = \frac{T_L L/4}{GJ_1} \qquad \theta_{C/B} = \frac{(T_L - T_1)L/2}{GJ_2} \qquad \theta_{C/D} = \frac{T_R L/4}{GJ_1}$$

Because ends A and D are fixed, the amount by which the cross section at C rotates with respect to A must equal the amount by which it rotates with respect to D. Thus,

$$\frac{T_L L}{4GJ_1} + \frac{(T_L - T_1)L}{2GJ_2} = \frac{T_R L}{4GJ_1}$$

or

$$T_L = \frac{2T_1 J_1 + T_R J_2}{J_2 + 2J_1} \tag{2}$$

For the given numerical values, (11.3) yields

$$J_1 = \frac{\pi(0.030 \text{ m})^4}{32} \qquad \text{and} \qquad J_2 = \frac{\pi(0.050 \text{ m})^4}{32}$$

so that (2) becomes

$$T_L = \frac{2(1000)(0.030)^4 + T_R(0.050)^4}{(0.050)^4 + 2(0.030)^4} = 205.8 + 0.794 T_R$$

Substituting this in (1), we find that $T_L = 1221$ N·m and $T_R = 1278$ N·m. The angle of twist at C is then

$$\theta_{C/D} = \frac{(1278 \text{ N·m})(0.125 \text{ m})}{(84 \times 10^9 \text{ N/m}^2)(\pi/32)(0.030 \text{ m})^4} = 0.0239 \text{ rad or } 1.37°$$

Figure 11-8 indicates that, because $T_R > T_L$, the peak shearing stress occurs at the outer fibers of CD; its value is given by (11.1):

$$\tau_{max} = \frac{T\rho}{\Psi} = \frac{(1278 \text{ N·m})(0.015 \text{ m})}{(\pi/32)(0.030 \text{ m})^4} = 241 \times 10^6 \text{ N/m}^2 = 241 \text{ MPa}$$

11.6   A shaft rotates at constant angular velocity ω. Derive a relationship between the twisting moment **T** acting on the shaft and the power P transmitted by it, assuming action in the elastic range.

Formulas involving rotary motion may be given in terms of the angular velocity ω, in radians per second, or in terms of frequency f, in revolutions per second or hertz, since $\omega = 2\pi f$. The units of power can also add complexity.

In 1 s, the twisting moment **T** does an amount of work given (by definition) as the product of its magnitude and the angular displacement in radians. Since power P is the time rate at which work is being done, we have

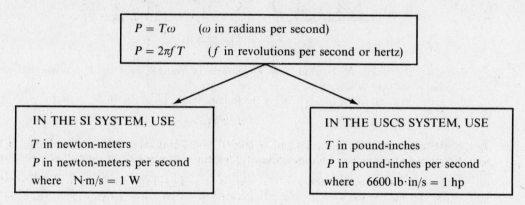

To use the SI units, you should know that $1 \text{ N·m} = 1 \text{ J}$ (joule), and so $1 \text{ W} = 1 \text{ J/s}$. Also, W denotes watt.

11.7 A solid, circular steel shaft is to transmit 40 kW at 900 rpm. For $G = 80 \text{ GPa}$ and a working stress in shear of 20 MPa, find the minimum diameter of the shaft.

The power transmitted at rotational frequency f is $P = 2\pi f T$. Hence, we write

$$40{,}000 \text{ N·m/s} = 2\pi(900 \text{ rpm}) \frac{1 \text{ min}}{60 \text{ s}} T$$

from which we find that $T = 424 \text{ N·m}$.

The shearing stress peaks at the outer fibers, at which $\rho = D/2$. Hence, from (11.1),

$$\tau_{max} = \frac{T\rho}{J} = \frac{TD/2}{\pi D^4/32} = \frac{16T}{\pi D^3} \tag{1}$$

Setting $\tau_{max} = 20 \times 10^6 \text{ N/m}^2$ and $T = 424 \text{ N·m}$ in this equation yields $D = 0.0475$ m or 47.5 mm.

11.8 A solid, circular steel shaft is to transmit 55 hp at 900 rpm. For $G = 12 \times 10^6 \text{ lb/in}^2$ and an allowable working stress in shear of 2900 lb/in², determine the minimum diameter of the shaft.

Substituting known values in the equation $P = 2\pi f T$ yields

$$55(6600 \text{ lb·in/s}) = 2\pi(900 \text{ rpm}) \frac{1 \text{ min}}{60 \text{ s}} T$$

which yields $T = 3850 \text{ lb·in}$.

The shearing stress peaks at the outer fibers of the shaft, where $\rho = \Lambda/2$. Hence, from (1) of Problem 11.7,

$$\tau_{max} = \frac{16T}{\pi D^3} \quad \text{or} \quad 2900 \text{ lb/in}^2 = \frac{16(3850 \text{ lb·in})}{\pi D^3}$$

from which $D = 1.89$ in.

11.9 A bar of circular cross section whose diameter varies along its length L is loaded in torsion at its ends, as shown in Fig. 11-9. The variation in the diameter may be known analytically, or

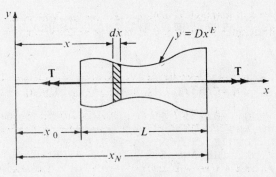

Fig. 11-9

through measurements at a number of locations along the axis of the shaft. Write a FORTRAN program to determine the angle of twist of one end of the bar with respect to the other end.

Equation (11.4) cannot be applied to the entire length L of the bar, since it was derived under the assumption that the bar has a constant circular cross section. However, we may divide the length of the bar into a number of segments, in each of which the cross section is regarded as constant. If we have an equation $y = f(x)$ for the profile of the bar in Fig. 11-9, we can divide the length of the bar into infinitesimal segments each of length dx, take the cross section to be constant along each segment, and then use the calculus to apply $\theta = TL/GJ$ to all the segments and sum the results. If the bar consists of a finite number of segments whose dimensions have been measured, we can employ these measurements to find and sum the angles of twist for all the segments.

This approach is represented by the FORTRAN program that follows. The program is applicable to bars of arbitrarily varying circular cross section, and the various quantities involved in the program are shown in Fig. 11-9. Note that in the equation $y = Dx^E$ describing the bar shape, E is an exponent and not the elastic modulus. The bar is assumed to be symmetrical about its longitudinal axis; if the profile is given as a set of measurements, they must have been taken at equal intervals along the bar.

```
00020C      PROGRAM TORSION1 ---- TORSION OF A VARIABLE RADIUS SOLID
00030C                            CIRCULAR CROSS-SECTION BAR
00040C
00050C      THE BAR HAS LENGTH L, SHEAR MODULUS G, IS DIVIDED INTO N
00060C      SEGMENTS ALONG THE TOTAL LENGTH, AND IS LOADED BY A TORQUE T
00070C      WHICH IS CONSTANT ALONG THE BAR LENGTH.
00080C      THE RADIUS MAY BE DESCRIBED EITHER ANALYTICALLY AS R = R(X)
00090C      WHERE X IS THE GEOMETRIC AXIS OF THE BAR, OR NUMERICALLY USING
00100C      THE MAGNITUDE OF R AT EACH END OF THE N SEGMENTS, MEANING AN
00110C      INPUT OF N+1 VALUE. THESE ARE THE CASES IN LINE 00230.
00120C
00130       DIMENSION  A(101),C(101)
00140       PRINT *,'  ENTER TOTAL LENGTH OF SHAFT'
00150       READ(*,*)  L
00160       PRINT *,'  ENTER THE SHEAR MODULUS'
00170       READ(*,*)  G
00180       PRINT *,'  ENTER THE TORQUE'
00190       READ(*,*)  T
00200       PRINT *,'  DO YOU KNOW THE FUNCTION DESCRIBING THE SHAFT ?'
00210       PRINT *,'  ENTER 1 : YES ;    2 : NO'
00220       READ(*,*)  YON
00230       IF ( YON.EQ.2.) GO TO 10
00240       PRINT *,'  F(X) =  D*X**E '
00250       PRINT *,'  ENTER D,E'
00260       READ(*,*)  D,E
00270       PRINT *,'  ENTER THE COORDINATE OF BOTH ENDS IN X-AXES'
00280       READ(*,*)  XO,XN
00290       ANG=2.*T/(3.14159*G*(-4.*E+1.)*D**4.)*(XN**(-4.*E+1.)-XO**(-4.*E+1.))

00300       GO TO 40
00310    10 PRINT *,'  ENTER NO. OF SECTIONS TO BE CALCULATED'
```

```
00320        READ(*,*)  N
00330        PRINT *,'  ENTER THE RADII OF THE ENDS FOR SECTION 1 TO N'
00340        DO 20 I =  1,N+1.
00350    20  READ(*,*)  A(I)
00360        ANG = 0.
00370        DO 30 I = 1,N
00380        C(I) = (32.*T*L/N)/(3.14159*G *((A(I)+A(I+1))**4))
00390    30  ANG = ANG + C(I)
00400    40  DEGRE = ANG*180/3.14159
00410        PRINT 100,ANG
00420        PRINT 200,DEGRE
00430   100  FORMAT(/,5X,'THE ANGLE OF TWIST AT END IS ',F9.5,' RADIANS')
00440   200  FORMAT(/,5X,'                            OR ',F9.5,' DEGREES')
00450        END
```

READY.

11.10 A solid shaft of circular cross section lies along the x axis and has a contour described by the equation $x = 150y^{2.5}$ from $x = 50$ in to $x = 75$ in. The material has a shear modulus of 12×10^6 lb/in^2, and the bar is subject to a twisting moment of 6000 lb·in at each end. Find the angle of twist between the ends, using the FORTRAN program of Problem 11.9.

It is necessary first to rewrite the equation of the profile in the form $y = Dx^E$, which is how it appears in the program. This is accomplished by dividing both sides of the equation by 150 and then taking the "2.5th root" of both sides. The result is

$$y = \frac{x^{1/2.5}}{150^{1/2.5}} = \frac{x^{0.4}}{150^{0.4}} = 0.1348x^{0.4}$$

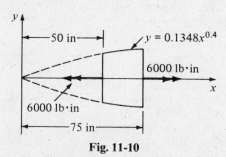

Fig. 11-10

as is shown in Fig. 11-10, which also contains the required input data. The computer run, including responses to prompts, is as follows:

```
ENTER THE TOTAL LENGTH OF THE ROD (IN M OR INCHES):
? 25
ENTER THE SHEAR MODULUS (IN PASCALS OR PSI) :
? 12E+6
ENTER THE UNIFORM TORQUE (IN N-M OR LB-IN) :
? 6000
DO YOU KNOW THE FUNCTION DESCRIBING THE ROD?
ENTER  1--YES  ;   2--NO
? 1
F(X) = D*(X**E)
ENTER D,E:
? 0.1348,0.4
ENTER THE X-COORDINATE FOR BOTH ENDS OF THE ROD:
(IN M OR INCHES):
? 50,75
THE ANGLE OF TWIST IS:       1.929 DEGREES.
```

11.11 A bar of solid circular cross section is subject to torsion. The material is considered to be elastic–perfectly plastic; i.e., the shear stress-strain diagram has the appearance of Fig. 11-11a. Determine the distance from the center at which plastic flow begins, in terms of the twisting moment. Also determine the twisting moment that produces fully plastic action throughout the cross section.

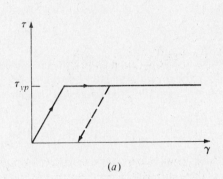

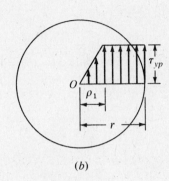

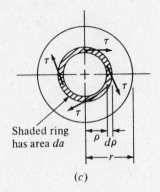

Shaded ring has area da

(a)   (b)   (c)

Fig. 11-11

Even after torsion has caused the outer portion of the bar to yield, it is still realistic to assume that sections of the bar that were plane and normal to its axis prior to loading remain plane after the torques have been applied, and further that a diameter in such a section before deformation remains a diameter, or a straight line, after deformation. Consequently, the shearing strains of longitudinal fibers vary linearly with their distance from the center of the bar.

Let us assume that plastic action begins at a distance ρ_1 from the center of the bar, so that the stress distribution appears as in Fig. 11-11b. Then the shearing stresses vary linearly with the distance ρ from the center O until ρ_1 is reached, after which they are constant and equal to the yield point in shear.

From Fig. 11-11b we have, for $\rho < \rho_1$,

$$\frac{\tau}{\rho} = \frac{\tau_{yp}}{\rho_1} \qquad \text{or} \qquad \tau = \frac{\rho}{\rho_1}\tau_{yp}$$

For $\rho > \rho_1$, $\tau = \tau_{yp} = $ constant.

The moment of all shearing stresses acting over the cross section may be found by considering the thin shaded ring in Fig. 11-11c. The shearing stress at a distance ρ from the center is τ, and this stress acts over the area da of the ring. The moment of this stress about the center is given by $\tau\rho\,da$, and the sum of the moments of the stresses acting on all such rings from the center to the outer fibers is $\int_0^r \tau\rho\,da$. Because this must equal the applied twisting moment T for equilibrium, we have

$$T = \int_0^r \tau\rho\,da$$

For the values of shearing stress computed above, this is

$$T = \int_0^{\rho_1} \frac{\rho}{\rho_1}\tau_{yp}\rho\,da + \int_{\rho_1}^r \tau_{yp}\rho\,da = \frac{\tau_{yp}}{\rho_1}\int_0^{\rho_1}\rho^2\,da + \tau_{yp}\int_{\rho_1}^r \rho\,da$$

$$= \frac{\tau_{yp}}{\rho_1}\int_0^{\rho_1}\rho^2 2\pi\rho\,d\rho + \tau_{yp}\int_{\rho_1}^r \rho 2\pi\rho\,d\rho = \tau_{yp}\left(\frac{\pi}{2} - \frac{2\pi}{3}\right)\rho_1^3 + \frac{2\pi}{3}\tau_{yp}r^3$$

This yields
$$\rho_1 = \left(4r^3 - \frac{6T}{\pi\tau_{yp}}\right)^{1/3} \tag{1}$$

as the distance from the center at which plastic flow begins. For fully plastic action, that is, for $\tau = \tau_{yp}$ at all points of the cross section, we set $\rho_1 = 0$ to obtain the fully plastic twisting moment T_p:

$$T_p = \tfrac{2}{3}\pi r^3\tau_{yp} \tag{2}$$

But if only the outer fibers of the bar are stressed to the yield point of the material and all interior fibers are in the elastic range of action, we have the maximum possible elastic twisting moment T_e:

$$T_e = \frac{\tau_{yp}}{2} \pi r^3 \qquad (3)$$

Comparison of (2) and (3) indicates that $T_p = 4T_e/3$; that is, fully plastic action occurs with the application of a twisting moment $33\frac{1}{3}$ percent greater than the twisting moment that just causes plastic action to begin in the outer fibers.

11.12 A twisting moment of 50,000 lb·in is applied to a 2-in-diameter shaft having a yield point in shear of 26,000 lb/in². Find the distance from the center of the shaft to the elastoplastic boundary, and determine the distribution of *residual* shearing stresses that remains after the torsional load has been removed.

From (1) of Problem 11.11 we have

$$\rho_1 = \left[4(1 \text{ in})^3 - \frac{6(50,000 \text{ lb·in})}{\pi(26,000 \text{ lb/in}^2)} \right]^{1/3} = 0.688 \text{ in}$$

as the radius of the elastoplastic boundary. The torsional shearing stress distribution then appears as in Fig. 11-12a.

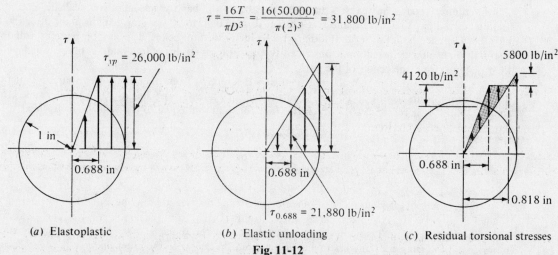

(a) Elastoplastic   (b) Elastic unloading   (c) Residual torsional stresses

Fig. 11-12

When the external twisting moment is removed, the material "relaxes" linearly, following the dashed line in Fig. 11-11a. This linear unloading has the stress distribution shown in Fig. 11-12b, for which the ordinates may be determined with (11.1) because the torsional stresses are in the elastic range.

To obtain the final stress state, i.e., the residual stresses after removal of the load, we merely superpose the stress states of Fig. 11-12a and b to obtain that shown in Fig. 11-12c. In that figure it is clear that some of the residual stresses produce a clockwise moment whereas others produce a counterclockwise moment. This must be the case, because the net torque over the cross section must be zero after the applied load is removed.

Supplementary Problems

11.13 A composite shaft (Fig. 11-13) is made up of a solid aluminum rod of diameter 30 mm with $G = 27$ GPa rigidly joined to a hollow brass cylinder of outer diameter 30 mm with $G = 39$ GPa. Find the inner diameter of the brass cylinder if the angle of twist per unit length of the brass portion of the shaft is 80 percent of that of the aluminum portion.   *Ans.*   18.2 mm

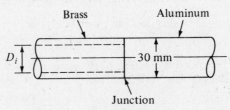

Fig. 11-13

11.14   The horizontal shaft in Fig. 11-14 has three pulleys keyed to it, as shown. The system may be considered weightless. The shaft rotates at constant angular velocity and has the belt pulls indicated. If the working stress of the shaft in shear is 9500 lb/in², determine the required shaft diameter. (Neglect bending of the shaft.)   *Ans.* $D = 0.99$ in $\approx 1/$in

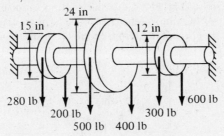

Fig. 11-14

11.15   A shaft of solid circular cross section and 1.375-in diameter is subject to a torque of 3500 lb·in that causes an angle of twist of 3.5° in a 6-ft length. What is the shear modulus of the material?

Ans. $G = 11.76 \times 10^6$ lb/in²

11.16   A solid circular shaft has a slight taper extending uniformly from one end to the other. The radius at the small end is a, and that at the large end is b. Using integration, determine the angle of twist in a length L.

Ans. $\dfrac{2TL}{3G\pi(b-a)}\left(\dfrac{1}{a^3} - \dfrac{1}{b^3}\right)$

11.17   A stepped solid shaft of circular cross section is loaded by a twisting moment that is uniformly distributed over the right half of the bar (Fig. 11-15). The narrower portion BC has a polar moment of inertia of J_1, and the wider portion AB has a polar moment of $1.5J_1$. Determine the angle of twist at the free end C.

Ans. $\frac{7}{24} tL^2/GJ_1$

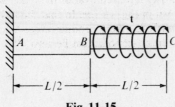

Fig. 11-15

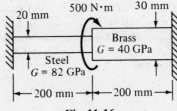

Fig. 11-16

11.18   The solid circular steel and brass portions of the composite shaft in Fig. 11-16 are rigidly clamped at their ends and securely brazed where they join. The shaft is subject to an applied twisting moment of 500 N·m, as shown. Determine the maximum torsional shearing stress in each material.

Ans.   91.5 MPa in steel;   67 MPa in brass

11.19 Determine the minimum diameter of a solid circular steel shaft that will transmit 22 kW at 1800 rpm. Take G to be 80 GPa and the maximum allowable shearing stress to be 24 MPa.   *Ans.*   29 mm

11.20 Find the diameter of a solid circular steel shaft that will transmit 45 kW at 1000 rpm if the allowable angle of twist is not to exceed 1.0° per meter of length. Take $G = 80$ GPa.   *Ans.*   42 mm

11.21 A hollow steel shaft with an outside diameter of 50 mm and an inside diameter of 30 mm rotates at 900 rpm. Find the maximum power that can be transmitted if the peak shearing stress is not to exceed 65 MPa.

Ans.   131 kW

11.22 A solid shaft with circular cross section lies along the x axis and has a profile described by the equation $x = 100y^2$.   The shaft extends from $x = 1$ m   to $x = 1.5$ m   and has a shear modulus of $G = 80$ GPa.   It is loaded by a twisting moment of 157 kN·m at each end. Use the FORTRAN program of Problem 11.9 to find the angle of twist of one end with respect to the other end.   *Ans.*   0.239°

11.23 A solid shaft of conical shape (Fig. 11-17) extends from $x = 200$ mm   to $x = 600$ mm   and has end radii of 40 mm and 60 mm. A twisting moment of 4000 N·m is applied at each end. If the shear modulus is $G = 80$ GPa,   find the angle of twist from end to end using the FORTRAN program of Problem 11.9.

Ans.   0.732°

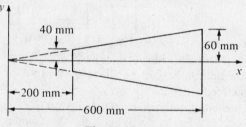

Fig. 11-17

11.24 A solid, circular steel shaft of diameter 1.60 in is subject to a twisting moment of 28,000 lb·in. The yield point of the material in shear is 27,000 lb/in². Determine the radius of the circular boundary between the resulting elastic and plastic zones.

Ans.   0.41 in

11.25 In Problem 11.24 determine the residual stress distribution if the twisting moment of 28,000 lb·in is completely released.   *Ans.*   Fig. 11-18

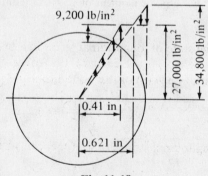

Fig. 11-18

Chapter 12

Stresses in Beams

BEAMS

A *beam* is a long, relatively slender bar subject to forces and couples that lie in a plane containing the longitudinal axis of the bar. The forces act perpendicular to the longitudinal axis of the beam. We shall assume that a beam is made up of a large number of longitudinal fibers, each acting in either tension or compression. We also assume that there are no lateral pressures from fiber to fiber, so each acts independently of the others. Further, the plane containing the forces and couples is a plane of symmetry of the cross section of the beam; and, lastly, we assume that cross sections of the beam normal to the longitudinal axis remain plane and normal to that axis after the beam has deflected due to the applied loads.

NEUTRAL AXIS

In any beam, there is one longitudinal surface whose fibers do not undergo any extension or compression. This surface is called the *neutral surface* of the beam.

The intersection of the neutral surface of a beam with any cross section of the beam perpendicular to its longitudinal axis is called a *neutral axis* (N.A.) of the beam. All fibers to one side of a neutral axis are in tension, those on the other side are in compression.

BENDING MOMENT AND SHEARING FORCE

The definitions and discussions of these quantities in Chapter 7 apply to beams as well.

ELASTIC BENDING OF BEAMS

The following statements apply only if *all* fibers of a beam are stressed within the linear elastic range of the material of the beam.

Normal Stresses

It is possible to express the state of longitudinal stress in a beam (tensile or compressive, to one side or the other of the neutral surface) by means of the stress function of (9) of Problem 8.20 with $A_3 = B_3 = C_3 = 0$. Substitution into (3) of the same problem leads to

$$\sigma_x = \frac{\partial^2 (D_3 y^3)}{\partial y^2} = 6D_3 y \qquad (12.1)$$

For the moments of all the longitudinal stresses about the neutral axis to be equal to the bending moment **M**, it must be that

$$\sigma_x = \sigma = \frac{My}{I} \qquad (12.2)$$

where $M = |\mathbf{M}|$; I denotes the moment of inertia of the cross section about the neutral axis, computed by the methods of Chapter 6; and y denotes the distance of a longitudinal fiber from the neutral axis.

From (12.2) it is obvious that the magnitude of the normal stress varies linearly with the distance y. For a bending moment that leads to tensile stresses below the neutral axis and compressive stresses above, the normal stress distribution appears as shown in Fig. 12-1. For equilibrium of normal forces over the cross section shown in that figure, the neutral axis must pass through the centroid of the cross section.

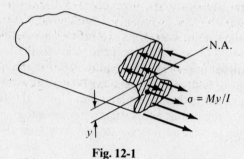

Fig. 12-1

Section Modulus

The value of the coordinate y (measured positive downward in this book) at the outer fibers of a beam is often denoted by the symbol c. In that case the maximum normal stress is given by

$$\sigma_{max} = \frac{Mc}{I} = \frac{M}{I/c} \tag{12.3}$$

The ratio I/c is called the *section modulus* of the cross section and is usually denoted by Z. Its units are those of a length to the third power. The maximum bending stress may then be represented as

$$\sigma_{max} = M/Z \tag{12.4}$$

This form is convenient because values of Z for many common structural shapes are tabulated in structural manuals. (See Problem 12.1.)

Shearing Stresses

A beam that is loaded by a transverse shearing force V (in pounds or newtons) is subject to both vertical and horizontal shearing stresses τ. The magnitude of the vertical shearing stress at any cross section is such that the resultant of all such stresses is the shearing force V.

For a beam having a rectangular cross section as in Fig. 12-2, let the vertical plane of symmetry

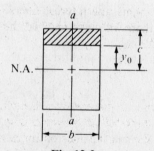

Fig. 12-2

(*a-a*) contain the applied forces. The shearing stress on the fibers at a distance y_0 from the neutral axis is then given by

$$\tau = \frac{V}{Ib} \int_{y_0}^{c} y \, dA \qquad (12.5)$$

where b denotes the width of the beam at the location where the shearing stress is sought. The integral in (*12.5*) represents the first moment of the shaded area in Fig. 12-2 about the neutral axis (see Chapter 6). More precisely, the integral represents the first moment about the neutral axis of that part of the cross-sectional area of the beam that lies between the horizontal plane on which the stress τ is desired and the outer fibers of the beam. Moreover, (*12.5*) gives both vertical and horizontal shearing stresses at y_0.

From (*12.5*), it is clear that the peak shearing stresses occur at the neutral axis, whereas the shearing stresses at the outer fibers are zero. This is the opposite of the behavior of the normal stresses, as given by (*12.2*). (See Problem 12.7.)

Beams of Varying Cross Section

Stresses in such beams may be found with (*12.2*) and (*12.5*). Usually, if the cross section of a beam varies along its length, the maximum bending stress does not occur at the section where the bending moment is a maximum. (See Problem 12.6.)

ELASTOPLASTIC AND FULLY PLASTIC BENDING OF BEAMS

The following statements apply if the outer fibers of a beam have reached the material's yield point σ_{yp}, which is assumed to be the same in tension as in compression. The material is assumed to have a simplified stress-strain curve similar to that considered for inelastic torsion in Problem 11.11, with a horizontal plateau that extends indefinitely to the right. This implies a type of action that is termed *elastic–perfectly plastic* behavior. Unloading usually takes place along a straight line having a slope identical to that of the elastic loading region, as is represented by the dashed line in Fig. 12-3.

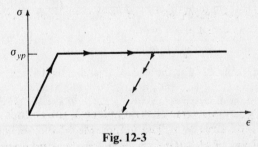

Fig. 12-3

Elastoplastic Action

For sufficiently large bending moments, the interior fibers of a beam will be stressed in the elastic range of the material while the outer fibers will have reached the yield point, as shown in Fig. 12-4*a*. (See Problems 12.10 and 12.12 through 12.14.)

Fully Plastic Action

As the bending moment on a beam is increased, a limiting case is approached in which all fibers are stressed to the yield point of the material, as shown in Fig. 12-4*b*. (See Problems 12.11 and 12.15.)

During this fully plastic action, the neutral axis assumes a position such that it divides the total cross-sectional area into two equal parts. (See Problem 12.15.)

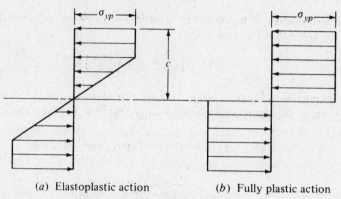

(*a*) Elastoplastic action   (*b*) Fully plastic action

Fig. 12-4

Residual Stresses

If transverse loadings are applied to a beam and they are sufficiently large so that the stresses in the outer fibers reach the yield point (as in Fig. 12-4*a*), after which the external loadings are completely released, then residual tensile and compressive stresses will remain. The resultant of these stresses over any cross section in the direction of the longitudinal axis of the beam will be zero. (See Problem 12.12.)

Solved Problems

Elastic Bending of Beams

12.1   Select a commercially available steel wide-flange beam capable of resisting a bending moment of 150 kN·m if the maximum allowable working stress in tension and compression is 160 MPa.

From (*12.4*), the maximum outer-fiber bending stresses are given by $\sigma_{max} = M/Z$. Hence,

$$Z = \frac{M}{\sigma_{max}} = \frac{150{,}000 \text{ N·m}}{160 \times 10^6 \text{ N/m}^2} = 937.5 \times 10^{-6} \text{ m}^3 = 937.5 \times 10^3 \text{ mm}^3$$

We now must examine Table 12-2 at the end of this chapter to find a beam having a section modulus Z of at least $937.5 \times 10^3 \text{ mm}^3$. Evidently a W 305×66 is adequate, since it has $Z = 952 \times 10^3 \text{ mm}^3$. The W 254×79, a beam of lesser depth having $Z = 988 \times 10^3 \text{ mm}^3$, is more than adequate.

12.2   A simply supported beam of length 3 m is loaded by a uniformly distributed load of 6 kN/m. The cross section of the beam is rectangular, 7 cm by 15 cm. (See Fig. 12-5.) Determine the maximum bending stress in the beam, neglecting its weight. Also find the bending stress 2 cm below the upper surface of the beam at the section midway between the supports.

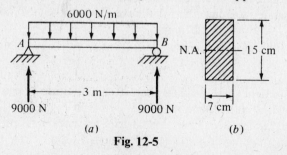

(*a*)   (*b*)

Fig. 12-5

The support reactions are, by symmetry, each 9000 N. The bending moment at any distance x from the left end of the beam thus has magnitude

$$M = \left(9000x - 6000x\frac{x}{2}\right) \text{N·m}$$

Hence the bending moment diagram has the shape of a parabola and, as is easily verified, is symmetric about the midpoint of the beam. It thus appears as in Fig. 12-6. The magnitude of the bending moment at the midpoint of the beam is

$$M_{1.5\,m} = (9000)(1.5) - (6000)(1.5)(0.75) = 6750 \text{ N·m}$$

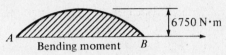

A   Bending moment   B

6750 N·m

Fig. 12-6

The moment of inertia of the rectangular cross section, which we shall need shortly, is

$$I = \tfrac{1}{12}bh^3 = \tfrac{1}{12}(0.07 \text{ m})(0.15 \text{ m})^3 = 19.69 \times 10^{-6} \text{ m}^4$$

Since the bending moment diagram shows that the maximum moment occurs at the midpoint of the beam, the maximum bending stresses must occur at the outermost fibers there. These stresses are given by

$$\sigma_{max} = \frac{Mc}{I} = \frac{(6750 \text{ N·m})(0.075 \text{ m})}{19.69 \times 10^{-6} \text{ m}^4} = 25.7 \text{ MPa}$$

at the lower fibers where c is positive, indicating tensile stress, and

$$\sigma_{min} = \frac{(6750 \text{ N·m})(-0.075 \text{ m})}{19.69 \times 10^{-6} \text{ m}^4} = -25.7 \text{ MPa}$$

at the upper fibers where c is negative, indicating compressive stress.

At a point 2 cm below the upper surface, we have $y = -(7.5 - 2.0) = -5.5 \text{ cm}$,   so the normal stress there is

$$\sigma = \frac{My}{I} = \frac{(6750 \text{ N·m})(-0.055 \text{ m})}{19.69 \times 10^{-6} \text{ m}^4} = -18.8 \text{ MPa}$$

the minus sign indicating compression for fibers that lie above the neutral axis.

12.3   A fiber-optic cable is coiled around a cylinder that is 1 cm in diameter. If the cable has a diameter of 0.5 mm and $E = 2 \text{ GPa}$,   find the peak bending stress in the cable.

We consider two adjacent cross sections of the cable that, prior to bending, are parallel to each other. After the cable is bent, these cross sections appear as a-a and b-b in Fig. 12-7, where O represents

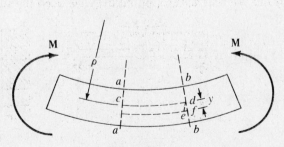

Fig. 12-7

the center of curvature of the bent cable. The elongation of a longitudinal fiber at a distance y (measured positive downward) is found by drawing line de parallel to section a-a. If ρ denotes the radius of curvature of the bent cable, then from similar triangles cOd and edf we have, as the strain for this fiber,

$$\varepsilon = \frac{ef}{cd} = \frac{de}{cO} = \frac{y}{\rho} \tag{1}$$

But since each longitudinal fiber is in uniaxial tension or compression, we have, by Hooke's law, $q = E\varepsilon$. Then the stress in the cable at a distance y from the neutral axis is

$$\sigma = E\frac{y}{\rho} \tag{2}$$

For the given numerical values, the peak bending stress (at the outer fibers) is

$$\sigma_{\max} = (2 \times 10^9 \text{ N/m}^2)\frac{0.25 \text{ mm}}{5 \text{ mm}} = 100 \text{ MPa}$$

12.4   The simply supported W 10 × 49 beam in Fig. 12-8a is subject to a uniformly varying load having a maximum intensity of w lb per foot of length at the right support. Find w if the working stress for the section is 18,000 lb/in² in either tension or compression. Neglect the weight of the beam.

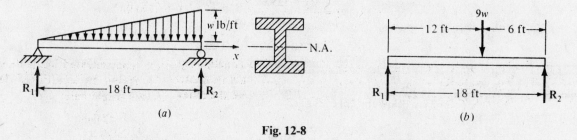

Fig. 12-8

The reactions R_1 and R_2 may readily be determined in terms of the unknown w by replacing the distributed load by its resultant. Since the average value of the distributed load is $w/2$ lb/ft acting over a length of 18 ft, the resultant is a force of magnitude $18(w/2) = 9w$ lb acting through the centroid of the triangular loading diagram, that is, 12 ft to the right of R_1. This resultant thus appears as in Fig. 12-8b. From statics we immediately have $R_1 = 3w$ and $R_2 = 6w$.

Let us introduce an x axis coinciding with the beam and having its origin at the left support (Fig. 12-9a). Then at a distance x to the right of the left reaction, the intensity of the loading is found from similar triangles to be $(x/18)w$ lb/ft. Using the procedure of Problem 7.4, we find, for the shearing force V at a distance x from the left support,

$$V = 3w - \frac{1}{2}\frac{x}{18}wx = 3w - \frac{1}{36}wx^2$$

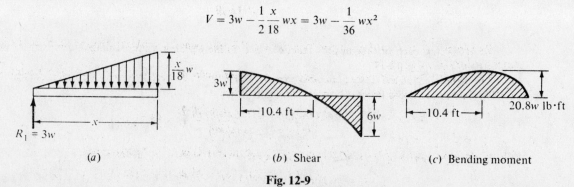

Fig. 12-9

This equation holds for all values of x, and from it the shear diagram in Fig. 12-9b is readily plotted. The point of zero shear is found by setting

$$3w - \frac{1}{36}wx^2 = 0 \qquad \text{from which} \qquad x = \sqrt{108} = 10.4 \text{ ft}$$

This is also the point where the bending moment assumes its maximum value.

Again using Problem 7.4, we find that the bending moment M at a distance x from the left support is given by

$$M = 3wx - \frac{1}{2}\frac{x}{18}wx\frac{x}{3} = 3wx - \frac{1}{108}wx^3$$

This equation too holds for all values of x, and from it the bending moment diagram of Fig. 12-9c may be plotted. At the point of zero shear, $x = 10.4$ ft, the bending moment is found by substitution in the above equation to be

$$M_{10.4} = 3w\sqrt{108} - \frac{1}{108}w(\sqrt{108})^3 = 2w\sqrt{108} \text{ lb-ft} = 250w \text{ lb·in}$$

This is the maximum bending moment in the beam.

The bending stress on any fiber at a distance y from the neutral axis of the beam is given by $\sigma = My/I$. The moment of inertia of the beam is found from Table 12-1 to be 272.9 in^4. The maximum tensile stress occurs at the lower fibers of the beam, where $y = 5$ in, at the section where the bending moment is a maximum. If this stress is 18,000 lb/in^2, then (12.2) becomes

$$18,000 = \frac{My}{I} = \frac{(250w)(5)}{272.9} \qquad \text{or} \qquad w = 3930 \text{ lb/ft}$$

12.5 The simply supported T beam in Fig. 12-10a is subject to three concentrated loads as shown. The material of the beam is titanium alloy having allowable working stresses of 600 MPa in tension and 700 MPa in compression. Determine the maximum allowable value of **P**.

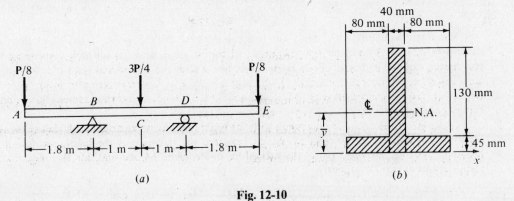

Fig. 12-10

By symmetry, each of the support reactions is **P**/2; the bending moment diagram consists of straight lines as shown in Fig. 12-11.

The properties of the T section must next be determined. If we place an x axis as indicated in Fig. 12-10b, then the centroid lies a distance $\bar{y}$ above it, where

$$\bar{y} = \frac{(160)(45)(45/2) + (175)(40)(175/2)}{(160)(45) + (175)(40)} = 54.5 \text{ mm}$$

The moment of inertia of the entire T section about the x axis is, from Problem 6.9,

$$I_x = \tfrac{1}{3}(160)(45)^3 + \tfrac{1}{3}(40)(175)^3 = 71.46 \times 10^6 \text{ mm}^4$$

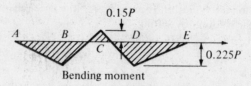

Bending moment

Fig. 12-11

Using the parallel-axis theorem to transfer the moment of inertia from the x axis to the N.A., which extends through the centroid, we obtain

$$I_{\text{N.A.}} = 71.46 \times 10^6 \text{ mm}^4 - (14{,}200 \text{ mm}^2)(54.5 \text{ mm})^2 = 29.28 \times 10^6 \text{ mm}^4$$

Now we shall calculate four values for P, based upon the maximum allowable tensile and compressive stresses at points B and C; the least of these four values will be the maximum allowable value.

We begin with point B. Since the bending moment there is negative, the beam is concave downward there, as shown in Fig. 12-12a. The upper fibers are thus in tension, and the lower fibers in compression. If the allowable tensile stress of 600 MPa is realized in the upper fibers, then (12.3) yields

$$600 \times 10^6 \text{ N/m}^2 = \frac{0.225 P_1 [(175 - 54.5)(1/10^3) \text{ m}]}{29.28 \times 10^{-6} \text{ m}^4} \qquad \text{or} \qquad P_1 = 648 \text{ kN}$$

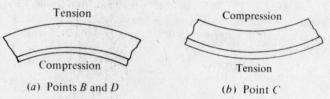

Tension

Compression

Compression

Tension

(a) Points B and D (b) Point C

Fig. 12-12

If the allowable compressive stress of 700 MPa is realized in the lower fibers, then (12.3) yields

$$700 \times 10^6 \text{ N/m}^2 = \frac{0.225 P_2 [54.5(1/10^3) \text{ m}]}{29.28 \times 10^{-6} \text{ m}^4} \qquad \text{or} \qquad P_2 = 1671 \text{ kN}$$

We next examine point C. Since the bending moment there is positive, the beam is concave upward there (Fig. 12-12b). The upper fibers are thus in compression, and the lower in tension. If the allowable tensile stress of 600 MPa is realized in the lower fibers, then

$$600 \times 10^6 \text{ N/m}^2 = \frac{0.15 P_3 [54.5(1/10^3) \text{ m}]}{29.28 \times 10^{-6} \text{ m}^4} \qquad \text{or} \qquad P_3 = 2149 \text{ kN}$$

and, finally, if the allowable compressive stress of 700 MPa is realized in the upper fibers, then

$$700 \times 10^6 \text{ N/m}^2 = \frac{0.15 P_4 [(175 - 54.5)(1/10^3) \text{ m}]}{29.28 \times 10^{-6} \text{ m}^4} \qquad \text{or} \qquad P_4 = 1133 \text{ kN}$$

The least of these four values is $P_1 = 648$ kN. Thus the tensile stress at B and D is the controlling stress, and the maximum allowable load is **$P = 648$ kN.**

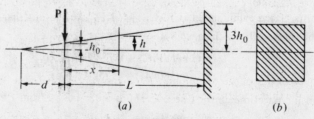

(a)   (b)

Fig. 12-13

12.6   A tapered cantilever beam has the dimensions shown in Fig. 12-13 and is loaded by a force **P** at its free end. The beam has square cross sections all along its length; that is, both width and height vary linearly from the free end to the clamped end. Find the maximum normal stress in the beam.

We should first determine where the top and bottom surfaces of the beam would intersect, so that the geometry of the problem is clear. From similar triangles,

$$\frac{h_0}{d} = \frac{3h_0}{d+L} \qquad \text{or} \qquad d = \frac{L}{2}$$

Next, we consider a cross section of the beam at a distance x from the left end (Fig. 12-13a). The half-height h at that section is, from the geometry,

$$h = \frac{x + L/2}{L/2} h_0 = \left(\frac{2x}{L} + 1\right)h_0$$

The plane moment of inertia of the cross section at x is thus

$$I = \frac{1}{12}\left[2\left(\frac{2x}{L}+1\right)h_0\right]\left[2\left(\frac{2x}{L}+1\right)h_0\right]^3 = \frac{4}{3}\left(\frac{2x}{L}+1\right)^4 h_0^4$$

and the section modulus Z is

$$Z = \frac{I}{c} = \frac{\frac{4}{3}(2x/L+1)^4 h_0^4}{(2x/L+1)h_0} = \frac{4}{3}\left(\frac{2x}{L}+1\right)^3 h_0^3$$

The bending stresses at the outer fibers of the section are therefore given by

$$\sigma_{max} = \frac{M}{Z} = \frac{Px}{\frac{4}{3}(2x/L+1)^3 h_0^3} = \frac{3P}{4h_0^3}\left[\frac{x}{(2x/L+1)^3}\right] \tag{1}$$

There is no reason to assume that these outer-fiber stresses reach their peak value at the clamped end of the bar. Instead, we must first find the location along the beam where they are a maximum, and then evaluate (1) at that location. We begin by setting $d\sigma_{max}/dx = 0$. Working only with the quantity in brackets in (1), we obtain

$$\left(\frac{2x}{L}+1\right)^3 - (x)(3)\left(\frac{2x}{L}+1\right)^2\left(\frac{2}{L}\right) = 0$$

which yields $x = L/4$ as the location of the section at which the outer-fiber stresses are a maximum. Substituting this value of x in (1) yields, for the peak outer-fiber stresses,

$$\sigma_{max} = \frac{1}{18}\frac{PL}{h_0^3}$$

[By direct computation with (1), the outer-fiber stresses at the clamped end may be found to be $\sigma_L = \frac{1}{36}(PL/h_0^3)$, only half those at the section where the normal stresses are a maximum.]

12.7   The cantilever beam in Fig. 12-14 has a T-shaped cross section and is subject to a concentrated load as shown. Determine the maximum shearing stress in the beam, and determine the shearing stress 1 in from the top surface of the beam at a section adjacent to the supporting wall.

The shear force is 12,000 lb all along the length of the beam; hence, no shear diagram need be drawn.

With the x axis placed as indicated in Fig. 12-14b, the location of the centroid of the cross section is

$$\bar{y} = \frac{(3\text{ in})(2\text{ in})(1\text{ in})(2) + (7\text{ in})(2\text{ in})(3.5\text{ in})}{(3\text{ in})(2\text{ in})(2) + (7\text{ in})(2\text{ in})} = 2.35\text{ in}$$

The moment of inertia of the section about the x axis is found as the sum of the moments of inertia about that axis of the three rectangles indicated in Fig. 12-14b:

$$I_x = \frac{1}{3}(3\text{ in})(2\text{ in})^3(2) + \frac{1}{3}(2\text{ in})(7\text{ in})^3 = 245\text{ in}^4$$

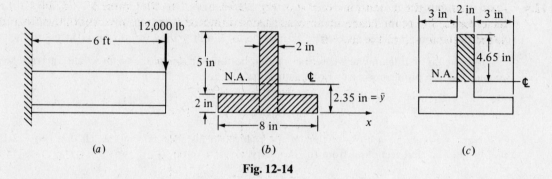

Fig. 12-14

We use the parallel-axis theorem to transfer the moment of inertia to the N.A., which passes through the centroid:

$$I_{N.A.} = I_x - A\bar{y}^2 = 245 \text{ in}^4 - (26 \text{ in}^2)(2.35 \text{ in})^2 = 101 \text{ in}^4$$

The shearing stress at a distance y_0 from the neutral axis is, from (12.5),

$$\tau = \frac{V}{Ib} \int_{y_0}^{c} y \, dA \tag{1}$$

Inspection of this equation reveals that the shearing stress is a maximum at the neutral axis, since at that point $y_0 = 0$ and consequently the integral assumes its largest possible value. We need not integrate here, however, since we know the integral (with $y_0 = 0$) represents the first moment of the area between the neutral axis and the outer fibers of the beam about the neutral axis. This area is represented by the shaded region in Fig. 12-14c, and its first moment about the neutral axis is $2(4.65)(2.33) = 21.6 \text{ in}^3$. The shearing stress at the neutral axis, where $b = 2$ in, is found by substitution in (1):

$$\tau = \frac{12,000}{101(2)} 21.6 = 1290 \text{ lb/in}^2$$

The maximum shearing stress of 1290 lb/in^2 occurs at all points on the neutral axis, along the entire length of the beam, since the shearing force is constant along the entire length of the beam.

The shearing stress 1 in from the top surface of the beam is again given by (1). Now, however, the integral represents the first moment of the shaded area shown in Fig. 12-15 about the neutral axis. Again it is not necessary to integrate to evaluate the integral, since the coordinate of the centroid of this area is known: It is 4.15 in above the neutral axis. Thus the first moment of this area about the neutral axis is $2(1)(4.15) = 8.30 \text{ in}^3$, and the shearing stress 1 in below the top fibers is

$$\tau = \frac{12,000}{101(2)} (8.30) = 495 \text{ lb/in}^2$$

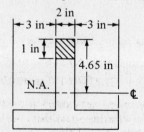

Fig. 12-15

Again, b is taken to be 2 in because that is the width of the beam at the point where the shearing stress is being evaluated. Since the shearing force is equal to 12,000 lb everywhere along the length of the beam, the shearing stress 1 in below the top fibers is 495 lb/in^2 everywhere along the beam.

12.8 An I beam has the dimensions shown in Fig. 12-16, and a shearing force of   25,000 N   acts over the cross section of the beam. Determine the maximum and minimum values of the shearing stress in the vertical web of the section.

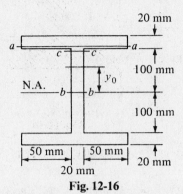

Fig. 12-16

The moment of inertia of the entire cross section about the N.A. is

$$I_{\text{N.A.}} = \tfrac{1}{12}(20 \text{ mm})(240 \text{ mm})^3 + 2[\tfrac{1}{12}(100 \text{ mm})(20 \text{ mm})^3 + (100 \text{ mm})(20 \text{ mm})(110 \text{ mm})^2]$$
$$= 71.57 \times 10^6 \text{ mm}^4 = 71.57 \times 10^{-6} \text{ m}^4$$

From (*12.5*), the shearing stress τ at any point in the cross section is

$$\tau = \frac{V}{Ib} \int_{y_0}^{c} y \, dA \tag{1}$$

where y_0 is the distance from the N.A. to the location at which τ acts, and I is the moment of inertia of the *entire* cross section about the N.A., which passes through the centroid. As we noted in Problem 12.7, the shearing stress is a maximum at the N.A. (where $y_0 = 0$). Moreover, it is not necessary to integrate to obtain $\int_0^c y \, dA$,   since this integral represents the first moment of the area between the N.A. and the outer fibers (shown shaded in Fig. 12-17). This first moment is

$$(20 \text{ mm})(120 \text{ mm})(60 \text{ mm}) + (100 \text{ mm})(20 \text{ mm})(110 \text{ mm}) = 3.64 \times 10^{-4} \text{ m}^3$$

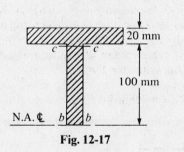

Fig. 12-17   **Fig. 12-18**

The maximum shearing stress occurs along section   *b-b*   and is, by (*1*),

$$\tau_{\max} = \frac{(25,000 \text{ N})(3.64 \times 10^{-4} \text{ m}^3)}{(71.57 \times 10^{-6} \text{ m}^4)(0.02 \text{ m})} = 6.36 \text{ MPa}$$

The minimum shearing stress in the web occurs at the point in the web that is farthest from the N.A., which is section   *c-c*.   To find the shearing stress there, we need the first moment of the area of the flange, shown shaded in Fig. 12-18, about the N.A. This is

$$(120 \text{ mm})(20 \text{ mm})(110 \text{ mm}) = 0.264 \times 10^{-3} \text{ m}^3$$

The shearing stress at   *c-c*   is then, by (*1*),

$$\tau_{c\text{-}c} = \frac{(25,000 \text{ N})(2.64 \times 10^{-4} \text{ m}^3)}{(71.57 \times 10^{-6} \text{ m}^4)(0.02 \text{ m})} = 4.61 \text{ MPa}$$

Note that there is not a great difference between the maximum and minimum web shearing stresses. As a result, it is not unusual to find only an approximate value of the shearing stress, calculated by dividing the shearing force by the cross-sectional area of the web. Here,

$$\tau_{mean} = \frac{25,000 \text{ N}}{(0.240 \text{ m})(0.020 \text{ m})} = 5.21 \text{ MPa}$$

Finally, we may determine the shearing stress just inside the flange, at section *a-a*. There, $b = 120$ mm and we have

$$\tau_{a\text{-}a} = \frac{(25,000 \text{ N})(2.64 \times 10^{-4} \text{ m}^3)}{(71.57 \times 10^{-6} \text{ m}^4)(0.120 \text{ m})} = 0.768 \text{ MPa}$$

Plastic Bending of Beams

12.9   Consider a beam of arbitrary doubly symmetric cross section, such as that in Fig. 12-19*a*, subject to pure bending. The material is considered to be elastic–perfectly plastic; i.e., the stress-strain diagram is like that in Fig. 12-19*b* and its stress-strain characteristics in tension and compression are identical. Determine the moment acting on the beam when all fibers at a distance y_1 from the neutral axis have reached the yield point of the material.

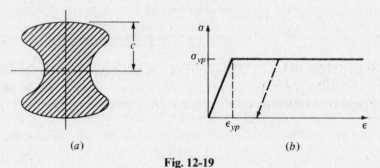

(a)   (b)

Fig. 12-19

Even though bending of the beam may have caused the outer fibers to yield, it is still realistic to assume that plane sections of the beam that were normal to its axis before loads were applied remain plane and normal to the axis after loading. Consequently, normal strains of the longitudinal fibers of the beam still vary linearly with the distance of the fibers from the neutral axis.

As the value of the applied bending moment is increased from zero, the extreme fibers of the beam are the first to reach the yield point of the material; at that value of the load, the normal stresses on all interior

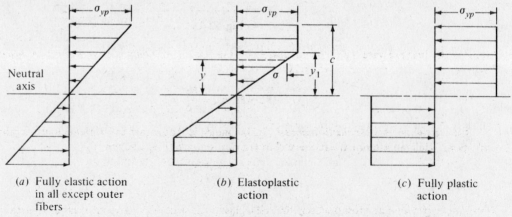

(*a*) Fully elastic action
in all except outer
fibers

(*b*) Elastoplastic
action

(*c*) Fully plastic
action

Fig. 12-20

fibers vary linearly with the distance of the fiber from the neutral axis, as indicated in Fig. 12-20a. A further increase in the value of the moment puts interior fibers at the yield point, with yielding progressing from the outer fibers inward, as indicated in Fig. 12-20b. In the limiting case when all fibers (except those along the neutral axis) are stressed to the yield point, the normal stress distribution appears as in Fig. 12-20c. The bending moment corresponding to Fig. 12-20c is termed a *fully plastic moment*. For the type of stress-strain curve shown in Fig. 12-19b, no greater moment is possible.

For a beam in pure bending, the sum of the normal forces over the cross section must vanish. Hence, for a doubly symmetric section, it is evident from inspection of Fig. 12-20b that the neutral axis must pass through the centroid of the section. However, this is not necessarily so for a more general nonsymmetric cross section.

From Fig. 12-20b we have, for $y < y_1$,

$$\frac{\sigma}{y} = \frac{\sigma_{yp}}{y_1} \qquad \text{or} \qquad \sigma = \frac{y}{y_1}\sigma_{yp}$$

For $y > y_1$, we have $\sigma = \sigma_{yp} = \text{constant}$. Thus the required bending moment is

$$M = \int \sigma y \, dA = 2\int_0^{y_1} \frac{y}{y_1}\sigma_{yp} y \, dA + 2\int_{y_1}^{c} \theta_{yp} y \, dA$$

$$= \frac{2\sigma_{yp}}{y_1}\int_0^{y_1} y^2 \, dA + 2\sigma_{yp}\int_{y_1}^{c} y \, dA$$

12.10 For a beam of rectangular cross section, determine the moment acting when all fibers at a distance y_1 from the neutral axis have reached the yield point of the material.

From the results of Problem 12.9 for the geometry indicated in Fig. 12-21,

$$M = \frac{2\sigma_{yp}}{y_1}\left(\frac{1}{3}by_1^3\right) + 2\sigma_{yp}b(c - y_1)\frac{c + y_1}{2} = \left(bc^2 - \frac{b}{3}y_1^2\right)\sigma_{yp} \qquad (1)$$

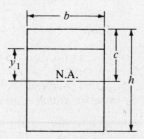

Fig. 12-21

For the limiting case $y_1 = 0$, indicated by Fig. 12-20c, the *fully plastic moment* of this rectangular beam is

$$M_p = bc^2\sigma_{yp} = \frac{bh^2}{4}\sigma_{yp} \qquad (2)$$

The *maximum possible elastic moment*, i.e., the moment that causes the extreme fibers to just reach the yield point while all interior fibers are still in the elastic range (Fig. 12-20a), is

$$M_e = \frac{bh^2}{6}\sigma_{yp} \qquad (3)$$

Thus, for a rectangular cross section, the fully plastic moment is 50 percent greater than the maximum possible elastic moment.

12.11 Find the fully plastic moment of a rectangular beam that is 35 mm by 70 mm in cross section. The steel has a yield point of 250 MPa. Also find the maximum elastic moment that this beam can carry.

From (2) of Problem 12.10, the fully plastic moment is

$$M_p = \frac{bh^2}{4}\,\sigma_{yp} = \frac{(0.035\text{ m})(0.070\text{ m})^2}{4}\,(250 \times 10^6\text{ N/m}^2) = 10.72\text{ kN·m}$$

From (3) of Problem 12.10, the maximum possible elastic moment is

$$M_e = \frac{bh^2}{6}\,\sigma_{yp} = \frac{(0.035\text{ m})(0.070\text{ m})^2}{6}\,(250 \times 10^6\text{ N/m}^2) = 7.15\text{ kN·m}$$

12.12 The beam of Problem 12.11 is subject to a bending moment of 9 kN·m. Determine the location of the boundary between the regions of elastic and plastic action. Also determine the stress distribution that remains after the 9-kN·m moment is removed.

Applying (1) of Problem 12.10, we have

$$9000\text{ N·m} = \left[(0.035\text{ m})(0.070\text{ m})^2 - \frac{0.035\text{ m}}{3}\,y_1^2\right](250 \times 10^6\text{ N/m}^2)$$

from which we find $y_1 = 0.1077$ m or 10.77 mm. Thus, the 9-kN·m bending moment produces the stress distribution shown in Fig. 12-22b.

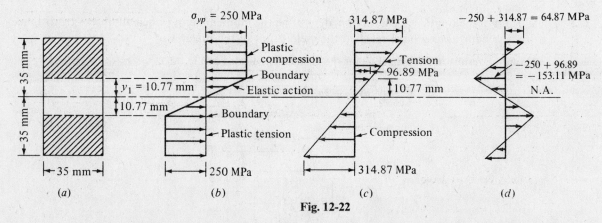

Fig. 12-22

The residual stresses are determined with the procedure developed for torsion in Problem 11.12. When the bending moment is removed, unloading occurs linearly, following the dashed arrow in Fig. 12-19b. This unloading produces, at the outer fibers, bending stresses

$$\sigma = \frac{Mc}{I} = \frac{(9000\text{ N·m})(0.035\text{ m})}{\frac{1}{12}(0.035\text{ m})(0.070\text{ m})^3} = 314.87\text{ MPa}$$

The stress distribution due to unloading is shown in Fig. 12-22c, where fibers above the neutral axis are now stressed in tension.

To determine the final stress state, we superpose the elastoplastic stresses of Fig. 12-22b on the elastic unloading stresses of Fig. 12-22c to obtain the residual stresses shown in Fig. 12-22d. The sum of the residual tensile and compressive forces over the cross section must, of course, be zero because there is no net axial load.

12.13 For a beam of rectangular cross section (Fig. 12-23), determine the relation between the bending moment and the radius of curvature when all fibers at a distance y_1 from the neutral axis have reached the yield point of the material.

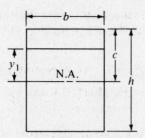

Fig. 12-23

We assume that sections that are plane before loading remain plane and normal to the beam axis after loading. Because of this, normal strains of the longitudinal fibers vary linearly as the distance of the fibers from the neutral axis. Thus, if ε_{yp} denotes the strain of the fibers at a distance y_1 from the neutral axis and ε_c represents the outer-fiber strain, we have

$$\frac{\varepsilon_c}{c} = \frac{\varepsilon_{yp}}{y_1} \tag{1}$$

Consideration of the geometry of an originally rectangular element of length dx along the beam axis, as shown in Fig. 12-24a, reveals that after bending it assumes the configuration indicated in Fig. 12-24b.

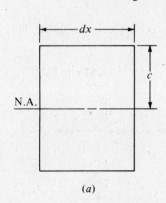

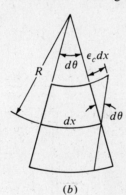

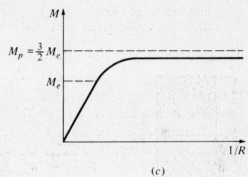

(a)   (b)   (c)

Fig. 12-24

From that sketch we have

$$\frac{1}{R} = \frac{d\theta}{dx} = \frac{\varepsilon_c}{c} \tag{2}$$

Thus,

$$\frac{d\theta}{dx} = \frac{\varepsilon_{yp}}{y_1} = \frac{\sigma_{yp}}{Ey_1} \tag{3}$$

since the fibers at a distance y_1 from the neutral axis obey Hooke's law: $\sigma_{yp} = E\varepsilon_{yp}$. From Problem 12.10, the moment corresponding to these strains is

$$M = \left(bc^2 y_1 - \frac{b}{3} y_1^3\right)\frac{\sigma_{yp}}{y_1} \tag{4}$$

Thus, from (3) and (4),

$$\frac{d\theta}{dx} = \frac{M}{Eby_1(c^2 - \frac{1}{3}y_1^2)} \tag{5}$$

Finally, from (2) and (5) we have

$$\frac{1}{R} = \frac{M}{EI(M/M_e)\sqrt{3 - 2M/M_e}} \tag{6}$$

where $M_e = bh^2\sigma_{yp}/6$ as in Problem 12.10. This is the desired relation between the bending moment M and the radius of curvature R. Figure 12.24c is a plot of (6).

12.14 A steel beam of rectangular cross section, with $b = 1$ in and $h = \frac{1}{2}$ in, has $\sigma_{yp} = 30,000$ lb/in^2 and $E = 30 \times 10^6$ lb/in^2. Determine the radius of curvature corresponding to the maximum possible elastic moment and the radius of curvature corresponding to a moment of 1850 lb·in.

From (3) of Problem 12.10, the maximum possible elastic moment is

$$M_e = \frac{1(1/2)^2}{6}\,30,000 = 1250 \text{ lb·in}$$

The radius of curvature corresponding to this moment is found with (6) of Problem 12.13:

$$\frac{1}{R} = \frac{1250}{(30 \times 10^6)\dfrac{(1)(1/2)^3}{12}\sqrt{3-2}} = 0.004 \quad \text{or} \quad R = 250 \text{ in}$$

The value of y_1 corresponding to a moment of 1850 lb·in may be found with (1) of Problem 12.10 to be 0.05 in. The curvature corresponding to this value is

$$\frac{1}{R} = \frac{1850}{(30 \times 10^6)\dfrac{(1)(1/2)^3}{12}\left(\dfrac{1850}{1250}\right)\sqrt{3 - \dfrac{3700}{1250}}} = 0.02 \quad \text{or} \quad R = 50 \text{ in}$$

12.15 For the T section shown in Fig. 12-25a, find the location of the neutral axis for fully plastic action. Also determine the fully plastic moment M_p and the maximum possible elastic moment M_e.

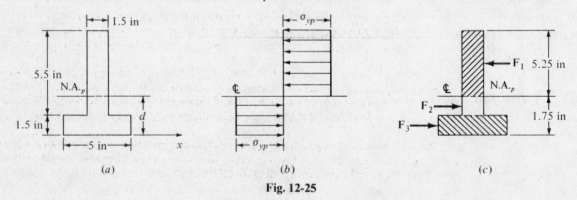

Fig. 12-25

We know that the neutral axis N.A.$_p$ for fully plastic action divides the cross section into two equal areas. If we designate by d the distance of this axis from the x axis, we have

$$(5 \text{ in})(1.5 \text{ in}) + (1.5 \text{ in})[(d - 1.5)\text{ in}] = (1.5 \text{ in})[(7 - d)\text{ in}]$$

from which $d = 1.75$ in.

The fully plastic bending moment is the bending moment resulting from the fully plastic normal stress distribution, which is shown in Fig. 12-25b. If we divide the cross section into three rectangles as shown in Fig. 12-25c, then we may designate as F_1, F_2, and F_3 the forces corresponding to this normal stress distribution. The sum of the moments of these forces about the neutral axis is the bending moment for fully plastic action:

$$M_p = \sigma_{yp}(5.25 \text{ in})(1.5 \text{ in})(5.25/2 \text{ in}) + \sigma_{yp}(0.25 \text{ in})(1.5 \text{ in})(0.125 \text{ in})$$
$$+ \sigma_{yp}(5 \text{ in})(1.5 \text{ in})[(0.25 + 0.75)\text{ in}] = 28.22\sigma_{yp}$$

To determine the value of the maximum possible elastic bending moment, we must first determine the location of the neutral axis N.A.$_e$ for fully elastic action. We know that it passes through the centroid of the cross section; we divide the cross section into three rectangles as shown in Fig. 12-26a and use the methods of Chapter 7 to find

$$\bar{y} = \frac{(7\text{ in})(1.5\text{ in})(3.5\text{ in}) + 2(1.5\text{ in})(1.75\text{ in})(0.875\text{ in})}{(7\text{ in})(1.5\text{ in}) + 2(1.5\text{ in})(1.75\text{ in})} = 2.62\text{ in}$$

Using these same three rectangles, we find that the moment of inertia of the cross section about the x axis is

$$I_x = \tfrac{1}{3}(1.5\text{ in})(7\text{ in})^3 + 2[\tfrac{1}{3}(1.75\text{ in})(1.5\text{ in})^3] = 175.44\text{ in}^4$$

We then use the parallel-axis theorem to find the moment of inertia about the neutral axis:

$$I_{\text{N.A.}_e} = I_x - A\bar{y}^2 = 175.44\text{ in}^4 - (15.75\text{ in}^2)(2.62\text{ in})^2 = 67.33\text{ in}^4$$

The fibers above N.A.$_e$ are in compression, and those below that axis are in tension. The elastic stress distribution is thus as shown in Fig. 12-26b. If we take the moments about the neutral axis N.A.$_e$ of the forces corresponding to this stress distribution, we find $M_e = 15.92\sigma_{yp}$.

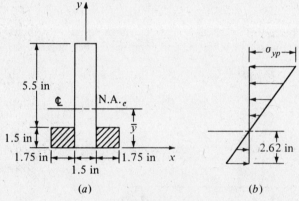

Fig. 12-26

Supplementary Problems

12.16 A titanium beam has a rectangular cross section, 35 mm by 70 mm, with a yield point of 825 MPa. If the peak bending stress in the outer fibers is 700 MPa, find the corresponding bending moment.

Ans.   23.6 kN·m

12.17 A cantilever beam has a length of 10 ft and carries a uniformly distributed load of 2000 lb/ft over its entire length. For a working stress in bending of 20,000 lb/in^2, select a wide-flange section capable of carrying this load.   *Ans.*   W 10 × 54

12.18 A strip of steel 1 mm thick is bent into an arc of a circle of radius 1 m. Determine the maximum bending stress. Take $E = 200$ GPa.   *Ans.*   100 MPa

12.19 The cantilever T beam in Fig. 12-27 carries a concentrated load at its tip as shown. Determine the peak compressive and tensile stresses due to bending.   *Ans.* $-19,600$ lb/in^2;   8820 lb/in^2

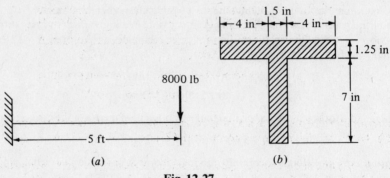

Fig. 12-27

12.20 For the beam of Problem 12.19, keep the same depth of flange (1.25 in), but vary the height of the web. Determine the overall height H of the section (web plus flange) such that the numerical value of the peak compressive stress is twice that of the peak tensile stress.

Ans. $H = 11.18$ in

12.21 The cantilever T beam in Fig. 12-28 is subject to a uniformly distributed load of 7000 N/m, including its own weight. Determine the peak tensile and compressive bending stresses.

Ans. 27.5 MPa; -49.1 MPa

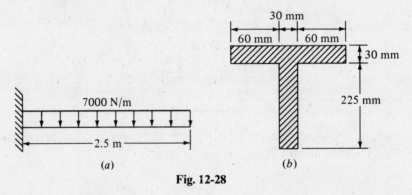

Fig. 12-28

12.22 The simply supported beam in Fig. 12-29 is subject to two concentrated forces as shown. The material is steel having a working stress in tension or compression of 180 MPa, and the cross section is rectangular with the height being 1.75 times the width. Determine the width of the beam necessary to support the loads.   *Ans.*   50.7 mm

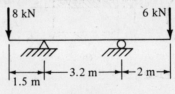

Fig. 12-29

12.23 In Problem 12.22, replace the 8-kN force with one of 64 kN, and the 6-kN force with one of 48 kN. Select a wide-flange section capable of carrying this load if the working stress in bending is 160 MPa.

Ans. W 254 × 54

12.24 The simply supported beam in Fig. 12-30 is subject to the uniformly distributed loads shown. The beam is wood having a working stress in bending of 1500 lb/in^2 (in tension as well as in compression) and a working

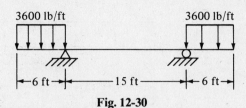

Fig. 12-30

stress in shear of 90 lb/in². The beam is of rectangular cross section with the height 50 percent greater than the width. Determine the necessary height of the beam.   *Ans.*   23.2 in

12.25 Consider the loading shown in Fig. 12-29 to act on a steel wide-flange beam having a working stress in bending of 24,000 lb/in². Select a suitable section for the beam.   *Ans.*   W 8 × 40

12.26 The extruded beam in Fig. 12-31 has two symmetrically placed webs as shown. It acts as a cantilever with its load being a tip moment M. If the allowable working stress in tension is 80 MPa, determine the maximum allowable moment M.   *Ans.*   102.6 kN·m

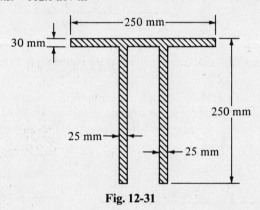

Fig. 12-31

12.27 The T beam in Fig. 12-32 is loaded in pure bending as shown. If the working stress in compression is 2.5 times that in tension, find the flange width b.   *Ans.*   10.09 cm

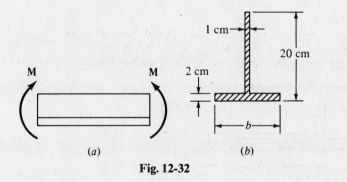

Fig. 12-32

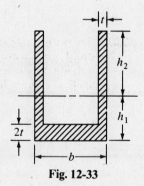

Fig. 12-33

12.28 The U-shaped extruded beam in Fig. 12-33 has $b = 30$ cm and $t = 2$ cm. The existing peak elastic stress in compression is 2.5 times the tensile stress. Locate the neutral axis by finding h_1 and h_2.

   Ans.   There are two solutions: (1) $h_1 = 7.12$ cm, $h_2 = 17.81$ cm; (2) $h_1 = 2.78$ cm, $h_2 = 6.95$ cm

12.29 Beam ABC in Fig. 12-34 is simply supported at A and B and overhangs in region BC. It is subject to a uniformly distributed load of 20 kN/m. If the material is titanium alloy having a working stress in tension or compression of 600 MPa and the beam is square in cross section, determine the length of a side of the cross section.   *Ans.*   80.3 mm

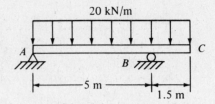

Fig. 12-34

12.30 The overhanging beam in Fig. 12-35 is simply supported and is subject to a uniformly distributed load and a couple. Select a wide-flange section capable of carrying these loads with bending stresses not to exceed 22,000 lb/in². *Ans.* W 8 × 24

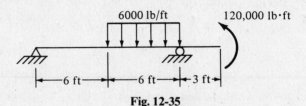

Fig. 12-35

12.31 The overhanging beam in Fig. 12-36 is simply supported and loaded with concentrated and distributed loads as shown. The beam is steel, having a working stress in bending of 22,000 lb/in², and it has a rectangular cross section whose height is twice its width. Determine the required width of the cross section to carry the loads. *Ans.* 1.94 in

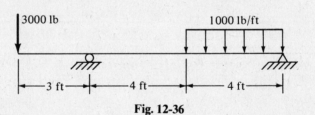

Fig. 12-36

12.32 A simply supported steel beam of channel-type cross section is loaded by a uniformly distributed load and a couple, as shown in Fig. 12-37. Determine the maximum tensile and compressive stresses produced in the beam. *Ans.* 3020 lb/in²; −5520 lb/in²

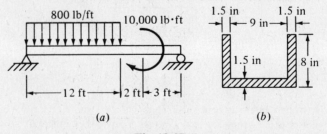

Fig. 12-37

12.33 The simply supported overhanging beam in Fig. 12-38 is subject to three concentrated forces. The cross section of the beam is T-shaped; the material is gray cast iron having an allowable working stress in tension of 5000 lb/in², and in compression of 20,000 lb/in². Determine the maximum allowable value of **P**.

Ans. P = 12,000 lb

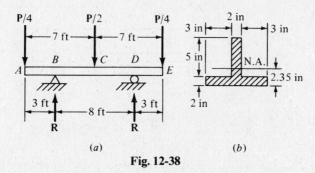

Fig. 12-38

12.34 A cantilever beam of variable circular cross section, bounded by the curve $y = Cx^{1/3}$, is subject to a vertical concentrated force **P** at its free end (Fig. 12-39). Determine the maximum normal stress.

Ans. $4P/\pi C^3$ = constant in all outer fibers

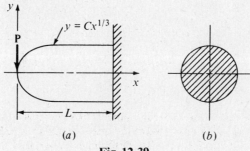

Fig. 12-39

12.35 Determine (a) the maximum bending stress and (b) the maximum shearing stress in the simply supported beam shown in Fig. 12-40.   *Ans.*   (a) 30 MPa;   (b) 3 MPa

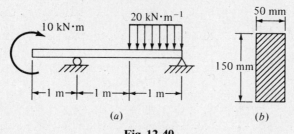

Fig. 12-40

12.36 For the T section shown in Fig. 12-41, determine the location of the neutral axis for fully plastic action.   *Ans.*   155 mm above the lowest fibers of the section

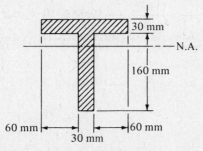

Fig. 12-41

12.37 For a W 8 × 40 wide-flange steel section having a yield point of 38,000 lb/in², determine the fully plastic moment. Find the maximum possible elastic moment that the section can carry.

Ans. $M_p = 1,516,200$ lb·in; $M_e = 1,349,000$ lb·in

Table 12-1 Properties of Selected Wide-Flange Sections, USCS Units

Designation*	Weight per Foot (lb/ft)	Area (in²)	I (about x-x axis) (in⁴)	Z (in³)	I (about y-y axis) (in⁴)	Zₚ (plastic section modulus) (in³)
W 18 × 70	70.0	20.56	1153.9	128.2	78.5	144.7
W 18 × 55	55.0	16.19	889.9	98.2	42.0	111.6
W 12 × 72	72.0	21.16	597.4	97.5	195.3	108.1
W 12 × 58	58.0	17.06	476.1	78.1	107.4	86.5
W 12 × 50	50.0	14.71	394.5	64.7	56.4	72.6
W 12 × 45	45.0	13.24	350.8	58.2	50.0	64.9
W 12 × 40	40.0	11.77	310.1	51.9	44.1	57.6
W 12 × 36	36.0	10.59	280.8	45.9	23.7	51.4
W 12 × 32	32.0	9.41	246.8	40.7	20.6	45.0
W 12 × 25	25.0	7.39	183.4	30.9	14.5	35.0
W 10 × 89	89.0	26.19	542.4	99.7	180.6	114.4
W 10 × 54	54.0	15.88	305.7	60.4	103.9	67.0
W 10 × 49	49.0	14.40	272.9	54.6	93.0	60.3
W 10 × 45	45.0	13.24	248.6	49.1	53.2	55.0
W 10 × 37	37.0	10.88	196.9	39.9	42.2	45.0
W 10 × 29	29.0	8.53	157.3	30.8	15.2	34.7
W 10 × 23	23.0	6.77	120.6	24.1	11.3	33.7
W 10 × 21	21.0	6.19	106.3	21.5	9.7	24.1
W 8 × 40	40.0	11.76	146.3	35.5	49.0	39.9
W 8 × 35	35.0	10.30	126.5	31.1	42.5	34.7
W 8 × 31	31.0	9.12	109.7	27.4	37.0	30.4
W 8 × 28	28.0	8.23	97.8	24.3	21.6	27.1
W 8 × 27	27.0	7.93	94.1	23.4	20.8	23.9
W 8 × 24	24.0	7.06	82.5	20.8	18.2	23.1
W 8 × 19	19.0	5.59	64.7	16.0	7.9	17.7
W 6 × 15½	15.5	4.62	28.1	9.7	9.7	11.3

*The first number after the W is the nominal depth of the section in inches. The second number is the weight in pounds per foot of length.

Table 12-2 Properties of Selected Wide-Flange Sections, SI Units

Designation*	Mass per Meter (kg/m)	Area (mm²)	I (about x-x axis) (10⁶ mm⁴)	Z (10³ mm³)	I (about y-y axis) (10⁶ mm⁴)	Z_p (plastic section modulus) (10³ mm³)
W 460 × 103	102.9	13,200	479	2100	32.6	2,370
W 460 × 81	80.9	10,400	369	1610	17.4	1,820
W 305 × 106	105.8	13,600	248	1590	81.0	1,770
W 305 × 85	85.3	11,000	198	1280	44.6	1,410
W 305 × 74	73.5	9,480	164	1060	23.4	1,190
W 305 × 66	66.2	8,530	146	952	20.7	1,060
W 305 × 59	58.8	7,580	129	849	18.3	942
W 305 × 53	52.9	6,820	117	750	9.83	840
W 305 × 47	47.0	6,060	102	665	8.55	736
W 305 × 37	36.8	4,760	76.1	505	6.02	572
W 254 × 131	130.8	16,900	225	1630	74.9	1,870
W 254 × 79	79.4	10,200	127	988	43.1	1,100
W 254 × 72	72.0	9,280	113	893	38.6	986
W 254 × 66	66.2	8,530	103	803	22.1	899
W 254 × 54	54.4	7,010	81.7	652	17.5	736
W 254 × 43	42.6	5,490	65.3	504	6.31	567
W 254 × 34	33.8	4,360	50.0	394	4.69	551
W 254 × 31	30.9	3,990	44.1	352	4.02	394
W 203 × 59	58.8	7,580	60.7	580	20.3	652
W 203 × 51	51.4	6,630	52.5	508	17.6	567
W 203 × 46	45.6	5,870	45.5	448	15.4	497
W 203 × 41	41.2	5,300	40.6	397	8.96	443
W 203 × 40	39.7	5,110	39.0	383	8.63	391
W 203 × 35	35.3	4,550	34.2	340	7.55	378
W 203 × 28	27.9	3,600	26.8	262	3.28	290
W 152 × 23	22.8	2,980	11.7	159	4.02	185

* The first number after the W is the nominal depth of the section in millimeters. The second number is the mass in kilograms per meter of length.

Chapter 13

Beam Deflections

In Chapter 12 we considered various loads on an initially straight bar. Besides giving rise to the stresses examined there, those loads cause the beam to deflect in the plane of symmetry, which contains the applied forces and moments. Several methods exist for finding the magnitudes of the deflections.

METHOD OF DOUBLE INTEGRATION

The method of double integration involves straightforward double integration of the differential equation describing the deflection of the midsurface of an initially straight elastic beam. That equation is

$$EI \frac{d^2y}{dx^2} = M \tag{13.1}$$

where E represents Young's modulus, I the moment of inertia of the beam cross section about its neutral axis (see Chapter 6), and M the magnitude of the bending moment at any section along the length of the beam (see Chapter 7).

The customary sign convention for the bending moment M is again illustrated in Fig. 13-1. A force or couple that tends to bend a beam so that it is concave upward is said to produce a positive bending moment, and such a couple is regarded as positive.

(a) Positive bending   (b) Negative bending

Fig. 13-1

In (13.1), x represents a coordinate scale that extends along the longitudinal axis of the beam, which is usually drawn horizontal (see Fig. 13-2); y is perpendicular to x and positive upward. By this sign convention, then, the deflections at B and C in Fig. 13-2 are negative.

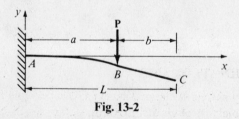

Fig. 13-2

Recall from Chapter 7 that the analytical expression for $M(x)$ changes from load to load along a beam. For example, there is a separate and distinct equation for $M(x)$ in each of the two parts AB and BC of the beam in Fig. 13-2. Double integration of (13.1) then would lead to a different algebraic equation for each of these regions and, unfortunately, to two constants of integration for each; thus, for the simple loading in Fig. 13-2, there would be four constants of integration to be determined by boundary conditions involving support reactions (at *A*) as well as continuity of deflection and continuity of slope at common points such as *B*. Here, this process results in the deflection-curve equations

$$EIy = \begin{cases} \dfrac{P}{6}x^3 - \dfrac{Pa}{2}x^2 & \text{for } 0 < x < a \qquad\qquad (13.2) \\[2em] \dfrac{-Pa^2}{2}x + \dfrac{Pa^3}{6} & \text{for } a < x < L \qquad\qquad (13.3) \end{cases}$$

Clearly, this can become an exceedingly tedious procedure if more than one load acts on a beam. Hence, the method of double integration is suitable only for relatively simple loadings. (See Problem 13.4.)

METHOD OF SINGULARITY FUNCTIONS

Singularity (or bracket) functions were introduced in Chapter 7. The singularity function

$$f_n(x) = \langle x - a \rangle^n$$

is defined to be zero if the quantity in pointed brackets is zero or negative, and to be $x - a$ if that quantity is positive. Singularity functions provide a simple means for writing a *single* equation that yields the deflection at any point over the entire length of a beam. The imposition of boundary conditions is usually exceedingly simple and direct. (See Problems 13.5 through 13.11.)

COMPUTER SOLUTION

Singularity functions make possible the use of relatively simple FORTRAN programs for determining beam deflections in terms of the magnitudes of applied loads, the beam geometry, and material properties. The simplicity stems from the correspondence between the definition of the singularity function and the IF statement in FORTRAN. Such a program is presented in Problem 13.12, and an example of its use in Problem 13.13.

BEAMS OF VARYING CROSS SECTION

Either of these methods (double integration and singularity functions) may be applied to beams of varying cross section, provided the variation can be described with a relatively simple analytical expression. (See Problem 13.4.) If the variation is complex, it is necessary to resort to advanced numerical methods.

STATICALLY INDETERMINATE BEAMS

In analyzing certain fairly simple structural systems, it is possible to determine the reactions arising from external applied loads solely through the use of the equations of static equilibrium. These are called *statically determinate* systems. More complex systems give rise to more unknown reaction components than there are equations of static equilibrium. To determine the external reactions in such systems, which are termed *statically indeterminate*, it is necessary to supplement the available equations of statics with additional equations stemming from deformations of the elastic system. The double-integration and singularity-function approaches are both well suited to the development of such additional equations. (See Problems 13.14 through 13.20.)

Solved Problems

Statically Determinate Systems: Double-Integration Method

13.1   Find the equation of the deflection curve for a cantilever beam subject to a uniformly varying load, as shown in Fig. 13-3.

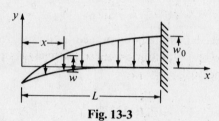

Fig. 13-3

We place the x coordinate along the undeflected beam, and the y coordinate perpendicular to that, as shown. Now we must determine the intensity w of the load at any distance x from the free end of the beam. Because the load diagram would have a triangular shape if the beam did not deflect, we have, from the geometry,

$$\frac{w}{x} = \frac{w_0}{L} \quad \text{or} \quad w = \frac{x}{L} w_0$$

At this distance x from the free end, the bending moment is that due to the triangular load to the left of x. Its magnitude is the area of the triangle, and its resultant acts at a distance $2x/3$ from the tip. Thus, the bending moment at x is

$$\left(\frac{1}{2} x \frac{x}{L} w_0\right)\frac{x}{3} = \frac{w_0}{6L} x^3$$

The differential equation of the deflected beam is, then,

$$EI \frac{d^2 y}{dx^2} = -\frac{w_0}{6L} x^3$$

Integrating this equation once yields

$$EI \frac{dy}{dx} = -\frac{w_0}{6L} \frac{x^4}{4} + C_1 \tag{1}$$

The constant of integration C_1 may be found by noting that at $x = L$ the slope of the beam is zero. This yields, from (*1*),

$$0 = -\frac{w_0 L^3}{24} + C_1 \quad \text{or} \quad C_1 = \frac{w_0 L^3}{24}$$

Hence, (*1*) becomes

$$EI \frac{dy}{dx} = -\frac{w_0}{24L} x^4 + \frac{w_0 L^3}{24}$$

Integrating once again, we obtain

$$EIy = -\frac{w_0}{24L} \frac{x^5}{5} + \frac{w_0 L^3}{24} x + C_2 \tag{2}$$

The constant C_2 is evaluated by using the fact that the deflection is zero at $x = L$. This yields, from (2),

$$0 = -\frac{w_0 L^4}{120} + \frac{w_0 L^4}{24} + C_2 \quad \text{or} \quad C_2 = -\frac{w_0 L^4}{30}$$

The desired equation for the deflection curve is thus

$$EIy = \frac{w_0}{120L}x^5 - \frac{w_0L^3}{24}x - \frac{w_0L^4}{30}$$

We can use this equation, for example, to find the deflection at the tip, where $x = 0$:

$$EIy_{x=0} = -\frac{w_0L^4}{30} \quad \text{or} \quad y_{x=0} = -\frac{w_0L^4}{30EI}$$

13.2 Determine the equation of the deflection curve for a simply supported beam loaded by a couple M_1 at its left end, as shown in Fig. 13-4.

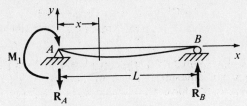

Fig. 13-4

From the equilibrium of moments about A, we have

$$+\circlearrowright \Sigma M_A = M_1 - R_BL = 0 \quad \text{or} \quad R_B = \frac{M_1}{L}$$

Next, by summing forces vertically, we find R_A to be numerically equal to R_B but directed downward. Thus, $\mathbf{R}_A$ and $\mathbf{R}_B$ constitute a couple that holds the applied couple $\mathbf{M}_1$ in equilibrium.

We place a coordinate system as shown in Fig. 13-4, with origin at A. At any section a distance x from A, the bending moment has magnitude

$$M = M_1 - R_Ax$$

where M_1 is assumed positive because it produces positive (concave upward) curvature.

The differential equation of the deflected beam is

$$EI\frac{d^2y}{dx^2} = M_1 - \frac{M_1}{L}x$$

Integrating this once yields

$$EI\frac{dy}{dx} = M_1x - \frac{M_1}{L}\frac{x^2}{2} + C_1$$

We know nothing about the slope at either end of the beam, and so are unable to determine C_1 immediately. Instead, we integrate again to obtain

$$EIy = M_1\frac{x^2}{2} - \frac{M_1}{2L}\frac{x^3}{3} + C_1x + C_2 \tag{1}$$

We may now make use of our two boundary conditions, which are that the deflections at both ends are zero. For the boundary condition at A, we substitute $x = 0$ and $y = 0$ in (1) and obtain $C_2 = 0$. For the boundary condition at B, we then substitute $x = L$ and $y = 0$, obtaining

$$0 = \frac{M_1L^2}{2} - \frac{M_1L^2}{6} + C_1L \quad \text{or} \quad C_1 = -\frac{M_1L}{3}$$

The equation of the deflection curve is thus

$$EIy = \frac{M_1}{2}x^2 - \frac{M_1}{6L}x^3 - \frac{M_1L}{3}x \tag{2}$$

and the slope of the beam at any point is given by

$$EI\frac{dy}{dx} = M_1 x - \frac{M_1}{2L}x^2 - \frac{M_1 L}{3} \tag{3}$$

13.3   Assume that the beam of Problem 13.2 is made of steel for which $E = 30 \times 10^6$ lb/in^2 and has a rectangular cross section, 2 in by 3 in. Its length is 8 ft. Determine the location of the point of maximum deflection and the amount of this deflection when the applied moment $M_1 = 90,000$ lb·in.

First we must investigate the state of stress to ascertain whether the action is entirely elastic. The bending moment diagram appears as in Fig. 13-5, with the peak value of A equal to M_1. The outer-fiber bending stresses are thus

$$\sigma_{max} = \frac{6M_1}{bh^2} = \frac{6(90,000 \text{ lb·in})}{(2 \text{ in})(3 \text{ in})^2} = 30,000 \text{ lb/in}^2$$

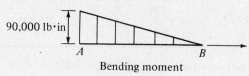

90,000 lb·in

A B

Bending moment

Fig. 13-5

Since this is within the elastic range of any steel, we are justified in using the deformation equations of Problem 13.2.

The point of maximum deflection of the beam in Fig. 13-4 is the point at which the slope of the deflected beam is zero. Setting $dy/dx = 0$ in (3) of Problem 13.2 yields

$$0 = M_1 x - \frac{M_1}{2L}x^2 - \frac{M_1 L}{3}$$

which leads to the quadratic equation

$$x^2 - 2Lx + \tfrac{2}{3}L^2 = 0$$

Only one root of this equation, namely, $x = 0.423L$, is of interest; the other root gives a point that lies to the right of B. The peak deflection thus occurs at $x = 0.423L = 40.6$ in.

The magnitude of the peak deflection is found by substituting in (2) of Problem 13.2:

$$(30 \times 10^6 \text{ lb/in}^2)[\tfrac{1}{12}(2 \text{ in})(3 \text{ in})^3]y = \frac{(90,000 \text{ lb·in})}{2}(40.6 \text{ in})^2$$

$$-\frac{90,000 \text{ lb·in}}{6(96 \text{ in})}(40.6 \text{ in})^3 - \frac{(90,000 \text{ lb·in})(96 \text{ in})}{3}(40.6 \text{ in})$$

which yields $y = 0.24$ in.

13.4   A cantilever beam when viewed from the top has the configuration indicated in Fig. 13-6a and is of constant thickness h as indicated in Fig. 13-6b. Find the equation of the deflection curve as well as the deflection at the tip due to the action of a vertical force P applied at the tip. Neglect the weight of the beam.

This problem differs from our earlier beam deflection studies because the moment of inertia of the cross-section varies along the length of the beam. Thus, I is a function of x. To find this moment of inertia at any distance x from the clamped end, we must first determine the constant f and g in the equation $z^2 = fx + g$. We accomplish this by realizing that when $x = 0, z = a$, so that $g = a^2$. Also, when $x = L, z = 0$, which leads to $f = -a^2/L$. Thus, the contour of the beam is defined by the relation

$$z^2 = -\frac{a^2}{L}x + a^2 = a^2\left(1 - \frac{x}{L}\right)$$

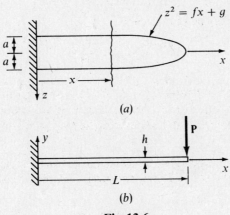

Fig. 13-6

The moment of inertia about a neutral axis parallel to the z-axis of the cross-section a distance x from the clamped end is thus

$$I = \frac{1}{12}(2z)h^3 = \frac{ah^3}{6\sqrt{L}}(L-x)^{1/2} \tag{1}$$

The differential equation of the deformed beam, eq. (5) of Problem 14.1 becomes:

$$\frac{Eah^3}{6\sqrt{L}}(L-x)^{1/2}\frac{d^2y}{dx^2} = -P(L-x) \tag{2}$$

For brevity, let

$$K = \frac{Eah^3}{6\sqrt{L}}$$

so we may write Eq. (2) in the form

$$K\frac{d^2y}{dx^2} = -P(L-x)^{1/2} \tag{3}$$

Integrating the first time we obtain

$$K\frac{dy}{dx} = -P\left\{\frac{2}{(-3)}(L-x)^{3/2}\right\} + c, \tag{4}$$

We may determine c, using the boundary condition that when $x = 0$, the slope is zero. Thus from (4) we have

$$0 = \frac{2P}{3}(L)^{3/2} + c,$$

or

$$c_1 = -\frac{2P}{3}L^{3/2} \tag{5}$$

Integrating again we have

$$Ky = \frac{2P}{3}\left\{-\frac{2}{5}[L-x]^{5/2}\right\} + \frac{2P}{3}L^{3/2}x + c_2 \tag{6}$$

As a second boundary condition we know that when $x = 0$, $y = 0$. From Eq. (6) we now have

$$0 = -\frac{4P}{15}L^{5/2} - 0 + c_2$$

from which

$$c_2 = \frac{4PL^{5/2}}{15}$$ (7)

The equation of the deflection curve is thus

$$y = \frac{6\sqrt{L}P}{Eah^3}\left\{-\frac{4}{15}[L-x]^{5/2} - \frac{2}{3}L^{3/2}x + \frac{4L^{5/2}}{15}\right\}$$ (8)

and from Eq. (8) the deflection at the tip $x = L$ is:

$$y]_{x=L} = -\frac{12PL^3}{5Eah^3}$$

Statically Determinate Systems: Method of Singularity Functions

13.5 Use singularity functions to determine the deflection equation for the simply supported beam in Fig. 13-7, which is subject to a single concentrated force **P**.

First we use statics to determine the reactions. From the moment equilibrium about A, we find that $R_C = Pa/L$; from the equilibrium of vertical forces, we find $R_A = Pb/L$.

Next we use the singularity functions of Chapter 7 to write for a single equation the bending moment along the entire length of the beam:

$$M = \frac{Pb}{L}\langle x \rangle - P\langle x - a \rangle$$

The differential equation of deformation (13.1) thus becomes

$$EI\frac{d^2y}{dx^2} = M = \frac{Pb}{L}\langle x \rangle - P\langle x - a \rangle$$ (1)

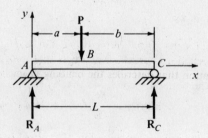

Fig. 13-7

Integration of (1) yields

$$EI\frac{dy}{dx} = \frac{Pb}{2L}\langle x \rangle^2 - \frac{P}{2}\langle x - a \rangle^2 + C_1$$

where C_1 is a constant of integration. A second integration gives

$$EIy = \frac{Pb}{6L}\langle x \rangle^3 - \frac{P}{6}\langle x - a \rangle^3 + C_1x + C_2$$ (2)

where C_2 is a second constant of integration. These two constants are found from the conditions that $y = 0$ at $x = 0$ and at $x = L$. Substituting these in (2), in turn, we find that

$$C_2 = 0 \quad \text{and} \quad C_1 = -\frac{PbL}{6} + \frac{Pb^3}{6L}$$

The desired deflection equation is thus

$$EIy = \frac{Pb}{6L}\langle x \rangle^3 - \frac{P}{6}\langle x - a \rangle^3 + \left(-\frac{PbL}{6} + \frac{Pb^3}{6L}\right)x$$

13.6   Using singularity functions, determine the deflection equation for a simply supported beam subject to a single applied moment (Fig. 13-8a).

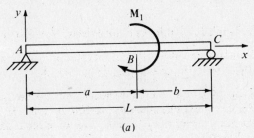

(a)

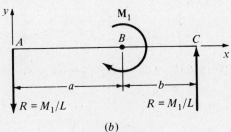

(b)

Fig. 13-8

We use the equations of static equilibrium to find the reactions at A and C, whose magnitudes are shown in Fig. 13-8b; these reactions constitute a couple that holds the applied couple M_1 in equilibrium. Then we write a single equation that describes the bending moment along the entire length of the beam:

$$M(x) = -\frac{M_1}{L}\langle x \rangle^1 + M_1\langle x - a \rangle^0$$

Next, we use (13.1) to write the differential equation of the bent beam:

$$EI\frac{d^2y}{dx^2} = -\frac{M_1}{L}\langle x \rangle^1 + M_1\langle x - a \rangle^0$$

Integrating once yields

$$EI\frac{dy}{dx} = -\frac{M_1}{2L}\langle x \rangle^2 + M_1\langle x - a \rangle^1 + C_1$$

Integrating once more yields

$$EIy = -\frac{M_1}{6L}\langle x \rangle^3 + \frac{M_1}{2}\langle x - a \rangle^2 + C_1x + C_2$$

For boundary conditions, we have $y = 0$ at $x = 0$ and at $x = L$. Using these boundary conditions in turn, we find that

$$C_2 = 0 \quad \text{and} \quad C_1 = \frac{M_1 L}{6} - \frac{M_1 b^2}{2L}$$

The deflection equation is thus

$$EIy = -\frac{M_1}{6L}\langle x \rangle^3 + \frac{M_1}{2}\langle x - a \rangle^2 + \left(\frac{M_1 L}{6} - \frac{M_1 b^2}{2L}\right)x \qquad (1)$$

Note that there is no reason to assume that the deflection at B, the point of application of the couple, is zero. In fact, the deflection at that point, as given by (1), is definitely nonzero.

13.7 Consider a simply supported beam subject to a uniform load distributed over a portion of its length (Fig. 13-9). Use singularity functions to determine the deflection equation for the beam.

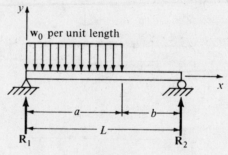

Fig. 13-9

From the static equilibrium equations, the reactions are found to be

$$R_1 = \frac{w_0}{2L}(L^2 - b^2) \qquad R_2 = w_0 a - \frac{w_0}{2L}(L^2 - b^2)$$

The bending moment at all points along the length of the beam is described by the single equation

$$M = R_1\langle x \rangle^1 - \frac{w_0}{2}\langle x \rangle^2 + \frac{w_0}{2}\langle x - a \rangle^2 \qquad (1)$$

The last term on the right in (1) is required to cancel the distributed load $-(w_0/2)\langle x \rangle^2$ for all values of x greater than $x = a$.

Now, (13.1) gives

$$EI\frac{d^2 y}{dx^2} = R_1\langle x \rangle^1 - \frac{w_0}{2}\langle x \rangle^2 + \frac{w_0}{2}\langle x - a \rangle^2$$

Hence,

$$EI\frac{dy}{dx} = \frac{R_1}{2}\langle x \rangle^2 - \frac{w_0}{6}\langle x \rangle^3 + \frac{w_0}{6}\langle x - a \rangle^3 + C_1$$

and

$$EIy = \frac{R_1}{6}\langle x \rangle^3 - \frac{w_0}{24}\langle x \rangle^4 + \frac{w_0}{24}\langle x - a \rangle^4 + C_1 x + C_2 \qquad (2)$$

To determine C_1 and C_2, we impose the boundary conditions that $y = 0$ at $x = 0$ and at $x = L$. From (2) we thus find that

$$C_2 = 0 \quad \text{and} \quad C_1 = \frac{w_0 L^3}{24} - \frac{w_0 b^4}{24L} - \frac{w_0 L}{12}(L^2 - b^2)$$

The deflection equation is, accordingly,

$$EIy = \frac{w_0}{12L}(L^2 - b^2)\langle x \rangle^3 - \frac{w_0}{24}\langle x \rangle^4 + \frac{w_0}{24}\langle x - a \rangle^4 + \left(-\frac{w_0 L^3}{24} - \frac{w_0 b^4}{24L} + \frac{w_0 L b^2}{12}\right)x$$

13.8 A uniform load acts over a portion of a simply supported beam as indicated in Fig. 13-10a. Use singularity functions to determine the deflection equation for the beam.

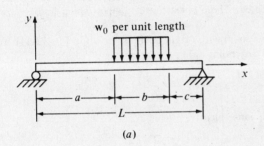
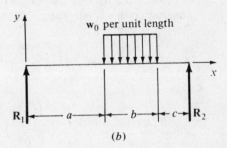

(a)   (b)

Fig. 13-10

The reactions, indicated in Fig. 13-10b, have magnitudes

$$R_1 = \frac{w_0 b}{L}\left(\frac{b}{2} + c\right) \quad \text{and} \quad R_2 = \frac{w_0 b}{L}\left(\frac{b}{2} + a\right)$$

Using singularity functions, we may now write a single equation that gives the bending moment all along the beam:

$$M = R_1\langle x \rangle^1 - \frac{w_0}{2}\langle x - a \rangle^2 + \frac{w_0}{2}\langle x - a - b \rangle^2$$

Then

$$EI\frac{d^2y}{dx^2} = R_1\langle x \rangle^1 - \frac{w_0}{2}\langle x - a \rangle^2 + \frac{w_0}{2}\langle x - a - b \rangle^2$$

so

$$EI\frac{dy}{dx} = \frac{R_1}{2}\langle x \rangle^2 - \frac{w_0}{6}\langle x - a \rangle^3 + \frac{w_0}{6}\langle x - a - b \rangle^3 + C_1$$

and

$$EIy = \frac{R_1}{6}\langle x \rangle^3 - \frac{w_0}{24}\langle x - a \rangle^4 + \frac{w_0}{24}\langle x - a - b \rangle^4 + C_1 x + C_2 \tag{1}$$

For boundary conditions we have $y = 0$ at $x = 0$ and at $x = L$. Applying these conditions in turn to (1) yields

$$C_2 = 0 \qquad C_1 = \frac{w_0}{24L}[(L-a)^4 - (L-c)^4] - \frac{w_0 bL}{6}\left(\frac{b}{2} + c\right)$$

The desired deflection curve is thus

$$EIy = \frac{w_0 b}{6L}\left(\frac{b}{2} + c\right)\langle x \rangle^3 - \frac{w_0}{24}\langle x - a \rangle^4 + \frac{w_0}{24}\langle x - a - b \rangle^4 + \left\{\frac{w_0}{24L}[(L-a)^4 - (L-c)^4] - \frac{w_0 bL}{6}\left(\frac{b}{2} + c\right)\right\}x$$

13.9   The beam in Fig. 13-11 is simply supported at B and C and loaded by couples at ends A and D. Using singularity functions, determine the deflection equation for the beam and the deflection at $x = 3a/2$, the midpoint of its length.

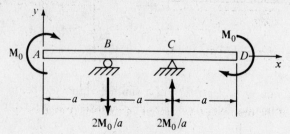

Fig. 13-11

From the equations of statics, the vertical reactions at B and C are readily found to be equal and opposite, each of magnitude $2M_0/a$ as indicated. These constitute a couple which holds the applied end couples in equilibrium.

Having introduced a cartesian coordinate system with origin at A (as shown in Fig. 13-11), we may write a single equation for the bending moment at any point along the beam:

$$M = M_0\langle x\rangle^0 - \frac{2M_0}{a}\langle x - a\rangle + \frac{2M_0}{a}\langle x - 2a\rangle$$

The differential equation of the bent beam is, consequently,

$$EI\frac{d^2y}{dx^2} = M_0\langle x\rangle^0 - \frac{2M_0}{a}\langle x - a\rangle + \frac{2M_0}{a}\langle x - 2a\rangle \tag{1}$$

Two successive integrations of (1) then yield

$$EI\frac{dy}{dx} = M_0\langle x\rangle - \frac{2M_0}{a}\frac{\langle x - a\rangle^2}{2} + \frac{2M_0}{a}\frac{\langle x - 2a\rangle^2}{2} + C_1 \tag{2}$$

and

$$EIy = M_0\frac{\langle x\rangle^2}{2} - \frac{M_0}{a}\frac{\langle x - a\rangle^3}{3} + \frac{M_0}{a}\frac{\langle x - 2a\rangle^3}{3} + C_1\langle x\rangle + C_2 \tag{3}$$

One boundary condition is that $y = 0$ at $x = a$. Substituting these values in (3), we obtain

$$0 = \frac{M_0a^2}{2} + C_1a + C_2 \tag{4}$$

A second boundary condition is that $y = 0$ at $x = 2a$. Again substituting in (3), we get

$$0 = \frac{M_0}{2}4a^2 - \frac{M_0}{3a}a^3 + 2C_1a + C_2 \tag{5}$$

Solving (4) and (5) simultaneously yields $C_1 = -\frac{7}{6}M_0a$ and $C_2 = \frac{2}{3}M_0a^2$. Hence, the equation of the deflection curve is

$$EIy = \frac{M_0}{2}\langle x\rangle^2 - \frac{M_0}{3a}\langle x - a\rangle^3 + \frac{M_0}{3a}\langle x - 2a\rangle^3 - \frac{7}{6}M_0a\langle x\rangle + \frac{2}{3}M_0a^2 \tag{6}$$

The deflection at $x = 3a/2$ is now found by substituting this value of x in (6) to obtain $y = 0$. The symmetry of the loading and support reactions indicates that this value is reasonable.

13.10   Use singularity functions to determine the equation of the deflection curve for the simply supported overhanging beam in Fig. 13-12a.

The free-body diagram for the beam is shown in Fig. 13-12b. From the static equilibrium equations, the vertical reactions are found to be $R_1 = 225\,\text{N}$ and $R_2 = 525\,\text{N}$. The bending moment at any point

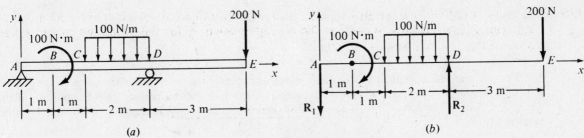

(a)   (b)

Fig. 13-12

along the length of the beam is then, in terms of singularity functions,

$$M = -225\langle x \rangle + 100\langle x-1 \rangle^0 - \frac{100}{2}\langle x-2 \rangle^2 + \frac{100}{2}\langle x-4 \rangle^2 + 525\langle x-4 \rangle \qquad (1)$$

In this equation the applied moment of 100 N·m is considered positive because it tends to produce curvature (of the portion of the beam to the right of the point of application of the moment) which is concave upward and hence positive according to our sign convention. Also, the third term on the right side of (1), corresponding to the uniformly distributed load of 100 N/m, carries that load to the right end E of the beam. To remove this effect between D and E, we must apply an upward uniform load of 100 N/m there so that the net uniform load on DE is zero. This is accomplished by the fourth term in (1).

From (13.1) and (1), the differential equation of the deflected beam is

$$EI \frac{d^2y}{dx^2} = -225\langle x \rangle^1 + 100\langle x-1 \rangle^0 - 50\langle x-2 \rangle^2 + 50\langle x-4 \rangle^2 + 525\langle x-4 \rangle^1 \qquad (2)$$

Integrating (2) twice yields

$$EI \frac{dy}{dx} = -\frac{225}{2}\langle x \rangle^2 + 100\langle x-1 \rangle^1 - \frac{50}{3}\langle x-2 \rangle^3 + \frac{50}{3}\langle x-4 \rangle^3 + \frac{525}{2}\langle x-4 \rangle^2 + C_1 \qquad (3)$$

and
$$EIy = -\frac{225}{6}\langle x \rangle^3 + \frac{100}{2}\langle x-1 \rangle^2 - \frac{50}{12}\langle x-2 \rangle^4 + \frac{50}{12}\langle x-4 \rangle^4 + \frac{525}{6}\langle x-4 \rangle^3 + C_1 x + C_2 \quad (4)$$

The boundary conditions are $y = 0$ at $x = 0$ and at $x = 4$. Using these conditions in (4) yields $C_1 = 504$ and $C_2 = 0$. The desired deflection equation is thus

$$EIy = -\frac{225}{6}\langle x \rangle^3 + \frac{100}{2}\langle x-1 \rangle^2 - \frac{50}{12}\langle x-2 \rangle^4 + \frac{50}{12}\langle x-4 \rangle^4 + \frac{525}{6}\langle x-4 \rangle^3 + 504x$$

13.11 A simply supported beam is subject to a uniformly varying load over its left half, as shown in Fig. 13-13a. Use singularity functions to determine the equation of the beam's deflection curve.

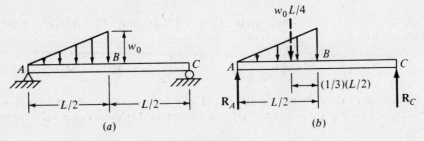

(a)   (b)

Fig. 13-13

For the purpose of determining the support reactions, it is permissible to replace the distributed load with its resultant, $(\frac{1}{2})(w_0)(L/2) = w_0 L/4$. Since the loading is triangular, the resultant acts through the centroid of the triangle, which is located a distance $(1/3)(L/2)$ from the midpoint of the bar as indicated in

Fig. 13-13*b*. A moment equation about point *C* now yields

$$+\circlearrowleft \Sigma M_C = R_A L - \frac{w_0 L}{4}\left(\frac{L}{2}+\frac{L}{6}\right) = 0 \quad \text{or} \quad R_A = \frac{w_0 L}{6}$$

We must next determine the bending moment at every point along the length of the beam. In the portion *AB* of the beam, we consider a section at a distance *x* from *A*, and we replace only the portion of the distributed load to the *left* of *x* with its resultant (Fig. 13-14). The load intensity at *x* is found from the geometry to be

$$w = \frac{w_0}{L/2}x = \frac{2w_0}{L}x \tag{1}$$

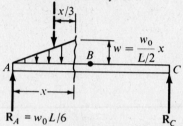

Resultant of load *left* of *x*

$R_A = w_0 L/6$

R_C

Fig. 13-14

Thus, the resultant of the distributed load to the left of *x* is

$$\frac{1}{2}x\,\frac{2w_0}{L}x = \frac{w_0 x^2}{L}$$

and is represented by the dashed vector in Fig. 13-14. The resultant acts at a distance *x*/3 to the left of the section at *x*, as shown. The bending moment it produces in *AB* is

$$\frac{w_0}{L}\langle x\rangle^2\,\frac{\langle x\rangle}{3} = \frac{w_0}{3L}\langle x\rangle^3 \tag{2}$$

Expression (2) implies that the distributed load continues to act over the right portion *BC* of the beam, as indicated in Fig. 13-15. Thus, it is necessary to introduce, in *BC*, oppositely directed loads (i.e., directed upward) corresponding to the rectangle ① and the triangle ②, so that the net effect will be zero loading in *BC*. Figure 13-15 indicates how expressions (in terms of *x*) may be written for these loads.

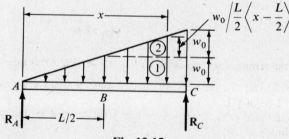

Fig. 13-15

We are now in a position to write, using singularity functions, the equation for the bending moment anywhere along the beam. It is

$$M = \frac{w_0 L}{6}\langle x\rangle - \frac{w_0}{3L}\langle x\rangle^3 + w_0\left\langle x-\frac{L}{2}\right\rangle\frac{\left\langle x-\frac{L}{2}\right\rangle}{2} + \frac{1}{2}\left(\frac{2w_0}{L}\left\langle x-\frac{L}{2}\right\rangle\right)\left\langle x-\frac{L}{2}\right\rangle\frac{\left\langle x-\frac{L}{2}\right\rangle}{3}$$

The differential equation of the bent beam is thus

$$EI \frac{d^2 y}{dx^2} = \frac{w_0 L}{6} \langle x \rangle - \frac{w_0}{3L} \langle x \rangle^3 + \frac{w_0}{2} \left\langle x - \frac{L}{2} \right\rangle^2 + \frac{w_0}{3L} \left\langle x - \frac{L}{2} \right\rangle^3$$

which may be integrated twice to yield the deflection equation

$$EIy = \frac{w_0 L}{36} \langle x \rangle^3 - \frac{w_0}{60L} \langle x \rangle^5 + \frac{w_0}{24} \left\langle x - \frac{L}{2} \right\rangle^4 + \frac{w_0}{60L} \left\langle x - \frac{L}{2} \right\rangle^5 + C_1 \langle x \rangle + C_2 \qquad (3)$$

The boundary conditions are that $y = 0$ at $x = 0$ (point A) and at $x = L$ (point C). Substitution of these values, in turn, into (3) yields $C_2 = 0$ and $C_1 = -0.01416\, w_0 L^3$. Thus, the equation of the deflected beam is, finally,

$$EIy = \frac{w_0 L}{36} \langle x \rangle^3 - \frac{w_0}{60L} \langle x \rangle^5 + \frac{w_0}{24} \left\langle x - \frac{L}{2} \right\rangle^4 + \frac{w_0}{60L} \left\langle x - \frac{L}{2} \right\rangle^5 - 0.01416 w_0 L^3 \langle x \rangle$$

Statically Determinate Systems: Computer Solution

13.12 Write a FORTRAN program that will calculate the deflections and slope at various points along a beam of constant cross section, simply supported at its ends, and subject to arbitrary concentrated forces, moments, and uniformly distributed loads, all acting at known points on the beam.

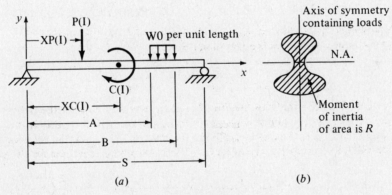

Fig. 13-16

We employ the terminology indicated in Fig. 13-16 and in the following list:

P(I) = numerical value of concentrated force I, taken positive downward
XP(I) = x coordinate of P(I)
C(I) = numerical value of concentrated couple I, taken positive clockwise
XC(I) = x coordinate of C(I)
W0 = intensity of uniformly distributed load, taken positive downward
A, B = beginning, ending x coordinates of W0
E = Young's modulus
R = moment of inertia of beam about its neutral axis
S = beam length
N = number of equally spaced points along the beam length at which the deflections are required (including ends), less 1
NP = number of concentrated forces acting
NC = number of concentrated couples acting

What follows is a FORTRAN program for the numerical solution of (*13.1*). The program provides the lateral deflections at the ends of the beam and at N − 1 stations along the beam. Positive and negative values indicate upward and downward deflections, respectively. The user does not have to calculate the end reactions, and any consistent system of units may be used.

```
00001         PROGRAM BEAMDEF
00002C        DEFLECTIONS OF A SIMPLY SUPPORTED BEAM SUBJECTED
00003C        TO CONCENTRATED MOMENTS, CONCENTRATED FORCES
00004C        AND UNIFORMLY DISTRIBUTED LOADING
00005C            REACTIONS MUST BE AT END POINTS OF THE BEAM,
00006C        THIS PROGRAM DETERMINES BEAM REACTIONS.
00007         DIMENSION P(15),XP(15),C(15),XC(15),XN(100)
00008         DIMENSION Y(100),SL(100)
00009C            P(I) & C(I) ARE VALUES OF CONCENTRATED FORCES &  COUPLES
00010C            XP(I) & XC(I) ARE COORDINATES OF P(I) & C(I)
00011C            FROM LEFT ENDPOINT OF BEAM
00012C            XN(I) ARE COORDINATES OF SEGEMENT NODES FROM LEFT END OF BEAM
00013C            INCLUDING LEFT & RIGHT ENDPOINTS
00014C            Y(I) & SL(I) ARE DEFLECTIONS & SLOPES AT NODES XN(I)
00015         LP=1
00016         DO 420 LT=1,LP
00017         PRINT*,'ENTER THE VALUES E,R,S,N,NC,NP:'
00018         READ(*,*) E,R,S,N,NC,NP
00019C            E IS YOUNGS MODULUS, R IS MOMENT OF INERTIA
00020C            S  IS  LENGTH OF SPAN, N IS NUMBER OF SEGEMENTS OF SPAN
00021C            NC IS NUMBER OF CONCENTRATED COUPLES
00022C            NP IS NUMBER OF CONCENTRATED FORCES
00023         PRINT*,'ENTER THE VALUES A,B,W0:'
00024         READ(*,*) A,B,W0
00025C            A & B ARE COORDINATES OF DISTRIBUTED LOADING FROM LEFT END
00026C            W0 IS DISTRIBUTED LOADING-DOWNWARD IS POSITIVE
00027         IF(NC.EQ.0) GO TO 400
00028C            INPUT COORDINATES OF CONCENTRATED COUPLES
00029C            THEN INPUT THEIR VALUES-CLOCKWISE IS POSITIVE
00030         PRINT*,'ENTER THE ALL VALUES XC(I) & THEN ALL C(I):'
00031         READ(*,*) (XC(I),I=1,NC),(C(I),I=1,NC)
00032 400     IF(NP.EQ.0) GO TO 410
00033C            INPUT COORDINATES OF CONCENTRATED FORCES
00034C            THEN INPUT THEIR VALUES-DOWNWARD IS POSITIVE
00035         PRINT*,'ENTER ALL THE VALUES XP(I) & THEN ALL P(I):'
00036         READ(*,*) (XP(I),I=1,NP),(P(I),I=1,NP)
00037 410     DX=S/N
00038         PRINT 20
00039 20      FORMAT(38HDEFLECTIONS OF A SIMPLY SUPPORTED BEAM)
00040         PRINT 21,E,R,S
00041 21      FORMAT(1X,2HE=,E10.3,2X,2HI=,E10.3,2X,2HL=,E10.3)
00042         DO 110 I=1,N+1
00043         XN(I)=DX*(I-1)
00044   110   CONTINUE
00045         EI=E*R
00046         IF(NC.LE.0) GO TO 200
00047         PRINT 22
00048         PRINT 23
00049 22      FORMAT(45H CONCENTRATED COUPLES-  CLOCKWISE IS POSITIVE)
00050 23      FORMAT(14H LOCATION - IN,7X,15H COUPLE - IN*LB)
00051         DO 450 KT=1,N+1
00052         SL(KT)=0.0
00053         Y(KT)=0.0
00054 450     CONTINUE
00055         DO 140 K=1,NC
00056         PRINT 24,XC(K),C(K)
00057 24      FORMAT(F10.3,12X,E10.3)
00058         C1=S/6.0-(S-XC(K))**2/(2.0*S)

00059         DO 140 I=1,N+1
```

```
00060           SL(I)=SL(I)+(C(K)/EI)*(-XN(I)**2/(2.0*S)+C1)
00061           Y(I)=Y(I)+(C(K)/EI)*(-XN(I)**3/(6.0*S)+C1*XN(I))
00062           IF(XN(I)-XC(K)) 140,140,135
00063     135   SL(I)=SL(I)+(C(K)/EI)*(XN(I)-XC(K))
00064           Y(I)=Y(I)+(0.5*C(K)/EI)*(XN(I)-XC(K))**2
00065     140   CONTINUE
00066     200   IF(NP.LE.0) GO TO 300
00067           PRINT 25
00068     25    FORMAT(41H CONCENTRATED FORCES-DOWNWARD IS POSITIVE)
00069           PRINT 251
00070     251   FORMAT(14H LOCATION - IN,7X,11H FORCE - LB)
00071           DO 220 K=1,NP
00072           PRINT 26,XP(K),P(K)
00073     26    FORMAT(F10.3,12X,E10.3)
00074           C2=(-S*(S-XP(K))*S+(S-XP(K))**3)/(6.0*S)
00075           DO 220 I=1,N+1
00076           IF(XN(I)-XP(K)) 221,221,215
00077     221   SL(I)=SL(I)+(P(K)/EI)*((S-XP(K))*XN(I)**2/(2.0*S)+C2)
00078           Y(I)=Y(I)+(P(K)/EI)*((S-XP(K))*XN(I)**3/(6.0*S)+C2*XN(I))
00079           GO TO 220
00080     215   SL(I)=SL(I)+(P(K)/EI)*((S-XP(K))*XN(I)**2-S*(S-XP(K))*S/3.0
00081+          +(S-XP(K))**3/3.0-(XN(I)-XP(K))**2*S)/(2.0*S)
00082           Y(I)=Y(I)+(P(K)/EI)*((S-XP(K))*XN(I)*(XN(I)**2-S**2)
00083+          +(S-XP(K))**3*XN(I)-(XN(I)-XP(K))**3*S)/(6.0*S)
00084     220   CONTINUE
00085     300   IF(W0.EQ.0.0) GO TO 170
00086           PRINT 430
00087     430   FORMAT(40HDISTRIBUTED LOADING-DOWNWARD IS POSITIVE)
00088           PRINT 440,A,B,W0
00089     440   FORMAT(1X,2HA=,F10.3,2X,2HB=,F10.3,2X,3HW0=,E10.3)
00090           C3=(-(2.0*S-A-B)*(B-A)*S**2*2+((S-A)**4-(S-B)**4))/(24.0*S)
00091           DO 160 I=1,N+1
00092           SL(I)=SL(I)+(W0/EI)*((2.0*S-A-B)*(B-A)*XN(I)**2/(4.0*S)+C3)
00093           Y(I)=Y(I)+(W0/EI)*((2.0*S-A-B)*(B-A)*XN(I)**3/(12.0*S)+C3*XN(I))
00094           IF(XN(I).GT.A) GO TO 120
00095           GO TO 160
00096     120   SL(I)=SL(I)-(W0/EI)*(XN(I)-A)**3/6.0
00097           Y(I)=Y(I)-(W0/EI)*(XN(I)-A)**4/24.0
00098     130   IF(XN(I).GE.B) GO TO 150
00099           GO TO 160
00100     150   SL(I)=SL(I)+(W0/EI)*(XN(I)-B)**3/6.0
00101           Y(I)=Y(I)+(W0/EI)*(XN(I)-B)**4/24.0
00102     160   CONTINUE
00103     170   PRINT 27
00104           PRINT 28
00105     27    FORMAT(44H NODE    LOCATION        SLOPE       DEFLECTION)
00106     28    FORMAT(42H  NO         IN         IN/IN          IN)
00107           DO 305 I=1,N+1
00108           PRINT 29,I,XN(I),SL(I),Y(I)
00109     29    FORMAT(1H ,I3,4X,F8.3,4X,E10.3,5X,E10.3)
00110     305   CONTINUE
00111     420   CONTINUE
00112           STOP
00113           END
```

13.13 A simply supported W 250×115 beam having $I = 190 \times 10^6$ mm^4 and $E = 200$ GPa is subject to the concentrated and distributed loads shown in Fig. 13-17. Use the FORTRAN program of Problem 13.12 with $N = 24$ to determine the deflection of the beam.

We input $E = 200E + 9$, $R = 190E - 6$ [after converting the given value to (meters)^4], $S = 18$, $N = 24$, $NC = 0$, $NP = 1$, $A = 12$, $B = 18$, $W0 = 600$, $XP = 6$, and $P = 8000$. The computer output that follows shows a peak downward deflection of approximately 0.0272 m.

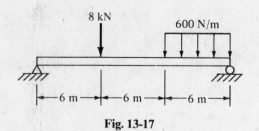

Fig. 13-17

```
ENTER THE VALUES E,R,S,N,NC,NP:
? 200E+9,190E-6,18,24,0,1
ENTER THE VALUES A,B,WO:
? 12,18,600
ENTER ALL THE VALUES XP(I) & THEN ALL P(I):
? 6,8000
DEFLECTIONS OF A SIMPLY SUPPORTED BEAM
E=  .200E+12  I=  .190E-03  L=  .180E+02
CONCENTRATED FORCES-DOWNWARD IS POSITIVE
LOCATION - IN        FORCE - LB
     6.000             .800E+04
DISTRIBUTED LOADING-DOWNWARD IS POSITIVE
A=    12.000  B=     18.000  WO=  .600E+03
NODE    LOCATION       SLOPE      DEFLECTION
NO.       IN           IN/IN          IN
 1       .000        -.502E-02     .000E+00
 2       .750        -.497E-02    -.375E-02
 3      1.500        -.484E-02    -.744E-02
 4      2.250        -.462E-02    -.110E-01
 5      3.000        -.431E-02    -.143E-01
 6      3.750        -.392E-02    -.174E-01
 7      4.500        -.343E-02    -.202E-01
 8      5.250        -.286E-02    -.226E-01
 9      6.000        -.221E-02    -.245E-01
10      6.750        -.152E-02    -.259E-01
11      7.500        -.861E-03    -.268E-01
12      8.250        -.235E-03    -.272E-01
13      9.000         .361E-03    -.271E-01
14      9.750         .925E-03    -.266E-01
15     10.500         .146E-02    -.257E-01
16     11.250         .196E-02    -.245E-01
17     12.000         .244E-02    -.228E-01
18     12.750         .288E-02    -.208E-01
19     13.500         .328E-02    -.185E-01
20     14.250         .364E-02    -.159E-01
21     15.000         .395E-02    -.130E-01
22     15.750         .421E-02    -.998E-02
23     16.500         .439E-02    -.675E-02
24     17.250         .451E-02    -.340E-02
25     18.000         .455E-02     .347E-17
```

Statically Indeterminate Systems

13.14   The beam in Fig. 13-18 is clamped at the left end, simply supported at the right end, and subject to a single concentrated force as shown. Determine all reaction components.

The available equilibrium equations are

$$\Sigma F_y = R_A + R_B - P = 0 \tag{1}$$

$$+\!\!\curvearrowleft \Sigma M_A = -M_A + Pa - R_B L = 0 \tag{2}$$

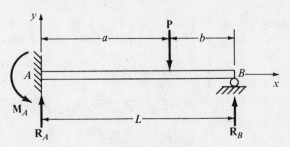

Fig. 13-18

We thus have two statics equations in the three unknowns R_A, R_B, and M_A. We must supplement these equations with one more, based upon the deformations of the beam.

Singularity functions seem ideally suited to this situation, and we use them to write (*13.1*) as

$$EI \frac{d^2y}{dx^2} = R_A \langle x \rangle - M_A \langle x \rangle^0 - P \langle x - a \rangle$$

Integrating twice, we obtain

$$EI \frac{dy}{dx} = R_A \frac{\langle x \rangle^2}{2} - M_A \langle x \rangle - P \frac{\langle x - a \rangle^2}{2} + C_1$$

$$EIy = \frac{R_A}{2} \frac{\langle x \rangle^3}{3} - M_A \frac{\langle x \rangle^2}{2} - \frac{P}{2} \frac{\langle x - a \rangle^3}{3} + C_1 x + C_2 \qquad (3)$$

Imposition of the boundary conditions that at $x = 0$ we have $dy/dx = 0$ and $y = 0$ yields $C_1 = C_2 = 0$. There is a third boundary condition: $y = 0$ at $x = L$. Substituting these values for x and y in (*3*) gives us the equation

$$0 = \frac{R_A L^3}{6} - \frac{M_A L^2}{2} - \frac{Pb^3}{6} \qquad (4)$$

This equation, which stems from the deformations of the beam, is the desired third equation. Now, solving (*1*), (*2*), and (*4*) simultaneously yields

$$R_A = \frac{Pb}{2L^3}(3L^2 - b^2) \qquad R_B = \frac{Pa^2}{2L^3}(2L + b) \qquad M_A = \frac{Pb}{2L^3}(L^2 - b^2)$$

13.15 The cantilever beam in Fig. 13-19 is supported by a spring having spring constant k and is loaded by a single concentrated force, as shown. Determine the deflection of point B.

Fig. 13-19

Let us denote the magnitude of the force acting within the spring as P_s. Then the desired deflection Δ_B is the sum of a deflection due to **P** and one due to $\mathbf{P}_s$. From (*13.3*), the deflection of the tip of the beam due to the force at a (but with *no* spring support) is given by

$$EI[y]_{x=L} = -\frac{Pa^2 L}{2} + \frac{Pa^3}{6}$$

Using *(13.3)* again, this time with $a = x = L$, we find the deflection of point B due to the upward spring force to be $P_s L^3 / 3EI$. Hence, we have the situation shown in Fig. 13-20.

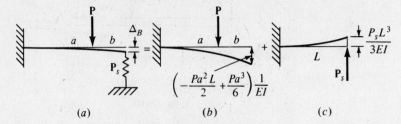

Fig. 13-20

Because the beam exerts a force of magnitude P_s on the spring, the spring contracts by an amount P_s/k, as shown in Fig. 13-21. Since the downward displacement of the tip of the beam must equal the net contraction of the spring, we have

$$-\frac{P_s}{k} = \Delta_B = \left(-\frac{Pa^2 L}{2} + \frac{Pa^3}{6}\right)\frac{1}{EI} + \frac{P_s L^3}{3EI} \tag{1}$$

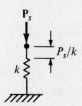

Fig. 13-21

Note that, in *(1)*, we show the contraction of the spring as being negative because the top of the spring moves downward—in the negative y direction.

Solving, we find that

$$P_s = \frac{\left(\dfrac{Pa^2 L}{2} - \dfrac{Pa^3}{6}\right)\dfrac{1}{EI}}{\dfrac{1}{k} + \dfrac{L^3}{3EI}} \tag{2}$$

The deflection Δ_B of the tip of the beam is thus

$$\Delta_B = -\frac{P_s}{k} = \frac{-\dfrac{Pa^2 L}{2} + \dfrac{Pa^3}{6}}{EI\left(1 + \dfrac{kL^3}{3EI}\right)} \tag{3}$$

If the spring is infinitely stiff so that $k \to \infty$, then *(3)* yields $\Delta_B = 0$. In this special case, the spring reaction coincides with the simple support of Problem 13.14, and *(2)* gives the same value for R_B as was found in Problem 13.14.

13.16 Cantilever beam AB in Fig. 13-22 is clamped at B and supported through a hinge by a partially submerged (in water) pontoon at A. The beam is of rigidity EI and length L. It is loaded by a vertical concentrated force $\mathbf{F}$ at A. Determine the reactive moment at B.

This problem is a variation of Problem 13.15. When the force $\mathbf{F}$ is applied and the pontoon submerges a distance Δ, then according to the law of Archimedes, the pontoon is buoyed up by a force $\mathbf{R}_A$ of magnitude

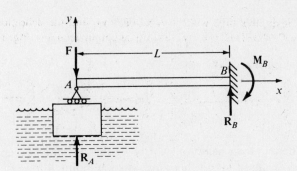

Fig. 13-22

equal to the weight of the additional water displaced during the motion through Δ. If the cross-sectional area of the pontoon is A_0 and the weight of the water per unit volume is γ, then

$$A_0 \Delta \gamma = -R_A \tag{1}$$

For a coordinate system as shown in Fig. 13-22, we have, from (13.1),

$$EI \frac{d^2 y}{dx^2} = R_A x - Fx$$

Integration yields

$$EI \frac{dy}{dx} = R_A \frac{x^2}{2} - F \frac{x^2}{2} + C_1 \tag{2}$$

Because $dy/dx = 0$ when $x = L$, we have, from (2),

$$C_1 = \frac{FL^2}{2} - \frac{R_A}{2} L^2$$

Integrating (2) now yields

$$EIy = \frac{R_A}{2} \frac{x^3}{3} - \frac{F}{2} \frac{x^3}{3} + \left(\frac{FL^2}{2} - \frac{R_A}{2} L^2 \right) x + C_2 \tag{3}$$

As a second boundary condition we have $y = 0$ when $x = L$. This gives us

$$C_2 = \frac{R_A L^3}{3} - \frac{FL^3}{3}$$

The equation of the deflected beam is thus

$$EIy = \frac{R_A}{6} x^3 - \frac{F}{6} x^3 + \left(\frac{FL^2}{2} - \frac{R_A L^2}{2} \right) x + \frac{R_A L^3}{3} - \frac{FL^3}{3} \tag{4}$$

We need to find the deflection y at $x = 0$. It is, from (1),

$$y = \Delta = -\frac{R_A}{A_0 \gamma}$$

Then, at $x = 0$ we have, from (4),

$$-\frac{R_A EI}{A_0 \gamma} = \frac{R_A L^3}{3} - \frac{FL^3}{3} \quad \text{or} \quad R_A = \frac{FL^3/3}{\dfrac{L^3}{3} + \dfrac{EI}{A_0 \gamma}} \tag{5}$$

From (5) it is clear that for $\gamma \to \infty$ (that is, for a solid, pinned support at A) the value of R_A approaches F, which indeed it must.

Now, for moment equilibrium about B, we have

$$+\circlearrowleft \Sigma M_B = R_A L - FL + M_B = 0 \tag{6}$$

Solving (5) and (6) simultaneously yields

$$M_B = \frac{3FLEI}{L^3 A_0 \gamma + 3EI}$$

13.17 Consider an infinitely long beam of rigidity EI that is initially completely in contact with a rigid plane. The beam is raised up off the plane at some point A by a force $2F$ (Fig. 13-23). Determine the length $2L$ of beam that is no longer in contact with the plane if the weight of the beam per unit length is w.

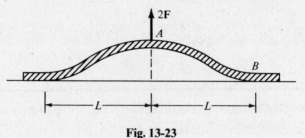

Fig. 13-23

Because the vertical line of action of the force $2\mathbf{F}$ is an axis of symmetry, we need consider only the portion of the beam to one side of that line. The free-body diagram for the portion of the beam between the axis of symmetry and the right-hand point on the beam that is just breaking contact with the rigid plane is shown in Fig. 13-24.

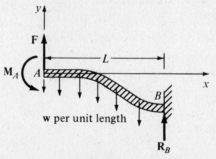

Fig. 13-24

Several aspects of Fig. 13-24 need explanation. First, only the force $\mathbf{F}$ acts at the left end of the free body. Also, due to the symmetry, the slope of the deflected beam must be zero at the point of application of $\mathbf{F}$. Most important, since the plane is flat, the beam must have zero curvature to the right of point B. Then, from (13.1), it immediately follows that *the bending moment must be zero at point B* as well as at all points to the right of B. However, there must be a nonzero bending moment in the lifted beam to the left of B, and this moment can only be caused by a concentrated force acting at B. That force is designated $\mathbf{R}_B$ in Fig. 13-24.

We can write two equations of static equilibrium involving the three unknowns R_B, L, and M_A. However, only one of these is of direct value, and it is

$$+\circlearrowleft \Sigma M_B = -M_A - \frac{wL^2}{2} + FL = 0 \tag{1}$$

Now we make use of the method of double integration. From (13.1), we write the general equation

$$EI\frac{d^2y}{dx^2} = -wx\frac{x}{2} + Fx - M_A \tag{2}$$

Substituting M_A from (1) into (2) yields

$$EI\frac{d^2y}{dx^2} = -\frac{wx^2}{2} + Fx + \left(\frac{wL^2}{2} - FL\right) \qquad (3)$$

and one integration gives us

$$EI\frac{dy}{dx} = -\frac{w}{2}\frac{x^3}{3} + F\frac{x^2}{2} + \left(\frac{wL^2}{2} - FL\right)x + C_1 \qquad (4)$$

One boundary condition is that $dy/dx = 0$ when $x = 0$, and it yields $C_1 = 0$.

 We need not perform a second integration. We simply note that $dy/dx = 0$ when $x = L$, and substitute these values in (4) to obtain

$$0 = -\frac{wL^3}{6} + \frac{FL^2}{2} + \frac{wL^3}{2} - FL^2$$

from which $L = 3F/2w$. Note that this value is independent of the rigidity EI.

13.18 The propped cantilever beam in Fig. 13-25 is subject to a uniform load distributed over the left half of its span, as shown. Determine the peak bending moment in the beam.

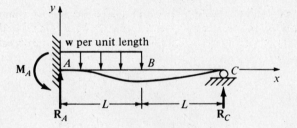

Fig. 13-25

We have only two equations of static equilibrium in the three unknowns R_A, R_C, and M_A:

$$\Sigma F_y = R_A + R_C - wL = 0 \qquad (1)$$

$$+\!\!\curvearrowleft \Sigma M_C = -M_A + R_A(2L) - wL\left(\frac{3L}{2}\right) = 0 \qquad (2)$$

Because the loading extends over only a portion of the beam, the method of singularity functions should be employed to obtain a third equation. As in Problem 13.7, we must be careful to add a term that cancels the load in region BC; the last term in the following differential equation does just that:

$$EI\frac{d^2y}{dx^2} = -M_A\langle x\rangle^0 + R_A\langle x\rangle - \frac{w}{2}\langle x\rangle^2 + w\frac{\langle x-L\rangle^2}{2} \qquad (3)$$

Integrating (3) yields

$$EI\frac{dy}{dx} = -M_A\langle x\rangle + R_A\frac{\langle x\rangle^2}{2} - \frac{w}{2}\frac{\langle x\rangle^3}{3} + \frac{w}{2}\frac{\langle x-L\rangle^3}{3} + C_1 \qquad (4)$$

For one boundary condition, we have $dy/dx = 0$ when $x = 0$, and substituting those values in (4) yields $C_1 = 0$. Integrating a second time, we obtain

$$EIy = -M_A\frac{\langle x\rangle^2}{2} + \frac{R_A}{2}\frac{\langle x\rangle^3}{3} - \frac{w}{6}\frac{\langle x\rangle^4}{4} + \frac{w}{6}\frac{\langle x-L\rangle^4}{4} + C_2 \qquad (5)$$

As a second boundary condition, we have $y = 0$ when $x = 0$. These values yield $C_2 = 0$, so the equation of the deflected beam is

$$EIy = -\frac{M_A\langle x\rangle^2}{2} + \frac{R_A\langle x\rangle^3}{6} - \frac{w\langle x\rangle^4}{24} + \frac{w\langle x - L\rangle^4}{24} \tag{6}$$

A third boundary condition is that $y = 0$ when $x = 2L$. With these values substituted, (6) becomes

$$0 = -\frac{M_A}{2}(2L)^2 + \frac{R_A}{6}(2L)^3 - \frac{w}{24}(2L)^4 - \frac{wL^4}{24} \tag{7}$$

Now, solving (1), (2), and (7) simultaneously, we find that

$$R_A = \frac{55}{64}wL \qquad R_C = \frac{9}{64}wL \qquad M_A = \frac{7}{32}wL^2 \tag{8}$$

Having these values, we can now construct the shear and moment diagrams (see Fig. 13-26). The bending moment in region AB is, from (3) and (8),

$$M = -\frac{7}{32}wL^2 + \frac{55}{64}wLx - \frac{wx^2}{2} \tag{9}$$

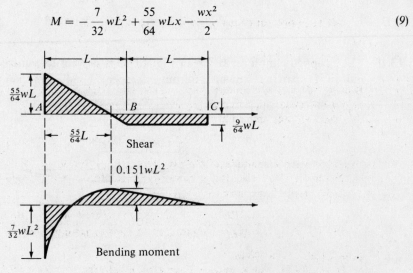

Fig. 13-26

By differentiating (9), the point of zero shear is found to be $x = 55L/64$. The bending moment curve has a horizontal tangent at this point, and the value of the bending moment there is readily found to be $0.151wL^2$ (a positive bending moment). However, the reactive moment M_A at the wall has a larger absolute value of $7wL^2/32$ and is the required peak bending moment.

13.19 Beam AB in Fig. 13-27 is clamped at the left end A and loaded by a force of 1000 lb at the right tip B. With no load at B, there is a 0.3-in gap between the tip of the beam and the top of a linear

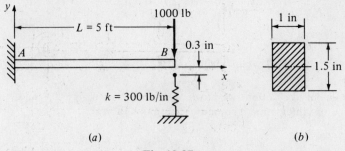

Fig. 13-27

spring of constant 300 lb/in. The beam is steel, with $E = 30 \times 10^6$ lb/in², and of rectangular cross section, 1 in by 1.5 in. Determine the force that is developed in the spring when the load is applied at B.

Free-body diagrams for the beam and the spring are shown in Fig. 13-28. There, P_s represents the force that the spring exerts upward on the beam, as well as the downward force that the tip of the beam exerts on the spring.

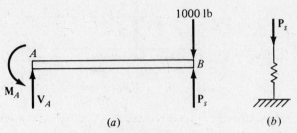

(a) (b)

Fig. 13-28

We have two equations of static equilibrium for beam AB:

$$\Sigma F_y = V_A + P_s - 1000 = 0 \tag{1}$$

$$+\circlearrowleft \Sigma M_A = -M_A + 5(1000 - P_s) = 0 \tag{2}$$

Because (1) and (2) contain three unknowns, M_A, V_A, and P_s, they must be supplemented with a deformation relation. Here, we may use (13.2) to write an equation for the deflection at the tip $(x = L)$ due to a vertical force applied at $a = L$:

$$3EIy = -PL^3 \tag{3}$$

In (3), P is the magnitude of the *net* force acting downward on the beam; Fig. 13-28a shows that this is $(1000 - P_s)$ lb. Also, the amount by which the spring is compressed is $(P_s$ lb)/(300 lb/in).

Now, from (3), we have for point B,

$$y = \frac{-PL^3}{3EI} = \frac{-(1000 - P_s)(60 \text{ in})^3}{3(30 \times 10^6 \text{ lb/in}^2)(1/12)(1 \text{ in})(1.5 \text{ in})^3} = -0.3 \text{ in} - \frac{P_s}{300 \text{ lb/in}}$$

from which $P_s = 694$ lb.

Knowing this value, we can, if we wish, obtain the remaining reactions from (1) and (2).

13.20 The initially straight beam AB in Fig. 13-29 is supported by a linear spring at each end, as well as by a torsion spring at end B. The linear springs have constants k_A and k_B, and the torsion spring (which tends to restrain angular rotation at end B) has constant k_T (newton-meters per radian in SI units or pound-inches per radian in USCS units). An applied load P acts at a distance a from the left end. Determine the deflection of the beam at A, neglecting the weight of the beam.

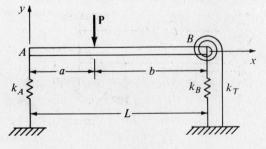

Fig. 13-29

The free-body diagram for the beam is shown in Fig. 13-30, where the forces exerted on the beam by the linear springs are denoted $\mathbf{R}_A$ and $\mathbf{R}_B$. We assume that the ends of the beam are displaced downward; hence we must write

$$R_A = -k_A y_A \quad \text{and} \quad R_B = -k_B y_B \tag{1}$$

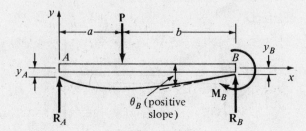

Fig. 13-30

where y_A and y_B are the displacements at A and B, and the minus signs indicate that the forces and displacements occur in opposite directions. The moment $\mathbf{M}_B$ due to the torsion spring must have the sense indicated in Fig. 13-30 because a torsion spring has the property that its resistance, as measured by M_B, increases as the angle θ increases. Hence we may write

$$M_B = k_T \theta_B \tag{2}$$

We may write two equations of static equilibrium:

$$\Sigma F_y = R_A + R_B - P = 0 \tag{3}$$

$$+\circlearrowleft \Sigma M_B = M_B + R_A L - Pb = 0 \tag{4}$$

Upon substituting (1) and (2) in (3) and (4), we find that

$$y_A = \frac{1}{k_A}(-k_B y_B - P) \qquad y_B = \frac{1}{k_B}(y_A k_A + P) \tag{5}$$

and

$$\theta_B = \frac{1}{k_T}(k_A y_A L + Pb) = \frac{1}{k_T}(-k_B y_B L - Pa) \tag{6}$$

The method of singularity functions and (13.1) now yield

$$EI\frac{d^2y}{dx^2} = R_A\langle x\rangle - P\langle x - a\rangle \tag{7}$$

$$EI\frac{dy}{dx} = R_A\frac{\langle x\rangle^2}{2} - P\frac{\langle x - a\rangle^2}{2} + C_1 \tag{8}$$

$$EIy = \frac{R_A}{2}\frac{\langle x\rangle^3}{3} - \frac{P}{2}\frac{\langle x - a\rangle^3}{3} + C_1 x + C_2 \tag{9}$$

As boundary conditions, we have

1. $y = y_A$ when $x = 0$.
2. $y = y_B$ when $x = L$.
3. $dy/dx = \theta_B$ when $x = L$.

Substituting these values in (8) and (9), we obtain, after lengthy algebraic manipulations,

$$y_A = \frac{\dfrac{PEI}{Lk_B} - \dfrac{Pb^2}{2} - \dfrac{Pb^3}{6L} - \dfrac{PbEI}{k_T}}{\dfrac{EIk_A L}{k_T} + \dfrac{2}{3}k_A L^2 + \dfrac{EI}{L} - \dfrac{EIk_A}{Lk_B}}$$

Supplementary Problems

13.21 When viewed from the top, a cantilever beam has the configuration shown in Fig. 13-31a. The beam is of constant thickness h, as indicated in Fig. 13-31b. Determine the deflection at the tip of the beam due to a concentrated force **P** applied at that point.

Ans. $\dfrac{PL^3}{Eah^3}[15 - 24\ln(2L) + 24\ln(L)]$

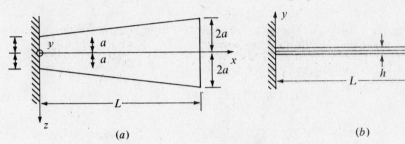

(a)   (b)

Fig. 13-31

13.22 When viewed from above, a cantilever beam appears as a triangle, as shown in Fig. 13-32a; the beam is of constant thickness h, as indicated in Fig. 13-32b. If a load **w** per unit area is uniformly distributed over the surface of the beam, determine the deflection of its tip.   *Ans.* $wL^4/2Eh^3$

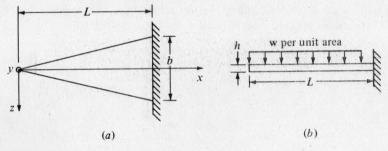

(a)   (b)

Fig. 13-32

13.23 Determine the equation of the deflection curve for the simply supported beam of Fig. 13-33, which is subject to a load of uniformly varying intensity.

Ans. $EIy = \dfrac{wL}{2}\left(-\dfrac{x^5}{60L^2} + \dfrac{x^3}{18} - \dfrac{7L^2x}{180}\right)$

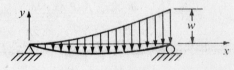

Fig. 13-33

13.24 The simply supported beam AB in Fig. 13-34 is subject to a normal load whose intensity per unit length varies in the form of half a loop of a sine curve, as shown. Determine the equation of the deflection curve of the beam. [*Hint*: Instead of using (13.1), start with $EI\,d^4y/dx^4 = -w$, which may be obtained by differentiating (13.1) twice and then substituting for w and V from (7.1) and (7.2).]

Ans. $EIy = \dfrac{16w_0L^4}{\pi^4}\sin\dfrac{\pi x}{2L} + \dfrac{2Lw_0}{3\pi^2}x^3 - w_0L^3\left(\dfrac{16}{\pi^4} + \dfrac{2}{3\pi^2}\right)x$

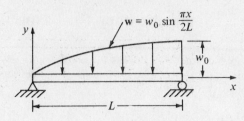

Fig. 13-34

13.25 The simply supported beam *AD* in Fig. 13-35 is subject to a couple and a uniformly distributed load, as shown. Determine the equation of its deflection curve.

Ans. $EIy = -402.8\langle x \rangle^3 + 5000\langle x - 1.333 \rangle^2 - 5.208\langle x - 1.333 \rangle^4 + 5.208\langle x - 2.667 \rangle^4 - 8185\langle x \rangle$

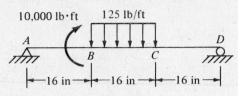

Fig. 13-35

13.26 Consider the beam in Problem 13.25 to be commercially available TS-7 × 4 rectangular tubing having the cross section shown in Fig. 13-36. The moment of inertia about the neutral axis is 57.6 in⁴, and $E = 30 \times 10^6$ lb/in². Determine the deflection at point *B*.   *Ans.*   −0.0116 in

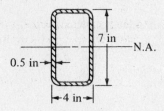

Fig. 13-36

13.27 The beam in Fig. 13-37 has constant cross section, is simply supported at *A* and *B*, and is loaded by two concentrated forces as shown. Determine the deflection of point *C*.   *Ans.* $PL^3/48EI$, upward

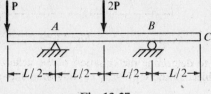

Fig. 13-37

13.28 The double-overhanging beam in Fig. 13-38 is simply supported at *C* and *D*. The loading is a single couple **M₀**, applied as shown. Write the equation of the deflection curve due to this load. If the beam is a titanium bar of circular cross section and diameter 20 mm, $E = 115$ GPa, $L = 0.5$ m,   and $M_0 = 300$ N·m,   find the deflection at end *E*.

Ans. $EIy = \dfrac{M_0}{2}\left\langle x - \dfrac{L}{2} \right\rangle^2 - \dfrac{M_0}{6L}\langle x - L \rangle^3 + \dfrac{M_0}{6L}\langle x - 2L \rangle^3 - \dfrac{5}{6}M_0 L\langle x \rangle + \dfrac{17}{24}M_0 L^2$; $y_E = 13.8$ mm

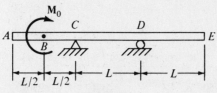

Fig. 13-38

13.29 The simply supported beam in Fig. 13-39 is loaded by an upwardly directed uniform load in region *AB*, together with two couples. Determine the equation of the deflection curve for the beam.

Ans. $EIy = \dfrac{w}{24}\langle x\rangle^4 - \left(\dfrac{M_1}{9a} + \dfrac{7}{36}wa\right)\langle x-a\rangle^3 + \dfrac{M_1}{2}\langle x-a\rangle^2 - \dfrac{w}{24}\langle x-a\rangle^4 + \dfrac{M_1}{2}\langle x-4a\rangle^2$

$+ \left(\dfrac{M_1}{9a} + \dfrac{wa}{36}\right)\langle x-4a\rangle^3 - (0.668wa^3 + 0.5M_1a)\langle x\rangle + 0.626wa^4 + 0.5M_1a^2$

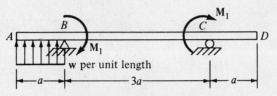

Fig. 13-39

13.30 In Problem 13.6 let the beam be a W 250 × 58 section having $I = 87.4 \times 10^6$ mm^4, and let $M_1 = 60$ kN·m, $a = 3$ m, and $b = 2$ m. Find the peak bending stress and the deflection under the point of application of the couple.   *Ans.* $\sigma = 85.8$ MPa; $y_B = 1.37$ mm (upward)

13.31 The cantilever beam of Fig. 13-40 is loaded by a uniform load over part of its length. Use singularity functions to determine the equation of the deflection curve for the beam.

Ans. $EIy = -\dfrac{w_0}{24}\langle x\rangle^4 + \dfrac{w_0}{24}\langle x-a\rangle^4 + \dfrac{w_0}{6}(L^3 - b^3)x + \dfrac{w_0}{24}(L^4 - b^4) - \dfrac{w_0 L}{6}(L^3 - b^3)$

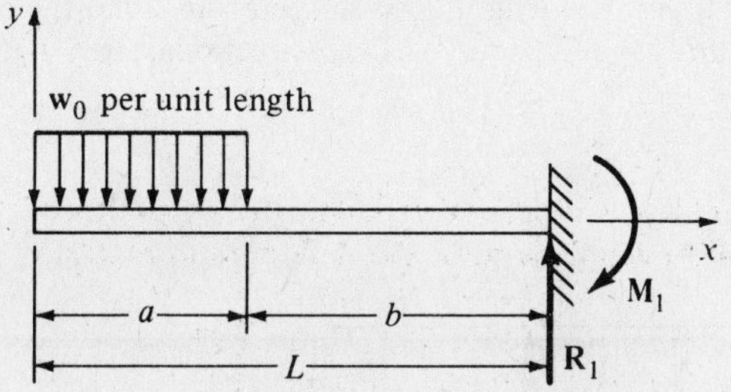

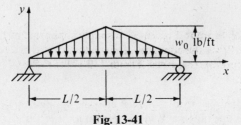

Fig. 13-40

13.32 Use singularity functions to determine the equation of the deflection curve of the simply supported beam in Fig. 13-41, which is subject to the uniformly varying load shown. Also find the central deflection of the beam.

Fig. 13-41

Ans. $EIy = \dfrac{w_0 L}{24} \langle x \rangle^3 - \dfrac{w_0}{60L} \langle x \rangle^5 + \dfrac{w_0}{24L} \left\langle x - \dfrac{L}{2} \right\rangle^4 - \dfrac{5}{192} w_0 L^3 x; \quad y_{L/2} = -\dfrac{w_0 L^4}{120 EI}$

13.33 Use singularity functions to determine the equations of the deflection curve for the beam in Fig. 13-42.

Ans. $EIy = \dfrac{230}{3} \langle x \rangle^3 - 500 \langle x - 4 \rangle^2 - \dfrac{100}{12} \langle x - 4 \rangle^4 - 6930x$

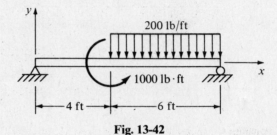

Fig. 13-42

13.34 Use singularity functions to determine the equation of the deflection curve for the beam in Fig. 13-43.

Ans. $EIy = -\dfrac{w_0 a}{24} \langle x \rangle^3 - \dfrac{w_0}{24} \langle x \rangle^4 + \dfrac{w_0}{24} \langle x - a \rangle^4 + \dfrac{w_0 a^2}{2} \langle x - a \rangle^2 + \dfrac{9}{24} w_0 a \langle x - 2a \rangle^3 + \dfrac{11}{48} w_0 a^3 x$

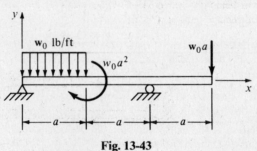

Fig. 13-43

13.35 Beam AB in Fig. 13-44 is supported at A through a pin to a pontoon floating in water, and it is pinned at B. A uniform load of q per unit length acts on the beam. Find the slope of the beam at A if the beam has stiffness EI and length L, the pontoon has cross-sectional area A_0, and the weight of the water per unit volume is γ.

Ans. $\dfrac{q}{2A_0 \gamma} - \dfrac{qL^3}{24EI}$

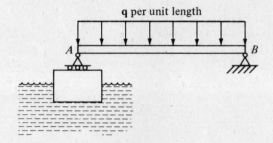

Fig. 13-44

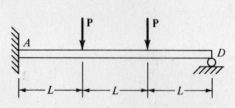

Fig. 13-45

13.36 The propped cantilever AD in Fig. 13-45 is loaded by two concentrated forces. Determine the vertical reaction at D.   *Ans.* $R_D = 2P/3$

13.37 The beam in Fig. 13-46 is clamped at the left end and spring-supported at the right end. When the beam is unloaded, the spring is free of force. When a vertical force of 1 ton is applied at point C with *no spring* there, the deflection at C is 2 in. The spring constant k is 1 ton/in. Determine the deflection at point C when a load of 2 tons is applied at the midpoint B and the spring *is* attached to the beam.   *Ans.*   5/12 in

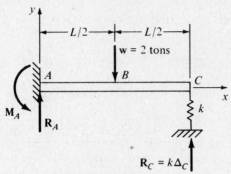

Fig. 13-46

13.38   A very long bar of constant cross section rests on a rigid plane. A vertical force **P**, applied at one end of the bar, causes a length L of the bar to lift up, i.e., to break contact with the plane. The weight of the bar per unit length is w. Determine the length L of the bar that is no longer in contact with the plane, as well as the vertical deflection of the end of the bar that is being lifted up.   *Ans.* $L = 2P/w$; $EIy_L = 2P^4/3w^3$

13.39   The propped cantilever beam AC in Fig. 13-47 is subject to a uniformly distributed load over its right half. Determine the vertical reaction at support C.

Ans. $R_C = \dfrac{7wL}{10}$

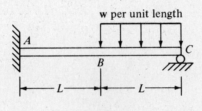

Fig. 13-47

13.40   Return to Problem 13.6, and let $M_1 = 4500$ lb·in, $a = 2$ ft,   and $b = 6$ ft.   Let the beam be of circular cross section, 1 in in diameter, with $E = 30 \times 10^6$ lb/in^2.   Use the FORTRAN program of Problem 13.12 to determine the beam deflections at 25 points along the length of the beam. What is the midpoint deflection?   *Ans.* -1.32 in

Chapter 14

Combined Loadings: Theories of Failure and Design Methodology

To this point we have discussed mainly the stresses and deformations arising from the application of a single type of load to a structural member—a sequence of concentrated forces acting normal to a beam, for example, or a shaft with several twisting moments applied to it. In real situations, however, several quite different types of loading are usually acting on the member. A shaft subject to the simultaneous action of bending moments and twisting moments (Fig. 14-1) is a common example. So too is a bar subject to axial loading and torsion (Fig. 14-2), or a liquid storage tank subject to internal hydrostatic pressure together with lateral wind loading (Fig. 14-3). In each case, the member must be designed to withstand the simultaneous action of the multiple loadings.

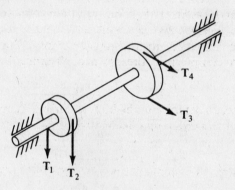

Fig. 14-1

Design for combined loading is more complex than design for a single type of load. The design must be based on the experimentally determined mechanical properties of the materials, but these properties cannot be determined for all possible combinations of loadings. Hence, designers must rely on mechanical characteristics that are determined in simple single-load tensile, compressive, or shear tests. The problem then arises as to how to relate the strength of an elastic body subject to combined loadings to these strength characteristics known only for simpler loadings. Relations that link strength under various combined loads and simple mechanical properties of materials are termed *theories of failure*. Many such theories (or criteria) are available, but we shall discuss only the three that are most commonly used—one applicable to brittle materials and two suitable for use with ductile materials.

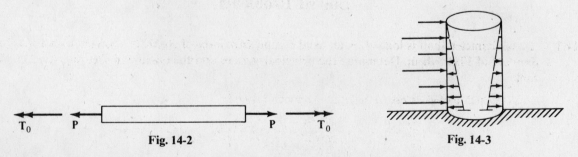

Fig. 14-2

Fig. 14-3

Theories of failure are usually expressed in terms of principal stresses. Hence the first step in designing a member for combined loading is to determine the principal stresses at a carefully selected critical point (or points) of the member. The procedure outlined in Chapter 8 is then employed to evaluate the principal stresses. (See Problems 14.1 and 14.2.)

MAXIMUM NORMAL STRESS THEORY

According to this theory, a material subject to biaxial or triaxial tensile stresses fails when the maximum normal stress reaches the value at which failure occurs in a simple tension test on the same material. Alternatively, if the loading is compressive, failure occurs when the minimum normal stress reaches the value at which failure occurs in a simple compression test. Failure is usually defined as either yielding or fracture—whichever occurs first. This theory is in good agreement with experimental evidence on brittle materials.

MAXIMUM SHEARING STRESS (TRESCA) THEORY

According to this theory, a material subject to biaxial or triaxial stresses fails when the maximum shearing stress reaches the value at which failure occurs in a simple tension or compression test on the same material. Using the concepts of Chapter 8, it can be shown that the maximum shearing stress at a point is one-half the difference between the maximum and minimum principal stresses at that point and always occurs on a plane inclined at $45°$ to the principal planes. Thus, if σ_{yp} denotes the yield point of the material in simple tension or compression, the maximum shearing stress criterion may be stated as

$$\sigma_{\max} - \sigma_{\min} = \sigma_{yp} \qquad (14.1)$$

Judgment must be used in analyses to determine which of the three principal stresses leads to the greatest difference on the left-hand side of this equation. (See Problems 14.3 to 14.5.)

HUBER–VON MISES–HENCKY (MAXIMUM ENERGY OF DISTORTION) THEORY

For an element subject to the principal stresses $\sigma_1, \sigma_2, \sigma_3$ this theory states that yielding begins when

$$(\sigma_1 - \sigma_2)^2 + (\sigma_2 - \sigma_3)^2 + (\sigma_1 - \sigma_3)^2 = 2(\sigma_{yp}^2) \qquad (14.2)$$

where σ_{yp} is the yield point of the material. This theory is in excellent agreement with experiments on ductile materials. (See Problems 14.4 and 14.6.)

Design criteria based upon these theories of failure assume that all loads are slowly applied (i.e., no impact or shock loads are involved) and that the loadings are not of a cyclical nature.

Solved Problems

14.1   A 2-in-diameter shaft is loaded by an axial compressive force of 50,000 lb together with a twisting moment of 30,000 lb·in. Determine the principal stresses and the maximum shearing stress in the shaft.

The axial load gives rise to uniform compressive stresses

$$\sigma_x = \frac{P}{A} = -\frac{50,000 \text{ lb}}{(\pi/4)(2 \text{ in})^2} = -15,900 \text{ lb/in}^2 \qquad \text{and} \qquad \sigma_y = 0 \qquad (1)$$

According to (11.1), the twisting moment gives rise to torsional shear stresses $\tau = T\rho/J$. These are maximal at the outer fibers of the shaft, where they are equal to

$$\tau_{xy} = \tau = \frac{T\rho}{J} = \frac{(30,000 \text{ lb·in})(1 \text{ in})}{(\pi/32)(2 \text{ in})^4} = 19,100 \text{ lb/in}^2 \tag{2}$$

Thus, an element at the outer surface of the shaft is subject to the compressive and shearing stresses shown in Fig. 14-4. From (8.5), the principal stresses are

$$\sigma_{1,2} = \frac{\sigma_x + \sigma_y}{2} \pm \sqrt{\left(\frac{\sigma_x - \sigma_y}{2}\right)^2 + \tau_{xy}^2} \tag{3}$$

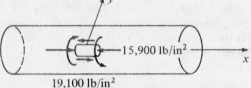

Fig. 14-4

After substituting (1) and (2) into (3) and solving, we find that

$$\sigma_{\max} = 12,740 \text{ lb/in}^2 \qquad \sigma_{\min} = -28,640 \text{ lb/in}^2$$

From (1) of Problem 8.7, the maximum shearing stress is

$$\tau_{\max} = \pm\sqrt{\left(\frac{\sigma_x - \sigma_y}{2}\right)^2 + \tau_{xy}^2} = \pm\sqrt{\left(\frac{-15,900 - 0}{2}\right)^2 + (19,100)^2} = \pm 20,690 \text{ lb/in}^2$$

14.2   The shaft shown in Fig. 14-5a rotates with constant angular velocity, and the belt pulls create a state of combined bending and torsion. The diameter of the shaft is 1.25 in. Determine the principal stresses in the shaft, neglecting the weight of the shaft and pulleys and assuming that the bearings can exert only concentrated force reactions.

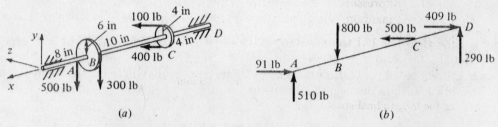

Fig. 14-5

The transverse forces acting on the shaft are not parallel, and the bending moments they cause must be added vectorially to obtain the resultant bending moment. This vector addition need be carried out at only a few apparently critical points along the length of the shaft. The loads causing bending, together with the reactions they produce, are shown in Fig. 14-5b; they are considered as passing through the axis of the shaft. The upper and lower shaded portions of Fig. 14-6 represent the bending moment diagrams for a vertical and a horizontal plane, respectively.

The resultant bending moments at B and C have magnitudes

$$M_B = \sqrt{(4080)^2 + (728)^2} = 4140 \text{ lb·in} \qquad M_C = \sqrt{(1160)^2 + (1636)^2} = 2000 \text{ lb·in}$$

The twisting moment between the two pulleys is constant and equal to

$$T = (400 - 100)(4) = 1200 \text{ lb·in}$$

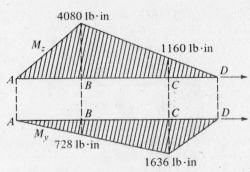

Fig. 14-6

Since this torque is the same at B and C, the maximum stress occurs at the outer fibers of the shaft at point B. The maximum bending stress is given by

$$\sigma_x = \frac{My}{I} = \frac{(4140)(1.25/2)}{\pi(1.25)^4/64} = 21{,}500 \text{ lb/in}^2 \qquad \sigma_y = 0$$

The maximum shearing stress, occurring at the outer fibers of the shaft, is given by

$$\tau_{xy} = \frac{T\rho}{J} = \frac{1200(1.25/2)}{\pi(1.25)^4/32} = 3100 \text{ lb/in}^2$$

From (8.5) with $\sigma_y = 0$, the principal stresses are

$$\sigma_{\max} = \tfrac{1}{2}\sigma_x + \sqrt{(\tfrac{1}{2}\sigma_x)^2 + (\tau_{xy})^2} = 21{,}500/2 + \sqrt{(21{,}500/2)^2 + (3100)^2} = 22{,}000 \text{ lb/in}^2$$

$$\sigma_{\min} = \tfrac{1}{2}\sigma_x - \sqrt{(\tfrac{1}{2}\sigma_x)^2 + (\tau_{xy})^2} = 21{,}500/2 - \sqrt{(21{,}500/2)^2 + (3100)^2} = -400 \text{ lb/in}^2$$

14.3 A closed, thin-walled cylindrical shell that is used as a pressure vessel has a mean diameter of 200 mm and a wall thickness of 3 mm. The shell is subject to a twisting moment of 1 kN·m, along with the internal pressure. If the allowable working stress in tension and compression is 160 MPa, determine the maximum allowable internal pressure using the maximum shearing stress theory.

From Problem 10.1 we have, for the circumferential (hoop) stress,

$$\sigma_c = \sigma_y = \frac{pr}{h} = \frac{p(100 \text{ mm})}{3 \text{ mm}} = 33.33p$$

and for the longitudinal stress,

$$\sigma_l = \sigma_x = \frac{pr}{2h} = \frac{p(100 \text{ mm})}{2(3 \text{ mm})} = 16.67p$$

where p is the unknown internal pressure. By (11.1), the torsional shearing stress is $\tau = T\rho/J$, where J is the polar moment of inertia of the cross section of the shell. By definition, $J = \int \rho^2 \, da$, but for a thin shell ρ is essentially the same for all points of the cross section and hence can be taken outside the integral; then, since $\rho \approx r$, we have $J \approx r^2 \int da$. But $\int da$ is the cross-sectional area of the thin shell, which may be approximated as $2\pi rh$. Thus, the polar moment of inertia of a thin-walled cylindrical shell becomes

$$J \approx 2\pi r^3 h$$

The torsional shearing stress is then

$$\tau_{xy} = \frac{T\rho}{J} = \frac{(1000 \text{ N·m})(0.1 \text{ m})}{2\pi(0.1 \text{ m})^3(0.003 \text{ m})} = 5.308 \times 10^6 \text{ N/m}^2 \text{ or } 5.308 \text{ MPa}$$

From (8.5) we now have, for the principal stresses,

$$\sigma_{1,2} = \frac{\sigma_x + \sigma_y}{2} \pm \sqrt{\left(\frac{\sigma_x - \sigma_y}{2}\right)^2 + \tau^2} = \frac{16.67p + 33.33p}{2} \pm \sqrt{\left(\frac{16.67p - 33.33p}{2}\right)^2 + (5.308 \times 10^6)^2} \quad (1)$$

Since we are to use the maximum shearing stress theory, we need (8.9):

$$\tau_{max} = \pm \tfrac{1}{2}(\sigma_{max} - \sigma_{min}) \tag{2}$$

It is important to realize that every element of this cylindrical shell is subject to three-dimensional stress. Not only are there normal stresses in the circumferential and longitudinal directions, and shearing stresses in the plane of the cylindrical wall, but there are also normal stresses that act *radially*, i.e., perpendicular to the shell wall. These vary from zero at the outside of the wall to a compressive stress numerically equal to the internal pressure at the inside of the wall. The following question then arises: In the application of (2), what minimum normal stress σ_{min} should be employed? We must investigate three possibilities: the zero stress at the outside of the shell; a compressive stress numerically equal to the internal pressure at the inside of the wall; and the in-plane stress σ_2 found by using the minus sign in (1).

In most (but not all) problems involving pressurized thin-walled shells, the last of these possibilities is the proper one to use. Here, this choice yields, for (2),

$$\tfrac{1}{2}(160 \times 10^6) = \frac{1}{2}\left\{ \frac{16.67p + 33.33p}{2} + \sqrt{\left(\frac{16.67p - 33.33p}{2}\right)^2 + (5.308 \times 10^6)^2} \right.$$
$$\left. - \left[\frac{16.67 + 33.33p}{2} - \sqrt{\left(\frac{16.67 - 33.33p}{2}\right)^2 + (5.308 \times 10^6)^2}\right] \right\} \tag{3}$$

On the left side of (3) 160×10^6 is the given working stress; the factor 2 is required because, according to the maximum shearing stress theory, failure under biaxial or triaxial loading occurs when the maximum shearing stress reaches the value of the shearing stress at failure in a simple tension test—and this is known from Chapter 8 to be one-half the value of the tensile allowable stress.

Equation (3) yields $p = 4.79$ MPa. Investigation of the other two possibilities for the assumed minimum normal stress shows that they would lead to considerably greater values of p. Naturally, the lowest of the three values, 4.79 MPa, is the required pressure.

14.4 A thin-walled cylindrical pressure vessel is subject to an internal pressure of 600 lb/in². The mean radius of the cylinder is 15 in. If the material has a yield point of 39,000 lb/in² and a safety factor of 3 is employed, determine the required wall thickness using (a) the maximum normal stress theory and (b) the Huber–von Mises–Hencky theory.

The hoop and meridional stresses were determined in Problem 10.1. Since they are principal stresses, we have

$$\sigma_1 = \sigma_c = \frac{pr}{h} = \frac{600(15)}{h} = \frac{9000}{h}$$

$$\sigma_2 = \sigma_l = \frac{pr}{2h} = \frac{600(15)}{2h} = \frac{4500}{h}$$

The third principal stress varies from zero at the outside of the shell to the value $-p$ at the inside. It is customary to neglect this third component in thin-shell design, so we shall assume that $\sigma_3 = 0$.

(a) Using the maximum normal stress theory, we have

$$\frac{9000}{h} = \frac{39,000}{3} \quad \text{from which} \quad h = 0.69 \text{ in}$$

(b) Using the Huber–von Mises–Hencky theory we have, from (14.2),

$$\left(\frac{9000}{h} - \frac{4500}{h}\right)^2 + \left(\frac{4500}{h} - 0\right)^2 + \left(\frac{9000}{h} - 0\right)^2 = 2\left(\frac{39,000}{3}\right)^2$$

whence $h = 0.60$ in.

14.5 One end of a horizontal shaft projects beyond the last of a series of bearings (thus acting as a cantilever) and is subject to a vertical force of 36 kN, as shown in Fig. 14-7. Simultaneously, the shaft is subject to a twisting moment T_0. If the allowable working stress in tension and compression is 150 MPa, determine the maximum allowable value of T_0 on the basis of the maximum shearing stress theory.

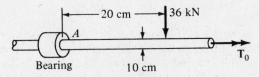

Fig. 14-7

Consideration of the bending effect indicates that the uppermost and lowermost elements at the point of support A are most highly stressed in tension and compression, respectively. From (12.3), the peak bending stress (in tension) is

$$\sigma_x = \frac{Mc}{I} = \frac{(36{,}000 \text{ N})(0.20 \text{ m})(0.05 \text{ m})}{(\pi/64)(0.10 \text{ m})^4} = 73.3 \times 10^6 \text{ N/m}^2 \tag{1}$$

Also, $\sigma_y = 0$.

The torsional shearing stress at the outer fibers is, by (11.1),

$$\tau = \frac{T\rho}{J} = \frac{T_0(0.05 \text{ m})}{(\pi/32)(0.10 \text{ m})^4} = 5093T_0 \tag{2}$$

Since the outer fibers of the shaft are free of additional loads, we are concerned only with an element of the top surface of the shaft, at A, loaded in two dimensions. The principal stresses are thus given by (8.5):

$$\sigma = \frac{\sigma_x + \sigma_y}{2} \pm \sqrt{\left(\frac{\sigma_x - \sigma_y}{2}\right)^2 + \tau^2} \tag{3}$$

Substituting (1), (2), and $\sigma_y = 0$ in (3) yields

$$\sigma_{1,2} = \frac{73.3 \times 10^6 + 0}{2} \pm \sqrt{\left(\frac{73.3 \times 10^6 - 0}{2}\right)^2 + (5093T_0)^2}$$

The maximum shearing stress is given by (8.9) as $\tau_{max} = \pm\frac{1}{2}(\sigma_{max} - \sigma_{min})$, which here becomes

$$\frac{\dfrac{73.3 \times 10^6}{2} + \sqrt{\left(\dfrac{73.3 \times 10^6}{2}\right)^2 + (5093T_0)^2} - \left[\dfrac{73.3 \times 10^6}{2} - \sqrt{\left(\dfrac{73.3 \times 10^6}{2}\right)^2 + (5093T_0)^2}\right]}{2} = \frac{150}{2} \times 10^6$$

yielding $T_0 = 12.84 \text{ kN·m}$.

14.6 A bar has solid circular cross section, and its base is rigidly clamped at the origin of an x, y, z coordinate system (Fig. 14-8). The bar, which has a 20-mm diameter, is bent so that one part CD lies in the xy plane and is parallel to the x axis, and the remainder OC lies along the y axis. At point D, a force P acts on the bar in a plane parallel to the yz plane and in a direction 25° below the z axis. For the bar material, the yield point is 200 MPa. Determine the magnitude of P that causes yielding at point A, which lies on the z axis at coordinates $(0, 0, 10)$. Use the Huber–von Mises–Hencky theory.

Let us first determine the components of the force P along the y and z axes, and then consider their effects. They are

$$P_y = -P \sin 25° = -0.423P \qquad P_z = P \cos 25° = 0.906P$$

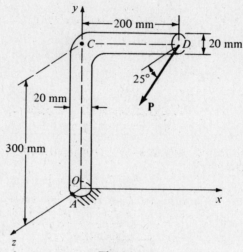

Fig. 14-8

At point A, component P_y causes direct axial compressive stress given by

$$\sigma'_y = -\frac{0.423P}{(\pi/4)(0.02 \text{ m})^2} = -1346P \text{ N/m}^2$$

Component P_z causes bending of the vertical portion OC about the x axis. That is, the x axis serves as a neutral axis, so that peak compression arises at A (with the compressive stress vector being directed in the negative y direction). The compressive stress is

$$\sigma''_y = \frac{Mc}{I} = \frac{-0.906P(0.3 \text{ m})(0.01 \text{ m})}{(\pi/64)(0.02 \text{ m})^4} = (-0.346 \times 10^6)P \text{ N/m}^2$$

Thus, the net compressive stress at A is $\sigma_y = \sigma'_y + \sigma''_y = -347,346P \text{ N/m}^2$.

Component P_z also causes torsion about the y axis. The torsional shearing stresses in the xz plane are given by

$$\tau_{xz} = \frac{(0.906P)(0.2 \text{ m})(0.01 \text{ m})}{(\pi/32)(0.02 \text{ m})^4} = (0.115 \times 10^6)P \text{ N/m}^2$$

Finally, we note that there are no applied loads in the x direction; hence, at A we have $\sigma_x = 0$.

The stresses at A are thus those shown in Fig. 14-9. Since there is no stress in the z direction, this is a two-dimensional situation and we may use (8.5) to write the principal stresses as

$$\sigma = \frac{\sigma_x + \sigma_y}{2} \pm \sqrt{\left(\frac{\sigma_x - \sigma_y}{2}\right)^2 + \tau_{xz}^2}$$

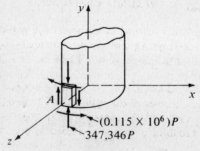

$(0.115 \times 10^6)P$
$347,346P$

Fig. 14-9

Substituting the calculated values of σ_y and τ_{xy}, along with $\sigma_x = 0$,   in this equation, we obtain

$$\sigma_{max} = \sigma_1 = (0.380 \times 10^6)P \qquad \text{and} \qquad \sigma_{min} = \sigma_3 = (-0.032 \times 10^6)P$$

Further, as noted above, $\sigma_z = \sigma_2 = 0$.

Now, by substituting the computed values of σ_1, σ_2, and σ_3, as well as $\sigma_{yp} = 200$ MPa   in (14.2), we find that $P = 499$ N.

Supplementary Problems

14.7   Determine the maximum tensile stress in a block that is loaded by an eccentric tensile force as shown in Fig. 14-10.   *Ans.*   1200 lb/in^2

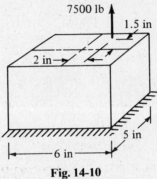

Fig. 14-10

14.8   A cast-iron machine part has a tensile strength of 300 MPa and a compressive strength of 800 MPa. For the two loadings shown in Fig. 14-11, determine the safety factor based upon (a) maximum normal stress theory, (b) maximum shearing stress theory, and (c) Huber–von Mises–Hencky theory.

Ans.   I: (a) 3.75, (b) 3.75, (c) 4.17;   II: (a) 3.75, (b) 2.31, (c) 2.64

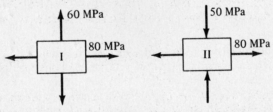

Fig. 14-11

14.9   A shaft of 50-mm diameter is subject to an axial tension of 200 kN together with a twisting moment of 4 kN·m. Determine the principal stresses in the shaft and the maximum shearing stress.

Ans. $\sigma_{max} = 273$ MPa; $\sigma_{min} = -69$ MPa; $\tau = 171$ MPa

14.10   A solid circular shaft is subject to a twisting moment of 2 kN·m together with a bending moment of 3 kN·m. The diameter of the shaft is 100 mm. Determine the principal stresses and the maximum shearing stress in the shaft.   *Ans.* $\sigma_{max} = 33.7$ MPa; $\sigma_{min} = -3.1$ MPa; $\tau = 18.4$ MPa

14.11   A thin-walled cylindrical shell is subject to an axial compression of 50,000 lb together with a torsional moment of 30,000 lb·in. The diameter of the cylinder is 12 in, and the wall thickness is 0.125 in. Determine the principal stresses in the shell and the maximum shearing stress. Neglect the possibility of buckling of the shell.   *Ans.* $\sigma_{max} = 120$ lb/in^2; $\sigma_{min} = -10,680$ lb/in^2; $\tau = 5400$ lb/in^2

14.12   The shaft shown in Fig. 14-12 rotates with constant angular velocity and is subject to combined bending and torsion due to the indicated belt pulls. The weights of the shaft and pulleys may be neglected, and the bearings can exert only concentrated force reactions. The diameter of the shaft is 50 mm. Determine the principal stresses in the shaft.   *Ans.* $\sigma_{max} = 147.7$ MPa; $\sigma_{min} = -0.7$ MPa

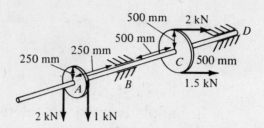

Fig. 14-12

14.13   A shaft transmitting 12 hp at 200 rpm is supported in a series of bearings (Fig. 14-13). The end of the shaft overhangs the leftmost bearing by 8 in and supports a 50-lb pulley with belt pulls having a tension ratio of 1:2. If the working tensile stress is 20,000 lb/in², find the minimum allowable shaft diameter based upon the stress condition at the left bearing and the maximum shearing stress theory.   *Ans.*   1.60 in

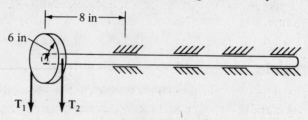

Fig. 14-13

14.14   A solid steel shaft of diameter 6.5 cm is subject to a bending moment of 1600 N·m together with a twisting moment **T**. The material has a tensile yield point of 425 MPa, and a safety factor of 1.5 is to be employed. Determine the allowable twisting moment based upon the maximum shearing stress criterion.

Ans. $T = 7.44$ kN·m

14.15   Repeat Problem 14.14 using the Huber–von Mises–Hencky criterion.   *Ans.*   8.5 kN·m

14.16   A solid steel shaft of diameter 3.5 in is loaded by a twisting moment of 55,000 lb·in and a bending moment of 12,500 lb·in. Determine the principal stresses. If the tensile yield point of the material is 44,000 lb/in², find the safety factor on the basis of the maximum shearing stress theory.   *Ans.*   3.28

14.17   Repeat Problem 14.5 using the Huber–von Mises–Hencky criterion.   *Ans.*   14.8 kN·m

Chapter 15

Columns

A long, slender bar subject to axial compression is called a *column*. Some writers use the term *column* only to describe a vertical member, and the word *strut* for an inclined bar. We shall use the term in its more general meaning.

Many aircraft structural components, structural connections between stages of boosters for space vehicles, and certain members in bridge trusses and structural frameworks of buildings are common examples of columns. Linkages in oscillating or reciprocating machines may also behave as columns, especially as regards failure.

FAILURE OF A COLUMN

A column fails by buckling, i.e., by lateral deflection of the bar. (For comparison, a short compression member fails by yielding of the material.) Buckling, and hence failure, of a column may occur even though the maximum stress in the bar is below the yield point of the material.

SLENDERNESS RATIO

The ratio of the length of a column to the minimum radius of gyration of its cross-sectional area is termed the *slenderness ratio* of the bar. This ratio is dimensionless. The method of determining the radius of gyration of an area was discussed in Chapter 6.

If the column is free to rotate at each end, then buckling takes place about that axis for which the radius of gyration is a minimum.

CRITICAL LOAD

The *critical load* for a long, slender bar subject to axial compression is that value of the axial force that is just sufficient to keep the bar in a slightly deflected configuration. Figure 15-1 shows a pin-ended bar in a buckled configuration due to the critical load P_{cr}.

Fig. 15-1

If a long, slender bar of constant cross section is pinned at each end and subject to axial compression (Fig. 15-1), the load P_{cr} that will cause buckling is given by

$$P_{cr} = \frac{\pi^2 EI}{L^2} \qquad (15.1)$$

where E denotes the modulus of elasticity, I the minimum second moment of area (moment of inertia) of the cross-sectional area about an axis through the centroid, and L the length of the bar.

Formula (*15.1*) was first obtained by the Swiss mathematician Leonhard Euler (1707–1783), and the load P_{cr} is called the *Euler buckling load*. As discussed in Problem 15.1, this formula is not immediately

265

applicable if the corresponding axial stress, found from the expression $\sigma_{cr} = P_{cr}/A$, where A represents the cross-sectional area of the bar, exceeds the proportional limit of the material. For example, for a steel bar having a proportional limit of 210 MPa, (15.1) is valid only for columns whose slenderness ratio exceeds 100. The value of P_{cr} represented by this formula is a failure load; consequently, a safety factor must be introduced to obtain a design load. (See Problems 15.3 to 15.5.)

For supports other than that shown in Fig. 15-1, the Euler formula (15.1) can be modified to

$$P_{cr} = \frac{\pi^2 EI}{(KL)^2} \qquad (15.2)$$

where KL is an *effective length* of the column, defined to be a portion of the deflected bar between points corresponding to zero curvature. As an example, for a column pinned at both ends, $K = 1$. If both ends are rigidly clamped, $K = 0.5$. If one end is clamped and the other is pinned, $K = 0.7$. And for a cantilever-type column loaded at its free end, $K = 2$.

INELASTIC COLUMN BUCKLING

Equation (15.1) may be extended into the inelastic range of action by replacing Young's modulus with the *tangent modulus E_t*. The resulting *tangent modulus formula* is

$$P_{cr} = \frac{\pi^2 E_t I}{L^2} \qquad (15.3)$$

The tangent modulus is actually the slope of the stress-strain curve in the inelastic range (to the right of point A in Fig. 15-2). E_t obviously varies with strain, and it must be determined by materials tests.

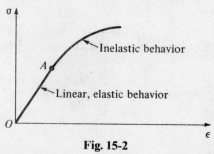

Fig. 15-2

When (15.3) is used, the axial stress immediately prior to buckling is given by

$$\sigma_{cr} = \frac{\pi^2 E_t}{(L/r)^2} \qquad (15.4)$$

This is another form of the *tangent modulus formula*; the load $P_{cr} = A\sigma_{cr}$ is often called the *Engesser load*. This approach (see Problem 15.7) indicates a load only slightly smaller than the inelastic buckling load found experimentally. The theory has certain inconsistencies (that will not be discussed here), so it is not the best approach to rational column design.

Tests on axially compressed bars produce three modes of failure. The first, compressive yielding of short columns, was discussed in Chapter 9. Another, Euler column behavior, is treated here in Problem 15.1. The third is inelastic buckling of intermediate-length bars, and the rational design of such bars is discussed in Problems 15.7 to 15.10.

DESIGN FORMULAS FOR COLUMNS HAVING INTERMEDIATE SLENDERNESS RATIOS

Compression members having large slenderness ratios are designed on the basis of (15.1), together with an appropriate safety factor. For the design of shorter compression members, it is customary to employ one of the many semiempirical relationships between the yield stress and the slenderness ratio of the bar.

For steel columns, one commonly employed design formula is that due to the American Institute of Steel Construction (AISC), which gives the allowable (working) axial stress σ_a on a steel column having slenderness ratio L/r as

$$\sigma_a = \begin{cases} \dfrac{\left[1 - \dfrac{(KL/r)^2}{2C_c^2}\right]\theta_{yp}}{\dfrac{5}{3} + \dfrac{3KL/r}{8C_c} - \dfrac{(KL/r)^3}{8C_c^3}} & \text{for } \dfrac{KL}{r} < C_c \\[4mm] \dfrac{\pi^2 E}{\dfrac{23}{12}\left(\dfrac{KL}{r}\right)^2} & \text{for } \dfrac{KL}{r} > C_c \end{cases} \tag{15.5}$$

where

$$C_c = \sqrt{\frac{2\pi^2 E}{\sigma_{yp}}} \tag{15.6}$$

σ_{yp} is the yield point of the material, and E is Young's modulus. (See Problem 15.8.)

Aluminum columns are usually designed according to a code developed by The Aluminum Association, Inc. The formulas for allowable stresses take into account such details as the type of alloy, heat treatment, and temper. As an example, the formulas for allowable axial compressive stresses for 6061-T6 aluminum alloy are as follows*: In SI units,

$$\sigma_a = \begin{cases} 131 \text{ MPa} & \text{for } 0 < \dfrac{L}{r} \leqslant 9.5 \\[3mm] \left(139 - 0.869\dfrac{L}{r}\right) \text{MPa} & \text{for } 9.5 < \dfrac{L}{r} \leqslant 66 \\[3mm] \dfrac{352{,}000}{(L/r)^2} \text{ MPa} & \text{for } \dfrac{L}{r} > 66 \end{cases} \tag{15.7}$$

In USCS units,

$$\sigma_a = \begin{cases} 19{,}000 \text{ lb/in}^2 & \text{for } 0 < \dfrac{L}{r} \leqslant 9.5 \\[3mm] \left(20{,}200 - 126\dfrac{L}{r}\right) \text{lb/in}^2 & \text{for } 9.5 < \dfrac{L}{r} \leqslant 66 \\[3mm] \dfrac{51{,}000{,}000}{(L/r)^2} \text{ lb/in}^2 & \text{for } \dfrac{L}{r} > 66 \end{cases} \tag{15.8}$$

These allowable stresses (based on the stress just prior to buckling) incorporate safety factors which vary from approximately 1.60 to 2.25, depending upon the slenderness ratio. (See Problem 15.9.)

BUCKLING OF RIGID SPRING-SUPPORTED BARS

The columns discussed above are *flexible* members; they are capable of undergoing lateral bending immediately after buckling. A related type of buckling involves one or more *rigid* bars pinned to fixed supports or to each other and supported by one or more transverse springs. In certain situations, the

---

* *Specifications for Aluminum Structures* (Washington, D.C.: The Aluminum Association, Inc., 818 Connecticut Ave. N.W., 1982).

applied loads may cause such a bar system to suddenly move to an alternative equilibrium position. This, like buckling of columns, is a form of instability. (See Problem 15.12.)

Solved Problems

15.1   Determine the axial stress in the column considered in Equation 15.1.

In the derivation of (13.1), which we use to determine the critical load (15.1), we assume that there is a linear relationship between stress and strain. Thus the critical load (15.1) is correct only if the proportional limit of the material has not been exceeded.

The axial stress in the bar just before the bar assumes its buckled configuration is given by

$$\sigma_{cr} = P_{cr}/A \qquad (1)$$

where A is the cross-sectional area of the bar. Substituting for P_{cr} from (15.1), we find that

$$\sigma_{cr} = \frac{\pi^2 EI}{AL^2} \qquad (2)$$

But from Chapter 6 we know that $I = Ar^2$,   where r represents the radius of gyration of the cross-sectional area. Substituting this in (2) yields

$$\sigma_{cr} = \frac{\pi^2 EAr^2}{AL^2} = \pi^2 E\left(\frac{r}{L}\right)^2 \qquad \text{or} \qquad \sigma_{cr} = \frac{\pi^2 E}{(L/r)^2} \qquad (3)$$

where the ratio L/r is the *slenderness ratio* of the column.

Let us consider a steel column having a proportional limit of 210 MPa and $E = 200\,\text{GPa}$.   The stress of 210 MPa marks the upper limit of stress for which (3) may be used. To find the value of L/r corresponding to these constants, we substitute in (3) and obtain

$$210 \times 10^6 = \frac{\pi^2(200 \times 10^9)}{(L/r)^2} \qquad \text{or} \qquad \frac{L}{r} \approx 100$$

Thus for this material the buckling load as given by (15.1) and the axial stress as given by (3) are valid only for those columns having $L/r \geqslant 100$. For columns having $L/r < 100$, the compressive stress exceeds the proportional limit before elastic buckling takes place and the above equations are not valid.

Equation (3) is plotted in Fig. 15-3. For the particular values of proportional limit and modulus of elasticity assumed above, point A marks the upper limit of applicability of the curve.

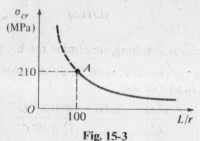

Fig. 15-3

15.2   Determine the critical load for a long slender bar clamped at each end and loaded by an axial compressive force at each end.

The critical load is that axial compressive force **P** that is just sufficient to keep the bar in a slightly deformed configuration, as shown in Fig. 15-4. The moments $\mathbf{M_0}$ at the ends of the bar represent the actions of the supports on the column; these moments prevent angular rotation of the bar at both ends.

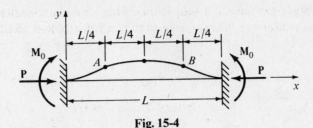

Fig. 15-4

Inspection of the deflection curve for the buckled column indicates that the central portion of the bar, between points A and B, corresponds to the deflection curve for the pin-ended column in Fig. 15-1. Thus for the fixed-end column, the length $L/2$ corresponds to the entire length L for the pin-ended bar. Hence the critical load for a clamped-end bar may be found from (15.1) by replacing L with $L/2$. This yields

$$P_{cr} = \frac{\pi^2 EI}{(L/2)^2} = \frac{4\pi^2 EI}{L^2}$$

This formula, derived here on an intuitive basis, could be derived more rigorously by solving the usual differential equation for the bent bar.

15.3 A steel bar of rectangular cross section, 40 mm by 50 mm, is pinned at each end and is subject to axial compression. If the proportional limit of the material is 230 MPa and $E = 200$ GPa, determine the minimum length for which Euler's equation (15.1) may be used to determine the buckling load.

The minimum second moment of area is $I = \frac{1}{12}bh^3 = \frac{1}{12}(50)(40)^3 = 2.67 \times 10^5$ mm⁴. Hence the least radius of gyration is

$$r = \sqrt{\frac{I}{A}} = \sqrt{\frac{2.67 \times 10^5}{(40)(50)}} = 11.5 \text{ mm}$$

The axial stress just before buckling for such an axially loaded bar was found in Problem 15.1 to be

$$\sigma_{cr} = \frac{\pi^2 E}{(L/r)^2} \qquad (1)$$

The minimum length for which Euler's equation may be applied is found by letting $\sigma_{cr} = 230$ MPa in (1) to obtain

$$230 \times 10^6 = \frac{\pi^2(200 \times 10^9)}{(L/11.5)^2} \qquad \text{or} \qquad L = 1.065 \text{ m}$$

15.4 If the bar of Problem 15.3 is 2 m long, determine the buckling load using Euler's formula.

The minimum second moment of area of the cross section was found in Problem 15.3 to be 2.67×10^5 mm⁴. Applying (15.1), we find that

$$P_{cr} = \frac{\pi^2 EI}{L^2} = \frac{\pi^2(200 \times 10^9)(10^{-6})(2.67 \times 10^5)}{(2 \times 10^3)^2} = 132 \text{ kN}$$

15.5 Use (15.1) to determine the critical load for a W 10×21 section acting as a pinned-end column. The bar is 12 ft long, and $E = 30 \times 10^6$ lb/in².

From Table 12-1, the minimum moment of inertia is 9.7 in⁴. Thus,

$$P_{cr} = \frac{\pi^2 EI}{L^2} = \frac{\pi^2(30 \times 10^6 \text{ lb/in}^2)(9.7 \text{ in}^4)}{(144 \text{ in})^2} = 138,000 \text{ lb}$$

15.6 A long, thin bar AB of length L and rigidity EI is pinned at end A; at end B, rotation is resisted by a restoring moment of magnitude λ per radian of rotation at that end. Neither A nor B can be displaced laterally, but A is free to approach B. Derive an equation that gives the axial load **P** that causes buckling.

The buckled bar is shown in Fig. 15-5, where M_L represents the restoring moment. The differential equation of the buckled bar is

$$EI \frac{d^2y}{dx^2} = Vx - Py \qquad \text{or} \qquad \frac{d^2y}{dx^2} + \frac{P}{EI} y = \frac{V}{EI} x$$

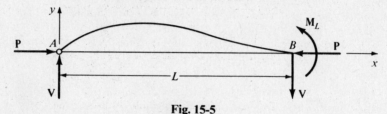

Fig. 15-5

Let $\alpha^2 = P/EI$. Then the last equation becomes

$$\frac{d^2y}{dx^2} + \alpha^2 y = \frac{V}{EI} x$$

The general solution of this equation is easily found to be

$$y = A \sin \alpha x + B \cos \alpha x + \frac{V}{P} x \tag{1}$$

As one boundary condition, we have $y = 0$ when $x = 0$. Hence $B = 0$. As a second boundary condition, $y = 0$ when $x = L$. Hence, from (1) we obtain

$$0 = A \sin \alpha L + \frac{VL}{P} \qquad \text{or} \qquad \frac{V}{P} = -\frac{A}{L} \sin \alpha L$$

Thus,
$$y = A\left(\sin \alpha x - \frac{x}{L} \sin \alpha L \right) \tag{2}$$

From (2), the slope at $x = L$ is found to be

$$\left[\frac{dy}{dx} \right]_{x=L} = A\left(\alpha \cos \alpha L - \frac{1}{L} \sin \alpha L \right)$$

From the definition of λ, we see that the restoring moment at end B is

$$M_L = A\lambda\left(\alpha \cos \alpha L - \frac{1}{L} \sin \alpha L \right) \tag{3}$$

Also, since in general $M = EI(d^2y/dx^2)$, we have from (2)

$$M_L = -A\alpha^2 EI \sin \alpha L \tag{4}$$

Equating (3) and (4) after noting that as M_L increases, dy/dx at point B decreases (necessitating the insertion of a negative sign), we have

$$-A\alpha^2 EI \sin \alpha L = -A\lambda\alpha \cos \alpha L + \frac{A\lambda}{L} \sin \alpha L$$

or, after simplifying,

$$\frac{PL}{\lambda} - \alpha L \cot \alpha L + 1 = 0$$

This equation would have to be solved numerically for specific values of EI, L, and λ.

15.7 A pinned-end column, 275 mm long and having a solid circular cross section, must support an axial load of 250 kN. Determine the minimum radius for the rod using the tangent modulus theory and the experimentally determined curve in Fig. 15-6, which relates tangent modulus to axial stress.

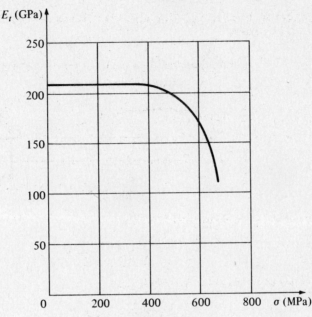

Fig. 15-6

According to (*15.3*) and (*15.4*), the critical load is given by

$$P_{cr} = A \frac{\pi^2 E_t}{(L/r)^2} = \frac{\pi^2 E_t I}{L^2} \tag{1}$$

For a solid circular cross section of radius R, $I = \pi R^4/4$ and (*1*) may be rearranged to yield

$$E_t = \frac{(250,000 \text{ N})(0.275 \text{ m})^2}{\pi^2(\pi R^4/4)} = \frac{2439}{R^4} \text{ N/m}^2 \tag{2}$$

For any radius R, the axial stress due to the load is

$$\sigma = \frac{P}{A} = \frac{250,000}{\pi R^2} \tag{3}$$

and for any value of σ we can ascertain the corresponding value of E_t from Fig. 15-6. Thus, (*2*) and (*3*) can be solved for R by trial and error.

Let us try $R = 0.012$ m. From (*3*), we get $\sigma = 250,000/\pi(0.012 \text{ m})^2 = 553$ MPa. For this value of σ, Fig. 15-6 yields $E_t = 175$ GPa. However, from (*2*) we have

$$E_t = \frac{2439}{(0.012 \text{ m})^4} = 117 \text{ GPa}$$

Clearly these values of E_t do not agree, and the assumed radius is too large.

Next we try $R = 0.011$ m. From (*3*), we get $\sigma = 250,000/\pi(0.011 \text{ m})^2 = 658$ MPa. For this value of σ, Fig. 15-6 yields $E_t = 125$ GPa. However, from (*2*) we obtain

$$E_t = \frac{2439}{(0.011 \text{ m})^4} = 167 \text{ GPa}$$

This time the assumed radius is too small.

Clearly, an acceptable value of R lies between 0.011 m and 0.012 m. For $R = 0.0112$ m, (3) yields $\sigma = 634$ MPa and Fig. 15-6 then gives $E_t = 152$ GPa. The value found from (2) is $E_t = 155$ GPa. These two values of E_t are sufficiently close so that we may assume the radius to be 0.0112 m or 11.2 mm.

15.8 Use the AISC recommendation (15.5) to determine the allowable axial load on a W 203 × 28 section that is 3 m long if its ends are pinned, the yield point is 250 MPa, and $E = 200$ GPa.

From Table 12-2 we have, for the W 203 × 28 section, $I_{min} = 3.28 \times 10^6$ mm^4 and $A = 3600$ mm^2.

The radius of gyration for the section is then $r = \sqrt{3.28 \times 10^6 \text{ mm}^4/3600 \text{ mm}^2} = 30.18$ mm, and $L/r = 3000/30.18 = 99.4$.

From (15.6),

$$C_c = \sqrt{\frac{2\pi^2 E}{\sigma_{yp}}} = \sqrt{\frac{2\pi^2(200 \times 10^9 \text{ N/m}^2)}{250 \times 10^6 \text{ N/m}^2}} = 125.7$$

Since both ends are pinned, $K = 1$ and, thus, $KL/r < C_c$. Then, by (15.5), the allowable axial stress is

$$\sigma_a = \frac{\left[1 - \frac{(KL/r)^2}{2C_c^2}\right]\sigma_{yp}}{\frac{5}{3} + \frac{3(KL/r)}{8C_c} - \frac{(KL/r)^3}{8C_c^3}} = \frac{\left[1 - \frac{(99.4)^2}{2(125.7)^2}\right]250 \times 10^6}{\frac{5}{3} + \frac{3(99.4)}{8(125.7)} - \frac{(99.4)^3}{8(125.7)^3}} = 90.35 \text{ MPa}$$

The allowable axial load is

$$P = A\sigma_a = (3600 \text{ mm}^2)\left(\frac{1 \text{ m}}{10^3 \text{ mm}}\right)^2 (90.35 \times 10^6 \text{ N/m}) = 325,000 \text{ N or } 325 \text{ kN}$$

15.9 A structural aluminum column is a rolled angle section with the cross-sectional dimensions shown in Fig. 15-7. The area A of the cross section is 1.43 in^2; the minimum moment of inertia of the cross-sectional area occurs about the inclined axis shown and is equal to 0.41 in^4. The length of the column is 25 in. Determine the allowable axial load.

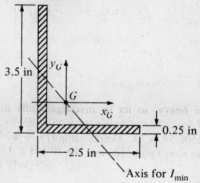

Fig. 15-7

The minimum radius of gyration is

$$r = \sqrt{\frac{I_{min}}{A}} = \sqrt{\frac{0.41 \text{ in}^4}{1.43 \text{ in}^2}} = 0.53 \text{ in}$$

so that the slenderness ratio is $L/r = 25/0.53 = 47.2$. Then the allowable stress is, from (15.8),

$$\sigma_a = 20,200 - 126(47.2) = 14,250 \text{ lb/in}^2$$

and the allowable axial load is

$$P_a = A\sigma_a = (1.43 \text{ in}^2)(14,250 \text{ lb/in}^2) = 20,400 \text{ lb}$$

15.10 Select a wide-flange section from Table 12-2 to carry an axial compressive load of 750 kN. The column is to be pinned at both ends and 3.5 m long, with a material yield point of 250 MPa and a modulus of 200 GPa. Use the AISC specifications.

For a first approximation, let us use $P = A\sigma$ to compute

$$A = \frac{750,000 \text{ N}}{250 \times 10^6 \text{ N/m}^2} = 0.0030 \text{ m}^2 \text{ or } 3000 \text{ mm}^2$$

This tells us that any wide-flange section having an area smaller than 3000 mm is unacceptable.

Next, let us try the W 203 × 28 section. In Table 12-2 we find $A = 3600 \text{ mm}^2$ and $I_{min} = 3.28 \times 10^6 \text{ mm}^4$. The minimum radius of gyration is thus $r = \sqrt{3.28 \times 10^6 \text{ mm}^4 / 3600 \text{ mm}^2} = 30.2 \text{ mm}$, and so the slenderness ratio is $L/r = 3500/30.2 = 116$.

From (15.6), we have

$$C_c = \sqrt{\frac{2\pi^2(200 \times 10^9 \text{ N/m}^2)}{250 \times 10^6 \text{ N/m}^2}} = 125.6$$

Thus, since $K = 1$ (both ends are pinned), $KL/r < C_c$ and, from (15.5),

$$\sigma_a = \frac{\left[1 - \dfrac{(116)^2}{2(125.6)^2}\right]250}{\dfrac{5}{3} + \dfrac{3(116)}{8(125.6)} - \dfrac{(116)^3}{8(125.6)^3}} = 74.95 \text{ MPa}$$

Hence, $P_a = (3600 \text{ mm}^2)(1 \text{ m}/10^3 \text{ mm})^2(74.95 \times 10^6 \text{ N/m}^2) = 270,000 \text{ N or } 270 \text{ kN}$ which indicates that this is far too light a section.

Let us now try the W 254 × 72 section having an area of 9280 mm² and $I_{min} = 38.6 \times 10^6 \text{ mm}^4$. The minimum radius of gyration is $r = \sqrt{38.6 \times 10^6 \text{ mm}^4 / 9280 \text{ mm}^2} = 64.5 \text{ mm}$ so the slenderness ratio is $3500/64.5 = 54.26$. Again we have $KL/r < C_c$ (which has not changed), so by (15.5) the allowable stress is

$$\sigma_a = \frac{\left[1 - \dfrac{(54.26)^2}{2(125.6)^2}\right]250}{\left[\dfrac{5}{3} + \dfrac{3(54.26)}{8(125.6)} - \dfrac{(54.26)^3}{8(125.6)^3}\right]} = 124.6 \text{ MPa}$$

and

$$P_a = (9280 \text{ mm}^2)\left(\frac{1 \text{ m}}{10^3 \text{ mm}}\right)^2(124.6 \times 10^6 \text{ N/m}^2) = 1.15 \times 10^6 \text{ N or } 1150 \text{ kN}$$

This section is rather heavy, so let us investigate one more—the W 254 × 54 section. Its area is 7010 mm², and $I_{min} = 17.5 \times 10^6 \text{ mm}^4$. The minimum radius of gyration works out to be 50.0 mm, and the slenderness ratio is $3500/50 = 70$. Again using (15.5), we find $\sigma_a = 114 \text{ MPa}$ and, from it, $P_a = 799 \text{ kN}$ Investigation of the next lighter section, the W 254 × 43, indicates that it can carry only 478 kN.

Thus, we choose the W 254 × 54 section, which can carry an axial load of 799 kN, slightly in excess of the 750-kN required load.

15.11 Two bars, *AB* and *BC*, are pinned at *B* as well as at ends *A* and *C* (Fig. 15-8). Each bar is initially of length *L*, and initially point *B* lies at a distance *h* above the line *AC*. The bars are identical, each having cross-sectional area *A* and Young's modulus *E*. A vertical force **P** is applied at *B*. Determine the relation between **P** and the displacement Δ under the point of application of **P**. Point *B* can move only vertically.

Let us denote by *S* the magnitude of the axial force in each bar after the displacement Δ has occurred; also let $L(1 - \varepsilon)$ denote the length of each bar at that same time. For equilibrium of the joint at *B*, we have $S = P/2 \sin \alpha$, where α is the angle the displaced system makes with the horizontal. From the

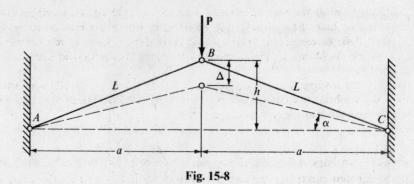

Fig. 15-8

geometry,

$$\sin \alpha = \frac{h - \Delta}{L(1 - \varepsilon)} \quad \text{so} \quad S = \frac{PL(1 - \varepsilon)}{2(h - \Delta)} \tag{1}$$

Also,

$$[L(1 - \varepsilon)]^2 = a^2 + (h - \Delta)^2 = L^2 - 2h\Delta + \Delta^2$$

so

$$\varepsilon = 1 - \frac{\sqrt{L^2 - 2h\Delta + \Delta^2}}{L} \tag{2}$$

The use of $\sigma = S/A$, where σ denotes the axial stress in the bars, and Hooke's law, $\sigma = E\varepsilon$, in (1) now yields

$$P = 2AE \frac{h - \Delta}{L} \frac{\varepsilon}{1 - \varepsilon} \tag{3}$$

Substituting (2) in (3) then yields

$$P = 2AE \frac{h - \Delta}{L} \left(\frac{L}{\sqrt{L^2 - 2h\Delta + \Delta^2}} - 1 \right) \tag{4}$$

Equation (4) is the required relation. Note that no assumptions have been made regarding the magnitude of the displacement Δ; that is, it need not be small compared to h. Equation (4) is plotted in Fig. 15-9, and from this plot it may be seen that the curve has both a maximum and a minimum. From (4) it is obvious that the curve intersects the horizontal axis when $\Delta = h$ and when $\Delta = 2h$. From the plot it may be seen that if the vertical force is gradually increased from zero to the value corresponding to point a, a maximum value will be attained. After that, the value of P required to increase Δ theoretically decreases until, when $\Delta = h$, no force is supposedly necessary to hold pin B on the horizontal line AC. However, in this configuration, and in fact at all points between a and d on the curve, the equilibrium is *unstable* (hence the curve is shown dashed). Spring action will tend to increase Δ further, and now a negative (upward) vertical force is required to keep the bars in position, as represented by portion bcd of the curve.

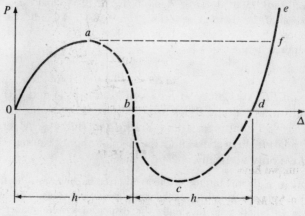

Fig. 15-9

When $\Delta = 2h$ (point d), the bars have reached the mirror image of their original configuration, and no force is necessary to hold the system in this position, in which the bars are stressfree. For still further downward vertical displacements the portion of the curve de represents the relationship between downward load P and vertical displacement. The portions of the curve shown in solid lines correspond to a state of *stable* equilibrium.

In reality, if the loading is a deadweight applied at B, some very small imperfection in the system of bars or some slight vibratory motion will cause the system to "jump" from position a on the curve directly to f. This is termed the *snap-through* phenomenon.

15.12 Two identical rigid bars AB and BC are pinned at B and C and supported at A by a pin in a frictionless roller that can move only vertically (Fig. 15-10). A spring having constant k is attached to bar BC as shown. Determine the critical vertical load for the system.

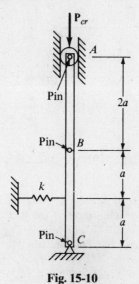

Fig. 15-10

The free-body diagram for the system of two rigid bars is shown in Fig. 15-11. The system is shown in a slightly buckled configuration characterized by the angle $\Delta\theta$. Because ends A and C are pinned, it is necessary to show two components of pin reaction at each of these points. The spring elongates an amount $a\Delta\theta$ and consequently exerts a force $ka\,\Delta\theta$ on bar BC. The pin at B is internal to this free body; hence no pin forces are shown at B.

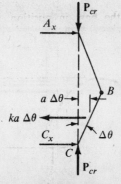

Fig. 15-11

For static equilibrium, we have

$$+\,\circlearrowleft\Sigma\,M_A = C_x(4a) - ka\,\Delta\theta(3a) = 0 \qquad \text{or} \qquad C_x = \frac{3ka\Delta\theta}{4}$$

The free-body diagram for bar BC is shown in Fig. 15-12. It includes the pin forces at B, because they are now external to the free body, and it yields

$$+\,\circlearrowleft\Sigma\, M_B = \frac{3ka\Delta\theta}{4}2a - P_{cr}a(2a\Delta\theta) - (ka\Delta\theta)a = 0 \qquad \text{or} \qquad P_{cr} = \frac{ka}{4}$$

It is impossible to determine $\Delta\theta$ with this approach.

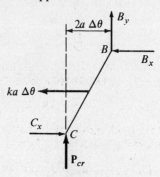

Fig. 15-12

Supplementary Problems

15.13 A steel bar of solid circular cross section has a 2-in diameter. The bar is pinned at each end and is subject to axial compression. If the proportional limit of the material of the bar is 36,000 lb/in² and $E = 30 \times 10^6$ lb/in², determine the minimum length for which Euler's formula (15.1) is valid. Also determine the Euler buckling load when the column has this minimum length. *Ans.* 45.5 in; 112,800 lb

15.14 Determine the slenderness ratio of a steel column of solid circular cross section that has a 4-in diameter and is 9 ft long. *Ans.* 108

15.15 The column shown in Fig. 15-13 is pinned at both ends and is free to expand into the opening at the upper end. The bar is steel, 25 mm in diameter, and occupies the position shown at 16°C. Determine the temperature to which the column may be heated before it will buckle. Take $\alpha = 12 \times 10^{-6}$ (°C)$^{-1}$ and $E = 200$ GPa, and neglect the weight of the column. *Ans.* 29.3°C

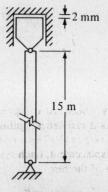

Fig. 15-13

15.16 A bar of length L is clamped at its lower end and subject to both vertical and horizontal forces at the upper end, as shown in Fig. 15-14. The magnitude of the vertical force is equal to one-fourth of the Euler load for this bar. Determine the lateral displacement of the upper end of the bar. *Ans.* $16(4 - \pi)RL^3/\pi^3 EI$

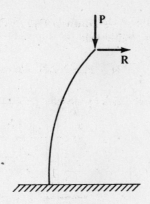

Fig. 15-14

15.17 Use the AISC formula to determine the allowable axial load on a W 8 × 40 column that is 12 ft long. The material yield point is 36,000 lb/in², and $E = 30 \times 10^6$ lb/in².   *Ans.*   194,000 lb

15.18 Use the AISC formula to determine the allowable axial load on a W 203 × 59 column that is 4 m long. The material is steel having a yield point of 250 MPa and $E = 200$ GPa.   *Ans.*   821 kN

15.19 Determine the allowable axial load on a 6061-T6 aluminum column whose cross section is identical to that shown in Fig. 15-7 and whose length is 50 in.   *Ans.* $P_a = 8200$ lb

15.20 Select a wide-flange section from Table 12-2 to act as a column 5 m long that will carry an axial load of 675 kN. The material has a yield point of 250 MPa and a Young's modulus of 200 GPa. Use the AISC formula.   *Ans.*   W 203 × 59

15.21 The rigid bar in Fig. 15-15 is pinned at the lower end and partially restrained against lateral motion at the top by a spring having spring constant k. The upper end of the bar is given a very slight lateral displacement. Determine the critical value of the load **P**.   *Ans.* $P_{cr} = kL$

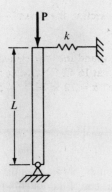

Fig. 15-15

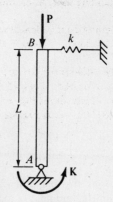

Fig. 15-16

15.22 An initially straight bar is elastically restrained by springs at its upper and lower ends, as shown in Fig. 15-16. The torsion spring at A offers a resistance against angular rotation equal to **K** newton-meters per radian of rotation at A. The linear spring at B offers a resistance against horizontal displacement there equal to k newtons per unit of horizontal displacement. Each spring force is zero when the bar is vertical. Determine the equation governing the buckling of the bar.

Ans. $\alpha L \cot \alpha L + \dfrac{kL}{P - kL} - \dfrac{PL}{K} = 0$, where $\alpha^2 = \dfrac{P}{EI}$

15.23 The system of two rigid vertical bars AB and BC in Fig. 15-17 is pinned at C and restrained against lateral displacement at A, but it is free to rotate at A. The bars are also pinned at B. Point B is partially restrained against lateral displacement by two linear springs, each offering k pounds of resistance per inch of lateral movement. If the springs are loadfree prior to the application of **P**, determine the buckling load P_{cr}.

Ans. $12k$

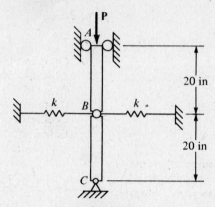

Fig. 15-17

15.24   The round aluminum bar AB in Fig. 15-18 is supported by two horizontal springs and subject to the vertical compressive load **P**. The spring constants are $k_1 = 4 \text{ N/mm}$ and $k_2 = 8 \text{ N/mm}$.   The length of the bar is 600 mm, its diameter is 16 mm, and $E = 70 \text{ GPa}$.   Determine the buckling load and the form of the buckled bar.

Ans. $P_{cr} = L\left(\dfrac{k_1 k_2}{k_1 + k_2}\right) = 1.6 \text{ kN}$; the bar remains straight and rotates about a point $x_0 = 400$ mm

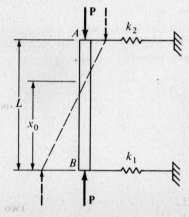

Fig. 15-18

15.25   A long thin bar of length L and rigidity EI is supported at each end in an elastic medium which exerts a restoring moment of magnitude λ per radian of angular rotation at that end. Find an equation from which the buckling loads $\mathbf{P}_{cr}$ may be determined.

Ans. $\tan \dfrac{\alpha L}{2} = -\dfrac{P_{cr}}{\alpha \lambda}$, where $\alpha^2 = \dfrac{P_{cr}}{EI}$

Index